SOUTH-WESTERN

AUTOMATED ACCOUNTING

6.0

DOS Version

Warren W. Allen, M.A.

Dale H. Klooster, Ed.D.

South-Western Publishing Co.

Developmental Editor: Janet Kinney
Senior Marketing Manager: Dick Walker
Product Manager: Gregory Getter
Production Editor: Thomas Bailey
Associate Director/Design: Darren K. Wright

ISBN: 0-538-62300-4

Library of Congress Catalog Card Number: 93-84724

1 2 3 4 5 6 7 8 9 KI 99 98 97 96 95 94 93

Printed in the United States of America

Preface

The 1980s were truly the decade of the personal computer. During this period personal computers were transformed from the small-capacity, high-priced machines of the 1970s into extraordinarily powerful, low-cost computer systems capable of meeting a wide variety of business record-keeping and accounting needs. The trend is continuing in the 1990s, with the appearance of ever-more-powerful, low-cost computer systems that offer better solutions to the computing needs of businesses. *Automated Accounting 6.0,* which accompanies this text, teaches how computers are used in today's accounting applications.

FEATURES OF THE AUTOMATED ACCOUNTING PACKAGE

The *Automated Accounting 6.0* package, consisting of the text, the workbook, Version 6.0 of the software, the reference guide, and a template disk, provides a realistic approach to computerized, integrated accounting principles. *Automated Accounting 6.0* represents a major revision to both the software and text. Because of technological changes, industry software innovations, and user feedback from previous editions, the following changes have been implemented:

1. The software has been redesigned with a new, easy-to-use, standard user interface involving pull-down menus, mouse support, buttons, and windowing.

2. Although the software fully supports the use of a mouse, a mouse is not required to run the software.

3. New, efficient methods of using the keyboard to operate the computer and move around the keyboard have been implemented.

4. "Quick keys" and "hot keys" can be activated during software execution to make computer operation easier and more efficient.

5. During data entry, students can use "List" and "Find" features of the software to locate data stored by the computer and to make corrections.

6. File maintenance activities may be performed during data entry without exiting the data entry window.

7. Data stored by the computer (such as account numbers and account titles) can be selected from list windows. This saves keying time and potential keying errors.

8. An extensive help system is available that provides information on the operational features of the software.

9. Reports are displayed in a scrollable window. The displayed report may be directed to an attached printer.

10. A template disk containing data and opening balances for the problems in this text accompanies this package. Because the template disk has additional free space, it may also be used as a data disk.

11. The software can now process a wider variety of accounting tasks (i.e., departmentalized/nondepartmentalized businesses, budgeting, service/merchandising businesses, an inventory system, and bank reconciliation).

12. The software now includes a complete plant assets system. Each plant asset can be entered into the computer and stored. This system generates depreciation schedules, monthly depreciation reports, and yearly depreciation reports. The depreciation journal entries may be exported directly to the accounting system.

13. The payroll system generates the journal entries resulting from payroll processing. The journal entries may be exported to the accounting system.

14. The text includes the following icons, which are used for easy identification of important activities and information.

 This icon identifies "Easy Steps," which are very brief step-by-step instructions for performing operational procedures.

 This icon identifies procedures performed with an optional mouse.

 This icon identifies procedures performed at the keyboard.

 This icon identifies tips, techniques, or useful operational information.

 This icon indicates special situations or circumstances where caution should be exercised.

15. Each new software feature introduced in the text is accompanied by a list of "Easy Steps," which are simple, step-by-step instructions for using the feature. This technique makes the software easy to learn and provides an easy-to-use reference.

16. Answers for the end-of-chapter audit test questions can be found in the student's most recently saved data files. Since the answers can be obtained from screen displays, the need to print reports and waste paper is eliminated. This feature, combined with the software design and the *Electronic Auditor* solution-checking software, makes it possible to complete the student problems entirely from screen displays and for the instructor to verify the results from screen displays (thereby conserving one of our precious natural resources—trees).

17. Students will be exposed to many types of accounting systems, including a wide variety of accounting procedures. Students will become very familiar with the software and its features before setting up an automated accounting system in the last chapter.

SYSTEM REQUIREMENTS

Automated Accounting 6.0 is available for the IBM PC, IBM Personal System/2,[1] and compatible computers. The minimum configuration to run the software is 512K of memory using DOS 2.1 or higher for the PC, DOS 3.3 or higher for the Personal System/2, and one disk drive. Access to an 80-column, continuous-feed printer is optional.

---

[1] IBM and Personal System/2 are registered trademarks of International Business Machines Corporation. Any reference to IBM, IBM PC, or Personal System/2 refers to this footnote.

Contents

CHAPTERS

1

Introduction

1. Identify and define the key terms associated with automated accounting systems.

2. Describe the various types of windows.

3. Operate the computer and the accounting software using a keyboard or a mouse.

4. Perform system start-up procedures.

5. Make menu selections.

6. Load data from disk.

7. Perform data entry activities.

8. Display and print reports.

9. Access Help information.

10. Save data to disk.

11. Define terms associated with computerized accounting.

INTRODUCTION

This text will teach you about computerized accounting using a hands-on approach. You will learn to operate the software by entering realistic accounting transactions for a variety of business applications and by generating financial statements as well as other management information reports.

The software makes use of a standard user interface that utilizes pull-down menus, movable overlapping windows, mouse support, list windows, and help windows. This standard interface is similar to the interface used in many other software applications. Most of the techniques you learn in this book can be applied to many other software packages. This will make the transition to other applications very easy. The *Automated Accounting 6.0* package contains the following: (1) the software, (2) a reference guide, (3) this textbook, (4) working papers, and (5) a template disk.

▶ The *Automated Accounting 6.0* Software

The *Automated Accounting 6.0* software contains three major modules: A1, A2, and A3. A1 contains the integrated accounting system software for general ledger, accounts payable, accounts receivable, financial statement analysis, and budgeting. A2 contains the software for plant asset accounting, bank reconciliation, and payroll. A3 contains the software for inventory processing.

▶ The *Automated Accounting 6.0* Reference Guide

The *Automated Accounting 6.0* Reference Guide comes with the software. It gives detailed operational information for the software. The *Automated Accounting* software has been designed so that it can be used for a variety of classes and a range of textbooks. Because a number of different textbooks may be used with the *Automated Accounting* software, none covers all features and capabilities of the software. The Reference Guide covers all of the features of the software and serves as a ready reference for its use.

▶ This Textbook

Each chapter begins with an introduction that describes the topics to be covered. The introduction is followed by a section on operating procedures. A tutorial problem follows the operating procedures section. If you have difficulty with an activity in the tutorial problem, refer back to the operational procedure that describes the activity. Page references are provided for each step of the tutorial problem.

This book uses features that will make learning the *Automated Accounting 6.0* software easier and allow you to locate reference information quickly and easily. These features are listed below.

1. Each pull-down menu is shown in the chapter.

2. Each data entry window is pictured with an explanation of each of the data fields.

3. Throughout the text, useful illustrations and notes are provided in the margins.

4. An illustration showing a partially completed input form is provided for many data entry screens.

5. Brief step-by-step procedures called **Easy Steps** are provided for each computer activity (such as menus, data entry, and report printing). The Easy Steps make the activities easier to learn and serve as a reference when you are working the end-of-chapter problems.

6. The following icons are used to identify important activities and information:

 This icon identifies Easy Steps, which are very brief, step-by-step instructions.

 This icon identifies procedures performed with an optional mouse pointing device.

 This icon identifies procedures performed at the keyboard.

 This icon identifies tips, techniques, or useful operational information.

 This icon indicates special situations where caution is necessary.

▶ The Working Papers

The working papers contain a set of input forms for each of the end-of-chapter problems and the **audit tests**. The audit tests are made up of questions relating to the end-of-chapter problems.

▶ The Template Disk

There is a file on the template disk containing the starting (or beginning) data for each problem in the textbook. Before a problem can be solved, the beginning data must be loaded from the template disk. On a hard disk or network system, the template files may have been copied into the directory containing the software. If you are using a floppy-based system, your instructor may give you a copy of the template disk. Once you have this copy, you will have: (1) template data and (2) storage space for your data files. If the template gets full (112 files), you can remove some of the early files.

OPERATING PROCEDURES

The operating procedures in this chapter include pull-down menus, mouse instructions, data entry windows, list windows, dialog windows, and report windows. In addition, the operating procedures for start-up, the File menu, the General Information data entry window, setting the display type, setting the colors, and using the Help menu will also be covered.

▶Using a Mouse

The *Automated Accounting 6.0* software works with a mouse. If you have a mouse connected to your computer, the pointer will be displayed on your screen as a small rectangle (■). The pointer moves on the screen as you move the mouse. The following functions can be performed with a mouse:

Point	Move the pointer to a specific location on the screen.
Click	Quickly press and release the left mouse button.
Drag	Press and hold down the left mouse button and move the mouse.
Point and click	Pointing to an object on the screen and clicking the mouse button is "clicking on the object." For example, if you are directed to "click on" the Ok button, you should point to the Ok button and click the left mouse button.

▶Pull-Down Menus

One of the ways you can communicate with the computer is with a menu. A **menu** is a list of commands. Figure 1.1 shows the parts of the *Automated Accounting 6.0* menu system.

MENU BAR.   The **menu bar** is the top line of the screen, which shows the menus that are available. The menu bar is different for the Accounting System, Plant Assets, Bank Reconciliation, Payroll, and Inventory.

MENU NAME.   Each of the words on the menu bar is the name of one of the pull down menus. If a menu name is "dimmed", it is not available.

PULL-DOWN MENU.   A pull-down menu is a list of commands that appears immediately below the selected menu.

MENU COMMAND.   The menu commands are the menu items, such as New and Open Accounting File shown in the File menu in Figure 1.1. They are referred to as commands because they command the computer to perform a particular action.

QUICK KEY.   Each menu name and each menu command has a quick key associated with it. The quick keys appear on the screen as either a bright or an underlined letter (within the menu or command name). Quick keys allow easy menu or menu command selection.

FIGURE 1.1
Pull-Down Menus

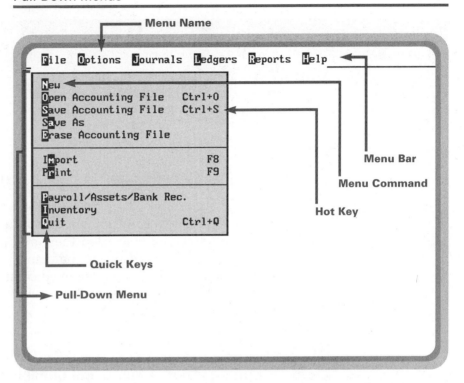

HOT KEY. Some menu options can be selected without pulling down a menu by using a key sequence called a "hot key." Frequently used menu commands can be selected quickly with hot keys. If a menu command has a hot key, it will be shown on the pull-down menu.

Table 1.1 describes keyboard keys that you will find useful when working with pull-down menus.

TABLE 1.1
Keys Used with Pull-Down Menus

Key	Function
Alt	Use this key to transfer control to the menu bar to select a pull-down menu.
Esc	Use this key to release control from the menu bar or to remove any pull-down menu.
Down Arrow	Use this key to pull down a menu. Each time this key is pressed while a menu is pulled down, the highlight bar will move down to the next menu command. If the highlight bar is on the last command, it will wrap around to the first command.
Up Arrow	Use this key to move the highlight bar up to the previous command within a pull-down menu.
Right Arrow	This key selects the next menu.

Continued

TABLE 1.1 (Continued)
Keys Used with Pull-Down Menus

Key	Function
Left Arrow	This key selects the previous menu.
Enter	Use this key to choose the currently highlighted menu or menu command.

▶Selecting and Choosing Menus and Menu Commands

With the *Automated Accounting 6.0* software, the terms **select** and **choose** have different meanings. When menus on the menu bar or menu commands are selected they are highlighted. When a highlighted (or selected) menu or command is *chosen*, the software will take the appropriate action. Dimmed commands are not available at the current time (you may need to select another command before using a dimmed command).

▶Pulling Down a Menu and Choosing a Menu Command

Keyboard

1   **Press the Alt key.**

When the Alt key is pressed, the first menu on the menu bar (File) is selected.

2   **Press the Left or Right Arrow key to select a menu.**

As you move through the menus with the left and right arrow keys, any menus that are inactive (dimmed) are skipped.

3   **Press Enter to choose the selected menu.**

The chosen menu will appear with the first menu command highlighted. For example, if the File menu is chosen, the screen will appear as shown in Figure 1.2.

 If the name in the menu bar has a highlighted or underlined letter, you can press Alt to select the menu bar, and then type the letter that is highlighted or underlined. For example, to pull down the Help menu, press Alt, then H.

4   **Use the Up and Down Arrow keys to select the menu command, then press Enter to choose the command.**

FIGURE 1.2
File Menu

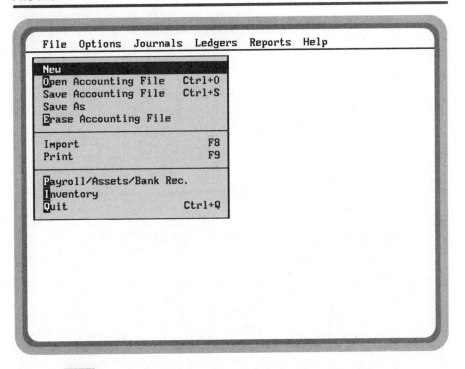

 If the menu command has a highlighted or underlined letter, you can choose a menu command by typing the letter that is highlighted or underlined. For example, to choose Open Accounting File, type O. As we have noted, these highlighted letters are called **"quick keys"** because they allow you to select menu commands quickly using the keyboard.

 Mouse

1 **Pull down the menu by pointing to the name of the menu on the menu bar and clicking the left mouse button.**

2 **Point to the menu command and click the left mouse button.**

To move directly to a menu item, point to the menu name and drag the highlight bar down the menu until the menu command is highlighted, and then release the mouse button.

▶Windows

You interact with the computer to perform the automated accounting procedures through windows. A **window** is a rectangular area of the screen in which the software is communicating with the user. Often the screen contains only one window. At times, two or more overlapping windows may appear on the screen. However, only one window is active at a time. The *Automated Accounting 6.0* software uses four different types of windows: data entry, list, dialog, and report windows.

To use the accounting software, it is important to understand how to work with each of these four types of windows. The following paragraphs describe how to use these windows with a mouse and the keyboard or with the keyboard alone.

DATA ENTRY WINDOWS. Data is keyed into the computer from the computer's keyboard and displayed in data entry windows as it is keyed. This process is called **data entry**. Figure 1.3 shows the parts of a data entry window.

FIGURE 1.3
Data Entry Window

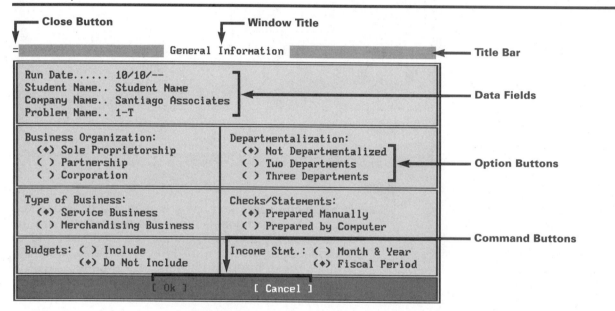

Window Title. The title of the data entry window appears at the top of the screen.

Close Button. The equals sign (=) in the upper left-hand corner of the screen is called the close button. Clicking on the close button with the mouse tells the computer to close the window. The window can be closed from the keyboard by pressing the Esc key.

Title Bar. Any data entry window with a wide title bar, like the one shown, in Figure 1.3, can be moved with the mouse. To move a window, point to the title bar with the mouse, then click-and-drag the window where desired. As the window is dragged, an outlined image of the window follows your movements. When the mouse button is released, the window moves to where the outlined image appeared. The window will remain in its new location during your computer session and until the software is restarted. The contents of a window underneath a movable window may be viewed by clicking-and-holding the mouse button down while the mouse is pointing to the title bar.

Data Fields. Data fields are used to enter data or change (edit) previously entered data.

Option Buttons. You can select only one option at a time. The selected option contains a diamond-shaped character in parentheses (◆).

Command Buttons. A command button initiates an immediate action. Choosing a command button is referred to as "pushing" the button. Command buttons are located along the bottom of the window. A command button is pushed by clicking on it with the mouse or by tabbing to it with the Tab key and pressing Enter. The default command button is always highlighted (selected). The default command button can be pushed from anywhere in the window by pressing Ctrl+Enter.

Data fields and buttons should be keyed or selected in the normal tab sequence. The **tab sequence** is the logical sequence in which the computer is expecting each data field and/or button to be entered. The sequence is usually left to right and top to bottom. The Tab key moves the cursor to the next data field or button in the tab sequence. Shift+Tab moves the cursor to the previous data field or button in the tab sequence. Table 1.2 describes keys that you will find useful when working with data entry windows.

TABLE 1.2
Keys Used with Data Entry Windows

Key	Function
Tab	Use this key to move the cursor to the next data field or button in the tab sequence.
Shift+Tab	Strike the Tab key while holding down the Shift key to move the cursor back to the previous data field or button in the tab sequence.
Enter	If the cursor is positioned on a command button, the command button will be executed. If the cursor is positioned on an option button, that option will be selected and the cursor will move to the next data field or button in the tab sequence. If the cursor is in a data field, the data will be accepted and the cursor will move to the next data field or button in the tab sequence.
Ctrl+Enter	Strike the Enter key while holding down the Ctrl key to select the action of the default (highlighted) command button regardless of the cursor location.
Home	Use the Home key to move the cursor to the first data field or button that appears in the data entry window.
Ctrl+Home	Strike the Home key while holding down the Ctrl key to move the cursor to the beginning of the *current* data field.
End	Use the End key to move the cursor to the last command button on the bottom (end) of the data entry window.
Ctrl+End	Strike the End key while holding down the Ctrl key to move the cursor to the end of the *current* data field.

(Continued)

TABLE 1.2 (Continued)
Keys Used with Data Entry Windows

Key	Function
Down Arrow	Use the Down Arrow key (↓) to move down to the next data field or button. If the cursor is positioned on one of the command buttons at the bottom of the window, it will wrap around to the first data field/button.
Up Arrow	Use the Up Arrow key (↑) to move up to the previous data field or button. If the cursor is located in the first data field/button, it will wrap around to the last button.
Right Arrow	Use the Right Arrow key (→) to move one position to the right within the current data field.
Left Arrow	Use the Left Arrow key (←) to move one position to the left within the current data field.
Insert	Use the Ins key to toggle between insert and overstrike modes. When a data field is selected, it always defaults to the insert mode. When in insert mode, the cursor is displayed as a blinking underscore (_). When in overstrike mode, the cursor appears as a blinking square (■).
Backspace	Within a data field, use this key to erase the character immediately to the left of the cursor.
Delete	Within a data field, use the Del key to erase the character at the current cursor position.
Space Bar	Use the Space Bar to select the button where the cursor is currently positioned.
Esc	Use the Esc key to close and remove the current window from the display screen.

LIST WINDOWS. List windows allow you to search lists and select items from the lists. Examples of available list windows include the chart of accounts, customers, vendors, journal entries, employees, plant assets, inventory items, inventory transactions, and directories. List windows are typically displayed on top of data entry windows. An example of a Chart of Accounts list window displayed on top of the General Journal data entry window is shown in Figure 1.4.

The **highlight bar** identifies the selected item. When a list window appears, the first item in the list is selected. The **scroll bar** is a bar on the right side of the list window that represents the range of items in the list window and is used in conjunction with the scroll box to view items that exist beyond the borders of the window. The **scroll box** indicates the relative position of the selected item within the range of items in the list.

When a list window is opened, no other menu commands can be chosen until the list window has been dismissed.

FIGURE 1.4
List Window

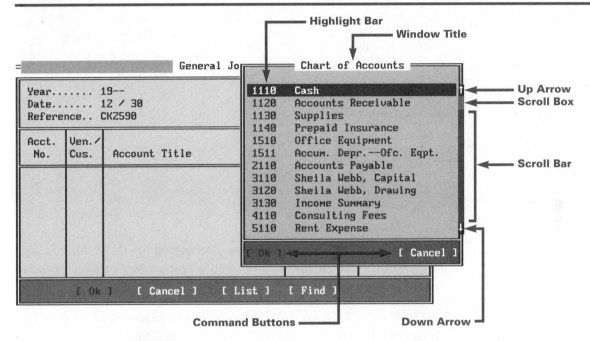

▶ **Selecting and Choosing Items from a List Window**

Keyboard

1   **Use the Up Arrow, Down Arrow, Page Up, Page Down, Home, and End keys to select the desired item from the list.**

2   **Press Enter to choose the selected item or press Esc to cancel the list window.**

When an item is chosen, the list window is closed and the item is inserted into the data entry window if the cursor is in an appropriate data field. For example, if the cursor is positioned on the account number data field and an account is chosen from the chart of accounts list window, the account number appears in the account number data field.

Mouse

1   **Use the mouse operations shown in Table 1.3 to select the desired item.**

TABLE 1.3
Mouse Operations for a List Window

Action	Mouse Operations
Scroll Up	Click on the up arrow (↑) located at the top of the scroll bar to scroll upward (you may also click on the line immediately above the first item in the list window).
Scroll Down	Click on the down arrow (↓) located at the bottom of the scroll bar to scroll downward (you may also click on the line immediately below the last item in the list window).
Scroll to Top	Click on the top of the scroll bar just below the up arrow.
Scroll to Bottom	Click on the bottom of the scroll bar just above the down arrow.
Scroll Anywhere	Click on the scroll bar at the relative position. For example, to scroll to the middle of the list, click on the middle of the scroll bar.

2   Choose the selected item by clicking on the Ok command button (click on the Cancel command button to exit without choosing an item).

DIALOG WINDOWS. The purpose of dialog windows is to provide informational and error messages. A decision from the user may be required. When a dialog window appears, one of the command buttons must be chosen before other menu commands can be selected. Figure 1.5 shows the dialog window that will appear if you quit the accounting system before saving data.

FIGURE 1.5
Dialog Window

```
Warning!  Data file currently
stored in memory has not been
saved.  Do you wish to save
data first?



[ Yes ]      [ No ]      [ Cancel ]
```

▶ **Selecting and Choosing Command Buttons from a Dialog Window**

Keyboard

1   Use the Right and Left Arrow keys or the Tab and Shift+Tab keys to select the desired command button.

2   Press Enter to choose the selected command button.

Mouse

Click on the desired command button.

REPORT WINDOWS. When a command is chosen from the Report menu or one of the Help commands is chosen, the corresponding information is displayed in a report window so that it can be viewed and/or printed on an attached printer. If one of the Report menu commands is chosen, a Report Selection window similar to the one shown in Figure 1.6 will appear.

FIGURE 1.6
Report Selection Window

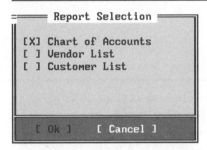

The Report Selection window uses **check boxes** to select the reports you want. There are brackets [ ] or check boxes to the left of each option that allow you to select or clear the option. You can select as many check box options as you wish. When a check box is selected, it contains an X.

▶ **Selecting Reports**

Keyboard

1   **Press Tab (or Down Arrow) to move to the check box you want to select or clear.**

2   **Press the Space Bar, Right Arrow, or Enter key to select the option.**

Press the Space Bar again to clear the option.

3   **Press Tab (or Down Arrow) to move to the Ok command button and press Enter (or press Ctrl+Enter from anywhere to choose the default command button).**

Tab to the Cancel command button and press Enter to close the Report Selection window without selecting any reports.

Mouse

  1   Click on each check box you want to select (or clear).

  2   Click on the Ok command button.

Click on the Cancel command button to dismiss the Report Selection window without selecting any reports.

Some reports have a **Selection Options** dialog like the one shown in Figure 1.7. You can restrict the data that appear on the report. For example, if the date range is 05/01/93 to 05/10/93, only transactions from May 1, 1993, to May 10, 1993, will be printed.

FIGURE 1.7
Selection Options

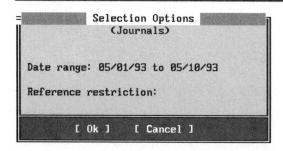

After pushing the Ok command button, the first of the selected reports will appear in the scrollable Report Window as illustrated in Figure 1.8. The report can be printed on an attached printer by either pulling down the File menu and choosing the Print command or by pressing the F9 key (the Hot Key for the Print command).

▶**Scrolling Data in a Report Window**

Keyboard

  1   Use the Up Arrow, Down Arrow, Page Up, Page Down, Home, and End keys to view the data in the report window.

  2   Press Esc to close the window.

Mouse

  1   Use the mouse operations in Table 1.4 to view the report.

FIGURE 1.8
Report Window

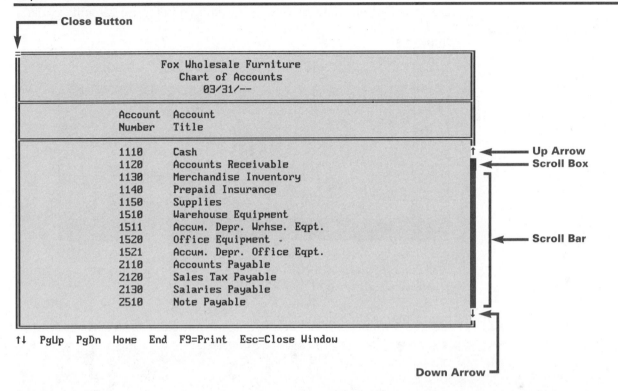

TABLE 1.4
Mouse Operations for a Report Window

Action	Mouse Operations
Scroll Up	Click on the up arrow (↑) located at the top of the scroll bar to scroll upward.
Scroll Down	Click on the down arrow (↓) located at the bottom of the scroll bar to scroll downward.
Scroll to Top	Click on the top of the scroll bar just below the up arrow.
Scroll to Bottom	Click on the bottom of the scroll bar just above the down arrow.
Scroll Anywhere	Click on the scroll bar at the relative position. For example, to scroll to the middle of the report, click on the middle of the scroll bar.

  2   **Close the window by clicking on the equals sign (=) in the upper left corner of the window.**

▶ Printing the Contents of a Report Window

At any time while a report is displayed in a report window, the contents of the report window can be printed by pulling down the File menu and selecting the Print command. As a shortcut, you can simply press the F9 function key. When the Print menu command is chosen, the Print Options data entry window shown in Figure 1.9 will appear.

FIGURE 1.9
Print Options

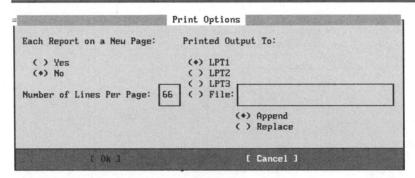

Each of the buttons and data fields on the Print Options data entry window are described in Table 1.5.

TABLE 1.5
Data Fields and Buttons for Print Options Data Entry Window

Button/Data Field	Explanation
Each Report on a New Page	If this option button is set to Yes, each report will be printed on a new page. If this button is set to No, the computer will space down several lines between reports, thus conserving paper.
Number of Lines Per Page	This number represents the number of print lines that will fit on each page of paper. This option is necessary for a printer that feeds individual sheets of paper.
Printed Output To	If your computer connects to several printers, this option allows you to direct the output to a specific printer. To direct the report to a file, you must: (1) key the file name of the disk file that is to receive the output and (2) set the option buttons to indicate whether the output is to be added to the end of an existing file (Append) or a new file is to be created (Replace). There are many uses for a file containing a printed report (for example, it could be printed later with the DOS Print command or it could be merged into a word processing document).
Ok	The Ok command button directs the computer to print the report. Once the report begins printing, it may be stopped by pressing the Esc key.
Cancel	The Cancel command button directs the computer to dismiss the Print Options data entry window and return to the Report Window

▶Initial Start-up

To bring up the Accounting System module of the *Automated Accounting 6.0* software, you must load a program named A1. The start-up procedure varies considerably depending on the type of computer system you are using. The procedure is different for (1) a floppy disk system, (2) a hard disk system, (3) a workstation on a network, or (4) a hard disk system with a graphics user interface, such as Microsoft Windows[1] or IBM's OS/2.[2] Whatever the environment, the start-up is quite simple.

▶ Floppy Disk Based System Start-up

1 At the Dos prompt (DOS Version 2.0 or higher), set the default drive to the drive containing the *Automated Accounting 6.0* software. For example, if you have the *Automated Accounting 6.0* disk in Drive A, you would key "A:" (without the quotation marks). A> will appear on your screen.

2 Key A1 and press the Enter key.

3 The program is large and will take some time to load from a floppy disk. After the program loads, the window shown in Figure 1.10 on page 18 will appear, displaying copyright information.

▶ Hard Disk Based System Start-up

1 From the C> prompt (assuming your hard disk is Drive C), set the default drive and directory to the drive and directory containing the *Automated Accounting 6.0* software.

For example, if the software is stored on Drive C in a directory called AutoAcct, you would:

(a) Key "C:" (without quotes) to set the default drive to Drive C.

(b) Key "CD C:\AutoAcct" (without quotes) to set the default directory to AutoAcct.

2 Key A1 and press the Enter key.

3 The window shown in Figure 1.10 on page 18 will appear, displaying copyright information.

▶ Network or Graphical User Interface

1 Because of the large number of networks available and because of the flexible program selection methods of the

---

[1] Microsoft and Windows are registered trademarks of Microsoft Corporation. Any reference to Microsoft or Windows refers to this footnote.

[2] IBM and OS/2 are registered trademarks of IBM Corporation. Any reference to IBM or OS/2 refers to this footnote.

graphical user interfaces, it is not possible to provide step-by-step procedures for start-up. Your instructor will provide you with the necessary start-up procedures.

2   After start-up is completed, the window shown in Figure 1.10 will appear displaying copyright information.

▶ Monitor Type

After program start-up has been completed, the opening screen window shown in Figure 1.10 will appear. The software automatically determines whether your computer has a color or monochrome monitor and adjusts the screen display. If your computer has a monochrome monitor with graphics capability, the software may incorrectly recognize it as a color monitor (the display may appear fuzzy and difficult to read). If this happens, key Ctrl+D and manually change the monitor type to monochrome.

FIGURE 1.10
Opening Screen

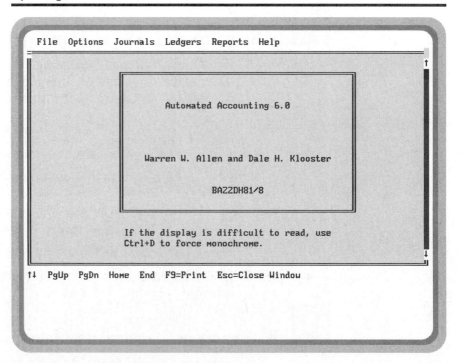

Scroll down to view the copyright information. Since the information is shown in a report window, you can follow the Easy Steps provided in the Report Window section earlier for instructions on how to print the data. Since pull-down menus can be chosen while you are in the Report Window, you can choose the menu command desired and the report window will close.

▶File Menu

When the File menu is selected from the menu bar, the menu shown in Figure 1.11 appears. The menu commands are described below.

FIGURE 1.11
File Menu

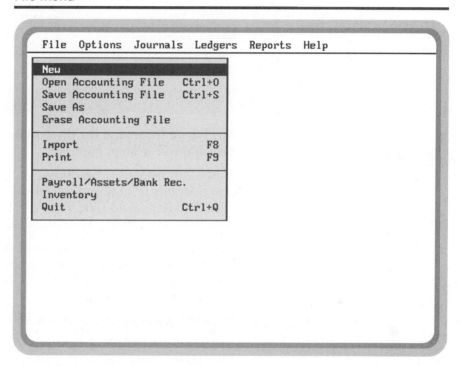

NEW.   The New menu command erases any existing data in the computer's memory and establishes empty accounting system files. The New menu command does *not* remove any data from disk.

OPEN ACCOUNTING FILE.   Before stored data can be processed, it must be loaded from disk into the computer's memory with the Open Accounting File menu command.

▶Open Accounting File

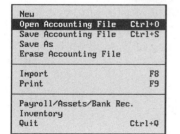

1   Choose the Open Accounting File menu command from the File menu.

The Open File data entry window shown in Figure 1.12 will appear. If you have previously entered a Path and File name during this session, they will appear in the Path and File data fields. If not, the Path field will default to the current path and the File field will be blank.

FIGURE 1.12
Open File Data Entry Window

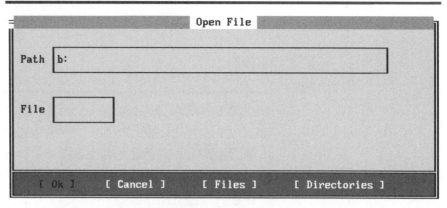

2   **Key the path name to the drive and directory that contains the data file you wish to load.**

If you are loading a template file, key the path to the drive and directory containing the template files. If you are loading a previously saved data file, key the path to the drive and directory containing your data files.

To view a list of subdirectories of the current path, push the Directories button by clicking on it with the mouse or pressing the End key to move the cursor to the Directory button and then pressing Enter.

3   **Key the file name you wish to load.**

To display a list of accounting system files, push the Files button by clicking on it with the mouse or pressing the End key to move the cursor to the Directory button, pressing the Left Arrow key to move to the Files button, and pressing Enter.

The path used depends on the configuration of your computer system and the location of the template files and data files. To obtain a list of subdirectories within the currently specified path, push the Directories button.

4   **To load the file, push the Ok command button by clicking on it with the mouse or pressing Ctrl+Enter.**

SAVE ACCOUNTING FILE.   The Save Accounting File command saves your data file to disk so that you can continue a problem in a later session. The file will be saved to disk with the path and file name currently displayed near the upper right corner of the screen.

```
New
Open Accounting File    Ctrl+O
Save Accounting File    Ctrl+S
Save As
Erase Accounting File

Import                  F8
Print                   F9

Payroll/Assets/Bank Rec.
Inventory
Quit                    Ctrl+Q
```

If you wish to save your data with a path or file name different from the current path and file, use the Save As command.

▶ Save Accounting File

Choose the Save Accounting File command from the File menu.

Before you use the Save Accounting File command, check the current file name in the upper right corner of the screen to make certain you want to save with this path and name (if not, use the Save As command to save with a different path or name).

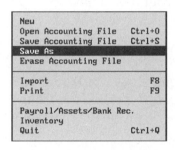

SAVE AS. The Save As command is the same as the Save Account File command except that the data can be saved with a path and/or file name different from the path and file name shown in the upper right corner of the screen. This menu command is useful for making a "backup," or a copy of a data file. For example, you may want to make a backup of your data file before performing period-end closing or before beginning processing for a new payroll period. To make a backup copy, load the data file you wish to back up and use the Save As command to save it under a different name.

▶ Save As Menu Command

1   **Choose the Save As menu command.**

2   **Key the path and file name under which you would like the data file saved.**

3   **Push the Ok button.**

ERASE ACCOUNTING FILE.   The Erase Accounting File command erases a data file stored on disk. You might want to delete a file that is no longer needed (perhaps to free up disk space). This command erases data from disk but not from memory. To erase data from memory, use the New menu command.

IMPORT.   The Import menu command allows you to import journal entries previously exported by either the plant asset or payroll system. When this option is selected, a screen appears that will allow you to supply the path and file name of the journal entries file you want to import.

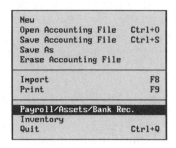

PRINT.   The purpose of the Print menu command is to print the report displayed in the Report Window. This process was described earlier under the Report Window section.

LOADING OTHER PROGRAM MODULES.   Choose the Payroll/Assets/ Bank Rec. menu command to load the second module, which contains the payroll system, plant assets system, and the bank reconciliation system. Choose the Inventory menu command to load the third module, which contains the inventory system.

QUIT.   The Quit menu command is used to exit the accounting software. When the Quit command is chosen, the computer checks to see if the current data in its memory has been saved. If not, a dialog window will appear asking if you wish to save your data to disk.

▶Options Menu

When the Options menu is chosen, the menu shown in Figure 1.13 will appear. The General Information, Display Type, and Set Colors menu commands are discussed below. (The other menu commands will be discussed in later chapters.)

FIGURE 1.13
Options Menu

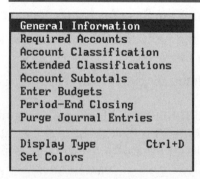

GENERAL INFORMATION.   The General Information data entry window shown in Figure 1.14 is used to give the computer information that appears on the reports as well as information needed to format the reports and to complete period-end closing.

FIGURE 1.14
General Information Data Entry Window

```
=                         General Information
┌────────────────────────────────────────────────────────────┐
│ Run Date...... 10/10/--                                      │
│ Student Name.. Student Name                                  │
│ Company Name.. Santiago Associates                           │
│ Problem Name.. 1-T                                           │
├──────────────────────────────┬───────────────────────────────┤
│ Business Organization:       │ Departmentalization:          │
│   (•) Sole Proprietorship    │   (•) Not Departmentalized    │
│   ( ) Partnership            │   ( ) Two Departments         │
│   ( ) Corporation            │   ( ) Three Departments       │
├──────────────────────────────┼───────────────────────────────┤
│ Type of Business:            │ Checks/Statements:            │
│   (•) Service Business       │   (•) Prepared Manually       │
│   ( ) Merchandising Business │   ( ) Prepared by Computer    │
├──────────────────────────────┼───────────────────────────────┤
│ Budgets: ( ) Include         │ Income Stmt.: ( ) Month & Year│
│          (•) Do Not Include  │               (•) Fiscal Period│
├──────────────────────────────┴───────────────────────────────┤
│           [ Ok ]              [ Cancel ]                      │
└────────────────────────────────────────────────────────────┘
```

Data Fields

Run Date — This date appears on the printed reports. The date is in the format mm/dd/yy.

Student Name — The student name is printed at the top of each report. Key your name carefully, as you will be unable to change it for the duration of the problem.

Company Name — The name of the company is printed as part of the heading for each report.

Problem Name — The problem name is printed at the top of the report along with the student name.

Option Buttons

Business Organization — This option button identifies whether the business is organized as a sole proprietorship, partnership, or corporation.

Type of Business — This option button indicates whether the business is set up as a service business or a merchandising business so that required account information can be collected and financial statements can be prepared.

Budgets — When the Budgets option is set to Include, a budgeting data entry window will be available. A performance report will also be available in the financial statement Report Selection window.

Departmentalization — For a nondepartmental business, this option is set to the Not Departmentalized option. Otherwise, select the number of departments (Two Departments or Three Departments).

Checks/Statements   If this option is set to have the computer prepare accounts payable checks and accounts receivable statements, the checks/statements option of the Reports menu is activated. Also the Check No. field of the cash payments journal is not accessible (since the check numbers are now assigned by the computer). When the checks are displayed, the cash payments transactions are updated to include the assigned check number.

Income Statement   If this option button is set to month and year, the income statement will include a column for the current month and column for the year. If the option button is set for fiscal period, the income statement will list only amounts for the fiscal period.

▶ General Information Data Entry

Keyboard

1   From the Options menu, choose the General Information menu command.

2   Key any changes to the data fields.

3   Set the option buttons (use the Up and Down Arrow keys to select the button option, then press the Space Bar to choose the option).

4   Push the Ok button to accept and store your changes.

Mouse

1   Click on the Options menu, then click on the General Information menu command.

2   Key any changes to the data fields.

3   Set the option buttons (point to the desired option and press the left mouse button).

4   Click on the Ok button.

DISPLAY TYPE.   The software checks the video card in your computer to determine whether you are using a monochrome or a color monitor. In some cases monochrome monitors with graphics capability are mistakenly identified by the software as color monitors. The result is a "fuzzy" display that is difficult to read. If this occurs, you can choose the Display Type menu command and force the correct display type. When this command is selected, the Dialog Window shown in Figure 1.15 will appear. Choose the display type desired by pushing either the "Color" or "Monochrome" command button.

FIGURE 1.15
Select Display Type

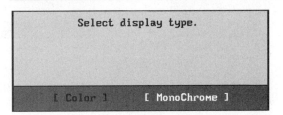

If the software recognizes that you are using a computer with a monochrome monitor, or the Display Type has been set to monochrome, the Set Colors command will be dimmed and unavailable.

SET COLORS.   If you are using a color monitor, you may modify the colors that appear on the screen with the Set Colors dialog window shown in Figure 1.16. Once set, color settings will remain in effect during your computer session and will be saved to disk along with your data.

▶ Setting the Colors

1   Push the Change button to change the colors.

A new, sample color combination will be displayed in the window boxes.

2   Continue pushing the Change button until the color combination appears that you prefer.

3   Push the Ok button to record your selection.

▶ Help Menu

The Help menu shown in Figure 1.17 provides help windows that offer a quick reference for operating the software and an on-screen calculator.

FIGURE 1.16
Set Colors Dialog Window

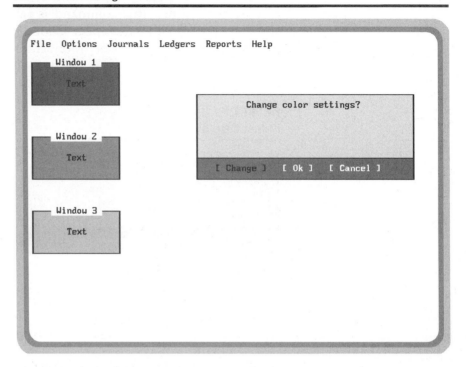

FIGURE 1.17
Help Menu

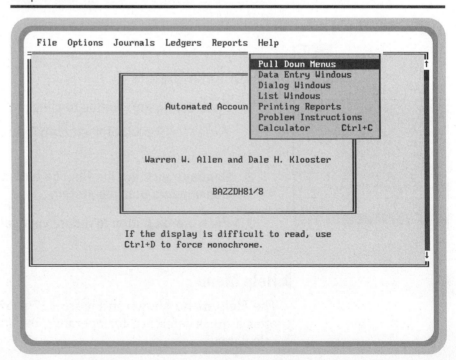

When any of the first six menu commands is chosen, useful information is given in the scrollable Report Window. When the Calculator menu command is chosen, the on-screen calculator shown in Figure 1.18 will appear. The calculator is operated like a hand-held calculator. The result of the calculations may be pasted into the current data field of a data entry screen.

FIGURE 1.18
Calculator

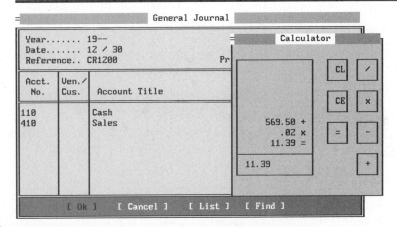

▶ **On-Screen Calculator (multiply $569.50 times 2%)**

1   Press C to clear the calculator (pressing E will clear the current entry).

2   Key 569.50.

3   Press x (for times).

4   Key .02 (for 2%).

5   Press = (to total the calculator).

6   Press F10 (to paste into a data entry field). Make sure the cursor is in the Debit or Credit column so that the program can accept the calculated total.

7   Close the calculator window by pressing Esc or clicking on the Close button.

TUTORIAL 1-T

In this tutorial, you will practice what you have learned in this chapter. Follow the step-by-step instructions. Each step lists a task to be completed at the computer. In case you need it, more detailed information on how to complete the task is provided immediately following the step. If you need additional operating instructions in order to complete the task, a page reference is provided that indicates the relevant page in the Operating Procedures section of the chapter.

Before starting this tutorial, be sure you have a properly formatted data disk (or established hard disk directory) for saving your data.

Step 1:   Start up the accounting system. (page 16)

Key A1 at the DOS prompt (or follow the instructions provided by your instructor).

Step 2:   Open the template file for Problem 1-T (the template file name is AA1-T. (page 19)

Pull down the File menu and choose the Open Accounting File menu command. When the Open File window shown in Figure 1.19 appears, key into the Path field the drive and directory containing the template files. Key a file name of AA1-T and press the Ok button.

FIGURE 1.19
Open File Window

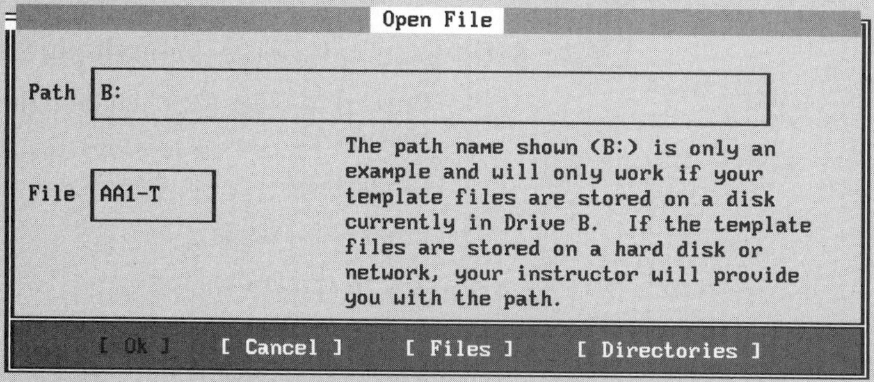

Step 3:   Save the data file to your disk drive or directory with a file name of XXX1-T (where XXX are your initials). (page 21)

Pull down the File menu, choose the Save As command, and save the data file to your disk drive or directory as XXX1-T (where XXX are your initials and 1-T represents Chapter 1, Tutorial Problem 1).

Step 4:   Access the help for dialog windows. (page 25)

Pull down the Help menu and choose the Dialog Windows command. After viewing the help information, close the report window by clicking on the Close button (=) or by pressing Esc.

Step 5: Access help for data entry windows. (page 25)

Pull down the Help menu and choose the Data Entry Windows menu command. Press Esc or click on the Close button to close the report window.

Step 6: Key the following data into the General Information data entry window. (page 24)

```
Run Date.........10/31/-- (--represents the current year)
Student Name.....Your name
Budgets..........Do not include
Income Statement.By Fiscal Period
```

Pull down the Option menu and choose the General Information menu command. Use the Backspace key to delete or the Insert key to overstrike the date. Key the above data in the appropriate data fields and set the option buttons. Check carefully that you have keyed your name correctly, because, you will not be able to change it for the duration of the problem. Press Ctrl+Enter or push the Ok button.

Step 7: Display a chart of accounts. (page 13)

Pull down the Reports menu and choose the Accounts command. When the Report Selection window shown in Figure 1.20 appears, select the Chart of Accounts check box by pressing the Space Bar when the cursor is in the bracket. Next press Ctrl+Enter. The report is shown in Figure 1.21.

FIGURE 1.20
Report Selection (Accounts)

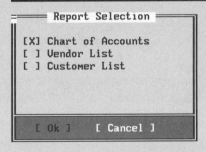

Step 8: Print the chart of accounts on an attached printer. (page 15)

To print the report currently displayed in the report window, press the F9 key, or pull down the File menu and choose the Print command. Unless instructed otherwise, set the print options as shown in Figure 1.22. The printed report is shown in Figure 1.23.

FIGURE 1.21
Displayed Chart of Accounts Report

```
                        Santiago Associates
                        Chart of Accounts
                            10/31/--

                  Account   Account
                  Number    Title

                    110     Cash
                    120     Supplies
                    130     Prepaid Insurance
                    210     Amos Business Forms
                    220     Business World
                    230     Cravens Computerware
                    240     Graphic Design Plus
                    250     Wilson Office Supplies
                    310     Luis Santiago, Capital
                    320     Luis Santiago, Drawing
                    330     Income Summary
                    410     Sales
                    510     Advertising Expense
```

FIGURE 1.22
Print Options

```
                          Print Options

  Each Report on a New Page:       Printed Output To:

     (*) Yes                          (*) LPT1
     ( ) No                           ( ) LPT2
                                      ( ) LPT3
  Number of Lines Per Page:  66      ( ) File: [            ]

                                      (*) Append
                                      ( ) Replace


        [ Ok ]                              [ Cancel ]
```

Step 9:   Display a trial balance. (page 13)

Pull down the Report menu and choose the Ledgers command. When the Report Selection window illustrated in Figure 1.24 appears, select the Trial Balance check box. The displayed report is shown in Figure 1.25.

FIGURE 1.23
Printed Chart of Accounts Report

```
                          Santiago Associates
                          Chart of Accounts
                               10/31/--

          ------------------------------------------
          Account   Account
          Number    Title
          ------------------------------------------
          110       Cash
          120       Supplies
          130       Prepaid Insurance
          210       Amos Business Forms
          220       Business World
          230       Cravens Computerware
          240       Graphic Design Plus
          250       Wilson Office Supplies
          310       Luis Santiago, Capital
          320       Luis Santiago, Drawing
          330       Income Summary
          410       Sales
          510       Advertising Expense
          520       Insurance Expense
          530       Miscellaneous Expense
          540       Rent Expense
          550       Supplies Expense
          560       Telephone Expense
```

FIGURE 1.24
Report Selection (Ledgers)

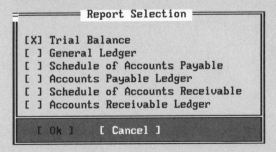

```
========= Report Selection =========

  [X] Trial Balance
  [ ] General Ledger
  [ ] Schedule of Accounts Payable
  [ ] Accounts Payable Ledger
  [ ] Schedule of Accounts Receivable
  [ ] Accounts Receivable Ledger

    [ Ok ]      [ Cancel ]
```

Step 10: If your computer has a printer attached, print the trial balance. (page 15)

To print the report currently displayed in the report window, press the F9 key, or pull down the File menu and choose the Print command. The report is shown in Figure 1.26.

FIGURE 1.25
Displayed Trial Balance

```
┌──────────────────────────────────────────────────────────────┐
│                      Santiago Associates                       │
│                        Trial Balance                           │
│                          10/31/--                              │
├──────────────────────────────────────────────────────────────┤
│      Acct.   Account                                           │
│      Number  Title                        Debit       Credit   │
├──────────────────────────────────────────────────────────────┤
│       110    Cash                       12796.54             ↑ │
│       120    Supplies                    1086.87              ▓│
│       130    Prepaid Insurance            431.91             ▓ │
│       220    Business World, Inc.                    266.90  ▓ │
│       240    Graphic Design Plus                     235.27  ▓ │
│       250    Wilson Office Supplies                  198.53  ▓ │
│       310    Luis Santiago, Capital               13779.28     │
│       410    Sales                                 1865.25     │
│       515    Charitable Contrib. Exp.      50.00               │
│       530    Miscellaneous Expense         15.00               │
│       540    Rent Expense                1711.00               │
│       560    Telephone Expense            253.91               │
│                                        ---------   ---------  ↓│
└──────────────────────────────────────────────────────────────┘
```

FIGURE 1.26
Printed Trial Balance

```
                    Santiago Associates
                      Trial Balance
                        10/31/--

   ----------------------------------------------------------------
   Acct.   Account
   Number  Title                          Debit        Credit
   ----------------------------------------------------------------
   110     Cash                          13355.40
   120     Supplies                        845.34
   130     Prepaid Insurance               157.00
   220     Business World                               266.90
   240     Graphic Design Plus                          235.27
   250     Wilson Office Supplies                       198.53
   310     Luis Santiago, Capital                     13779.28
                                         ----------   ----------
           Totals                        14357.74     14357.74
                                         ==========   ==========
```

Step 11:   Save the data file. (page 21)

Pull down the file menu and choose the Save Accounting File menu command. The file will be saved to disk with the path and file name currently displayed in the upper right corner of the screen.

Step 12:   End the session. (page 22)

Pull down the File menu and choose the Quit menu command.

CHAPTER 1 STUDENT EXERCISE

I. MATCHING

Directions: For each of the following definitions, write in the working papers or on a separate sheet of paper the number of the definition followed by the letter of the appropriate term.

(a) Easy Steps

(b) help windows

(c) option buttons

(d) command buttons

(e) point

(f) click

(g) drag

(h) mouse

(i) window

(j) list window

(k) menu bar

(l) report window

(m) tab sequence

(n) data fields

(o) hot keys

(p) quick keys

(q) dialog window

(r) pull-down menu

1. A pointing device used with the display screen.

2. Moving the mouse pointer to a specific location on the screen.

3. Quickly pressing and releasing the left mouse button.

4. Pressing and holding down the left mouse button and moving the mouse.

5. Text files that contain helpful information, which can be viewed in a report window.

6. The logical sequence in which the computer is expecting each data field and button to be accessed.

7. A bar displayed continuously on the top line of the screen, showing the menus available.

8. A list of commands that appears immediately below the selected menu.

9. Fields on a data entry screen that are used to enter or change data.

10. A window that displays reports so that they can be viewed or printed.

11. A highlighted or underlined letter within a menu command that may be keyed to choose that command.

12. A key sequence or function key that may be pressed at any time to choose the corresponding menu command.

13. A rectangular area of the screen in which the software is communicating with the user.

14. A window that allows you to search lists and select items from the lists.

15. Brief, step-by-step operating procedures.

16. A window that provides information and error messages, including the ability to respond to them.

17. Buttons representing options, where the selected option contains a diamond-shaped character and only one option may be selected.

18. A button that initiates an immediate action.

II. QUESTIONS

Directions: Write the answers to the following questions in the working papers or on a separate sheet of paper.

1. Explain how the terms *select* and *choose* differ with regard to the way they are used in *Automated Accounting 6.0*.
2. What is the purpose of the Alt key?
3. Each of the data entry and report windows has an equals sign (=) displayed as the upper left corner of the window. Explain its purpose.
4. Identify the four different types of windows used in *Automated Accounting 6.0*.
5. How can you tell which command button is the default command button?
6. Briefly describe how menu commands are chosen from a pull-down menu if your computer is configured with
   (a) A keyboard without a mouse.
   (b) A keyboard with a mouse.
7. Explain the difference between the Save Accounting File and Save As menu commands.
8. How is the on-screen calculator accessed?
9. What is the significance of a "dimmed" menu command?
10. Explain how to move a window with the mouse.
11. Explain how to close a window
    (a) From the keyboard
    (b) With a mouse

PRACTICE PROBLEM 1-P

In the following practice problem, you will practice what you have learned in this chapter. Practice problems are numbered with a chapter number and a "P" (1-P for Chapter 1 practice problem). To complete the problem, follow the step-by-step procedures provided.

Step 1:   Remove the Audit Test from the working papers for Chapter 1. Fill in the answers as you work through the following steps. If you are not using the working papers, fill in the answers on a separate sheet of paper.

Step 2:   Start up the accounting system.

Step 3:   Open the template file AA1-P.

Step 4:   Use the Save As menu command to save the data file to your disk drive or directory with a file name of XXX1-P (where XXX are your initials).

Step 5:   Access Help for pull-down menus.

Step 6:   Access Help for the data entry window.

Step 7:   Key the following data into the General Information data entry window.

Run Date ....12/31/-- (-- represents the current year)

Student Name .... Your name

Company Name .... Jackson Company

Business Organization... Partnership

Step 8:   Display a chart of accounts.

Step 9:   Display a trial balance.

Step 10:   Save the data file to disk.

Step 11:   Choose the Quit option of the File menu to end the session.

AUDIT TEST PROBLEM 1-P

Directions: Write the answers to the following questions in the working papers or on a separate piece of paper.

1. Based on the pull-down menu help screen, which keyboard key is used to activate menu selection?
2. Based on the file-handling data entry help information, what is the purpose of the Files command button?
3. From the General Information data entry window, what is the company's type of business?
4. What account number is assigned to Sales?
5. What is the balance of the Prepaid Insurance account shown on the trial balance report?
6. What are the total debits and total credits shown on the trial balance report?

2

General Ledger — Service Business

LEARNING OBJECTIVES ▶ UPON COMPLETION OF THIS CHAPTER, you will be able to:

1. Record additions, changes, and deletions to the chart of accounts on the chart of accounts input form.

2. Complete the general journal entries input form.

3. Perform chart of accounts maintenance.

4. Enter and correct general journal entries.

5. Display accounts, journal, and ledger reports.

INTRODUCTION

This chapter covers maintaining the chart of accounts, entering and correcting general journal entries, and generating the corresponding reports. Before the data is keyed into the computer, it can be recorded on input forms. Additions, changes, and deletions to the chart of accounts may be recorded on the chart of accounts input form, and journal entries may be recorded on the general journal input form.

Businesses might enter data into the computer directly from sales invoices, purchase invoices, and other source documents. Input forms are provided in the working papers, and their use is recommended because source documents are not available. Also, using input forms helps save computer time, because your data is organized and ready to key into the computer before you start a computer session.

▶ Chart of Accounts Input Forms

A business's chart of accounts must be maintained. New accounts must be added, account titles must be changed, and inactive accounts must be deleted whenever necessary. Each addition, change, or deletion may be recorded on a chart of accounts input form as illustrated in Figure 2.1. Both the Account Number and Account Title fields are completed whether you are adding or changing an account. When an account is to be deleted, enter the account number and (Delete).

FIGURE 2.1
Chart of Accounts Input Form

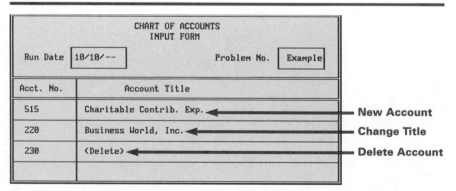

▶ General Journal Input Form

Any business transaction may be recorded in the general journal input form. Each debit part and each credit part of the transaction is recorded on a separate line, as shown in the partially completed general journal input form in Figure 2.2. The selected transactions listed below are recorded on the input form as examples. Additional examples of the various types of transactions are illustrated in Tutorial Problem 2-T at the end of this chapter.

Oct. 01   Paid cash for office rent, $1,711.00. Check no. 3611.

01   Paid cash for telephone bill, $253.91. Check no. 3612.

03   Received cash from sales, $1,865.25. Cash register tape 865.

FIGURE 2.2
General Journal Input Form

GENERAL JOURNAL INPUT FORM					
Run Date 10/10/--				Problem No. Example	
Date MM / dd	Reference	Account Number	Cust./ Vend No.	Debit	Credit
10 / 01	C3611	540		1711.00	
		110			1711.00
10 / 01	C3612	560		253.91	
		110			253.91
10 / 03	T865	110		1865.25	
		410			1865.25
Totals				3830.16	3830.16

Notice that the Date and Reference columns are completed only for the first part of each journal entry, and are left blank for each additional part of that journal entry.

Each line on the form represents one part of a transaction. Each column on the form matches one of the data fields in the General Journal data entry window. The field names and a description of each column on the input form are provided in Table 2.1. Additional examples of the recording of various types of journal transactions for a service business are given in Tutorial Problem 2-T at the end of this chapter.

The bottom of the form contains totals for the Debit and Credit columns. To prove the equality of debits and credits, these totals must be equal. When the general journal entries are displayed or printed, the total on the general journal input form must match the total on the computer-generated general journal report. If they do not match, a keying error has occurred.

TABLE 2.1
Field Names and Descriptions of the General Journal Input Form

Field Name	Description
Date	The Date field contains the two-digit month and day of the month on which the transaction occurred.
Reference	The Reference field contains a number or other information to identify the transaction and provide an audit trail for tracing a transaction back to its original source document. Typical entries would be a check number, sales invoice number, cash receipt number, purchase invoice number, or memorandum number.
Account Number	The general ledger account number from the chart of accounts to be debited or credited.
Customer/Vendor Number	This field should be left blank for now. The use of the Customer/Vendor Number field will be covered in Chapter 4.
Debit	The amount to be debited to the account specified in the Account Number field.
Credit	The amount to be credited to the account specified in the Account Number field.

OPERATING PROCEDURES

The operating procedures covered in this chapter include chart of accounts data entry, general journal data entry, corrections to general journal entries, finding previously entered journal entries, and displaying journal entries.

▶ Maintain Accounts Data Entry Window

When the Maintain Accounts menu command is chosen from the Ledgers menu, the data entry window shown in Figure 2.3 will appear.

```
Ledgers

Chart of Accounts      F1
Vendor List            F2
Customer List          F3

Maintain Accounts      F4
Maintain Vendors       F5
Maintain Customers     F6
```

FIGURE 2.3
Maintain Accounts Data Entry Window

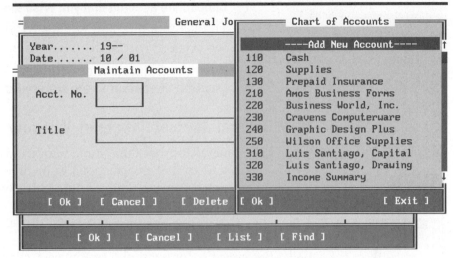

To exit from the Maintain Accounts data entry window, click on the Exit button or press the Right Arrow to select Exit and press Enter.

▶ Adding a New Account

1   **Choose the – – – –Add New Account– – – – item from the list window by pressing Enter or by clicking on the Ok button.**

The list window will be dismissed.

2   **Key the account number and title for the new account.**

3   **Push the Ok button (click on Ok with the mouse, or position the cursor to the Ok button and press Enter).**

▶ Changing an Account Title

1   **Choose the account that you wish to change from the list window.**

The list window will be dismissed and the data for the chosen account will be displayed in the data entry window.

The account number cannot be changed. An incorrect account number can be changed by deleting the account and adding it back with the correct number.

2   **Rekey the correct account title.**

3   **Push the Ok button (click on Ok with the mouse, or position the cursor to the Ok button and press Enter).**

▶Deleting an Account

1   Choose the account that you wish to delete from the list window.

The list window will be dismissed and the data for the chosen account will be displayed in the data entry window.

2   Push the Delete button (click on Delete with the mouse, or position the cursor to the Delete button and press Enter).

▶General Journal Data Entry Window

The General Journal data entry window is used to key new journal entries and to make corrections to or delete existing journal entries. A completed General Journal data entry window is shown in Figure 2.4. Notice that the last line of the screen contains a row of function keys that represent the "hot keys" for choosing menu commands with a single keystroke (without having to pull down the menu). Pressing F1, for example, produces a chart of accounts list window (on top of the General Journal data entry window). Pressing F4 calls up the Account Maintenance data entry window and allows you to add, change, or delete an account while in the middle of keying a journal entry. Shift+F3 calls up the Cash Payments Journal data entry window.

Journal entries are stored by the computer in date sequence. As new journal entries are entered, the computer will maintain the date sequence by inserting the new transaction into the journal file based on the transaction date.

▶Keying a Journal Entry

1   Key the two-digit day of the month (or press Tab if it is correct as is).

If the month or year is incorrect, use the Shift+Tab keys to move to the Month or Year field.

2   Key each of the data fields.

While the cursor is positioned at the Account Number field, you can press the F1 key to choose an account from a chart of accounts list window. Highlight the correct account and press Enter. The chosen account number will be inserted in the Account Number field. The cursor will skip over the Ven./Cus. (Vendor/Customer Number) field.

3   When the journal entry is complete, push the Ok button.

The Posting Summary dialog window shown in Figure 2.5 will appear. The purpose of this window is to show the journal entry in two-column format, giving you one last chance to verify the accuracy of your input and post the data.

General ledger accounts cannot be deleted unless the account being deleted has a zero balance.

```
Journals

Opening Balances

General Journal      S+F1
Purchases Journal    S+F2
Cash Payments Journal S+F3
Sales Journal        S+F4
Cash Receipts Journal S+F5
```

When the General Journal data entry window first appears, the Year and Date data fields will contain the year and date of the last transaction that was entered (even if it was entered in an earlier session). Similarly, the Reference data field will contain the reference for the last transaction that was entered. If there are no transactions on file, the Year and Date fields will contain the Run Date and the Reference field will be blank.

A new general ledger account can be added (or changed) while keying a journal entry. Press the function key (F4–F6) to call up the corresponding maintenance data entry window.

FIGURE 2.4

General Journal Data Entry Window

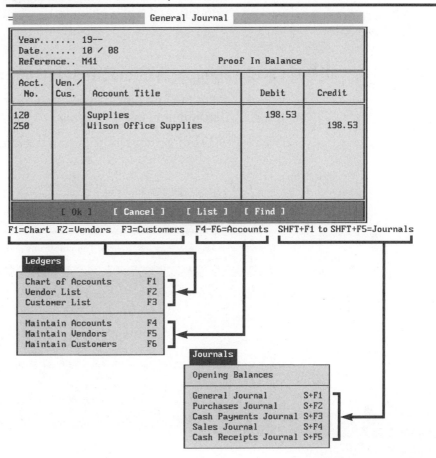

FIGURE 2.5

Posting Summary Dialog Window

4 **If the transaction is correct, push the Post button (push the Change button to return to the General Journal data entry window and make changes).**

▶Changing or Deleting General Journal Transactions

1 **Push the List command button near the bottom of the General Journal data entry window.**

A list of general journal transactions will appear in a list window as shown in Figure 2.6.

FIGURE 2.6
Journal Entries List

```
╔═══════════════════════ Transactions ═══════════════════════╗
║ Date  Refer.  Acct.  V/C Title                Debit    Credit ║
║ 10/01 C3611   540       Rent Expense          1711.00         ↑
║               110       Cash                            1711.00 ║
║ 10/01 C3612   560       Telephone Expense      253.91         ║
║               110       Cash                             253.91 ║
║ 10/03 T865    110       Cash                  1865.25         ║
║               410       Sales                           1865.25 ║
║ 10/06 C3613   515       Charitable Contrib. Exp. 50.00        ║
║               110       Cash                              50.00 ║
║ 10/07 C3614   250       Wilson Office Supplies   76.29        ║
║               110       Cash                              76.29 ║
║ 10/08 M41     120       Supplies               198.53         ║
║               250       Wilson Office Supplies           198.53 ↓
╠═══════════════════════════════════════════════════════════════╣
║ [ Ok ]                                           [ Cancel ]   ║
╚═══════════════════════════════════════════════════════════════╝
```

A transaction is chosen by using the Up and Down Arrow keys to select the transaction and then pressing Enter (or using the mouse to select the transaction and then clicking on Ok).

2 **Choose the transaction that you wish to change or delete.**

The chosen transaction will be displayed in the General Journal data entry window so that it may be changed or deleted.

3 **Key the corrections to the transaction and push the Ok button (or if you wish to delete the transaction, push the Delete command button).**

▶Finding a Journal Entry

1 **Push the Find command button.**

The Find What? dialog window shown in Figure 2.7 will appear.

2 **Key the date (month, day, and year), reference, amount, vendor/customer/chart number of the transaction you want to find.**

3   **If a matching transaction is found, it will be displayed in the General Journal data entry window so that it may be changed or deleted.**

FIGURE 2.7
Find What? Dialog Window

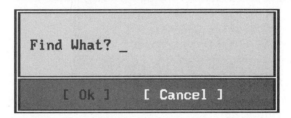

▶ General Journal Report

In Chapter 1 you learned how to choose several reports from the Reports menu. In this chapter you will learn how to select journal reports and to select which journal entries are to appear in the report. The report window in which the reports are displayed will hold a maximum of 400 lines. This is more information than the problems in this text require. However, if this capacity is exceeded, the message, "Insufficient memory. Narrow selection criteria." will appear in a dialog window. To display a report that exceeds the 400-line capacity, use the Selection Options window to shorten the date range, or choose other restriction criteria, in order to generate smaller portions of the report.

▶ Displaying the General Journal Report

1   **Choose the Journals menu command from the Reports menu.**

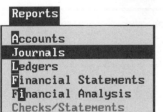

The Report Selection dialog window shown in Figure 2.8 will appear, allowing you to select which of the journal reports you want to be generated.

2   **Select the reports that you want to display (more than one may be selected).**

The reports are selected by clicking on the check box or by pressing the Space Bar (or Right Arrow) while the cursor is positioned to that check box.

3   **Push the Ok button.**

The Selection Options dialog window shown in Figure 2.9 will appear.

FIGURE 2.8
Report Selection Dialog Window

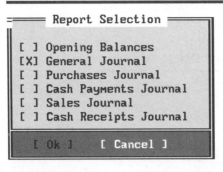

FIGURE 2.9
Selection Options for Journal Reports

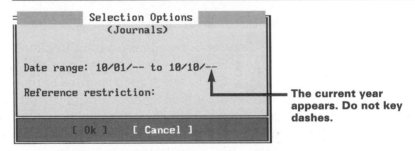

The current year appears. Do not key dashes.

4　Key the range of dates to be included in the journal report. Key a reference restriction if you wish to restrict the report to a particular reference. For example, you might want to display only adjusting entries, or only a certain invoice.

A journal entries report is shown in Figure 2.10. To print the displayed report on an attached printer, press F9.

FIGURE 2.10
General Journal Report Window

```
                        Santiago Associates
                         General Journal
                            10/10/--

Date   Refer.   V/C Acct.   Title                    Debit      Credit

10/01 C3611       540    Rent Expense              1711.00
10/01 C3611       110    Cash                                  1711.00

10/01 C3612       560    Telephone Expense          253.91
10/01 C3612       110    Cash                                   253.91

10/03 T865        110    Cash                      1865.25
10/03 T865        410    Sales                                 1865.25

10/06 C3613       515    Charitable Contrib. Exp.    50.00
10/06 C3613       110    Cash                                    50.00

10/07 C3614       250    Wilson Office Supplies      76.29
```

TUTORIAL 2-T

In this tutorial you will use the operating procedures introduced in this chapter. To complete the tutorial problem, follow the step-by-step instructions provided. Each step lists a task to be completed at the computer. In case you need it, more detailed information on how to complete the task is provided immediately following the step. If you need additional explanation for the task, a page reference is provided to the Operating Procedures section of this chapter (or a previous chapter).

The transactions for Santiago Associates occurred during the period of October 1 through October 10 of the current year. The general journal entries have already been recorded for you on a general journal entries input form illustrated within the step-by-step instructions in (see Figure 2.12). Any additions, changes, or deletions to the chart of accounts have also been recorded for you on a chart of accounts input form within the step-by-step instructions (see Figure 2.11).

Directions: The step-by-step instructions for solving the tutorial problem are listed below. Within the instructions, you will be directed to display various reports. If you have a printer attached to your computer and you wish to print the displayed report, pull down the File menu and choose the Print command while the desired report is displayed on the screen.

Step 1:   Bring up the accounting system. (page 16)

Key A1 at the DOS prompt (or follow the instructions provided by your instructor).

Step 2:   Load the opening balances template file, AA2-T. (page 19)

Pull down the File menu and choose the Open Accounting File command. When the Open File window appears, key the path and file name for the opening balances template file, AA2-T. Key into the Path field the drive and directory containing the template files. Key a file name of AA2-T and press the Ok button.

Step 3:   Save the opening balances file to your drive and directory with a file name of XXX2-T (where XXX are your initials). (page 21)

Pull down the File menu and choose the Save As menu command. Key the path to your drive and directory (for example, if you wish to save your data to drive B, key B: as the path name). Key a file name of XXX2-T where XXX are your initials. Push the Ok button.

Step 4: Set the run date and student name in the General Information data entry window. The run date is October 10 of the current year. (page 24)

Pull down the Options menu and choose the General Information menu command. Set the run date to October 10 of the current year. Key your name in the Student Name field. Verify that you have keyed your name correctly, since you will be unable to change it for the duration of this problem. Notice that the rest of the fields were automatically set when the balances were loaded. Leave these fields as they appear.

Step 5: Key the data from the chart of accounts input form. (page 40)

Pull down the Ledgers menu and choose the Maintain Accounts command. Key the data from the completed chart of accounts input form shown in Figure 2.11.

FIGURE 2.11
Completed Chart of Accounts Input Form

```
                    CHART OF ACCOUNTS
                       INPUT FORM

   Run Date  10/10/--              Problem No.   2-T

   Acct. No.            Account Title

     515       Charitable Contrib. Exp.

     220       Business World, Inc.

```

Step 6: Key the general journal entries. (page 42).

Pull down the Journal menu and choose the General Journal command (if not already displayed). Key the data from the completed general journal input form shown in Figure 2.12.

Transactions:

> Note: Do *not* key from these transaction statements, since they have already been recorded for you on the general journal entries input form in Figure 2.12. The reference numbers on the input forms are abbreviated as follows: Check no., C; Memorandum, M; Cash register tape, T.

Oct. 01 Paid cash for office rent, $1,711.00. C3611.
01 Paid cash for telephone bill, $253.91. C3612.
03 Received cash from sales, $1,865.25. T865.
06 Paid cash for charitable contribution, $50.00. C3613.

Sidebar notes:
After keying the date and your name, you may use Ctrl+Enter to push the Ok button and record the data.

After all entries have been keyed, push the Exit button on the chart of accounts list to close the Maintain Accounts window.

After all parts of the journal entry have been keyed, press Ctrl+Enter to Ok the transaction. To make corrections to journal entries, use the List command button to select the transaction to be corrected.

Note: Add Charitable Contrib. Exp. to the chart of accounts. Assign account number 515 to Charitable Contrib. Exp. so that it will be positioned immediately following Advertising Expense.

06 Change the account Business World to Business World, Inc.

07 Paid cash on account to Wilson Office Supplies, $76.29. C3614.

08 Bought supplies on account from Wilson Office Supplies, $198.53. M41.

09 Paid cash for miscellaneous expense, $15.00. C3615.

10 Paid cash for supplies, $43.00. C3616.

10 Paid cash for insurance, $274.91. C3617.

FIGURE 2.12
Completed Journal Entries Input Form

Date MM / dd	Reference	Account Number	Cust./ Vend No.	Debit	Credit
Run Date 10/10/--		GENERAL JOURNAL INPUT FORM		Problem No. 2-T	
10/01	C3611	540		1711.00	
	C3611	110			1711.00
10/01	C3612	560		253.91	
	C3612	110			253.91
10/03	T865	110		1865.25	
	T865	410			1865.25
10/06	C3613	515		50.00	
—	C3613	110			50.00
10/07	C3614	250		76.29	
	C3614	110			76.29
10/08	M41	120		198.53	
	M41	250			198.53
10/09	C3615	530		15.00	
	C3615	110			15.00
10/10	C3616	120		43.00	
	C3616	110			43.00
10/10	C3617	130		274.91	
	C3617	110			274.91
Totals				4487.89	4487.89

Step 7:   Display a chart of accounts. (page 13)

Pull down the Reports menu and choose the Accounts command. When the Report Selection window appears, choose the chart of accounts list. Examine the report in Figure 2.13 and verify that the data you keyed in Step 5 is correct.

> Note: Use the Up and Down Arrow keys or Page Up and Page Down keys to view the displayed report. If you have a mouse, click on the arrows at either end of the scroll bar to scroll the report data.
>
> To close a report window, press Esc or click on the close button (=) in the upper left corner of the window.
>
> To print the report currently displayed in the report window, use the F9 "hot key."

FIGURE 2.13
Chart of Accounts Report

```
                   Santiago Associates
                    Chart of Accounts
                       10/10/--

        ------------------------------------
        Account  Account
        Number   Title
        ------------------------------------
        110      Cash
        120      Supplies
        130      Prepaid Insurance
        210      Amos Business Forms
        220      Business World, Inc.
        230      Cravens Computerware
        240      Graphic Design Plus
        250      Wilson Office Supplies
        310      Luis Santiago, Capital
        320      Luis Santiago, Drawing
        330      Income Summary
        410      Sales
        510      Advertising Expense
        515      Charitable Contrib. Exp.
        520      Insurance Expense
        530      Miscellaneous Expense
        540      Rent Expense
        550      Supplies Expense
        560      Telephone Expense
```

Step 8:   Display the general journal report.

Pull down the Reports menu and choose the Journals command. When the Report Selection window shown in Figure 2.14 appears, select the general journal report. When the Selection Options window illustrated in Figure 2.15 appears, verify the date range of October 1 to October 10 of the current year. The report appears in Figure 2.16.

Note: If corrections are necessary, use the List button on the general journal data entry window to select the journal entry to be corrected. If a dialog window appears indicating that no journal entries were found, check the date range keyed on the Selection Option window. Only journal entries within the specified date range are included in the report.

FIGURE 2.14
Report Selection Window

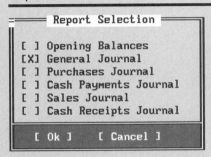

FIGURE 2.15
Selection Options

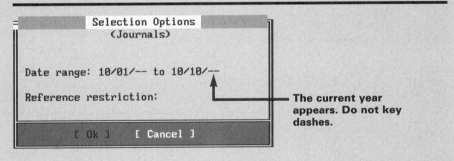

Step 9:   Display a trial balance. (page 13)

Pull down the Reports menu and choose the Ledgers command. When the Report Selection window appears, select the trial balance report. The report appears in Figure 2.17.

Step 10:   Save your data to disk with a file name of XXX2-T, where XXX are your initials.

Pull down the File menu and choose the Save menu command.

Step 11:   End your session.

Pull down the File menu and choose the Quit menu command.

FIGURE 2.16
General Journal Entries Report

```
                        Santiago Associates
                         General Journal
                            10/10/--

     .
     --------------------------------------------------------------
     Date   Refer. V/C Acct.  Title               Debit      Credit
     --------------------------------------------------------------
     10/01 C3611      540     Rent Expense        1711.00
     10/01 C3611      110     Cash                           1711.00

     10/01 C3612      560     Telephone Expense    253.91
     10/01 C3612      110     Cash                            253.91

     10/03 T865       110     Cash                1865.25
     10/03 T865       410     Sales                          1865.25

     10/06 C3613      515     Charitable Contrib. Exp.  50.00
     10/06 C3613      110     Cash                             50.00

     10/07 C3614      250     Wilson Office Supplies   76.29
     10/07 C3614      110     Cash                             76.29

     10/08 M41        120     Supplies             198.53
     10/08 M41        250     Wilson Office Supplies         198.53

     10/09 C3615      530     Miscellaneous Expense  15.00
     10/09 C3615      110     Cash                             15.00

     10/10 C3616      120     Supplies              43.00
     10/10 C3616      110     Cash                             43.00

     10/10 C3617      130     Prepaid Insurance    274.91
     10/10 C3617      110     Cash                            274.91

                                                ---------- ----------
                              Totals            4487.89    4487.89
                                                ========== ==========
```

FIGURE 2.17
Trial Balance Report

```
                        Santiago Associates
                          Trial Balance
                            10/10/--

     --------------------------------------------------------------
     Acct.  Account
     Number Title                          Debit       Credit
     --------------------------------------------------------------
     110    Cash                         12796.54
     120    Supplies                      1086.87
     130    Prepaid Insurance              431.91
     220    Business World, Inc.                       266.90
     240    Graphic Design Plus                        235.27
     250    Wilson Office Supplies                     198.53
     310    Luis Santiago, Capital                   13779.28
     410    Sales                                     1865.25
     515    Charitable Contrib. Exp.        50.00
     530    Miscellaneous Expense           15.00
     540    Rent Expense                  1711.00
     560    Telephone Expense              253.91
                                        ---------- ----------
            Totals                       16345.23   16345.23
                                        ========== ==========
```

CHAPTER 2 STUDENT EXERCISE

I. TRUE/FALSE

Directions: Answer the following questions in the working papers or on a separate sheet of paper. If the statement is true, write the question number followed by T. If the statement is false, write the question number followed by F.

1. An entry to add a new account is recorded on the chart of accounts input form.
2. Only transactions that do not involve cash may be recorded on the general journal input form.
3. General ledger accounts cannot be deleted unless the account balance is zero.
4. The Find command button in the General Journal data entry window could be used to find a transaction that contained a specified debit or credit amount.
5. The List command button on the general journal data entry window generates a chart of accounts list.
6. A new general ledger account can be added (or changed) while keying a journal entry.
7. Instead of keying an account number in the General Journal data entry window, you may select the account from a Chart of Accounts list window.

II. QUESTIONS

Directions: Answer each of the following questions in the working papers or on a separate sheet of paper.

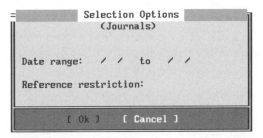

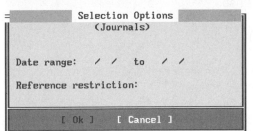

1. List the three kinds of entries that may be recorded on the chart of accounts input form.
2. Explain why the totals at the end of the general journal input form are compared to the totals at the end of the general journal entries report.
3. Describe the process for correcting a general journal entry.
4. Describe the process for deleting a general journal entry.
5. Explain how Shift+F1 to Shift+F5 are used with the General Journal data entry window.
6. Complete the date range section of the Selection Options dialog window shown on the left to display all journal entries from August 1 through August 31 of the current year.
7. Complete the Selection Options dialog window shown on the left to display all journal entries from September 1 through September 10 of the current year with a reference of C121.

PRACTICE PROBLEM 2-P

In this problem, you will process any additions, changes, and deletions to the chart of accounts as well as the general journal entries for the period October 12 through October 20 of the current year.

Directions: The step-by-step instructions for solving the practice problem are listed below.

Step 1:   Remove the input forms from the working papers. Record the following transactions for Santiago Associates on the general journal input form. Record any additions, changes, or deletions to the chart of accounts on the chart of accounts input form. Abbreviate the reference numbers on the input forms as follows: Check no., C; Memorandum, M; Cash register tape, T.

Oct. 14   Received cash from sales, $2,684.75. T866.

14   Bought a subscription on account from Brokerage News, $150.00. M42.

Note: Add Dues & Subscriptions Exp. to the chart of accounts. Assign account number 525 to Dues & Subscriptions Exp. so that it will be positioned immediately following Insurance Expense.

Add Brokerage News to the chart of accounts. Assign account number 260 to Brokerage News.

15   Paid cash for miscellaneous expense, $86.00. C3618.

15   Paid cash on account to Business World, Inc., $266.90. C3619.

15   Received cash from sales, $2,715.50. T867.

15   Change the account Graphic Design Plus to Graphic Designers.

16   Bought advertising on account from Business World, Inc., $575.00. M43.

17   Paid cash on account to Graphic Designers, $235.27. C3620.

17   Delete Cravens Computerware from the chart of accounts.

20   Paid cash for travel expense, $167.45. C3621.

Note: Add Travel & Entertain. Exp. to the chart of accounts. Assign account number 565 to Travel & Entertain. Exp. so that it will be positioned immediately following Telephone Expense.

Use the Files button to display a list box of all *Automated Accounting 6.0* files for the path currently displayed.

Step 2:   Bring up the accounting system.

Step 3:   Load the opening balances template file, AA2-P. Key into the Path field the drive and directory containing the template files. Key a file name of AA2-P.

Step 4:   Use the Save As menu command to save the opening balances file to your drive and directory with a file name of XXX2-P, where XXX are your initials.

After keying the date and your name, you may use Ctrl+Enter to activate the Ok button and record the data.

Step 5:   Set the run date and student name in the General Information data entry window. The run date is October 20 of the current year.

Step 6:   Key the data from the chart of accounts input form.

After all entries have been keyed, click on the Exit button on the chart of accounts list to close the Maintain Accounts window.

Step 7: Key the general journal entries.

Step 8: Display a chart of accounts report.

Step 9: Display the general journal report for the period October 11 to October 20.

> Note: If corrections are necessary, use the List button on the general journal data entry window to select the journal entry to be corrected. If a dialog window appears indicating that no journal entries were found, check the date range keyed on the Selection Option window. Only journal entries within the specified date range are included on the report.

After all parts of the journal entry have been keyed, press Ctrl+Enter to Ok the transaction. To make corrections to journal entries, use the List command button to select the transaction to be corrected.

Step 10: Display a trial balance.

Step 11: Save your data to disk with a file name of XXX2-P, where XXX are your initials.

Step 12: Remove the Audit Test from the working papers for Chapter 2. Display the reports necessary to fill in the answers. If you are not using the working papers, write the answers on a separate sheet of paper.

Step 13: End the session.

AUDIT TEST PROBLEM 2-P

Directions: Write the answers to the following questions in the working papers or on a separate sheet of paper.

1. What is the title of account number 525?
2. What are the debit and credit totals on the general journal report?
3. What is the amount of check number 3619 shown on the general journal report?
4. What is the balance in the Rent Expense account?
5. What is the balance in the Dues & Subscriptions Expense account?
6. What are the debit and credit totals on the trial balance report?

M MASTERY PROBLEM 2-M

In this problem, you will process any additions, changes, and deletions to the chart of accounts as well as the general journal entries for the period October 21 through October 31 of the current year.

Directions: To complete the mastery problem, record the transactions on the proper input form, load the opening balances file (AA2-M), set the run date, enter the transactions, and display the following reports:

Chart of Accounts
General Journal Report
Trial Balance

When you are finished, save your data file to disk with a file name of XXX2-M, where XXX are your initials. Display reports as necessary to answer the questions in the audit test.

Transactions:

Oct. 21   Bought supplies on account from Wilson Office Supplies, $210.20. M44.

     23   Paid cash for insurance, $310.50. C3622.

     23   Received cash from sales, $2,350.00. T868.

     27   Paid cash on account to Wilson Office Supplies, $198.53. C3623.

     27   Delete Amos Business Forms from the chart of accounts.

     28   Bought supplies on account from Graphic Designers, $410.15. M45.

     29   Received cash from sales, $2,442.20. T869.

     30   Paid cash for electric bill, $475.50. C3624.

          Note: Add Utilities Expense to the chart of accounts. Assign account number 570 to Utilities Expense so that it will be positioned immediately following Travel & Entertain. Exp.

     30   Paid cash for charitable contribution, $100.00. C3625.

     31   Paid cash for miscellaneous expense, $166.00. C3626.

     31   Paid cash to owner for personal use, $4,800.00. C3627.

AUDIT TEST PROBLEM 2-M

Directions: Write the answers to the following questions in the working papers or on a separate sheet of paper.

1. What is the title of account number 570?
2. What are the debit and credit totals on the general journal report?
3. What is the amount of check number 3626 shown on the general journal report?
4. What is the balance in the Advertising Expense account?
5. What is the balance in the Miscellaneous Expense account?
6. What are the debit and credit totals on the trial balance report?

3

General Ledger — End of Fiscal Period for a Service Business and Bank Reconciliation

LEARNING OBJECTIVES ▶ UPON COMPLETION OF THIS CHAPTER, you will be able to:

1. Record adjusting entries on the general journal input form.
2. Enter and correct adjusting entries.
3. Display adjusting entries.
4. Display financial statements.
5. Perform period-end closing.
6. Display a post-closing trial balance.
7. Enter bank reconciliation data.
8. Display the bank reconciliation report.

INTRODUCTION

In this chapter, you will learn how to complete the end-of-fiscal-period processing for a service business. In the previous chapter, you learned how to maintain the general ledger accounts and how to process the transactions. To complete the accounting cycle, adjusting entries are recorded on the general journal input form, keyed into the computer, and verified for accuracy. The financial statements can then be printed. Finally, period-end closing is performed and a post-closing trial balance is generated. In addition, you will learn how to use the computer to complete the bank reconciliation.

▶ Recording Adjusting Entries

Adjusting entries are recorded on the general journal input form. Adjusting entries, however, cannot be recorded until after all other transactions for the accounting period have been recorded, keyed into the computer, and posted. The trial balance is then displayed or printed. This trial balance and the period-end adjustment data are the basis for the adjusting entries. The adjusting entries are then recorded on the general journal input form, keyed into the computer, and posted. A journal entries report is then displayed to prove the equality of the debits and credits.

All the adjusting entries are recorded on the same day and have the same information in the reference column. Therefore, you record the date and reference only once on the input form. Record ADJ.ENT. in the Reference column. The adjustment data for Santiago Associates is shown below. The trial balance after the transactions for the period have been processed is shown in Figure 3.1. The adjusting entries have been recorded on the general journal input form illustrated in Figure 3.2.

FIGURE 3.1
Trial Balance (Before Adjusting Entries)

```
                        Santiago Associates
                           Trial Balance
                             10/31/—
        ------------------------------------------------------------
        Acct.    Account
        Number   Title                          Debit      Credit
        ------------------------------------------------------------
        110      Cash                           16182.84
        120      Supplies                        1707.22
        130      Prepaid Insurance                742.41
        220      Business World, Inc.                        575.00
        240      Graphic Designers                          410.15
        250      Wilson Office Supplies                     210.20
        260      Brokerage News                             150.00
        310      Luis Santiago, Capital                   13779.28
        320      Luis Santiago, Drawing          4800.00
```

(continued)

```
 --------------------------------------------------------
 Acct.    Account
 Number   Title                        Debit      Credit
 --------------------------------------------------------
 510      Advertising Expense          575.00
 515      Charitable Contrib. Exp.     150.00
 525      Dues & Subscriptions Exp.    150.00
 530      Miscellaneous Expense        267.00
 540      Rent Expense                1711.00
 560      Telephone Expense            253.91
 565      Travel & Entertain. Exp.     167.45
                                      --------- ---------
 570      Utilities Expense            475.50
                                      ========= =========
          Totals                     27182.33   27182.33
```

Supplies inventory $1,152.22

Value of insurance policies on October 31 ....492.41

The adjustment amounts are calculated as follows:

> Balance in Supplies from trial balance ($1,707.22)
> – current supplies inventory ($1,152.22)
> = supplies adjustment ($555.00)
>
> Balance in Prepaid Insurance from the trial balance ($742.41)
> – current value of insurance policies($492.41)
> = insurance adjustment ($250.00).

FIGURE 3.2
General Journal Input Form (Adjusting Entries)

	GENERAL JOURNAL INPUT FORM				
Run Date 10/31/--				Problem No.	3-T
Date MM / dd	Reference	Account Number	Cust./ Vend No.	Debit	Credit
10/31	ADJ. ENT.	550		555.00	
		120			555.00
		520		250.00	
		130			250.00
Totals				805.00	805.00

In a manual accounting system, a work sheet is used as a tool for analyzing the adjusting entries and preparing the financial statements. Since the computer generates the financial statements automatically from the general ledger data, a work sheet is not required for an auto-mated accounting system. Therefore, once the adjusting entries have been keyed, posted, and verified, the financial statements may be displayed.

OPERATING PROCEDURES

Operating procedures are covered in this chapter for performing period-end closing and displaying financial statements. Although adjusting entries are included in this chapter, the operating proce-dures for keying adjusting entries are identical to those given in Chapter 2 for keying general journal entries.

▶ Financial Statements

The financial statements available vary slightly depending on options set in the General Information data entry window. If the options are set to a nondepartmentalized business organized as a sole proprietor-ship, the three financial statements available are (1) income statement, (2) balance sheet, and (3) owner's equity statement.

▶ Displaying Financial Statements

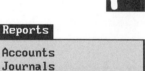

1   **Choose the Financial Statements menu command from the Reports menu.**

The Report Selection dialog window shown in Figure 3.3 will appear, allowing you to select which of the financial state-ments you would like generated.

FIGURE 3.3
Report Selection (Financial Statements)

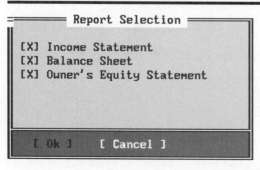

2   **Select the financial statements you would like to display (more than one may be selected).**

The reports are selected by clicking on the check box or by pressing the Space Bar (or Right Arrow) while the cursor is positioned in that check box.

3   **Push the Ok button.**

INCOME STATEMENT.   The income statement provides information on the profitability of the business. *Automated Accounting 6.0* offers two formats of the income statement. The format used by this chapter is illustrated in Figure 3.4. With this format the profitability of the business is shown from the beginning of the fiscal period until the time when the income statement is displayed. The second format of the income statement shows the profitability of the business for the current month as well as the profitability for the year to date. This second format will be further described and illustrated in later chapters. The format of the income statement is set with the Accounting System option button on the General Information data entry window illustrated on page 8 of Chapter 1.

FIGURE 3.4
Income Statement by
Fiscal Period

```
                  Santiago Associates
                   Income Statement
                For Period Ended 10/31/--

    O p e r a t i n g   R e v e n u e
    ---------------------------------
    Sales                              12057.70
                                       --------
    Total Operating Revenue            12057.70

    O p e r a t i n g   E x p e n s e s
    ---------------------------------
    Advertising Expense                  575.00
    Charitable Contrib. Exp.             150.00
    Insurance Expense                    250.00
    Dues & Subscriptions Exp.            150.00
    Miscellaneous Expense                267.00
    Rent Expense                        1711.00
    Supplies Expense                     555.00
    Telephone Expense                    253.91
    Travel & Entertain. Exp.             167.45
    Utilities Expense                    475.50
                                       --------
    Total Operating Expenses            4554.86
                                       --------
    Net Income                          7502.84
                                       ========
```

If the balance sheet is displayed or printed before period-end closing, the capital or equity section will include the drawing amount as well as the net income or loss. After period-end closing, these amounts will not appear because they will have been closed to the capital account.

BALANCE SHEET.   The balance sheet provides information on the overall financial strength of a business as of a specific date. While the balance sheet may be displayed at any time, it is typically displayed as of the end of a fiscal period. The balance sheet is illustrated in Figure 3.5.

FIGURE 3.5
Balance Sheet

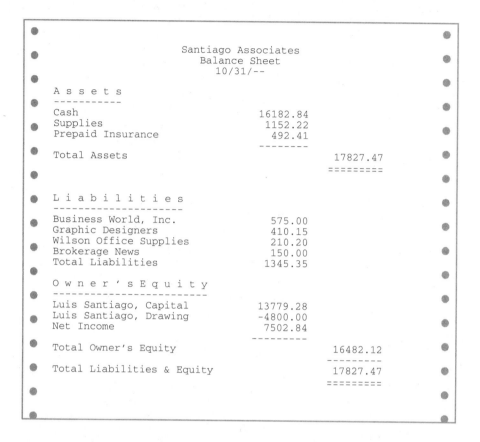

OWNER'S EQUITY STATEMENT.   The owner's equity statement shows the changes to owner's equity that have occurred during the fiscal period. The capital at the beginning of the period is shown, followed by additions and subtractions to capital and ending with the capital, at the end of the fiscal period. A sample owner's equity statement is shown in Figure 3.6.

FIGURE 3.6
Owner's Equity
Statement

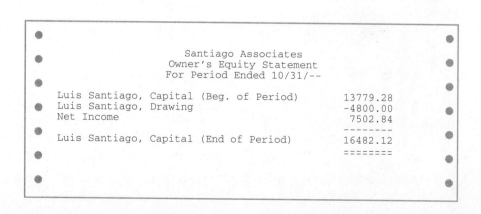

▶Period-End Closing

```
Options
General Information
Required Accounts
Account Classification
Extended Classifications
Account Subtotals
Enter Budgets
Period-End Closing
Purge Journal Entries

Display Type     Ctrl+D
Set Colors
```

At the end of the fiscal period in a manual accounting system, closing entries are recorded in the journal and posted to the general ledger. In an automated accounting system, the period-end closing process is performed automatically by the computer. During the period-end closing process, the computer closes all of the temporary income statement accounts to the income summary account, closes the income summary account to the capital account, closes the drawing account to the capital account, and purges (erases) the journal entries in preparation for the beginning of a new accounting period. During the period-end closing process the computer also copies the current account balances and stores them as the last fiscal period's account balances for use with financial statement analysis.

▶Performing Period-End Closing

1   Choose the Period-End Closing menu command from the Options menu.

The dialog window shown in Figure 3.7 will appear.

FIGURE 3.7
Perform Period-End Closing Dialog Window

```
        Perform period-end closing?



    [ Ok ]              [ Cancel ]
```

The procedure for displaying a post-closing trial balance is identical to the procedure for dislaying a regular trial balance (it is the same report). The only difference between a regular trial balance and a post-closing trial balance is *when* it is displayed.

2   Push the Ok button to perform period-end closing.

3   Display a post-closing trial balance report by choosing the Ledger menu command from the Reports menu and then selecting the trial balance report.

The post-closing trial balance for Santiago Associates is shown in Figure 3.8.

▶Bank Reconciliation

Each month, after the bank statement is received, the bank statement is reconciled to the checkbook balance (which should be the same as the Cash account balance). The bank reconciliation software is included in the second accounting system module, along with payroll and plant assets.

FIGURE 3.8
Post-Closing Trial Balance

```
                        Santiago Associates
                          Trial Balance
                            10/31/--

     -----------------------------------------------------------
     Acct.    Account
     Number   Title                             Debit      Credit
     -----------------------------------------------------------
     110      Cash                            16182.84
     120      Supplies                         1152.22
     130      Prepaid Insurance                 492.41
     220      Business World, Inc.                          575.00
     240      Graphic Designers                            410.15
     250      Wilson Office Supplies                       210.20
     260      Brokerage News                               150.00
     310      Luis Santiago, Capital                     16482.12
                                              ---------   --------
              Totals                          17827.47   17827.47
                                              =========   ========
```

▶Performing Bank Reconciliation

1   Choose the Payroll/Assets/Bank Rec. menu command from the File menu.

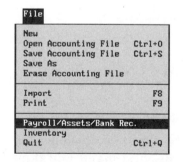

The second module of the accounting system, containing payroll, plant assets, and bank reconciliation, will be loaded. If you are running from a floppy disk and the second module is not on the disk currently in the drive, you will be prompted to insert the disk containing the second module. After the second module is loaded, the menu bar will change to that shown in Figure 3.9.

2   Load the opening balance template file for AA3-T.

Since each of the accounting system modules appends a different file extension to the file name, the file AA3-T in module 2 is not the same file as AA3-T loaded in module 1. Each module uses a unique file format.

3   Choose the General Information menu command from the Options menu and set the run date and student name in the General Information data entry window.

The module 2 General Information data entry window is illustrated in Figure 3.10. Notice that it is different from the General Information data entry window used in module 1 in that it contains fewer fields and buttons.

FIGURE 3.9
Module 2 Menu Bar

File   System   Options   Assets   Reports   Help

FIGURE 3.10
General Information Data Entry Window

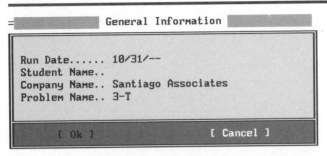

```
=              General Information

   Run Date......  10/31/--
   Student Name..
   Company Name..  Santiago Associates
   Problem Name..  3-T


        [ Ok ]                    [ Cancel ]
```

Reconciliation

Reconciliation Data

4   Choose the Bank Reconciliation Data menu command from the Reconciliation menu and key the reconciliation data.

The Bank Reconciliation data entry window is illustrated in Figure 3.11.

FIGURE 3.11
Bank Reconciliation Data Entry Window

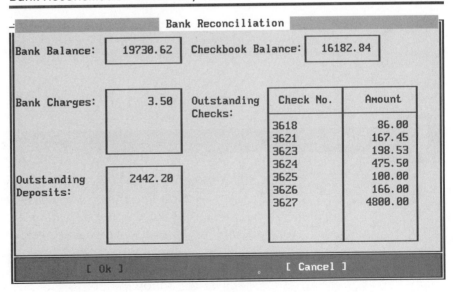

	Bank Reconciliation		
Bank Balance: 19730.62	Checkbook Balance: 16182.84		
Bank Charges: 3.50	Outstanding Checks:	Check No.	Amount
		3618	86.00
		3621	167.45
		3623	198.53
		3624	475.50
Outstanding Deposits: 2442.20		3625	100.00
		3626	166.00
		3627	4800.00
[Ok]		[Cancel]	

Report

Bank Reconciliation

5   Choose the Bank Reconciliation menu command from the Reports menu.

The resulting Bank Reconciliation is shown in Figure 3.12. Notice that the Adjusted Checkbook Balance is equal to the Adjusted Bank Balance.

FIGURE 3.12
Bank Reconciliation Report

```
                          Santiago Associates
                          Bank Reconciliation
                               10/31/--

   Checkbook Balance                                      16182.84
                                             3.50
                                           --------
   Less Bank Charges                                          3.50
                                                          --------
   Adjusted Checkbook Balance                             16179.34
                                                          ========


   Bank Balance                                           19730.62
                                          2442.20
   Plus Outstanding Deposits                               2442.20
                                    3618     86.00
                                    3621    167.45
                                    3623    198.53
                                    3624    475.50
                                    3625    100.00
                                    3626    166.00
                                    3627   4800.00
   Less Outstanding Checks                                 5993.48
                                                          --------
   Adjusted Bank Balance                                  16179.34
                                                          ========
```

TUTORIAL 3-T

In this tutorial problem, you will perform the operating procedures necessary to complete the end-of-fiscal-period processing for a service business by keying the adjusting entries, displaying the financial statements, and performing period-end closing for Santiago Associates. In addition, you will reconcile the bank statement balance to the checkbook balance.

Each of the following steps lists a task to be completed at the computer. In case you need it, more detailed information on how to complete the task is provided immediately following the step. If you need additional explanation for the task, a page reference is provided to the Operating Procedures section of this chapter (or a previous chapter).

Directions: Step-by-step instructions for completing the end-of-period processing for Santiago Associates for the fiscal period ended October 31 of the current year are as follows.

Step 1: Bring up the accounting system. (page 16)

At the Dos prompt, key A1 (or follow the instructions provided by your instructor).

Step 2: Load the opening balances template file, AA3-T. (Page 19)

Pull down the File menu and choose the Open Accounting File command. When the Open File window appears, key the path and file name for the opening balances template file, AA3-T. Key into the Path field the drive and directory containing the template files. Key a file name AA3-T and push the OK button.

Step 3: Save the opening balances file to your drive and directory with a file name of XXX3-T, where XXX are your initials. (page 21)

Pull down the File menu and choose the Save As menu command. Key the path to the drive and directory that contains your data files (for example, if you wish to save your data to Drive B, key B: as the path name). Key a file name of XXX3-T, where XXX are your initials. Push the Ok button.

Step 4: Enter the student name in the General Information data entry window and verify that the run date is set to October 31 of the current year. (page 24)

Pull down the Options menu and choose the General Information menu command. Set the run date to October 31 of the current year. Key your name in the Student Name field.

Step 5: Key the adjusting entries from the general journal input form shown in Figure 3.13. (page 42)

Pull down the Journal menu and choose the General Journal option (unless the General Journal is already on the screen). Key the adjusting entries.

The adjusting entries have been recorded for you and are illustrated in Figure 3.13.

Adjustment Data: The adjustment data for the month of October for Santiago Associates is listed below.

```
Supplies inventory .......................$1,152.22
Value of insurance policies on October 31 ....492.41
```

FIGURE 3.13
General Journal Input Form (Adjusting Entries)

Run Date 10/31/--	GENERAL JOURNAL INPUT FORM		Problem No. 3-T		
Date MM / dd	Reference	Account Number	Cust./ Vend No.	Debit	Credit
10/31	ADJ.ENT.	550		555.00	
		120			555.00
		520		250.00	
		130			250.00
Totals				805.00	805.00

Step 6: Display the adjusting entries. (page 45)

Pull down the Reports menu and choose the Journals command. When the Report Selection window appears, select the general journal report. When the selection options window is shown in Figure 3.14 appears, key a date range of October 31 through October 31 (of the current year) and a Reference restriction of ADJ.ENT. so that only the adjusting entries are reported. The report appears in Figure 3.15.

FIGURE 3.14
Selection Options

```
=        Selection Options
              (Journals)


 Date range: 10/01/-- to 10/31/--

 Reference restriction: ADJ.ENT.


      [ Ok ]      [ Cancel ]
```

FIGURE 3.15
General Journal Report (Adjusting Entries)

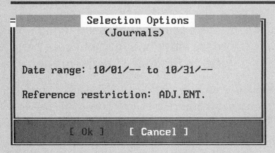

```
                    Santiago Associates
                     General Journal
                        10/31/--
        --------------------------------------------------
        Date   Refer.   V/C Acct. Title          Debit   Credit
        --------------------------------------------------
        10/31  ADJ.ENT.     550  Supplies Expense  555.00
        10/31  ADJ.ENT.     120  Supplies                  555.00

        10/31  ADJ.ENT.     520  Insurance Expense 250.00
        10/31  ADJ.ENT.     130  Prepaid Insurance         250.00
                                                   ------  ------
                                  Totals           805.00  805.00
                                                   ======  ======
```

Step 7:   Display the financial statements. (page 60)

Pull down the Reports menu and choose the Financial Statements menu command. When the Report Selection window shown in Figure 3.16 appears, select all three financial statements. The reports are shown in Figure 3.17.

FIGURE 3.16
Report Selection Dialog Window

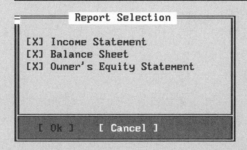

Step 8:   Save your data file to disk with a file name of XXX3-TBC, where XXX are your initials. (page 21)

Pull down the File menu and choose the Save As menu command. Save your file as XXX3-TBC, where XXX are your initials, 3-T is the problem number, and BC is "before closing." It is recommended that you *always* save a backup copy of your data file to disk before performing period-end closing. During the closing process, all of the journal entries for the current period are erased—thus making it difficult to make corrections after closing has been performed. If you discover an error after period-end closing, you can simply load the file saved in Step 8, make corrections, and proceed again with Step 9 below.

Step 9:   Perform the period-end closing. (page 63)

Pull down the Options menu and select the Period-End Closing menu command. When the dialog window appears asking if you want to perform period-end closing, push the Ok button.

Step 10:   Display a post-closing trial balance. (page 63)

Pull down the Report menu and select the Ledger menu command. When the Report Selection window appears, select the Trial Balance report and push the Ok button. The post-closing trial balance report appears in Figure 3.18.

Step 11:   Use the Save As menu command to save your data to disk with a file name of XXX3-T, where XXX are your initials. (page 21)

Pull down the File menu and choose the Save As menu command to save your file to disk.

FIGURE 3.17
Financial Statements

```
                         Santiago Associates
                          Income Statement
                       For Period Ended 10/31/--

O p e r a t i n g   R e v e n u e
-------------------------------
Sales                                 12057.70
                                      --------
Total Operating Revenue               12057.70

O p e r a t i n g   E x p e n s e s
-----------------------------------
Advertising Expense                     575.00
Charitable Contrib. Exp.                150.00
Insurance Expense                       250.00
Dues & Subscriptions Exp.               150.00
Miscellaneous Expense                   267.00
Rent Expense                           1711.00
Supplies Expense                        555.00
Telephone Expense                       253.91
Travel & Entertain. Exp.                167.45
Utilities Expense                       475.50
Total Operating Expenses               4554.86
Net Income                             7502.84
```

```
                         Santiago Associates
                           Balance Sheet
                       For Period Ended 10/31/--

A s s e t s
-----------
Cash                                  16182.84
Supplies                               1152.22
Prepaid Insurance                       492.41
                                      --------
Total Assets                                        17827.47
                                                    ========

L i a b i l i t i e s
--------------------
Business World, Inc.                    575.00
Graphic Designers                       410.15
Wilson Office Supplies                  210.20
Brokerage News                          150.00
                                      --------
Total Liabilities                                    1345.35

O w n e r ' s   E q u i t y
-----------------------
Luis Santiago, Capital                13779.28
Luis Santiago, Drawing                -4800.00
Net Income                             7502.84
                                      --------
Total Owner's Equity                                16482.12
                                                    --------
Total Liabilities & Equity                          17827.47
                                                    ========
```

```
                         Santiago Associates
                       Statement of Owner's Equity
                       For Period Ended 10/31/--

Luis Santiago, Capital (Beg. of Period)      13779.28
Luis Santiago, Drawing                       -4800.00
Net Income                                    7502.84
                                             --------
Luis Santiago, Capital (End of Period)       16482.12
                                             ========
```

FIGURE 3.18
Post Closing Trial
Balance

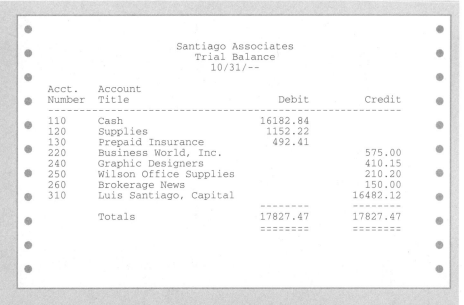

```
                          Santiago Associates
                             Trial Balance
                               10/31/--

     Acct.     Account
     Number    Title                        Debit          Credit
     ----------------------------------------------------------------
     110       Cash                       16182.84
     120       Supplies                    1152.22
     130       Prepaid Insurance            492.41
     220       Business World, Inc.                          575.00
     240       Graphic Designers                             410.15
     250       Wilson Office Supplies                        210.20
     260       Brokerage News                                150.00
     310       Luis Santiago, Capital                      16482.12
                                          --------        --------
               Totals                     17827.47        17827.47
                                          ========        ========
```

Step 12:   Load module 2 (Payroll/Assets/Bank Rec.). (page 64)

Pull down the File menu and choose the Payroll/Assets/Bank Rec. menu command.

Step 13:   Load the opening balance template file for AA3-T. (page 64)

Pull down the File menu and choose the Open File menu command. When the Open File window appears, key the path and file name for the opening balances template file, AA3-T. Key into the Path field the drive and directory containing the template files. Key a file name of AA3-T and push the OK button.

Step 14:   Set the run date and student name in the General Information data entry window. The run date is October 31 of the current year. (page 64)

Pull down the Options menu and choose the General Information menu command. Set the run date to October 31 of the current year. Key your name in the Student Name field.

Step 15:   Key the bank reconciliation data listed below. (page 65)

Choose the Bank Reconciliation Data menu command from the Reconciliation menu and key the reconciliation data.

Checkbook balance $16182.84

Bank charge 3.50

Balance shown on bank statement 19730.62

Outstanding deposit 2442.20

```
Outstanding checks as as follows:

Check No.      Amount
3618            $86.00
3621           $167.45
3623           $198.53
3624           $475.50
3625           $100.00
3626           $166.00
3627          $4800.00
```

Step 16:   Display the bank reconciliation report. (page 65)

Choose the Bank Reconciliation menu command from the Reports menu. The report is shown in Figure 3.19.

FIGURE 3.19
Bank Reconciliation Report

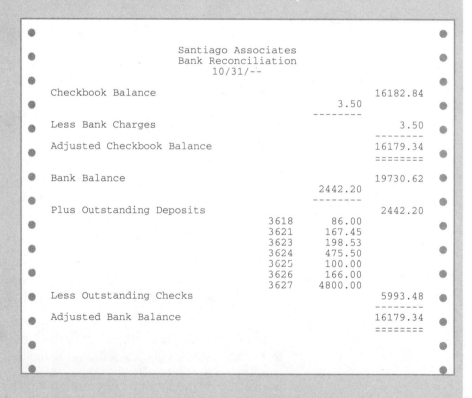

```
                    Santiago Associates
                    Bank Reconciliation
                         10/31/--

Checkbook Balance                                16182.84
                                      3.50
                                   --------
Less Bank Charges                                    3.50
                                                 --------
Adjusted Checkbook Balance                       16179.34
                                                 ========

Bank Balance                                     19730.62
                                   2442.20
                                   --------
Plus Outstanding Deposits                         2442.20
                            3618     86.00
                            3621    167.45
                            3623    198.53
                            3624    475.50
                            3625    100.00
                            3626    166.00
                            3627   4800.00
Less Outstanding Checks                           5993.48
                                                 --------
Adjusted Bank Balance                            16179.34
                                                 ========
```

Step 17:   Use the Save As menu command to save your data to disk with a file name of XXX3-T, where XXX are your initials. (page 21)

Pull down the File menu and choose the Save As menu command to save your file to disk.

Step 18:   End the session. (page 22)

Choose the Quit menu command from the File menu.

CHAPTER 3 STUDENT EXERCISE

I. TRUE/FALSE

Directions: Answer the following question in the working papers or on a separate sheet of paper. If the statement is true, write the question number followed by T. If the statement is false, write the question number followed by F.

1. When an automated accounting system is used, a work sheet is used to assist in the preparation of financial statements.
2. The income statement provides information on the profitability of a business.
3. The balance sheet provides information on the overall financial strength of the business.
4. One of the things that happens during the period-end closing process is that the balance sheet accounts are closed to the income summary account.
5. During the period-end closing all journal entries are purged (erased).
6. If the bank statement reconciles to the checkbook on the bank reconciliation report, the adjusted checkbook balance will equal the adjusted bank balance.

II. QUESTIONS

Directions: Write the answers to the following questions in the working papers or on a separate sheet of paper.

1. If the balance in the Supplies account after all transactions for the fiscal period have been processed and before adjusting entries is $1200.00 and the current supplies inventory is $900.00, what is the amount of the supplies adjusting entry?
2. What is the name of the report that shows the owner's equity at the beginning of the fiscal period, the changes to owner's equity that have occurred during the fiscal period, and the owners's equity at the end of the fiscal period?
3. Explain the processing that takes place during period-end closing.
4. Which one of the three accounting system modules (1, 2, or 3) contains the bank reconciliation software?
5. Why is it recommended that you save a backup copy of your accounting system data file to disk prior to completing the period-end closing?

P PRACTICE PROBLEM 3-P

In Practice Problem 3-P, you will process any additions, changes, and deletions to the chart of accounts. You will also process the monthly transactions for November, complete the end of fiscal period processing, and reconcile the bank statement.

Directions: The step-by-step instructions for solving this practice problem are listed below.

Step 1:   Remove the input forms from the working papers. Record the following transactions for Santiago Associates on the general journal input form. Record any additions, changes, or deletions to the chart of accounts on the chart of accounts input form. Abbreviate the reference numbers on the input forms as follows: check no., C; Memorandum, M; Cash register tape, T.

Nov. 03 Record the October bank service charge, $3.50. Charge Miscellaneous Expense. M46.

03 Paid cash for rent, $1,711.00. C3628.

04 Paid cash for telephone bill, $284.33. C3629.

06 Bought repairs on account from Williams Heating, $429.66. M47.

> Note: Add Repair Expense to the chart of accounts. Assign account number 545 for Repair Expense so that it will be positioned immediately following Rent Expense. Add Williams Heating to the chart of accounts. Assign account number 270 for Williams Heating so that it will be positioned immediately following Brokerage News.

07 Paid cash for insurance, $105.30. C3630.

10 Paid cash on account to Brokerage News, $150.00. C3631.

12 Change the account Wilson Office Supplies to Wilson Supply House.

14 Paid cash on account to Business World, Inc., $575.00. C3632.

17 Received cash from sales, $3,105.43. T870.

18 Bought supplies on account from Graphic Designers, $216.88. M48.

19 Paid cash on account to Wilson Supply House, $210.20. C3633.

20 Bought advertising on account from Brokerage News, $266.97. M49.

21 Received cash from sales, $3,678.99. T871.

21 Paid cash for travel expense, $64.33. C3634.

24 Paid cash on account to Graphic Designers, $410.15. C3635.

25 Paid cash for electric bill, $421.40. C3636.

26 Received cash from sales, $2,816.38. T872.

27 Paid cash to owner for personal use, $4,500.00. C3637.

28 Paid cash for charitable contribution, $75.00. C3638.

28 Paid cash for professional dues, $225.00. C3639.

Step 2:   Bring up the accounting system.

Step 3:   Load the opening balances template file for AA3-P.

Step 4:   Use the Save As menu command to save the opening balances file to your drive and directory with a file name of XXX3-P, where XXX are your initials.

Step 5:   Set the run date and student name in the General Information data entry window. The run date is November 30 of the current year.

Step 6:   Key the data from the chart of accounts input form prepared in Step 1.

Step 7:   Key the general journal entries from the general journal input form prepared in Step 1.

Step 8:   Display a chart of accounts report.

Step 9:   Display the general journal report for the period November 1 through November 30 of the current year. If errors are detected, use the List button on the General Journal data entry window to select the journal entry to correct.

Step 10:   Display a trial balance report.

Step 11:   Record the adjusting entries on a general journal input form. The adjustment data are shown below. Use the trial balance printed in the previous step as the basis for making the adjusting entries. Record "ADJ.ENT." as the reference.

```
Supplies inventory on November 30 ...........$644.10
Value of insurance policies on November 30 ...252.71
```

Step 12:   Key the adjusting entries recorded in the previous step.

Step 13:   Display the general journal report for the adjusting entries. Use a reference restriction of ADJ.ENT., so that only adjusting entries will be included on the report.

Step 14:   Display the financial statements.

Step 15:   Use the Save As menu command to save a backup copy of your data to disk with a file name of XXX3-PBC.

Step 16:   Perform period-end closing.

Step 17:   Display a post-closing trial balance.

Step 18:   Save your data to disk with a file name of XXX3-P, where XXX are your initials.

Step 19:   Load module 2 of the accounting system (Payroll/Assets/Bank Rec.).

Step 20:   Load the opening balance data for Practice Problem 3-P (AA3-P).

Step 21:   Set the run date and student name.

Step 22:   Key the bank reconciliation data based on the information provided below. The checkbook balance can be obtained from the trial balance report.

```
Bank charge ...............................$    3.50
Bank statement balance ....................20070.30
Outstanding deposit .......................2816.38
```

```
Outstanding checks:

Check No.    Amount
   3633    $ 210.20
   3635      410.15
   3636      421.40
   3637     4500.00
   3638       75.00
   3639      225.00
```

Step 23:   Display the bank reconciliation report.

Step 24:   Save your data to disk with a file name of XXX3-P, where XXX are your initials.

Step 25:   End the session.

AUDIT TEST PROBLEM 3-P

Directions: Write the answers to the following questions in the working papers or on a separate sheet of paper.

1. Based on the general journal report, what is the amount of check no. 3637?
2. What is the balance in the cash account at the end of the month?
3. What are the totals of the Debit and Credit columns of the adjusting entries shown on the general journal report for adjusting entries?
4. What is the total operating revenue?
5. What are the total operating expenses?
6. What is the net income?
7. What are the total assets?
8. What are the total liabilities?
9. What is the owner's equity at the end of the fiscal period?
10. What is the adjusted bank balance amount on the bank reconciliation report?

MASTERY PROBLEM 3-M

In this problem, you will process any additions, changes, and deletions to the chart of accounts. You will also process the monthly transactions for December, complete the end-of-fiscal-period processing, and reconcile the bank statement.

Directions: To solve the mastery problem, complete the tasks listed below using the *Automated Accounting 6.0* software.

Record the December transactions on the proper input form. Load the opening balances file (AA3-M).

Save the opening balances file to your data disk or directory (XXX3-M).

Set the run date to December 31 of the current year.

Key the December transactions.

Display a chart of accounts, general journal report of December transactions, and a trial balance.

Record the adjusting entries.

Key the adjusting entries.

Display the adjusting entries.

Display the financial statements.

Make a backup of your data file (XXX3-MBC)

Perform period-end closing.

Display a post-closing trial balance.

Save your data file (XXX3-MAC).

Load module 2 of the accounting system (Payroll/Assets/Bank Rec.).

Load the opening balances for module 2 for Mastery Problem 3-M (AA3-M)

Key the reconciliation data.

Display a bank reconciliation report.

Save your data to disk (XXX3-M).

End the session.

Transactions:

Dec. 01 Record the November bank charges, $3.50. Charge Miscellaneous Expense. M50.

02 Paid cash for rent, $1,711.00. C3640.

03 Paid cash for telephone bill, $295.41. C3641.

04 Bought supplies on account from Wilson Supply House, $363.03. M51.

05 Paid cash for travel expense, $50.97. C3642.

08 Received cash from sales, $3,222.80. T873.

09 Paid cash on account to Graphic Designers, $216.88. C3643.

10 Paid cash for charitable contribution, $150.00. C3644.

11 Paid cash for a subscription, $195.00. C3645.

12 Change the account Brokerage News to Brokerage News Today.

15 Paid cash for insurance, $477.27. C3646.

16 Paid cash on account to Williams Heating, $429.66. C3647.

17 Received cash from sales, $3,576.40. T874.

18 Bought advertising on account from Business World, Inc., $361.26. M52.

19 Paid cash on account to Brokerage News Today, $266.97. C3648.

22 Paid cash for miscellaneous expense, $81.50. C3649.

26 Paid cash for electric bill, $402.22. C3650.

26 Received cash from sales, $2,755.66. T875.

29 Bought repairs on account from Rundo Plumbing Service, $264.52. M53.

> Note: Add Rundo Plumbing Service to the chart of accounts. Assign account number 280 for Rundo Plumbing Service so that it will be positioned immediately following Williams Heating.

30 Paid cash to owner for personal use, $4,400.00. C3651.

Adjustment Data:

```
Supplies inventory on December 31 ...........$540.22
Value of insurance policies on December 31 ...168.52
```

Bank Statement Data: The checkbook balance can be obtained from the accounting reports.

```
Bank statement balance ...................$20,757.82
Bank charge ....................................3.50
Outstanding deposit .......................3,006.43
Outstanding checks
```

Check No.	Amount
3643	$ 216.88
3646	477.27
3648	266.97
3649	81.50
3650	402.22
3651	4,400.00

AUDIT TEST PROBLEM 3-M

Directions: Write the answers to the following questions in the working papers or on a separate sheet of paper.

1. Based on the general journal report, what is the amount of check no. 3648?
2. What is the balance in the cash account at the end of the month?
3. What are the totals of the Debit and Credit columns of the adjusting entries shown on the general journal report for adjusting entries?
4. What are the total sales for the period?
5. What is the total amount of telephone expense?
6. What is the net income?
7. What is the ending balance for supplies?
8. What are the total liabilities?
9. What is the owner's equity at the end of the fiscal period?
10. What is the total of outstanding checks on the bank reconciliation report?

C COMPREHENSIVE PROBLEM C-1

Shelby Linen Supply Company sells linens and uniforms. In Comprehensive Problem C-1, you will process the monthly transactions for April, complete the end-of-fiscal-period processing, and reconcile the bank statement for Shelby Linen Supply Company. Separate sales accounts are maintained for linens and uniforms. As you are recording the sales transactions, if the sale is for linens, record the account number for Sales--Linens. If the sale is for uniforms, record the account number for Sales--Uniforms.

Directions: The step-by-step instructions for solving this practice problem are listed below.

Step 1:

Remove the input forms from the working papers. Record the following transactions for Shelby Linen Supply Company on the general journal input form. Record any additions, changes, or deletions to the chart of accounts on the chart of accounts input form. Abbreviate the reference numbers on the input forms as follows: check no., C; memorandum, M; cash register tape, T. The chart of accounts for Shelby Linen Supply is shown below.

```
                    Shelby Linen Supply Co.
                       Chart of Accounts
                           04/01/--
        -------------------------------------------------------
        Account    Account
        Number     Title
        -------------------------------------------------------
        110        Cash
        120        Petty Cash
        130        Supplies
        140        Prepaid Insurance
        210        Clark Supply, Inc.
        220        Elsbrock Office Supplies
        230        Linnemann Press
        240        Baxter Chemicals, Inc.
        310        Eva Whalen, Capital
        320        Eva Whalen, Drawing
        330        Income Summary
        410        Sales--Linens
        420        Sales--Uniforms
        510        Insurance Expense
        520        Miscellaneous Expense
        530        Rent Expense
        540        Supplies Expense
        550        Telephone Expense
        560        Utilities Expense
```

Apr. 01 Received bank statement showing March bank service charge, $2.75. Charge miscellaneous expense. M63.

01 Paid cash on account to Elsbrock Office Supplies, $426.54. C188.

01 Paid cash for rent, $1,350.00. C189.

02 Change the account Linnemann Press to Pat Linnemann Company.

02 Paid cash for water bill, $76.51. C190.

02 Received cash from uniform sales, $891.66. T42.

02 Received cash from linen sales, $488.21. T43.

05 Bought supplies on account from Alabaster Supply Co., $461.13. M64.

> **Note:** Add Alabaster Supply Co. to the chart of accounts. Assign account number 250 for Alabaster Supply Co. so that it will be positioned immediately following Baxter Chemicals, Inc., in the chart of accounts.

05 Paid cash to owner for personal use, $250.00. C191.

06 Bought advertising on account from Pat Linnemann Company, $325.00. M65.

> **Note:** Add Advertising Expense to the chart of accounts. Assign account number 505 for Advertising Expense so that it will be positioned immediately following Sales––Uniforms in the chart of accounts.

06 Paid cash for miscellaneous expense, $71.60. C192.

07 Paid cash for repairs, $316.50. C193.

> **Note:** Add Repairs Expense to the chart of accounts. Assign account number 535 for Repairs Expense so that it will be positioned immediately following Rent Expense in the chart of accounts.

07 Paid cash for telephone bill, $163.53. C194.

08 Paid cash for miscellaneous expense, $15.00. C195.

09 Received cash from uniform sales, $963.31. T44.

09 Received cash from linen sales, $479.60. T45.

12 Paid cash on account to Clark Supply, Inc., $764.33. C196.

12 Paid cash on account to Baxter Chemicals, Inc., $966.81. C197.

12 Paid cash to owner for personal use, $250.00. C198.

13 Paid cash for electric bill, $345.21. C199.

13 Paid cash for miscellaneous expense, $28.90. C200.

14 Paid cash for repairs, $71.14. C201.

15 Bought supplies on account from Baxter Chemicals, Inc., $399.08. M66.

15 Paid cash for advertising, $83.63. C202.

16 Received cash from uniform sales, $1,100.69. T46.

16 Received cash from linen sales, $537.66. T47.

19 Paid cash to owner for personal use, $250.00. C203.

19 Bought supplies on account from Elsbrock Office Supplies, $397.16. M67.

19 Paid cash for professional dues, $150.00. C204.

Note: Add Dues & Subscriptions Exp. to the chart of accounts. Assign account number 515 for Dues & Subscriptions Exp. so that it will be positioned immediately following Insurance Expense in the chart of accounts.

20 Paid cash for insurance, $318.30. C205.

20 Paid cash for miscellaneous expense, $21.00. C206.

21 Paid cash on account to Pat Linnemann Company, $325.00. C207.

21 Bought supplies on account from Clark Supply, Inc., $206.56. M68.

21 Paid cash for advertising, $55.00. C208.

22 Paid cash on account to Alabaster Supply Co., $461.13. C209.

23 Received cash from uniform sales, $999.07. T48.

23 Received cash from linen sales, $514.29. T49.

26 Paid cash to owner for personal use, $250.00. C210.

26 Paid cash for miscellaneous expense, $42.00. C211.

26 Bought supplies on account from Alabaster Supply Co., $219.18. M69.

27 Paid cash on account to Clark Supply, Inc., $206.56. C212.

27 Paid cash for miscellaneous expense, $27.00. C213.

28 Paid cash for advertising, $188.88. C214.

28 Bought a subscription on account from Pat Linnemann Company, $76.00. M70.

28 Paid cash for repairs, $73.50. C215.

29 Paid cash for insurance, $168.99. C216.

29 Bought supplies on account from M & D Chemicals, $366.50. M71.

Note: Add M & D Chemicals to the chart of accounts. Assign account number 260 for M & D Chemicals so that it will be positioned immediately following Alabaster Supply Co. in the chart of accounts.

29 Paid cash on account to Baxter Chemicals, Inc., $399.08. C217.

30 Received cash from uniform sales, $1,108.75. T50.

30 Received cash from linen sales, $499.82. T51.

30 Paid cash to replenish the petty cash fund, $58.00: miscellaneous expense, $38.00; repairs, $20.00. C218.

Note: The two items (miscellaneous expense and repairs) are recorded on separate lines on the general journal input form.

30 Paid cash on account to Elsbrock Office Supplies, $397.16. C219.

Step 2:   Bring up the accounting system.

Step 3:   Load the opening balances template file for AAC-1.

Step 4:   Use the Save As menu command to save the opening balances file to your drive and directory with a file name of XXXC-1, where XXX are your initials.

Step 5:   Set the run date and student name in the General Information data entry window. The run date is April 30 of the current year.

Step 6:   Key the data from the chart of accounts input form prepared in Step 1.

Step 7:   Key the general journal entries from the general journal input form prepared in Step 1.

Step 8:   Display a chart of accounts report.

Step 9:   Display the general journal report for the period April 1 through April 30 of the current year. If errors are detected, use the List button on the General Journal data entry window to select the journal entry to correct.

Step 10:   Display a trial balance report.

Step 11:   Record the adjusting entries on a general journal input form. The adjustment data are shown below. Use the trial balance printed in the previous step as the basis for making the adjusting entries. Record "ADJ.ENT." as the reference.

```
Supplies inventory on April 30 .............$2426.88
Value of insurance policies on April 30 ......461.93
```

Step 12:   Key the adjusting entries recorded in the previous step.

Step 13:   Display the general journal report for the adjusting entries. Use a reference restriction of ADJ.ENT. so that only adjusting entries will be included on the report.

Step 14:   Display the financial statements.

Step 15:   Use the Save As menu command to save a backup copy of your data to disk with a file name of XXXC-1BC.

Step 16:   Perform period-end closing.

Step 17:   Display a post-closing trial balance.

Step 18:   Save your data to disk with a file name of XXXC-1, where XXX are your initials.

Step 19:   Load module 2 of the accounting system (Payroll/Assets/Bank Rec.).

Step 20: Load the opening balance data for Comprehensive Problem C-1 (AAC-1).

Step 21: Set the run date and student name.

Step 22: Key the bank reconciliation data based on the information provided below. The checkbook balance can be obtained from the trial balance report.

```
Bank charge ...................................$2.75
Bank statement balance ....................7910.82
```

Outstanding deposits are:

```
        $999.07
         514.29
        1108.75
         499.82
```

Outstanding checks are:

Check No.	Amount
211	$ 42.00
212	206.56
213	27.00
214	188.88
215	73.50
216	168.99
217	399.08
218	58.00
219	397.16

Step 23: Display the bank reconciliation report.

Step 24: Save your data to disk with a file name of XXXC-1, where XXX are your initials.

Step 25: End the session.

AUDIT TEST PROBLEM C-1

Directions: Write the answers to the following questions in the working papers or on a separate sheet of paper.

1. Based on the general journal report, what is the amount of check no. 193?
2. What are the totals of the debit and credit columns of the general journal report of the monthly transactions?
3. What is the balance in the cash account at the end of the month?

4. What are the totals of the Debit and Credit columns of the adjusting entries shown on the general journal report for adjusting entries?

5. What are the total sales for uniforms?

6. What is the total operating revenue?

7. What are the total operating expenses?

8. What is the net income?

9. What are the total assets?

10. What are the total liabilities?

11. What is the owner's equity at the end of the fiscal period?

12. What is the adjusted bank balance amount on the bank reconciliation report?

4

Purchases and Cash Payments

LEARNING OBJECTIVES ▶ UPON COMPLETION OF THIS CHAPTER, you will be able to:

1. Record additions, changes, and deletions to vendors on the vendors input form.

2. Record purchases-on-account transactions on the purchases journal input form.

3. Record cash payments on the cash payments journal input form.

4. Key vendor maintenance data.

5. Enter and correct purchases journal entries.

6. Enter and correct cash payments journal entries.

7. Display a vendor list report.

8. Display purchases and cash payments journal entries.

9. Display general ledger and accounts payable ledger reports.

10. Display a schedule of accounts payable report.

INTRODUCTION

In previous chapters, you learned about accounting activities for a service business. In this chapter, you will work with a merchandising business as you learn to add, change, or delete vendors and to enter and correct purchases and cash payments journal entries. A **merchandising business** is a business that purchases and resells goods. The goods purchased for resale are called **merchandise**. An asset account titled **Merchandise Inventory** is included in the chart of accounts for a merchandising business. Merchandise Inventory is the account that shows the value of the merchandise on hand. A merchandising business also has an account titled **Purchases**. The cost of the merchandise purchased for resale is recorded in the Purchases account.

The examples used in this chapter are for a merchandising business called Sun City Jewelers, a wholesale business. The business purchases merchandise directly from manufacturers, then sells merchandise wholesale to jewelry retailers.

▶ Vendors Input Form

Whenever necessary, new vendors must be added, vendor names must be changed, and inactive vendors deleted. Each addition, change, or deletion is recorded on a vendors input form as illustrated in Figure 4.1. Vendor Number and Vendor Name fields are completed whether you are adding or changing an account. When a vendor is to be deleted, record the vendor number and (Delete).

FIGURE 4.1
Vendors Input Form

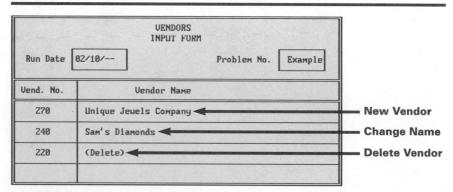

▶ Purchases Journal Input Form

In this accounting system, purchases on account are recorded on the purchases journal input form, then keyed into the computer using the Purchases Journal data entry window. Each line on the input form is used to record a purchase invoice or one part of a purchase invoice that contains multiple purchases. The field names and a description of each column of the input form are given in Table 4.1.

TABLE 4.1
Field Names and Descriptions of the Purchases Journal Input Form

Field Name	Description
Date	The date field contains the two-digit month and day of the month on which the transaction occurred.
Vendor Number	Record the vendor number from the vendor list.
Invoice Number	Record the number used to identify the purchases invoice.
Invoice Amount	Record the total amount of the purchase invoice.
Account Number	Record the general ledger account number from the chart of accounts that is to be charged for the purchase.
Debit	Record the amount to be debited to the account specified in the Account Number field.
Credit	Record the amount to be credited to the account specified in the Account Number field. Each debit or credit must be recorded on a separate line of the form. It is unusual to record an entry in the Credit column of this form.

On the first transaction, 220 is the vendor number for Superior Gold and 5110 is the account number for Purchases. On the second transaction, 260 is the vendor number for Martin Supply, Inc., and 1145 is the account number for Office Supplies.

The two sample transactions listed below are recorded on the purchases journal input form shown in Figure 4.2. The first transaction is an example of a purchase of merchandise on account, and the second transaction is an example of buying office supplies on account.

Feb. 01   Purchased merchandise on account from Superior Gold, $1,450.25. Invoice no. 22.

03   Bought office supplies on account from Martin Supply, Inc., $115.66. Memorandum no. 17.

FIGURE 4.2
Purchases Journal Input Form

PURCHASES JOURNAL INPUT FORM						
Run Date 02/10/--					Problem No.	Example
Date MM / dd	Vend. No.	Invoice No.	Invoice Amount	Acct. No.	Debit Amount	Credit Amount
02/01	220	P22	1450.25	5110	1450.25	
02/03	260	M17	115.66	1145	115.66	

▶ **Cash Payments Journal Input Form**

It is not necessary to record the credit to accounts payable on the purchases journal input form, because this entry is made automatically by the computer.

All cash disbursements are recorded on the Cash Payments Journal input form. Entries are keyed into the Cash Payments Journal data entry window from this input form. The field names and a description of each column of the input form are given in Table 4.2.

TABLE 4.2
Field Names and Descriptions of the Cash Payments Journal Input Form

Field Name	Description
Date	The date field contains the two-digit month and day of the month on which the transaction occurred.
Vendor Number	If an amount is recorded in the Accounts Payable Debit column, the number of the vendor's account is recorded in this column.
Check Number	This is the number of the manually written check used to pay the transactions.
Accounts Payable Debit	Record the total amount of the debit to accounts payable resulting from this cash payment.
Account Number	This is the general ledger account number from the chart of accounts that is to be either debited or credited in the next two columns.
Debit	This is the amount to be debited to the account specified in the Account Number field.
Credit	This is the amount to be credited to the account specified in the Account Number field. Each debit or credit must be recorded on a separate line of the form.

In the first transaction, 1150 is the account number for Store Supplies. In the second transaction, 1160 is the account number for Prepaid Insurance. In the third transaction, 210 is the vendor number for Sterling Supply House. In the last transaction, 3140 is the account number for Cory Knapp, Drawing.

Figure 4.3 illustrates a completed cash payments journal input form. Each line on the form may be used to record a cash payment or one part of a cash payment. The four transactions listed below are recorded on the form. Additional examples of the various types of cash payment transactions that may be recorded on this form are illustrated in Tutorial Problem 4-P.

Feb. 02   Paid cash for store supplies, $105.26. Check no. 46.

03   Paid cash for insurance, $165.75. Check no. 47.

04   Paid cash on account to Sterling Supply House, $1,867.13, covering P16. Check no. 48.

05   Cory Knapp, Partner, withdrew cash for personal use, $750.00. Check no. 49.

FIGURE 4.3
Cash Payments Journal Input Form

			CASH PAYMENTS JOURNAL INPUT FORM				
Run Date	02/10/--				Problem No.	Example	
Date mm / dd	Vend. No.	Check No.	Accounts Pay. Debit	Acct. No.	Debit Amount	Credit Amount	
02/02		C46		1150	105.26		
02/03		C47		1160	165.75		
02/04	210	C48	1867.13				
02/05		C49		3140	750.00		

It is not necessary to record the credit to cash, since the computer makes this entry automatically.

Ledgers

Chart of Accounts	F1
Vendor List	F2
Customer List	F3
Maintain Accounts	F4
Maintain Vendors	F5
Maintain Customers	F6

OPERATING PROCEDURES

Operating procedures are covered in this chapter for performing vendor maintenance data entry, purchases journal data entry, cash payments journal data entry, displaying journal entries, displaying detailed ledgers, and displaying a schedule of accounts payable.

▶ Maintain Vendors Data Entry Window

When the Maintain Vendors menu command is chosen from the Ledgers menu, the data entry window shown in Figure 4.4 will appear.

▶ Adding a New Vendor

1   Choose the ----Add New Vendor---- item from the list window by pressing Enter or by clicking on the Ok button.

2   Key the Vendor Number and Name for the new vendor.

3   Click on the Ok button.

▶ Changing a Vendor Name

1   Choose from the list window the vendor you wish to change.

    The list window will be dismissed, and the data for the chosen vendor will be displayed in the data entry window.

2   Key the correct vendor name.

3   Push the Ok button.

FIGURE 4.4
Maintain Vendors Data Entry Window

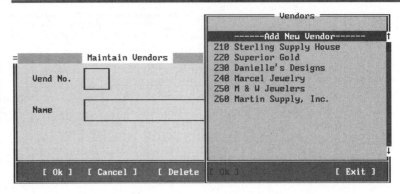

Vendor accounts cannot be deleted unless the account being deleted has a zero balance.

When you are finished with the Maintain Vendors data entry window, push the Exit button.

▶ Deleting a Vendor

1   **Choose from the list window the vendor you wish to delete.**

The list window will be dismissed, and the data for the chosen vendor will be displayed in the data entry window.

2   **Push the Delete button.**

▶ Purchases Journal Data Entry Window

Journals
Opening Balances
General Journal   S+F1
Purchases Journal   S+F2
Cash Payments Journal S+F3
Sales Journal   S+F4
Cash Receipts Journal S+F5

The Purchases Journal data entry window is used to key purchases-on-account transactions and to make corrections to or delete existing purchases journal entries. The Purchases Journal data entry window is shown in Figure 4.5. Only purchases-on-account transactions can be keyed. The computer automatically calculates and displays the accounts payable credit amount. The rest of the journal entry is completed in the General Accounts section. The entries in the General Accounts section will consist of one or more debits. The account debited reflects what was pur-chased on account (merchandise, office supplies, store supplies, advertising, etc.). On rare occasions, you may need to record a credit entry (a purchase discount recorded at the time of purchase, for example).

The Invoice Number field is automatically increased by one for each purchases journal entry.

▶ Keying a Purchases Journal Entry

1   **Key the two-digit day of the month (or press Tab if it is correct as is).**

FIGURE 4.5
Purchases Journal Data Entry Window

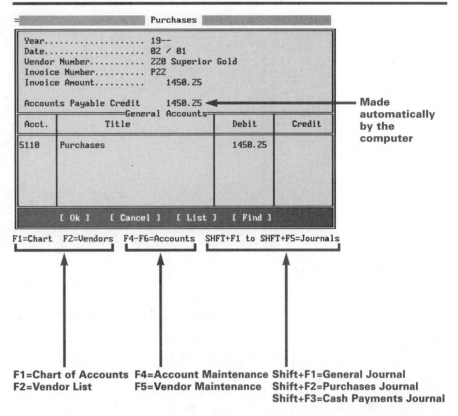

F1=Chart of Accounts F4=Account Maintenance Shift+F1=General Journal
F2=Vendor List   F5=Vendor Maintenance   Shift+F2=Purchases Journal
                                                Shift+F3=Cash Payments Journal

The Shift+F1 through Shift+F3 keys provide a quick and easy way to move among the three journals used in this chapter. The F4 and F5 keys provide an easy way to make changes to chart of accounts or vendor entries.

2 Key each of the data fields.

While the cursor is positioned to the Vendor Number field, you can press the F2 key to choose a vendor from a vendor list window. While the cursor is positioned to the Account Number field, you can press the F1 key to choose an account from a chart of accounts list window.

3 When the journal entry is complete, push the Ok button.

The Posting Summary dialog window shown in Figure 4.6 will appear. The purpose of this window is to show the journal entry in a two-column format, allowing you to verify the accuracy of your input and post the data.

4 If the transaction is correct, push the Post button (push the Change button to return to the Purchases Journal data entry window and make changes).

FIGURE 4.6
Purchases Journal Posting Summary Dialog Window

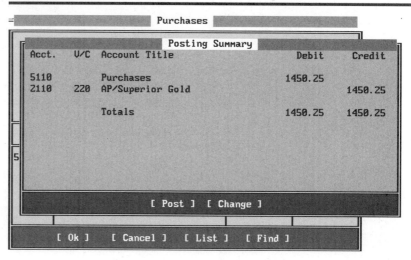

Cash Payments Journal Data Entry Window

The Cash Payments Journal data entry window is used to key all cash payments transactions and to make corrections to or delete existing cash payments journal entries. It is not necessary to key the credit to cash, because it is automatically calculated and displayed by the computer.

There are two types of cash payments: (1) direct payments and (2) payments on account. A **direct payment** is a cash disbursement that does *not* affect accounts payable. Examples of direct payments are checks written to pay expenses or purchase assets. **Payments on account** are cash disbursements that do affect accounts payable.

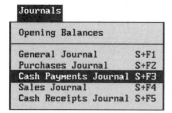

DIRECT PAYMENT. A Cash Payments data entry window with sample data for a direct cash payment is shown in Figure 4.7. Notice that the Vendor Number and Accounts Payable Debit fields are left blank. The vendor number is needed only for transactions that affect accounts payable. The cash credit amount is calculated and displayed by the computer. The account debited reflects why the cash was disbursed (miscellaneous expense, rent, etc.).

Keying a Direct Cash Payment

1   Key the two-digit day of the month (or press Tab if it is correct as is).

2   Key each of the data fields.

FIGURE 4.7
Cash Payments Data Entry Window (Direct Payment)

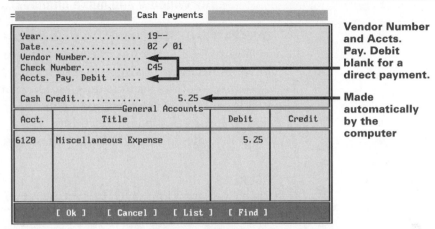

Leave the Vendor Number and Accts. Pay. Debit fields blank, since they do not apply to a direct payment. The cash credit amount is calculated and displayed automatically by the computer.

3   When the journal entry is complete, push the Ok button.

The Posting Summary dialog window shown in Figure 4.8 will appear. This window shows the journal entry in a two-column format. It allows you to verify the accuracy of your input and post the data.

FIGURE 4.8
Direct Cash Payment Posting Summary Dialog Window

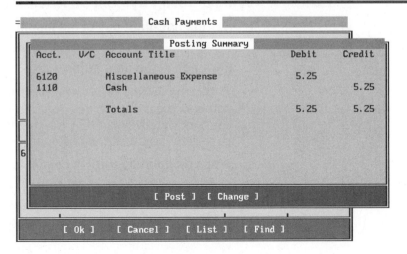

4   **If the transaction is correct, push the Post button (push the Change button to return to the Cash Payments Journal data entry window and make changes).**

CASH PAYMENT ON ACCOUNT.   A cash payment on account is illustrated in Figure 4.9. A vendor number is required because the accounts payable account is affected. For a cash payment on account, the General Accounts section may be left blank. In a later chapter, you will learn how to use the Credit column of the General Accounts section to record purchases discounts. The Cash Credit amount is automatically calculated and displayed by the computer.

FIGURE 4.9
Cash Payments Journal Data Entry Window (Payment on Account)

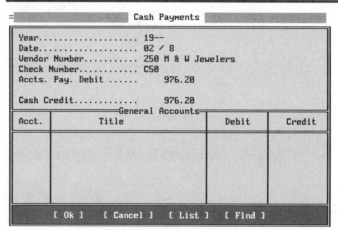

F1=Chart F2=Vendors F4-F6=Accounts SHFT+F1 to SHFT+F5=Journals

 ▶**Keying a Cash Payment on Account**

1   **Key the two-digit day of the month (or press Tab if it is correct as is).**

2   **Key each of the data fields.**

While the cursor is positioned to the Vendor Number field, you can press the F2 key to choose a vendor from a vendor list window. Because this is a payment on account, the Accts. Pay. Debit amount must be completed.

3   **When the journal entry is complete, push the Ok button.**

The Posting Summary dialog window shown in Figure 4.10 will appear. This window shows the journal entry in a two-column format. It allows you to verify the accuracy of your input and post the data.

4   **If the transaction is correct, push the Post button (push the Change button to return to the Cash Payments Journal data entry window and make changes).**

▶ **Changing or Deleting Journal Transactions**

1   **Push the List command button near the bottom of the Journal data entry window.**

The journal transactions will appear in a list window as shown in Figure 4.11.

When the List command button is pushed, only transactions for the current journal type will be displayed. If the List button at the bottom of the purchases journal is pushed, for example, only purchases transactions will be displayed.

FIGURE 4.10
Payment on Account Posting Summary Dialog Window

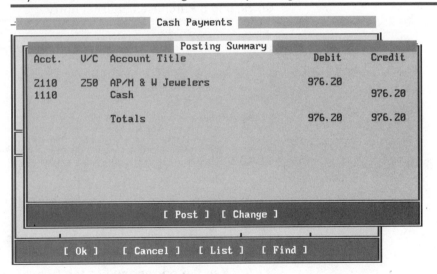

A transaction is chosen by using the Up and Down arrow keys to select the transaction and then pressing Enter (or using the mouse to select the transaction and then clicking on Ok).

2   **Choose the transaction you wish to change or delete.**

The chosen transaction will be displayed in the journal data entry window so that it may be changed or deleted. If the transaction chosen was originally entered in the Purchases Journal data entry window, for example, it would be displayed in the Purchases Journal for correction, as illustrated in Figure 4.12.

FIGURE 4.11
Journal Entries List

```
┌───────────────────────── Transactions ──────────────────────┐
│ Date   Refer.  Acct.  V/C Title                Debit   Credit│
│ 02/01  P22     5110       Purchases           1450.25        │1
│                2110   220 AP/Superior Gold             1450.25│
│ 02/03  P23     5110       Purchases            627.88        │
│                2110   250 AP/M & W Jewelers            627.88│
│ 02/03  M17     1145       Supplies--Office      115.66       │
│                2110   260 AP/Martin Supply, Inc.       115.66│
│ 02/08  P24     5110       Purchases            869.70        │
│                2110   240 AP/Marcel Jewelry            869.70│
│ 02/09  P25     5110       Purchases            855.15        │
│                2110   270 AP/Unique Jewels Company     855.15│
│ 02/10  M20     1150       Supplies--Store       327.89       │
│                2110   260 AP/Martin Supply, Inc.       327.89│↓
├──────────────────────────────────────────────────────────────┤
│ [ Ok ]                                              [ Cancel ]│
└──────────────────────────────────────────────────────────────┘
         [ Ok ]    [ Cancel ]    [ List ]    [ Find ]
```

FIGURE 4.12
Correcting a Purchases Journal Entry

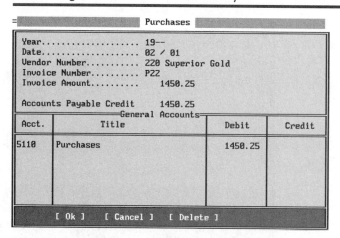

```
═══════════════════ Purchases ═══════════════════
Year.................. 19--
Date.................. 02 / 01
Vendor Number......... 220 Superior Gold
Invoice Number........ P22
Invoice Amount........    1450.25

Accounts Payable Credit   1450.25
───────────────── General Accounts ─────────────────
Acct. │        Title         │  Debit  │  Credit
5110  │ Purchases            │ 1450.25 │



       [ Ok ]    [ Cancel ]    [ Delete ]
```

3 Key the corrections to the transaction and push the Ok button (or if you wish to delete the transaction, push the Delete button).

▶ **Finding a Journal Entry**

1 Push the Find command button.

The Find What? dialog window shown in Figure 4.13 will appear.

2 Key the date, reference, amount, etc., of the transaction you want to find.

3 If a matching transaction is found, it will be displayed in the journal data entry window so that it may changed or deleted.

FIGURE 4.13
Find What? Dialog Window

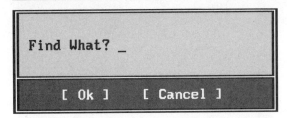

▶Journal Reports

Once the journal entries have been keyed, the journal reports may be displayed.

▶Displaying Journal Reports

1   Choose the Journals menu command from the Reports menu.

The Report Selection dialog window shown in Figure 4.14 will appear, allowing you to select journal reports.

2   Select the reports you would like to display (more than one may be selected).

The reports are selected by clicking on the check box or by pressing the Space Bar (or Right Arrow) while the cursor is positioned to that check box.

FIGURE 4.14
Report Selection Dialog Window

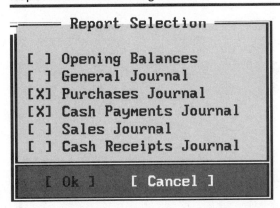

3   Push the Ok button.

The Selection Options dialog window shown in Figure 4.15 will appear.

FIGURE 4.15
Selection Options for Journal Reports

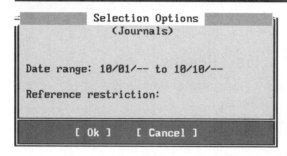

```
        Selection Options
            (Journals)


Date range: 10/01/-- to 10/10/--

Reference restriction:


        [ Ok ]     [ Cancel ]
```

4   Key the range of dates to be included in the journal report.

Key a reference restriction to limit the report to one particular reference. For example, you might want to display only a certain invoice.

A journal entries report is shown in Figure 4.16. To print the displayed report on an attached printer, press the F9 "hot key."

FIGURE 4.16
Purchases Journal Report Window

Sun City Jewelers
Purchases Journal
02/10/93

Date	Refer.	V/C	Acct.	Title	Debit	Credit
02/01	P22		5110	Purchases	1450.25	
02/01	P22	220	2110	AP/Superior Gold		1450.25
02/03	P23		5110	Purchases	627.88	
02/03	P23	250	2110	AP/M & W Jewelers		627.88
02/03	M17		1145	Supplies--Office	115.66	
02/03	M17	260	2110	AP/Martin Supply, Inc.		115.66
02/08	P24		5110	Purchases	869.70	
02/08	P24	240	2110	AP/Marcel Jewelry		869.70
02/09	P25		5110	Purchases	855.15	

▶Ledger Reports

If you notice errors in your reports (a financial statement, for example), the general ledger report can be the fastest way to discover the cause of the error, since it lists all journal activity by account.

Automated Accounting 6.0 uses three ledgers: (1) general ledger, (2) accounts payable ledger, and (3) accounts receivable ledger. There are two reports available for each. The general ledger reports are the trial balance and the general ledger. The two reports available for the accounts payable ledger are the schedule of accounts payable and the accounts payable ledger report. The accounts receivable ledger reports will be covered in Chapter 5.

▶Displaying Ledger Reports

Reports
Accounts
Journals
Ledgers
Financial Statements
Financial Analysis
Checks/Statements

1   **Choose the Ledgers menu command from the Reports menu.**

The Report Selection dialog window shown in Figure 4.17 will appear, allowing you to select which of the ledger reports you would like to be generated.

FIGURE 4.17
Report Selection Dialog Window (Ledgers)

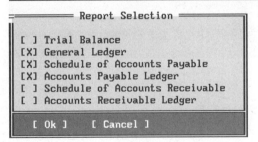

2   **Select the reports you would like to display.**

The reports are selected by clicking on the check box or by pressing the Space Bar (or Right Arrow) while the cursor is positioned to that check box.

3   **Push the Ok button.**

The general ledger, accounts payable ledger, and accounts receivable ledger reports can be quite lengthy and are most often used to locate journal recording errors.

GENERAL LEDGER REPORT. The general ledger report shows detailed journal entry activity by account. Any range of accounts may be displayed (from one account to all accounts). If you have determined that a particular account balance is incorrect, displaying all journal activity for that account can be very useful in locating the error.

▶ Displaying a General Ledger Report

1   **When the general ledger report is selected, the dialog window shown in Figure 4.18 will appear. Key the range of accounts to be included in the general ledger report.**

From the General Ledger Selection Options dialog window, you can press F1 to select an account number from the Chart of Accounts list window.

FIGURE 4.18
General Ledger Selection Options

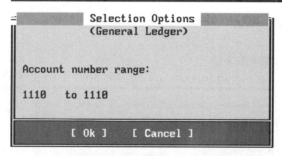

 If only one account is to be displayed, the "from" and "to" portions of the account number range can be the same. In the above example, account number 1110 is for the cash account. Since the account number range is from 1110 to 1110, only activity for the cash account will be displayed.

2   **Push the Ok button.**

The general ledger report is shown in Figure 4.19.

SCHEDULE OF ACCOUNTS PAYABLE. The schedule of accounts payable report lists each vendor that currently has a balance. A total of all vendor balances is shown at the end of the report. This total should equal the balance in the accounts payable account in the general ledger. A sample report is shown in Figure 4.20.

FIGURE 4.19

General Ledger Report for Cash Account

```
                          Sun City Jewelers
                           General Ledger
                             02/10/93

Account        Journal   Date  Refer.    Debit   Credit   Balance

1110-Cash
               Bal. Fwd.                                  35676.20
               Cash Pymt 02/01 C45                 5.25   35670.95
               Cash Pymt 02/02 C46               105.26   35565.69
               Cash Pymt 02/03 C47               165.75   35399.94
               Cash Pymt 02/04 C48              1867.13   33532.81
               Cash Pymt 02/05 C49               750.00   32782.81
               Cash Pymt 02/08 C50               976.20   31806.61
               Cash Pymt 02/09 C51              1326.41   30480.20
               Cash Pymt 02/10 C52               140.41   30339.79
               Cash Pymt 02/10 C53               520.00   29819.79
```

FIGURE 4.20

Schedule of Accounts Payable

```
                          Sun City Jewelers
                      Schedule of Accounts Payable
                             02/10/93

        Account
        Number    Name                       Balance

         220      Superior Gold               1450.25
         230      Danielle's Designs          1562.30
         240      Marcel Jewelry              1990.85
         250      M & W Jewelers               627.88
         260      Martin Supply, Inc.          893.76
         270      Unique Jewels Company        855.15
                                             ----------
                  Total                       7380.19
                                             ==========
```

ACCOUNTS PAYABLE LEDGER REPORT. The accounts payable ledger report shows detailed journal entry activity by vendor. The report is arranged in vendor number sequence. All the journal entries for the current fiscal period that affect each vendor are listed. This information is useful in locating errors, in obtaining status information about a specific vendor's activity, or in identifying transactions posted to the wrong vendor.

From the Accounts Payable Ledger Selection Options dialog window, you can press F2 to select an account number from the vendor list window.

▶ Displaying the Accounts Payable Ledger Report

1   When the accounts payable ledger report is selected, the dialog window shown in Figure 4.21 will appear. Key the range of vendors to be included in the accounts payable ledger report.

FIGURE 4.21
Accounts Payable Ledger Selection Options

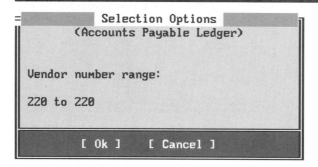

If only one account is to be displayed, the "from" and "to" portions of the vendor number range can be the same.

2   Push the Ok button.

The accounts payable ledger report for Vendor number 220 is shown in Figure 4.22.

FIGURE 4.22
Accounts Payable Ledger Report

```
                          Sun City Jewelers
                        Accounts Payable Ledger
                             02/10/--

Account          Journal   Date  Refer.    Debit    Credit   Balance

220-Superior Gold
                 Bal. Fwd.                                   1326.41
                 Purchases 02/01 P22                1450.25  2776.66
                 Cash Pymt 02/09 C51      1326.41            1450.25
```

TUTORIAL 4-T

In this tutorial problem you will learn the operating procedures for maintaining vendor accounts, as well as recording and keying purchases and cash payments journal entries. You will key the purchases and cash payments transactions from February 1 through February 10 for Sun City Jewelers.

The general, purchases, and cash payments journal entries have already been recorded for you and are illustrated in Figures 4.24 through 4.26. Any additions, changes, or deletions to vendors have also been recorded for you and are illustrated in Figure 4.23.

Each of the step-by-step instructions lists a task to be completed at the computer. In case you need it, more detailed information on how to complete the task is provided immediately following the step. If you need additional explanation for the task, a page reference is provided from the Operating Procedures section of this chapter (or a previous chapter).

Directions: The step-by-step instructions for processing the purchases and cash payments transactions for Sun City Jewelers for the first 10 days of February of the current year are listed below.

Step 1: Bring up the accounting system. (page 16)

At the DOS prompt, key A1 (or follow the instructions provided by your instructor).

Step 2: Load the opening balances template file, AA4-T. (page 19)

Pull down the File menu and choose the Open Accounting File command. Key into the Path field the drive and directory containing the template files. Key a file name of AA4-T and push the Ok button.

Step 3: Use the Save As command to save data to disk with a file name of XXX4-T (where XXX are your initials). (page 21)

Pull down the File menu and choose the Save As menu command. Key the path to the drive and directory that contains your data files. Key a file name of XXX4-T, where XXX are your initials. Push the Ok button.

Step 4: Enter your name in the General Information data entry window and set the run date to February 10 of the current year. (page 24)

Pull down the Options menu and choose the General Information menu command. Set the run date to February 10 of the current year. Key your name in the Student Name field.

Step 5: Key the data from the vendors input form shown in Figure 4.23.

Pull down the Ledgers menu and choose the Maintain Vendors command.

Step 6: Key the journal entries from the general purchases and cash payments input forms shown in Figures 4.24 through 4.26.

Transactions:

Note: Do not key from these transaction statements, since they have already been recorded for you on the journal input forms in Figures 4.24 through 4.26. The reference numbers have been abbreviated on the input forms as follows: check no., C; purchase invoice no., P; memorandum, M.

FIGURE 4.23
Vendors Input Form

VENDORS INPUT FORM		
Run Date 02/10/--		Problem No. 4-T
Vend. No.	Vendor Name	
270	Unique Jewels Company	

FIGURE 4.24
General Journal Input Form

Run Date 02/10/--		GENERAL JOURNAL INPUT FORM		Problem No.	4-T
Date MM / dd	Reference	Account Number	Cust./ Vend No.	Debit	Credit
02/04	M18	3120		230.50	
		5110			230.50
02/05	M19	1145		82.00	
		5110			82.00
Totals				312.50	312.50

FIGURE 4.25
Purchases Journal Input Form

PURCHASES JOURNAL INPUT FORM						
Run Date 02/10/--					Problem No. 4-T	
Date MM / dd	Vend. No.	Invoice No.	Invoice Amount	Acct. No.	Debit Amount	Credit Amount
02/01	220	P22	1450.25	5110	1450.25	
02/03	250	P23	627.88	5110	627.88	
02/03	260	M17	115.66	1145	115.66	
02/08	240	P24	869.70	5110	869.70	
02/09	270	P25	855.15	5110	855.15	
02/10	260	M20	327.89	1150	327.89	

FIGURE 4.26
Cash Payments Journal Input Form

CASH PAYMENTS JOURNAL INPUT FORM						
Run Date 02/10/--					Problem No. 4-T	
Date MM / dd	Vend. No.	Check No.	Accounts Pay. Debit	Acct. No.	Debit Amount	Credit Amount
02/01		C45		6120	5.25	
02/02		C46		1150	105.26	
02/03		C47		1160	165.75	
02/04	210	C48	1867.13			
02/05		C49		3140	750.00	
02/08	250	C50	976.20			
02/09	220	C51	1326.41			
02/10		C52		1145	140.41	
02/10		C53		3120	520.00	
/						

Feb. 01   Paid cash for miscellaneous expense, $5.25. C45.

01   Purchased merchandise on account from Superior Gold, $1,450.25. P22.

02 Paid cash for store supplies, $105.26. C46.

03 Purchased merchandise on account from M & W Jewelers, $627.88. P23.

03 Paid cash for insurance, $165.75. C47.

04 Joel Delano, partner, withdrew merchandise for personal use, $230.50. M18. Record this transaction in the general journal.

04 Paid cash on account to Sterling Supply House, $1,867.13, covering P16. C48.

05 Discovered that a transaction for office supplies bought for cash in January was journalized and posted in error as a debit to Purchases instead of Supplies—Office, $82.00. M19. Record this transaction in the general journal.

05 Cory Knapp, partner, withdrew cash for personal use, $750.00. C49.

08 Purchased merchandise on account from Marcel Jewelry, $869.70. P24.

08 Paid cash on account to M & W Jewelers, $976.20, covering P17. C50.

09 Purchased merchandise on account from Unique Jewels Company, $855.15. P25.

Note: Add Unique Jewels Company to the vendor list. Assign vendor number 270 for Unique Jewels Company so that it will be positioned immediately following Martin Supply, Inc., in the vendor list.

09 Paid cash on account to Superior Gold, $1,326.41, covering P18. C51.

10 Paid cash for office supplies, $140.41. C52.

10 Joel Delano, partner, withdrew cash for personal use, $520.00. C53.

10 Bought store supplies on account from Martin Supply, Inc., $327.89. M20.

Step 7: Display the general journal, purchases journal and cash payments journal reports. (page 97).

Pull down the Reports menu and choose the Journals command. When the Report Selection window shown in Figure 4.27 appears, select the general, purchases, and cash payments journals. When the Selection Options window illustrated in Figure 4.28 appears, key a date range of February 1 through February 10 of the current year. The reports appear in Figures 4.29 through 4.31.

FIGURE 4.27
Report Selection Window

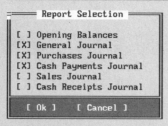

FIGURE 4.28
Selection Options

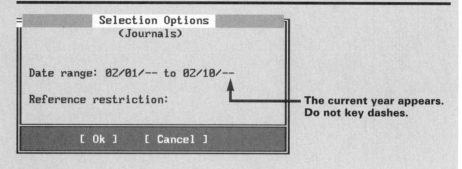

The current year appears.
Do not key dashes.

FIGURE 4.29
General Journal Report

```
                          Sun City Jewelers
                          General Journal
                             02/10/--

   ----------------------------------------------------------------
   Date   Refer.  V/C Acct.  Title              Debit      Credit
   ----------------------------------------------------------------
   02/04  M18          3120  Joel Delano, Drawing  230.50
   02/04  M18          5110  Purchases                        230.50

   02/05  M19          1145  Supplies--Office      82.00
   02/05  M19          5110  Purchases                         82.00

                                               ----------  ----------
                             Totals              312.50      312.50
                                               ==========  ==========
```

**Step 8:   Display a trial balance, a general ledger report
            for the Accounts Payable account, a schedule of
            accounts payable, and an accounts payable
            ledger report for all vendors. (pages 99-102)**

Pull down the Reports menu and choose the Ledgers command. When
the Report Selection window shown in Figure 4.32 appears, select the
trial balance, general ledger, schedule of accounts payable, and accounts
payable ledger reports. The reports appear in Figures 4.33 through 4.36.

FIGURE 4.30
Purchases Journal Report

```
                          Sun City Jewelers
                          Purchases Journal
                             02/10/--

  -----------------------------------------------------------------
  Date   Refer.   V/C Acct.  Title                    Debit    Credit
  -----------------------------------------------------------------
  02/01  P22          5110   Purchases              1450.25
  02/01  P22      220 2110   AP/Superior Gold                 1450.25

  02/03  P23          5110   Purchases               627.88
  02/03  P23      250 2110   AP/M & W Jewelers                 627.88

  02/03  M17          1145   Supplies--Office        115.66
  02/03  M17      260 2110   AP/Martin Supply, Inc.           115.66

  02/08  P24          5110   Purchases               869.70
  02/08  P24      240 2110   AP/Marcel Jewelry                869.70

  02/09  P25          5110   Purchases               855.15
  02/09  P25      270 2110   AP/Unique Jewels Company         855.15

  02/10  M20          1150   Supplies--Store         327.89
  02/10  M20      260 2110   AP/Martin Supply, Inc.           327.89
                                                   ---------- ----------
                             Totals                 4246.53  4246.53
                                                   ========== ==========
```

FIGURE 4.31
Cash Payments Journal Report

```
                          Sun City Jewelers
                        Cash Payments Journal
                             02/10/--

  -----------------------------------------------------------------
  Date   Refer.   V/C Acct.  Title                    Debit    Credit
  -----------------------------------------------------------------
  02/01  C45          6120   Miscellaneous Expense      5.25
  02/01  C45          1110   Cash                               5.25

  02/02  C46          1150   Supplies--Store          105.26
  02/02  C46          1110   Cash                             105.26

  02/03  C47          1160   Prepaid Insurance        165.75
  02/03  C47          1110   Cash                             165.75

  02/04  C48      210 2110   AP/Sterling Supply House 1867.13
  02/04  C48          1110   Cash                            1867.13

  02/05  C49          3140   Cory Knapp, Drawing      750.00
  02/05  C49          1110   Cash                             750.00

  02/08  C50      250 2110   AP/M & W Jewelers        976.20
  02/08  C50          1110   Cash                             976.20

  02/09  C51      220 2110   AP/Superior Gold        1326.41
  02/09  C51          1110   Cash                            1326.41

  02/10  C52          1145   Supplies--Office         140.41
  02/10  C52          1110   Cash                             140.41

  02/10  C53          3120   Joel Delano, Drawing     520.00
  02/10  C53          1110   Cash                             520.00
                                                   ---------- ----------
                             Totals                 5856.41  5856.41
                                                   ========== ==========
```

FIGURE 4.32
Report Selection (Ledgers)

```
╔═══════════ Report Selection ═══════════╗
║                                        ║
║  [X] Trial Balance                     ║
║  [X] General Ledger                    ║
║  [X] Schedule of Accounts Payable      ║
║  [X] Accounts Payable Ledger           ║
║  [ ] Schedule of Accounts Receivable   ║
║  [ ] Accounts Receivable Ledger        ║
║                                        ║
║    [ Ok ]        [ Cancel ]            ║
╚════════════════════════════════════════╝
```

FIGURE 4.33
Trial Balance

```
                        Sun City Jewelers
                          Trial Balance
                            02/10/--

        ----------------------------------------------------------
        Acct.   Account
        Number  Title                        Debit          Credit
        ----------------------------------------------------------
        1110    Cash                      29819.79
        1120    Petty Cash                  100.00
        1130    Accounts Receivable        1526.30
        1140    Merchandise Inventory    125325.20
        1145    Supplies--Office            874.48
        1150    Supplies--Store             866.82
        1160    Prepaid Insurance          1065.07
        2110    Accounts Payable                            7380.19
        2120    Sales Tax Payable                           1003.40
        3110    Joel Delano, Capital                       78095.15
        3120    Joel Delano, Drawing        750.50
        3130    Cory Knapp, Capital                        78095.15
        3140    Cory Knapp, Drawing         750.00
        5110    Purchases                  3490.48
        6120    Miscellaneous Expense          5.25
                                        ----------        ----------
                Totals                   164573.89         164573.89
                                        ==========        ==========
```

FIGURE 4.34
General Ledger Report

```
                        Sun City Jewelers
                         General Ledger
                            02/10/--

        ----------------------------------------------------------------
        Account         Journal   Date  Refer.  Debit   Credit   Balance
        ----------------------------------------------------------------
        2110-Accounts Payable
                        Bal. Fwd.                                 7303.40
                        Purchases 02/01 P22            1450.25    8753.65
                        Purchases 02/03 P23             627.88    9381.53
                        Purchases 02/03 M17             115.66    9497.19
                        Cash Pymt 02/04 C48   1867.13             7630.06
                        Purchases 02/08 P24             869.70    8499.76
                        Cash Pymt 02/08 C50    976.20             7523.56
                        Purchases 02/09 P25             855.15    8378.71
                        Cash Pymt 02/09 C51   1326.41             7052.30
                        Purchases 02/10 M20             327.89    7380.19
```

Step 9:   Save your data file to disk.

Pull down the File menu and choose the Save menu command.

FIGURE 4.35
Schedule of Accounts Payable

```
                    Sun City Jewelers
                Schedule of Accounts Payable
                        02/10/--

        -------------------------------------------------
        Account
        Number      Name                        Balance
        -------------------------------------------------
        220         Superior Gold               1450.25
        230         Danielle's Designs          1562.30
        240         Marcel Jewelry              1990.85
        250         M & W Jewelers               627.88
        260         Martin Supply, Inc.          893.76
        270         Unique Jewels Company        855.15
                                                ----------
                    Total                       7380.19
                                                ==========
```

FIGURE 4.36
Accounts Payable Ledger

```
                        Sun City Jewelers
                    Accounts Payable Ledger
                        02/10/--

  ---------------------------------------------------------------------
  Account        Journal  Date  Refer.   Debit    Credit   Balance
  ---------------------------------------------------------------------
  210-Sterling Supply House
                 Bal. Fwd.                                  1867.13
                 Cash Pymt 02/04 C48    1867.13

  220-Superior Gold
                 Bal. Fwd.                                  1326.41
                 Purchases 02/01 P22              1450.25   2776.66
                 Cash Pymt 02/09 C51    1326.41             1450.25

  230-Danielle's Designs
                 Bal. Fwd.    ******* No Activity *******   1562.30

  240-Marcel Jewelry
                 Bal. Fwd.                                  1121.15
                 Purchases 02/08 P24               869.70   1990.85

  250-M & W Jewelers
                 Bal. Fwd.                                   976.20
                 Purchases 02/03 P23               627.88   1604.08
                 Cash Pymt 02/08 C50     976.20              627.88

  260-Martin Supply, Inc.
                 Bal. Fwd.                                   450.21
                 Purchases 02/03 M17               115.66    565.87
                 Purchases 02/10 M20               327.89    893.76

  270-Unique Jewels Company
                 Purchases 02/09 P25               855.15    855.15
```

Step 10:   End your session.

Pull down the File menu and choose the Quit menu command.

CHAPTER 4 STUDENT EXERCISE

I. MATCHING

Directions: For each of the following definitions, write in the working papers or on a separate sheet of paper the number of the definition, followed by the letter of the appropriate term.

(a) merchandising business

(b) Merchandise Inventory

(c) Purchases

(d) purchases journal input form

(e) cash payments journal input form

(f) general ledger report

(g) accounts payable ledger report

(i) schedule of accounts payable

(j) vendors input form

1. A report that shows detailed journal entry activity by vendor.
2. A business that purchases and resells goods.
3. An input form used for recording additions, changes, and deletions to vendors.
4. An account that shows the value of the merchandise on hand.
5. An account in which merchandise purchased for resale is recorded.
6. A report that lists each vendor together with the balance owed to that vendor.
7. A report that shows detailed journal entry activity by account.
8. All purchases on account are recorded on this input form.
9. All disbursements of cash are recorded on this input form.

II. QUESTIONS

Directions: Write the answers to the following questions in the working papers or on a separate sheet of paper.

1. List the two types of cash payments.
2. If you have discovered that the general ledger account balance for accounts payable is incorrect, which report would be most useful in locating the problem?
3. If you have discovered that the balance in a particular vendor's account is incorrect, which report would be most useful in locating the error?
4. Explain how you could generate a purchases journal report that lists only invoice no. P23.

P PRACTICE PROBLEM 4-P

In this problem you will process any additions, changes, or deletions to vendors. You will also process the purchases and cash payments transactions for the period February 11 through February 20 of the current year.

Directions: The step-by-step instructions for solving this practice problem are listed below.

Step 1:   Remove the input forms from the working papers. Record the following transactions for Sun City Jewelers on the purchases and cash payments input forms. Record correcting entries on the general journal input form. Record additions, changes, or deletions to vendors in the vendors input form. Abbreviate the reference numbers on the input forms as follows: check no., C; purchase invoice no., P; memorandum, M. A chart of accounts and vendor list for Sun City Jewelers is shown below.

```
                        Sun City Jewelers
                        Chart of Accounts
                          02/10/--

    ---------------------------------------------------------
    Account    Account
    Number     Title
    ---------------------------------------------------------
    1110       Cash
    1120       Petty Cash
    1130       Accounts Receivable
    1140       Merchandise Inventory
    1145       Supplies--Office
    1150       Supplies--Store
    1160       Prepaid Insurance
    2110       Accounts Payable
    2120       Sales Tax Payable
    3110       Joel Delano, Capital
    3120       Joel Delano, Drawing
    3130       Cory Knapp, Capital
    3140       Cory Knapp, Drawing
    3150       Income Summary
    4110       Sales
    5110       Purchases
    6110       Insurance Expense
    6120       Miscellaneous Expense
    6130       Rent Expense
    6140       Supplies Expense--Office
    6150       Supplies Expense--Store
    6160       Utilities Expense
```

```
                        Sun City Jewelers
                          Vendor List
                          02/10/--

    ---------------------------------------------------------
    Vendor     Vendor
    Number     Name
    ---------------------------------------------------------
    210        Sterling Supply House
    220        Superior Gold
    230        Danielle's Designs
    240        Marcel Jewelry
    250        M & W Jewelers
    260        Martin Supply, Inc.
    270        Unique Jewels Company
```

Feb. 11 Paid cash for rent, $2,500.00. C54.

　　11 Paid cash on account to Danielle's Designs, $1,562.30, covering P19. C55.

　　11 Paid cash for store supplies, $254.68. C56.

　　12 Cory Knapp, partner, withdrew merchandise for personal use, $366.50. M21. Record this transaction in the general journal.

　　12 Purchased merchandise on account from Sterling Supply House, $2,106.48. P26.

12 Paid cash for miscellaneous expense, $96.53. C57.

15 Paid cash on account to Marcel Jewelry, $1,121.15, covering P20. C58.

15 Paid cash for office supplies, $131.62. C59.

15 Cory Knapp, partner, withdrew cash for personal use, $750.00. C60.

16 Discovered that a transaction for office supplies bought for cash in January was journalized and posted in error as a debit to Prepaid Insurance instead of Supplies—Office, $141.53. M22.

16 Bought store supplies on account from Martin Supply, Inc., $231.66. M23.

17 Paid cash on account to Martin Supply, Inc., $450.21, covering M15. C61.

17 Purchased merchandise on account from Superior Gold, $1,982.63. P27.

17 Purchased merchandise on account from Danielle's Designs, $1,699.54. P28.

18 Paid cash on account to M & W Jewelers, $627.88, covering P23. C62.

18 Purchased merchandise for cash, $2,509.61. C63.

18 Paid cash for miscellaneous expense, $15.00. C64.

18 Paid cash for insurance, $525.00. C65.

19 Paid cash for electric bill, $269.87. C66.

19 Paid cash on account to Superior Gold, $1,450.25, covering P22. C67.

19 Paid cash on account to Martin Supply, Inc., $115.66, covering M17. C68.

19 Bought store supplies on account from Supply Warehouse, $629.54. M24.

> Note: Add Supply Warehouse to the vendor list. Assign vendor number 280 for Supply Warehouse so that it will be positioned immediately following Unique Jewels Company in the vendor list.

19 Purchased merchandise on account from M & W Jewelers, $326.18. P29.

Step 2: Bring up the accounting system.

Step 3: Load the opening balances template file for AA4-P.

Step 4: Use the Save As menu command to save to your drive and directory with a file name of XXX4-P, where XXX are your initials.

Step 5:   Set the run date and student name in the General Information data entry window. The run date is February 20 of the current year.

Step 6:   Key the data from the vendors input form prepared in Step 1.

Step 7:   Key the journal entries (general journal, purchases journal, and cash payments journal input forms) prepared in Step 1.

Step 8:   Display the journal reports (general journal, purchases journal, and cash payments journal) for the period February 11 through February 19 of the current year. If errors are detected, use the List button of the data entry window for the journal with the error and select the journal entry to correct.

Step 9:   Display the following ledger reports:
                   Trial balance
                   General ledger report for the cash account
                   Schedule of accounts payable
                   Accounts payable ledger (all vendors)

Step 10:   Save your data file.

Step 11:   End the session.

AUDIT TEST PROBLEM 4-P

Directions: Write the answers to the following questions in the working papers or on a separate sheet of paper.

1. What are the totals of the debit and credit columns in the general journal report?
2. From the purchases journal report, what is the amount of invoice no. 29?
3. What is the amount of check no. 68 to Martin Supply, Inc.?
4. What is the current balance in Accounts Receivable?
5. What is the current balance in the office supplies account?
6. What was the balance at the beginning of the period in the Cash account?
7. What is the current balance owed to Superior Gold?
8. What is the total owed to all vendors on February 20?
9. What was the balance owed to Martin Supply, Inc., at the beginning of the period?
10. What is the total amount purchased by Martin Supply, Inc., during February?

MASTERY PROBLEM 4-M

In this problem you will process any additions, changes, or deletions to vendors. You will also process the purchases and cash payments transactions for the period February 21 through February 28 of the current year.

Directions: To solve the mastery problem, complete the tasks listed below using *Automated Accounting 6.0*. Abbreviate the reference numbers on the input forms as follows: check no., C; purchase invoice no., P; memorandum, M. The chart of accounts and vendor list needed to complete the input forms is shown below.

```
                        Sun City Jewelers
                        Chart of Accounts
                            02/20/--

         ----------------------------------------------------------
         Account   Account
         Number    Title
         ----------------------------------------------------------
         1110      Cash
         1120      Petty Cash
         1130      Accounts Receivable
         1140      Merchandise Inventory
         1145      Supplies--Office
         1150      Supplies--Store
         1160      Prepaid Insurance
         2110      Accounts Payable
         2120      Sales Tax Payable
         3110      Joel Delano, Capital
         3120      Joel Delano, Drawing
         3130      Cory Knapp, Capital
         3140      Cory Knapp, Drawing
         3150      Income Summary
         4110      Sales
         5110      Purchases
         6110      Insurance Expense
         6120      Miscellaneous Expense
         6130      Rent Expense
         6140      Supplies Expense--Office
         6150      Supplies Expense--Store
         6160      Utilities Expense
```

```
                        Sun City Jewelers
                          Vendor List
                           02/20/--

         ----------------------------------------------------------
         Vendor    Vendor
         Number    Name
         ----------------------------------------------------------
         210       Sterling Supply House
         220       Superior Gold
         230       Danielle's Designs
         240       Marcel Jewelry
         250       M & W Jewelers
         260       Martin Supply, Inc.
         270       Unique Jewels Company
         280       Supply Warehouse
```

1. Record the transactions on the proper input forms.

2. Load the opening balances file (AA4-M).

3. Save the opening balance data to your data disk or directory (XXX4-M).

4. Set the run date to February 28 of the current year.

5. Key the transactions.

6. Display the following reports:
    Journal reports
    Trial balance
    General ledger report for the office supplies and store sup-
    plies accounts
    Schedule of accounts payable
    Accounts payable ledger (all vendors)

7. Save your data to disk.

8. End the session.

Transactions:

Feb. 22 Purchased merchandise for cash, $563.29. C69.

22 Paid cash on account to Marcel Jewelry, $869.70, covering
    P24. C70.

22 Paid cash for miscellaneous expense, $21.00. C71.

23 Paid cash for store supplies, $99.10. C72.

23 Purchased merchandise on account from Sterling Supply
    House, $626.01. P30.

23 Paid cash on account to Unique Jewels Company, $855.15,
    covering P25. C73.

24 Paid cash for insurance, $128.62. C74.

24 Discovered that a payment for a miscellaneous expense was
    journalized and posted in error as a debit to Rent Expense
    instead of Miscellaneous Expense, $26.00. M25.

24 Purchased merchandise for cash, $290.03. C75.

24 Paid cash for office supplies, $136.43. C76.

25 Paid cash on account to Martin Supply, Inc., $327.89, cover-
    ing M20. C77.

25 Purchased merchandise on account from Aronoff Gems,
    $763.99. P31.

    Note: Add Aronoff Gems to the vendor list. Assign vendor
            number 290 for Aronoff Gems so that it will be posi-
            tioned immediately following Supply Warehouse in
            the vendor list.

25 Joel Delano, partner, withdrew cash for personal use,
    $800.00. C78.

25 Purchased merchandise on account from Marcel Jewelry,
    $603.22. P32.

26 Purchase office supplies on account from Supply
    Warehouse, $150.75. M26.

26   Paid cash to replenish the petty cash fund, $93.00: miscellaneous expense, $45.00; office supplies, $12.00; store supplies, $36.00. C79.

Note: Each of the items (miscellaneous expense, office supplies, etc) are recorded on separate lines on the cash payments input form.

26   Purchased merchandise on account from M & W Jewelers, $333.93. P33.

AUDIT TEST PROBLEM 4-M

Directions: Write the answers to the following questions in the working papers or on a separate sheet of paper.

1. On the purchases journal report, what is the amount credited to Marcel Jewelry for invoice no. 32?

2. On the purchases journal report, what is the amount of the debit to office supplies for memorandum no. 26?

3. What is the total of the debit column in the cash payments journal?

4. What is the balance in Cory Knapp's drawing account?

5. What is the balance in the Miscellaneous Expense account?

6. From the general ledger report, what is the amount of the office supplies purchase for memorandum no. 26?

7. From the general ledger report, was the amount of the office supply purchase for memorandum no. 26 mentioned in Question 6 debited or credited to office supplies?

8. What is the balance owed to Aronoff Gems on February 28?

9. What is the total amount owed to all vendors as of February 28?

10. From the accounts payable ledger report, what is the amount for memorandum no. 26 to Supply Warehouse?

5

Sales and Cash Receipts

LEARNING OBJECTIVES ▶ UPON COMPLETION OF THIS CHAPTER, you will be able to:

1. Record additions, changes, and deletions to customers on the customers input form.

2. Record sales on account transactions on the sales journal input form.

3. Record cash receipts transactions on the cash receipts journal input form.

4. Key customer maintenance data.

5. Enter and correct sales and cash receipts journal entries.

6. Display a customer list.

7. Display sales and cash receipts journal entries.

8. Display a schedule of accounts receivable.

9. Display an accounts receivable ledger report.

INTRODUCTION

In this chapter you will again work with the sample company, Sun City Jewelers, as you learn to add, change, and delete customers and to enter and correct sales and cash receipts journal entries. Sun City Jewelers is a wholesale merchandising business. This company sells merchandise on account to retail stores at wholesale prices. They also sell merchandise at retail prices to individuals for cash. The cash sales to individuals are subject to sales tax. Retailers do not pay that tax, since sales of merchandise for resale are not subject to sales tax. Occasionally, Sun City sells on account to individuals. Sales on account to individuals are subject to sales tax.

▶ Customers Input Form

Whenever necessary, new customers must be added, customer names must be changed, and inactive customers deleted. Each addition, change, or deletion is recorded on a customers input form as illustrated in Figure 5.1. Both the Customer Number and Customer Name fields are completed whether you are adding or changing an account. When a customer is to be deleted, record the customer number and (Delete).

FIGURE 5.1
Customers Input Form

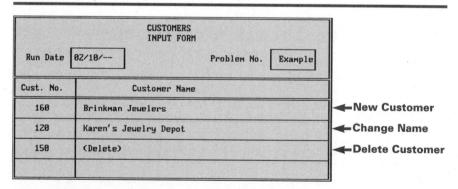

▶ Sales Journal Input Form

Sales on account are recorded on the sales journal input form, then keyed into the computer with the Sales Journal data entry window. Each line of the input form may be used to record a sales invoice or one part of a sales invoice that is charged to multiple revenue accounts. The field names and a description of each column of the input form are given in Table 5.1.

TABLE 5.1
Field Names and Descriptions of the Sales Journal Input Form

Field Name	Description
Date	The date field contains the two-digit month and day of the month on which the transaction occurred.
Customer Number	Record the customer number from the customer list, which identifies the customer to whom the transaction data belongs.
Invoice Number	Record the sales invoice number.
Invoice Amount	Record the total amount of the sales invoice.
Account Number	Record the general ledger account number from the chart of accounts that is to be charged for the purchase.
Debit	Record the amount that is to be debited to the account specified in the Account Number field. It is unusual to record an entry in the Debit column.
Credit	Record the amount that is to be credited to the account specified in the Account Number field (most often a revenue account or Sales Tax Payable).

For the first transaction, 140 is the customer number for Barber & Wolfe Jewelry and 4110 is the account number for sales. For the second transaction, 180 is the customer number for Chellis Lien and 2120 is the account number for sales tax payable.

The sample transaction shown below is recorded on the sales journal input form illustrated in Figure 5.2.

Feb. 02 Sold merchandise on account to Barber & Wolfe, $1,491.12. Sales invoice no. 82.

Feb. 10 Sold merchandise on account to Chellis Lien, $409.30; plus sales tax, $20.47; total, $429.77. Sales invoice no. 89.

FIGURE 5.2
Sales Journal Input Form

			SALES JOURNAL INPUT FORM				
Run Date	02/10/--					Problem No.	Example
Date MM / dd	Cust. No.	Invoice No.	Invoice Amount	Acct. No.	Debit Amount	Credit Amount
02/02	140	S82	1491.12	4110		1491.12
02/10	180	S89	433.86	4110		409.30
				2120		20.47

It is not necessary to record the debit to Accounts Receivable on the sales journal input form because this entry is made automatically by the computer.

▶ Cash Receipts Journal Input Form

All cash receipts are recorded on the cash receipts journal input form. Entries are keyed from this form. The field names and a description of each field in the input form are given in Table 5.2.

TABLE 5.2
Field Names and Descriptions of the Cash Receipts Journal Input Form

Field Name	Description
Date	The date field contains the two-digit month and day of the month on which the transaction occurred.
Customer Number	If an amount is recorded in the Accounts Receivable Credit column, the number of the customer's account is recorded in this column. Otherwise the Customer Number is left blank.
Reference	Record a reference that will identify the transaction, such as the sales invoice number or a cash register tape number.
Accounts Receivable Credit	Record the total amount of the credit to Accounts Receivable resulting from this cash receipt.
Account Number	The general ledger account number from the chart of accounts that is to be either debited or credited in the next two columns.
Debit	The amount that is to be debited to the account specified in the Account Number field.
Credit	The amount that is to be credited to the account specified in the Account Number field. Each debit or credit must be recorded on a separate line of the form.

In the first transaction, 110 is the customer number for Bayside Jewelry. In the second transaction, 4110 is the account number for sales and 2120 is the account number for sales tax payable.

It is not necessary to record the debit to Cash, since the computer makes this entry automatically.

Figure 5.3 illustrates a completed cash receipts journal input form. Each line of the form may be used to record a cash receipt transaction (or one part of a cash receipt transaction involving multiple parts). The two transactions listed below are recorded on the form. Additional examples of the various types of cash receipt transactions that may be recorded on this form are illustrated in Tutorial Problem 5-T.

Feb. 01 Received cash on account from Bayside Jewelry, $440.17, covering sales invoice no. 77. Cash receipt no. 136.

Feb. 01 Recorded cash and credit card sales, $3,341.07, plus sales tax, $167.05; total, $3,508.12. Cash register tape no. 1.

FIGURE 5.3
Cash Receipts Journal Input Form

		CASH RECEIPTS JOURNAL INPUT FORM				
Run Date 02/01/--					Problem No. Example	

Date MM / dd	Cust. No.	Refer.	Accounts Rec. Credit	Acct. No.	Debit Amount	Credit Amount
02/01	110	R136	440.17			
02/01		T1		4110		3341.07
				2120		167.05

OPERATING PROCEDURES

Operating procedures are covered in this chapter for performing data entry in customer maintenance, the sales journal, and the cash receipts journal, and displaying journal entries, an accounts receivable ledger, and a schedule of accounts receivable.

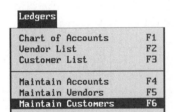

Ledgers	
Chart of Accounts	F1
Vendor List	F2
Customer List	F3
Maintain Accounts	F4
Maintain Vendors	F5
Maintain Customers	F6

▶Maintain Customers Data Entry Window

When the Maintain Customers menu command is chosen from the Ledgers menu, the data entry window shown in Figure 5.4 will appear.

▶Adding a New Customer

1   Choose the ----Add New Customer---- item from the list window by pressing Enter or by pushing the Ok button.

2   Key the Customer Number and Name for the new customer.

3   Push the Ok button.

▶Changing a Customer Name

1   Choose the customer you wish to change from the list window.

The list window will close, and the data for the chosen customer will appear in the data entry window.

2   Key the correct customer name.

3   Push the Ok button.

FIGURE 5.4
Maintain Customers Data Entry Window

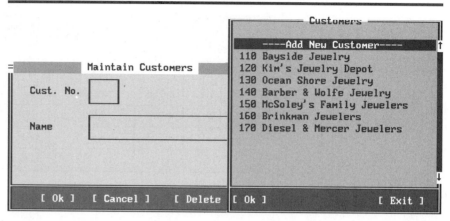

▶Deleting a Customer

> Customer accounts cannot be deleted unless the account being deleted has a zero balance.

1   Choose the customer you wish to delete from the list window.

The list window will be dismissed, and the data for the chosen customer will be displayed in the data entry window.

2   Push the Delete button.

▶Sales Journal Data Entry Window

Journals

Opening Balances	
General Journal	S+F1
Purchases Journal	S+F2
Cash Payments Journal	S+F3
Sales Journal	S+F4
Cash Receipts Journal	S+F5

The Sales Journal data entry window is used to key sales-on-account transactions and to make corrections to or delete existing sales journal entries. The Sales Journal data entry window is shown in Figure 5.5. Only sales-on-account transactions are keyed into the sales journal. The computer automatically calculates and displays the Accounts Receivable credit amount. The rest of the journal entry is completed in the General Accounts section. The entries in the General Accounts section most often consist of one or more credits. The account credited is usually a revenue account. On rare occasions, you may need to record a debit entry (a sales discount recorded at the time of sale, for example).

> The Invoice Number field is automatically increased by one for each sales journal entry.

FIGURE 5.5
Sales Journal Data Entry Window

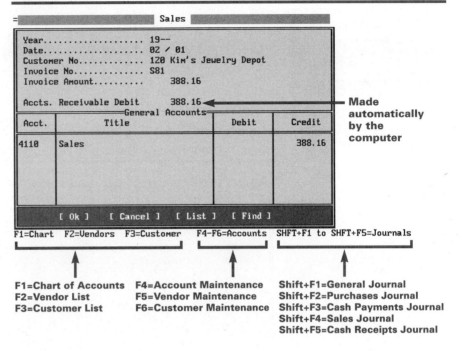

Made automatically by the computer

F1=Chart   F2=Vendors   F3=Customer   F4-F6=Accounts   SHFT+F1 to SHFT+F5=Journals

F1=Chart of Accounts	F4=Account Maintenance	Shift+F1=General Journal
F2=Vendor List	F5=Vendor Maintenance	Shift+F2=Purchases Journal
F3=Customer List	F6=Customer Maintenance	Shift+F3=Cash Payments Journal
		Shift+F4=Sales Journal
		Shift+F5=Cash Receipts Journal

▶ Keying a Sales Journal Entry

1 Key the two-digit day of the month.

2 Key each of the data fields.

While the cursor is positioned to the Customer Number field, you can press the F3 key to choose a customer from a customer list window.

3 When the journal entry is complete, push the Ok button.

The Posting Summary dialog window shown in Figure 5.6 will appear. It shows the journal entry in a two-column format. Verify the accuracy of your input and post the data.

4 If the transaction is correct, push the Post button (push the Change button to return to the Sales Journal data entry window and make changes).

The Shift+F1 through Shift+F5 keys provide a quick and easy way to move among the five journals. The F4 through F6 keys provide an easy way to make changes to the chart of accounts, vendors, or customers.

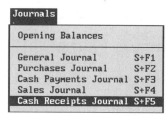

▶ Cash Receipts Journal Data Entry Window

The Cash Receipts Journal data entry window is used to key all cash receipts transactions and to make corrections to or delete previously entered cash receipts journal transactions. As the data is keyed, the computer automatically calculates and displays the debit to cash.

FIGURE 5.6

Sales Journal Posting Summary Dialog Window

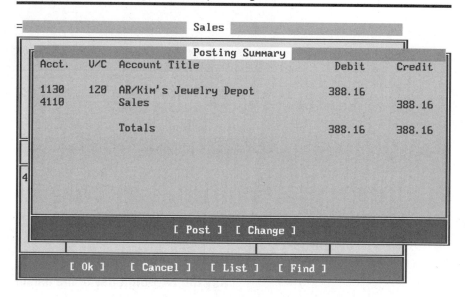

There are two types of cash receipts: (1) direct receipts and (2) receipts on account. A **direct receipt** is a cash receipt that does not affect accounts receivable. Examples of direct receipts are cash sales, cash received from the sale of an asset, or cash received for money borrowed. A **cash receipt on account** involves a receipt of cash from a customer on account.

DIRECT RECEIPT. A Cash Receipts data entry window with sample data for a direct cash receipt is shown in Figure 5.7. Notice that the Customer Number and Accounts Receivable Credit fields are left blank. The customer number is needed only for transactions that affect accounts receivable. The cash credit amount is calculated and displayed by the computer. The account(s) credited will vary depending on what the cash was received for. A typical transaction in shown in Figure 5.7, with credits to sales and sales tax payable.

FIGURE 5.7
Cash Receipts Data Entry Window (Direct Receipt)

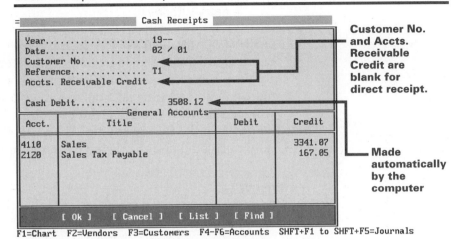

Keying a Direct Cash Receipt

1   **Key the two-digit day of the month.**

2   **Key each of the data fields.**

Leave the Customer Number and Accounts Receivable Credit fields blank, since they do not apply to a direct receipt. The cash debit is calculated and displayed automatically by the computer.

3   **When the journal entry is complete, push the Ok button.**

The Posting Summary dialog window shown in Figure 5.8 will appear.

FIGURE 5.8
Direct Cash Receipt Posting Summary Dialog Window

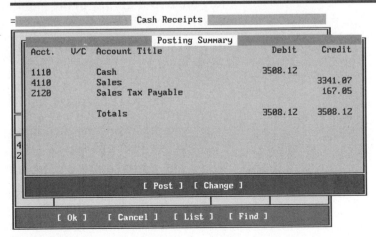

4   If the transaction is correct, push the Post button (push the Change button to return to the Cash Receipts Journal data entry window).

CASH RECEIPT ON ACCOUNT.   A cash receipt on account is illustrated in Figure 5.9. Notice that a customer number is required, because the accounts receivable account is affected. For a cash receipt on account, the General Accounts section may be blank. In a later chapter, you will learn how to use the Debit column of the General Accounts section to record sales discounts. The Cash Debit amount is automatically calculated and displayed by the computer.

FIGURE 5.9
Cash Receipts Journal Data Entry Window (Receipt on Account)

```
=▄▄▄▄▄▄▄▄▄▄▄▄▄▄        Cash Receipts        ▄▄▄▄▄▄▄▄▄▄▄▄▄▄
 ┌──────────────────────────────────────────────────────┐
 │ Year................. 19--                             │
 │ Date................. 02 / 01                          │
 │ Customer No.......... 110 Bayside Jewelry              │
 │ Reference............ R136                             │
 │ Accts. Receivable Credit      440.17                   │
 │                                                        │
 │ Cash Debit...........         440.17                   │
 │                    ─General Accounts─                  │
 │ Acct. │      Title       │    Debit    │   Credit      │
 │───────┼──────────────────┼─────────────┼───────────────│
 │       │                  │             │               │
 │       │                  │             │               │
 │       │                  │             │               │
 │       │                  │             │               │
 │       │                  │             │               │
 │                                                        │
 │     [ Ok ]    [ Cancel ]   [ List ]    [ Find ]        │
 └──────────────────────────────────────────────────────┘
```

▶**Keying a Cash Receipt on Account**

1   Key the two-digit day of the month (or press Tab if it is correct as is).

2   Key each of the data fields.

While the cursor is positioned to the Customer Number field, you can press the F3 key to choose a customer from a customer list window. Because this is a receipt on account, the Accounts Receivable Debit amount must be entered.

3   When the journal entry is complete, push the Ok button.

The Posting Summary dialog window shown in Figure 5.10 will appear. It shows the journal entry in a two-column format. Verify the accuracy of your input and post the data.

FIGURE 5.10
Cash Receipt on Account Posting Summary Dialog Window

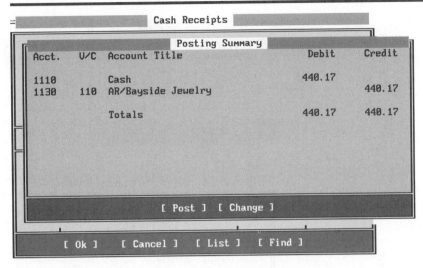

4   **If the transaction is correct, push the Post button (push the Change button to return to the Cash Receipts Journal data entry window and make changes).**

▶ Journal Reports

Once the journal entries have been keyed, the various journal reports may be displayed.

▶ Display the Journal Reports

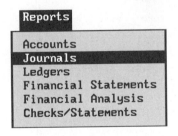

1   **Choose the Journals menu command from the Reports menu.**

The Report Selection dialog window shown in Figure 5.11 will appear, allowing you to select which of the journal reports you would like to be displayed.

2   **Select the reports you would like to display.**

The reports are selected by clicking on the check box or by pressing the Space Bar (or Right Arrow) while the cursor is positioned to that check box.

3   **Push the Ok button.**

The Selection Options dialog window shown in Figure 5.12 will appear.

FIGURE 5.11
Report Selection Dialog Window

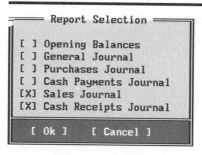

FIGURE 5.12
Selection Options for Journal Reports

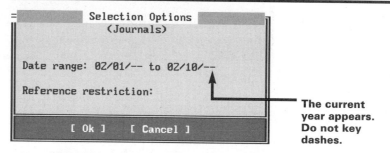

The current year appears. Do not key dashes.

4   Key the range of dates to be included on the journal report. Key a reference restriction to limit the report. You may want to display only a certain invoice.

A sales journal entries report is shown in Figure 5.13. To print the displayed report on an attached printer, press the F9 "hot key."

FIGURE 5.13
Sales Journal Entries Report

Sun City Jewelers
Sales Journal
02/10/--

Date	Refer.	V/C	Acct.	Title	Debit	Credit
02/01	S81	120	1130	AR/Kim's Jewelry Depot	388.16	
02/01	S81		4110	Sales		388.16
02/01	S81	120	1130	AR/Kim's Jewelry Depot	388.16	
02/01	S81		4110	Sales		388.16
02/02	S82	140	1130	AR/Barber & Wolfe Jewelry	1491.12	
02/02	S82		4110	Sales		1491.12
02/03	S83	110	1130	AR/Bayside Jewelry	1889.56	
02/03	S83		4110	Sales		1889.56
02/03	S84	160	1130	AR/Brinkman Jewelers	651.40	

▶ Accounts Receivable Ledger Reports

The two accounts receivable ledger reports available are the schedule of accounts receivable and the accounts receivable ledger report. The schedule shows the current balance for each customer. The report lists all journal activity by customer. This report can be very useful in locating errors in a customer account.

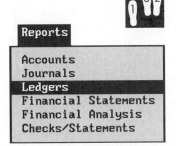

Reports

Accounts
Journals
Ledgers
Financial Statements
Financial Analysis
Checks/Statements

▶ Displaying the Accounts Receivable Ledger Report

1   Choose the Ledgers menu command from the Reports menu.

The Report Selection dialog window shown in Figure 5.14 will appear, allowing you to select which of the ledger reports you would like to be displayed.

2   Select the reports you would like to display.

The reports are selected by clicking on the check box or by pressing the Space Bar (or Right Arrow) while the cursor is positioned to that check box.

3   Push the Ok button.

The schedule of accounts receivable report is illustrated in Figure 5.15.

FIGURE 5.14
Report Selection Dialog Window

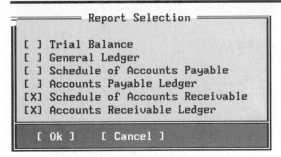

When the accounts receivable ledger report is selected, the dialog window shown in Figure 5.16 will appear.

4   Key the range of customers to be included in the accounts receivable ledger report.

The accounts receivable ledger report displaying customers 110 through 120 is shown in Figure 5.17.

FIGURE 5.15

Schedule of Accounts Receivable

```
                        Sun City Jewelers
                    Schedule of Accounts Receivable
                            02/10/--

        Account
        Number    Name                         Balance

          110     Bayside Jewelry              1989.56
          120     Kim's Jewelry Depot           388.16
          130     Ocean Shore Jewelry          1751.79
          150     McSoley's Family Jewelers    1665.18
          160     Brinkman Jewelers             651.40
          170     Diesel & Mercer Jewelers     1254.32
                                               -----------
                  Total                        7700.41
                                               ===========
```

F9=Print   Esc=Close Window

FIGURE 5.16

Selection Options for Accounts Receivable Ledger

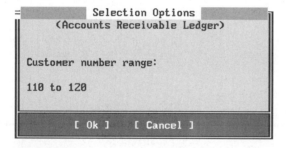

```
=========   Selection Options   =========
           (Accounts Receivable Ledger)


Customer number range:

110 to 120


           [ Ok ]      [ Cancel ]
```

FIGURE 5.17

Accounts Receivable Ledger Report

```
                        Sun City Jewelers
                    Accounts Receivable Ledger
                            02/10/--

Account          Journal   Date  Refer.     Debit    Credit    Balance

110-Bayside Jewelry
                 Bal. Fwd.                                       440.17
                 Cash Rcpt 02/01 R136                 440.17
                 Sales     02/03 S83      1889.56               1889.56
                 Sales     02/10 S89       100.00               1989.56

120-Kim's Jewelry Depot
                 Bal. Fwd.                                       175.26
                 Sales     02/01 S81       388.16                563.42
                 Cash Rcpt 02/03 R138                 175.26     388.16
                 Cash Rcpt 02/08 R141                 388.16
```

F9=Print   Esc=Close Window

T TUTORIAL 5-T

In this tutorial problem you will learn the operating procedures for maintaining customer accounts, and recording and keying sales and cash receipts journal entries for Sun City Jewelers. You will key the sales and cash receipts transactions that occurred during the period February 1 through 10 of the current year for Sun City Jewelers. These journal entries have already been recorded for you in Figures 5.19 and 5.20. Additions, changes, and deletions to customers have also been recorded for you and are illustrated in Figure 5.18.

Each of the steps listed below contains a task to be completed at the computer. In case you need it, more detailed information on how to complete the task is provided immediately following the step. If you need additional explanation for the task, a page number is shown that references that topic in the Operating Procedures section of this or a previous chapter.

Directions: The step-by-step instructions for processing the sales and cash receipts transactions for Sun City Jewelers for the first 10 days of February of the current year are listed below.

Step 1: Bring up the accounting system. (page 16)

At the DOS prompt, key A1 (or follow the instructions provided by your instructor).

Step 2: Load the opening balances template file, AA5-T. (page 19)

Pull down the File menu and choose the Open Accounting File command. Key into the Path field the drive and directory containing the template files. Key a file name of AA5-T and push the Ok button.

Step 3: Use the Save As command to save data to disk with a file name of XXX5-T (where XXX are your initials). (page 21)

Pull down the File menu and choose the Save As menu command. Key the path to the drive and directory that contains your data files. Key a file name of XXX5-T, where XXX are your initials. Push the Ok button.

Step 4: Enter your name in the General Information data entry window and set the run date to February 10 of the current year. (page 21)

Pull down the Options menu and choose the General Information menu command. Set the run date to February 10 of the current year. Key your name in the Student Name field.

Step 5: Key the data from the customers input form shown in Figure 5.18.

Pull down the Ledgers menu and choose the Maintain Customers command.

FIGURE 5.18
Customers Input Form

```
┌──────────────────────────────────────────────────────────┐
│                        CUSTOMERS                          │
│                       INPUT FORM                          │
│                                                          │
│   Run Date  │02/10/--│           Problem No.  │ 5-T │     │
│                                                          │
│  ┌─────────┬──────────────────────────────────────┐     │
│  │ Cust. No.│          Customer Name               │     │
│  ├─────────┼──────────────────────────────────────┤     │
│  │   150   │  McSoley's Family Jewelers            │     │
│  ├─────────┼──────────────────────────────────────┤     │
│  │   160   │  Brinkman Jewelers                    │     │
│  ├─────────┼──────────────────────────────────────┤     │
│  │   170   │  Diesel & Mercer Jewelers             │     │
│  ├─────────┼──────────────────────────────────────┤     │
│  │   125   │  (Delete)                             │     │
│  └─────────┴──────────────────────────────────────┘     │
└──────────────────────────────────────────────────────────┘
```

Step 6: Key the journal entries from the sales and cash receipts input forms shown in Figures 5.19 and 5.20.

Transactions:

> Note: Do not key from these transaction statements, since they have already been recorded for you on the journal input forms in Figures 5.19 and 5.20. The reference numbers have been abbreviated on the input forms as follows: sales invoice no., S; cash receipt no., C; cash register tape, T; memorandum, M.

Feb. 01   Sold merchandise on account to Kim's Jewelry Depot, $388.16. S81.

01   Received cash on account from Bayside Jewelry, $440.17, covering S77. R136.

01   Recorded cash and credit card sales, $3,341.07, plus sales tax, $167.05; total, $3,508.12. T1.

02   Change the name of the customer McSoley's, Inc., to McSoley's Family Jewelers.

02   Sold merchandise on account to Barber & Wolfe, $1,491.12. S82.

02   Received cash on account from Ocean Shore Jewelry, $289.22, covering S80. R137.

03   Received cash on account from Kim's Jewelry Depot, $175.26, covering S76. R138.

FIGURE 5.19
Sales Journal Input Form

SALES JOURNAL INPUT FORM						
Run Date 02/10/--					Problem No. 5-T	
Date MM / dd	Cust. No.	Invoice No.	Invoice Amount	Acct. No.	Debit Amount	Credit Amount
02/01	120	S81	388.16	4110		388.16
02/02	140	S82	1491.12	4110		1491.12
02/03	110	S83	1889.56	4110		1889.56
02/03	160	S84	651.40	4110		651.40
02/04	130	S85	596.14	4110		596.14
02/05	150	S86	1665.18	4110		
02/10	170	S87	1254.32	4110		1254.32
02/10	130	S88	1155.65	4110		1155.65
02/10	145	S89	429.77	4110		409.30
				2120		20.47

FIGURE 5.20
Cash Receipts Journal Input Form

CASH RECEIPTS JOURNAL INPUT FORM						
Run Date 02/10/--					Problem No. 5-T	
Date MM / dd	Cust. No.	Refer.	Accounts Rec. Credit	Acct. No.	Debit Amount	Credit Amount
02/01	110	R136	440.17			
02/01		T1		4110		3341.07
				2120		167.05
02/02	130	R137	289.22			
02/03	120	R138	175.26			
02/03	150	R139	296.47			
02/04	140	R140	325.18			
02/08		T8		4110		2841.50
				2120		142.08
02/08	120	R141	388.16			
02/09	140	R142	1491.12			

03 Received cash on account from McSoley Family Jewelers, $296.47, covering S78. R139

03 Sold merchandise on account to Bayside Jewelry, $1,889.56. S83.

03 Sold merchandise on account to Brinkman Jewelers, $651.40. S84.

Note: Add Brinkman Jewelers to the customer list. Assign customer number 160 for Brinkman Jewelers so that it will be positioned immediately following McSoley Family Jewelers in the customer list.

04 Received cash on account from Barber & Wolfe Jewelry, $325.18, covering S79. R140.

04 Sold merchandise on account to Ocean Shore Jewelry, $596.14. S85.

05 Sold merchandise on account to McSoley Family Jewelers, $1,665.18. S86.

08 Recorded cash and credit card sales, $2,841.50, plus sales tax, $142.08; total, $2,983.58. T8.

08 Received cash on account from Kim's Jewelry Depot, $388.16, covering S81. R141.

09 Received cash on account from Barber & Wolfe Jewelry, $1,491.12, covering S82. R142.

10 Sold merchandise on account to Diesel & Mercer Jewelers, $1,254.32. S87.

Note: Add Diesel & Mercer Jewelers to the customer list. Assign customer number 170 for Diesel & Mercer so that it will be positioned immediately following Brinkman Jewelers in the customer list.

10 Sold merchandise on account to Ocean Shore Jewelry, $1,155.65. S88.

10 Sold merchandise on account to Chellis Lien, $409.30, plus sales tax, $20.47; total, $429.77. S89.

Note: Enter 429.77 as the invoice amount. Enter 4110 as the account number, and change the sales credit from 429.77 to 409.30. Then enter the sales tax.

10 Delete Judy's Costume Jewelry from the customer list.

Step 7: Display the sales journal and cash receipts journal reports. (page 129).

Pull down the Reports menu and choose the Journals command. When the Report Selection window shown in Figure 5.21 appears, select the sales and cash receipts journals. When the Selection

Options window illustrated in Figure 5.22 appears, key a date range of February 1 through February 10 of the current year. The reports appear in Figure 5.23 and 5.24.

FIGURE 5.21
Report Selection Window

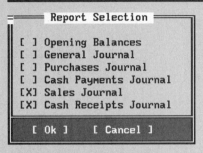

```
========= Report Selection =========

    [ ] Opening Balances
    [ ] General Journal
    [ ] Purchases Journal
    [ ] Cash Payments Journal
    [X] Sales Journal
    [X] Cash Receipts Journal

        [ Ok ]      [ Cancel ]
```

FIGURE 5.22
Selection Options

```
=============== Selection Options ===============
                   (Journals)


    Date range: 02/01/-- to 02/10/--

    Reference restriction:


            [ Ok ]      [ Cancel ]
```

When this screen appears on the computer, the current year will appear in place of the dashes.

FIGURE 5.23
Sales Journal Report

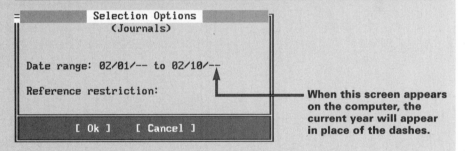

```
                        Sun City Jewelers
                          Sales Journal
                            02/10/--

    -----------------------------------------------------------------
    Date  Refer.  V/C Acct. Title                    Debit    Credit
    -----------------------------------------------------------------
    02/01 S81     120 1130  AR/Kim's Jewelry Depot   388.16
    02/01 S81         4110  Sales                              388.16

    02/02 S82     140 1130  AR/Barber & Wolfe Jewelry 1491.12
    02/02 S82         4110  Sales                             1491.12

    02/03 S83     110 1130  AR/Bayside Jewelry       1889.56
    02/03 S83         4110  Sales                             1889.56

    02/03 S84     160 1130  AR/Brinkman Jewelers     651.40
    02/03 S84         4110  Sales                              651.40

    02/04 S85     130 1130  AR/Ocean Shore Jewelry   596.14
    02/04 S85         4110  Sales                              596.14
```

(continued)

FIGURE 5.23 (Continued)
Sales Journal Report

```
    02/05 S86   150 1130  AR/McSoley's Family Jewelers  1665.18
    02/05 S86       4110  Sales                                    1665.18

    02/10 S87   170 1130  AR/Diesel & Mercer Jewelers   1254.32
    02/10 S87       4110  Sales                                    1254.32

    02/10 S88   130 1130  AR/Ocean Shore Jewelry        1155.65
    02/10 S88       4110  Sales                                    1155.65

    02/10 S89   145 1130  AR/Chellis Lien                429.77
    02/10 S89       4110  Sales                                     409.30
    02/10 S89       2120  Sales Tax Payable                          20.47
                                                        ---------- --------
                          Totals                         9521.30  9521.30
                                                        ========= ========
```

FIGURE 5.24
Cash Receipts Journal Report

```
                        Sun City Jewelers
                        Cash Receipts Journal
                             02/10/--
    -----------------------------------------------------------------
    Date  Refer.  V/C Acct. Title                    Debit    Credit
    -----------------------------------------------------------------
    02/01 R136       1110  Cash                      440.17
    02/01 R136   110 1130  AR/Bayside Jewelry                  440.17

    02/01 T1         1110  Cash                     3508.12
    02/01 T1         4110  Sales                              3341.07
    02/01 T1         2120  Sales Tax Payable                   167.05

    02/02 R137       1110  Cash                      289.22
    02/02 R137   130 1130  AR/Ocean Shore Jewelry              289.22

    02/03 R138       1110  Cash                      175.26
    02/03 R138   120 1130  AR/Kim's Jewelry Depot              175.26

    02/03 R139       1110  Cash                      296.47
    02/03 R139   150 1130  AR/McSoley's Family Jewelers        296.47

    02/04 R140       1110  Cash                      325.18
    02/04 R140   140 1130  AR/Barber & Wolfe Jewelry           325.18

    02/08 T8         1110  Cash                     2983.58
    02/08 T8         4110  Sales                              2841.50
    02/08 T8         2120  Sales Tax Payable                   142.08

    02/08 R141       1110  Cash                      388.16
    02/08 R141   120 1130  AR/Kim's Jewelry Depot              388.16

    02/09 R142       1110  Cash                     1491.12
    02/09 R142   140 1130  AR/Barber & Wolfe Jewelry          1491.12
                                                    ---------- ---------
                          Totals                     9897.28   9897.28
                                                    ========== =========
```

FIGURE 5.25
Report Selection (Ledgers)

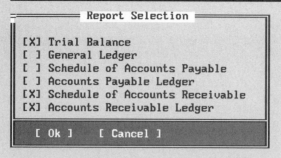

```
================ Report Selection ================

  [X] Trial Balance
  [ ] General Ledger
  [ ] Schedule of Accounts Payable
  [ ] Accounts Payable Ledger
  [X] Schedule of Accounts Receivable
  [X] Accounts Receivable Ledger

     [ Ok ]        [ Cancel ]
```

Step 8: Display a trial balance, a schedule of accounts receivable, and an accounts receivable ledger report for all customers. (page 131)

Pull down the Reports menu and choose the Ledgers command. When the Report Selection window shown in Figure 5.25 appears, select the trial balance, schedule of accounts receivable, and accounts receivable ledger reports. The reports appear in Figures 5.26 through 5.28.

FIGURE 5.26
Trial Balance Report

```
                        Sun City Jewelers
                         Trial Balance
                          02/10/--

        ------------------------------------------------------------
        Acct.   Account
        Number  Title                      Debit           Credit
        ------------------------------------------------------------
        1110    Cash                      23153.10
        1120    Petty Cash                  100.00
        1130    Accounts Receivable        7642.02
        1140    Merchandise Inventory    125325.20
        1145    Supplies--Office           1434.81
        1150    Supplies--Store            2081.80
        1160    Prepaid Insurance          1577.16
        2110    Accounts Payable                           9453.93
        2120    Sales Tax Payable                          1333.00
        3110    Joel Delano, Capital                      78095.15
        3120    Joel Delano, Drawing       1550.50
        3130    Cory Knapp, Capital                       78095.15
        3140    Cory Knapp, Drawing        1866.50
        4110    Sales                                     15683.40
        5110    Purchases                 14928.89
        6120    Miscellaneous Expense       208.78
        6130    Rent Expense               2474.00
        6160    Utilities Expense           317.87
                                         ----------        ----------
                Totals                   182660.63        182660.63
                                         ==========        ==========
```

FIGURE 5.27
Schedule of Accounts Receivable

```
                    Sun City Jewelers
              Schedule of Accounts Receivable
                       02/10/--

        ---------------------------------------------
        Account
        Number    Name                        Balance
        ---------------------------------------------
        110       Bayside Jewelry             1889.56
        130       Ocean Shore Jewelry         1751.79
        145       Chellis Lien                 429.77
        150       McSoley's Family Jewelers   1665.18
        160       Brinkman Jewelers            651.40
        170       Diesel & Mercer Jewelers    1254.32
                                             ----------
                  Total                       7642.02
                                             ==========
```

Step 9: Save your data file to disk.

Pull down the File menu and choose the Save menu command.

FIGURE 5.28
Accounts Receivable Ledger Report

```
                     Sun City Jewelers
                 Accounts Receivable Ledger
                        02/10/--

----------------------------------------------------------------
Account          Journal   Date  Refer.   Debit   Credit  Balance
----------------------------------------------------------------
110-Bayside Jewelry
                 Bal. Fwd.                                  440.17
                 Cash Rcpt 02/01 R136              440.17
                 Sales     02/03 S83    1889.56            1889.56

115-Oak Street Jewelry Shop       ******* No Activity *******

120-Kim's Jewelry Depot
                 Bal. Fwd.                                  175.26
                 Sales     02/01 S81     388.16             563.42
                 Cash Rcpt 02/03 R138              175.26   388.16
                 Cash Rcpt 02/08 R141              388.16

130-Ocean Shore Jewelry
                 Bal. Fwd.                                  289.22
                 Cash Rcpt 02/02 R137              289.22
                 Sales     02/04 S85     596.14             596.14
                 Sales     02/10 S88    1155.65            1751.79

135-Pete's Black Hills Gold       ******* No Activity *******

140-Barber & Wolfe Jewelry
                 Bal. Fwd.                                  325.18
                 Sales     02/02 S82    1491.12            1816.30
                 Cash Rcpt 02/04 R140              325.18  1491.12
                 Cash Rcpt 02/09 R142             1491.12
```

(continued)

FIGURE 5.28 (Continued)
Accounts Receivable Ledger Report

```
  145-Chellis Lien
                     Sales      02/10 S89    429.77                429.77

  150-McSoley's Family Jewelers
                     Bal. Fwd.                                     296.47
                     Cash Rcpt 02/03 R139              296.47
                     Sales      02/05 S86   1665.18               1665.18

  160-Brinkman Jewelers
                     Sales      02/03 S84    651.40                651.40

  170-Diesel & Mercer Jewelers
                     Sales      02/10 S87   1254.32               1254.32
```

Step 10:   End your session.

Pull down the File menu and choose the Quit menu command.

CHAPTER 5 STUDENT EXERCISE

I. TRUE/FALSE

Directions: Answer the following question in the working papers or on a separate sheet of paper. If the statement is true, write the question number followed by T. If the statement is false, write the question number followed by F.

1. Cash sales are recorded on the sales journal input form.
2. It is unusual to record a debit entry on the sales journal input form.
3. A cash sale with sales tax is recorded on the cash receipts journal input form.
4. It is not necessary to record the credit to sales on the cash receipts journal input form, since the computer makes this entry automatically.
5. Only sales on account are keyed into the Sales Journal data entry window.
6. In the Sales Journal data entry window, the account credited is usually an expense account.
7. The Invoice Number field is automatically increased by one for each sales journal entry.
8. A transaction in which the company borrowed money from a bank would be recorded on the cash receipts journal input form.
9. For a direct cash receipt, the customer number is keyed into the cash receipts journal data entry window.

II. QUESTIONS

Directions: Write the answers to the following questions in the working papers or on a separate sheet of paper.

1. List the two types of cash receipts.
2. List the two accounts receivable ledger reports.

3. Which of the two accounts receivable ledger reports lists all journal activity for a customer?

4. Which amount is automatically calculated as data is keyed into the Sales Journal data entry window?

5. Which amount is automatically calculated as data is keyed into the Cash Receipts Journal data entry window?

PRACTICE PROBLEM 5-P

In this problem you will process any additions, changes, or deletions to customers. You will also process the sales and cash receipts transactions for the period February 11 through February 20 of the current year.

Directions: The step-by-step instructions for solving this practice problem are listed below.

Step 1:

Remove the input forms from the working papers. Record the following transactions for Sun City Jewelers on the sales and cash receipts input forms. Record additions, changes, or deletions to vendors in the vendors input form. Abbreviate the reference numbers on the input forms as follows: sales invoice no., S; cash receipt no., C; cash register tape, T; memorandum, M. The chart of accounts and customer list needed to complete the input forms is shown below.

```
                    Sun City Jewelers
                    Chart of Accounts
                       02/10/--
    ------------------------------------------------
    Account   Account
    Number    Title
    ------------------------------------------------
    1110      Cash
    1120      Petty Cash
    1130      Accounts Receivable
    1140      Merchandise Inventory
    1145      Supplies--Office
    1150      Supplies--Store
    1160      Prepaid Insurance
    2110      Accounts Payable
    2120      Sales Tax Payable
    3110      Joel Delano, Capital
    3120      Joel Delano, Drawing
    3130      Cory Knapp, Capital
    3140      Cory Knapp, Drawing
    3150      Income Summary
    4110      Sales
    5110      Purchases
    6110      Insurance Expense
    6120      Miscellaneous Expense
    6130      Rent Expense
    6140      Supplies Expense—Office
    6150      Supplies Expense—Store
    6160      Utilities Expense
```

```
  ●                                                                              ●
  ●                              Sun City Jewelers                               ●
  ●                             Chart of Accounts                                ●
                                    02/10/--
  ●                                                                              ●
       ----------------------------------------------------------------
  ●    Customer    Customer                                                      ●
       Number      Name
  ●    ----------------------------------------------------------------          ●
  ●    110         Bayside Jewelry                                               ●
       115         Oak Street Jewelry Shop
  ●    120         Kim's Jewelry Depot                                           ●
       130         Ocean Shore Jewelry
  ●    135         Pete's Black Hills Gold                                       ●
       140         Barber & Wolfe Jewelry
  ●    145         Chellis Lien                                                  ●
       150         McSoley's Family Jewelers
  ●    160         Brinkman Jewelers                                             ●
       170         Diesel & Mercer Jewelers
  ●                                                                              ●
  ●                                                                              ●
```

Feb. 11 Received cash on account from Ocean Shore Jewelry, $596.14, covering S85. R143.

11 Sold merchandise on account to Ruter's Fashion Jewelry, $526.41. S90.

> Note: Add Ruter's Fashion Jewelry to the customer list. Assign customer number 180 for Ruter's Fashion Jewelry so that it will be positioned immediately following Diesel & Mercer Jewelers in the customer list.

12 Sold merchandise on account to Barber & Wolfe Jewelry, $329.86. S91.

12 Change the name of the customer Brinkman Jewelers to Brinkman's Fine Jewelry.

12 Sold merchandise on account to McSoley's Family Jewelers, $871.10. S92.

15 Recorded cash and credit card sales, $2,551.24, plus sales tax, $127.56; total, $2,678.80. T15.

15 Received cash on account from McSoley's Family Jewelers, $1,665.18, covering S86. R144.

15 Received cash on account from Brinkman's Fine Jewelry, $651.40, covering S84. R145.

16 Sold merchandise on account to Kim's Jewelry Depot, $499.61. S93.

16 Delete Pete's Black Hills Gold from the customer list.

16 Sold merchandise on account to Bayside Jewelry, $476.43. S94.

16 Received cash on account from Ocean Shore Jewelry, $1,155.65, covering S88. R146.

17 Sold merchandise on account to Diesel & Mercer Jewelers, $627.71. S95.

17   Sold merchandise on account to Brinkman's Fine Jewelry, $522.21. S96.

18   Recorded cash and credit card sales, $2,119.55, plus sales tax, $105.98; total, $2,225.53. T18.

18   Sold merchandise on account to Ocean Shore Jewelry, $299.61. S97.

18   Sold merchandise on account to Chellis Lien, $211.09, plus sales tax, $10.55; total, $221.64. S98.

19   Received cash on account from Diesel & Mercer Jewelers, $1,254.32, covering S87. R147.

19   Received cash on account from Ruter's Fashion Jewelry, $526.41, covering S90. R148.

19   Sold merchandise on account to Marci's Designer Jewelry, $465.44. S99.

Note: Add Marci's Designer Jewelry to the customer list. Assign customer number 190 for Marci's Designer Jewelry so that it will be positioned immediately following Ruter's Fashion Jewelry in the customer list.

19   Received cash on account from Chellis Lien, $429.77, covering S89. R149.

Step 2:   Bring up the accounting system.

Step 3:   Load the opening balances template file for AA5-P.

Step 4:   Use the Save As menu command to save to your drive and directory with a file name of XXX5-P, where XXX are your initials.

Step 5:   Set the run date and student name in the General Information data entry window. The run date is February 20 of the current year.

Step 6:   Key the data from the customers input form prepared in Step 1. Display a customer list.

Step 7:   Key the journal entries (sales journal and cash receipts journal input forms) prepared in Step 1.

Step 8:   Display the journal reports for the period February 11 through February 20 of the current year. If errors are detected, use the List button of the data entry window for the journal with the error and select the journal entry to correct.

Step 9:   Display the following ledger reports:

        Trial balance
        Schedule of accounts receivable
        Accounts payable ledger (all customers)

Step 10:   Save your data file.

Step 11:   End the session.

AUDIT TEST PROBLEM 5-P

Directions: Write the answers to the following questions in the working papers or on a separate sheet of paper.

1. What are the totals of the debit and credit columns in the sales journal report?
2. From the sales journal report, what is the amount of invoice no. 98?
3. What is the amount of cash received from Ruter's Fashion Jewelry under cash receipt no. 148?
4. What is the current balance in Accounts Receivable?
5. What is the current balance in the Sales Tax Payable account?
6. What is the current balance for Ocean Shore Jewelry?
7. What is the total due from customers on February 20?
8. List the amounts of the cash receipts transactions for Ocean Shore Jewelry for the period February 10 through February 20.
9. How many sales were made to McSoley Family Jewelers during the period February 10 through February 20?

 ## MASTERY PROBLEM 5-M

In this problem you will process any additions, changes, or deletions to vendors. You will also process the purchases and cash payments transactions for the period February 21 through February 28 of the current year.

Directions: To solve the mastery problem, complete the tasks listed below using *Automated Accounting 6.0*. Abbreviate the reference numbers on the input forms as follows: sales invoice no., S; cash receipt no., C; cash register tape, T; memorandum, M. The chart of accounts and customer list needed to complete the input forms is shown on the following page.

1. Record the transactions on the proper input forms.
2. Load the opening balances file (AA5-M).
3. Save the opening balance data to your data disk or directory (XXX5-M).
4. Set the run date to February 28 of the current year.
5. Key the transactions.

6. Display the following reports:

    Journal reports
    Trial balance
    Schedule of accounts receivable
    Accounts receivable ledger (all customers)

7. Save your data to disk.

8. End the session.

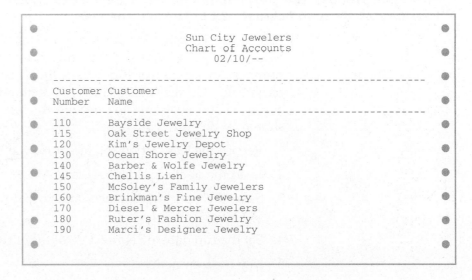

```
                        Sun City Jewelers
                        Chart of Accounts
                            02/10/--

       -----------------------------------------------------------
       Account  Account
       Number   Title
       -----------------------------------------------------------
       1110     Cash
       1120     Petty Cash
       1130     Accounts Receivable
       1140     Merchandise Inventory
       1145     Supplies--Office
       1150     Supplies--Store
       1160     Prepaid Insurance
       2110     Accounts Payable
       2120     Sales Tax Payable
       3110     Joel Delano, Capital
       3120     Joel Delano, Drawing
       3130     Cory Knapp, Capital
       3140     Cory Knapp, Drawing
       3150     Income Summary
       4110     Sales
       5110     Purchases
       6110     Insurance Expense
       6120     Miscellaneous Expense
       6130     Rent Expense
       6140     Supplies Expense--Office
       6150     Supplies Expense--Store
       6160     Utilities Expense
```

```
                        Sun City Jewelers
                        Chart of Accounts
                            02/10/--

       -----------------------------------------------------------
       Customer Customer
       Number   Name
       -----------------------------------------------------------
       110      Bayside Jewelry
       115      Oak Street Jewelry Shop
       120      Kim's Jewelry Depot
       130      Ocean Shore Jewelry
       140      Barber & Wolfe Jewelry
       145      Chellis Lien
       150      McSoley's Family Jewelers
       160      Brinkman's Fine Jewelry
       170      Diesel & Mercer Jewelers
       180      Ruter's Fashion Jewelry
       190      Marci's Designer Jewelry
```

Transactions:

Feb. 22 Sold merchandise on account to Barber & Wolfe Jewelry, $306.48. S100.

22 Delete Oak Street Jewelry Shop from the customer list.

22 Sold merchandise on account to Ruter's Fashion Jewelry, $405.83. S101.

23 Received cash on account from Bayside Jewelry, $1,889.56, covering S83. R150.

23 Sold merchandise on account to McSoley's Family Jewelers, $336.94. S102.

23 Recorded cash and credit card sales, $1,765.37, plus sales tax, $88.27; total, $1,853.64. T23.

24 Sold merchandise on account to Brinkman's Fine Jewelry, $485.66. S103.

24 Sold merchandise on account to Chellis Lien, $115.40, plus sales tax, $5.77; total, $121.17. S104.

24 Received cash on account from Barber & Wolfe Jewelry, $329.86, covering S91. R151.

24 Change the name of the customer Marci's Designer Jewelry to Marci's Accessories.

25 Received cash on account from McSoley's Family Jewelers, $871.10, covering S92. R152.

25 Received cash on account from Diesel & Mercer Jewelers, $627.71, covering S95. R153.

25 Sold merchandise on account to Sadie's Gift Shop, $308.76. S105.

> Note: Add Sadie's Gift Shop to the customer list. Assign customer number 155 for Sadie's Gift Shop so that it will be positioned immediately following McSoley's Family Jewelers in the customer list.

25 Sold merchandise on account to Diesel & Mercer Jewelers, $91.52. S106.

26 Recorded cash and credit card sales, $1,499.53, plus sales tax, $74.98; total, $1,574.51. T26.

26 Received cash on account from Bayside Jewelry, $476.43, covering S94. R154.

26 Received cash on account from Brinkman's Fine Jewelry, $522.21, covering S96. R155.

26 Sold merchandise on account to Kim's Jewelry Depot, $60.49. S107.

26 Received cash on account from Ocean Shore Jewelry, $299.61, covering S97. R156.

26 Sold merchandise on account to Marci's Accessories, $317.42. S108.

AUDIT TEST PROBLEM 5-M

Directions: Write the answers to the following questions in the working papers or on a separate sheet of paper.

1. In the sales journal report, what is the amount debited to Sadie's Gift Shop for invoice no. 105?
2. In the sales journal report, what is the amount of sales tax for invoice no. 104 to Chellis Lien?
3. What is the total of the debit column in the cash receipts journal?
4. What is the balance in the Sales Tax Payable account?
5. What is the balance in the Sales account?
6. What is the balance due from Brinkman's Fine Jewelry on February 28?
7. What is the total amount due from all customers as of February 28?
8. From the trial balance, what is the balance in the Accounts Receivable account?
9. From the accounts receivable ledger report, what is the amount of sales invoice no. 107 to Kim's Jewelry Depot?

6

End of Fiscal Period for a Partnership (Merchandising Business)

LEARNING OBJECTIVES ▶ UPON COMPLETION OF THIS CHAPTER, you will be able to:

1. Process the adjusting entries for a merchandising business.

2. Generate the financial statements for a merchandising business organized as a partnership.

3. Complete the period-end processing for a partnership.

INTRODUCTION

In previous chapters you performed computerized accounting activities for businesses that were organized as sole proprietorships. A **sole proprietorship** is a business that is owned by one individual. In this chapter you will learn how to complete the end-of-fiscal-period processing for a merchandising business that is organized as a partnership. A **partnership** is a business that is owned by two or more persons. Many small businesses are organized as partnerships in an effort to take advantage of the combined capital, managerial experience, and expertise of two or more individuals.

To complete the accounting cycle for a partnership, adjusting entries are recorded on the general journal input form, keyed into the computer, and verified for accuracy. The financial statements are then printed. After the financial statements have been generated, the period-end closing is performed.

For a partnership, the Business Organization option button on the General Information data entry window must be set to Partnership. The template data files used in the Chapter 6 problems were established with this option set to Partnership.

▶ Recording Adjusting Entries

Adjusting entries are recorded after all other transactions for the accounting period have been recorded, keyed into the computer, and posted. A trial balance is then generated. The trial balance and the period-end adjustment data are the basis for the adjusting entries.

The period-end adjustment data for Sun City Jewelers are as follows:

Merchandise inventory,	$118,400.00
Office supplies inventory,	$525.00
Store supplies inventory,	$795.00
Value of insurance policies on February 28,	$450.65

The trial balance after the transactions for the period have been processed is shown in Figure 6.1. The adjusting entries have been recorded on the general journal input form illustrated in Figure 6.2.

FIGURE 6.1
Trial Balance Before Adjusting Entries

```
                    Sun City Jewelers
                     Trial Balance
                       02/28/--
-------------------------------------------------------
Acct.   Account
Number  Title                          Debit      Credit
-------------------------------------------------------
1110    Cash                          42780.93
1120    Petty Cash                      100.00
1130    Accounts Receivable            3620.96
1140    Merchandise Inventory        125325.20
1145    SuppliesOffice                 1434.81
1150    SuppliesStore                  2081.80
1160    Prepaid Insurance              1577.16
```

(continued)

FIGURE 6.1 (Continued)
Trial Balance Before Adjusting Entries

2110	Accounts Payable		9453.93
2120	Sales Tax Payable		1746.11
3110	Joel Delano, Capital		78095.15
3120	Joel Delano, Drawing	1550.50	
3130	Cory Knapp, Capital		78095.15
3140	Cory Knapp, Drawing	1866.50	
4110	Sales		30877.06
5110	Purchases	14928.89	
6120	Miscellaneous Expense	208.78	
6130	Rent Expense	2474.00	
6160	Utilities Expense	317.87	
	Totals	198267.40	198267.40

FIGURE 6.2
General Journal Input Form (Adjusting Entries)

		GENERAL JOURNAL INPUT FORM			
Run Date 02/28/--				Problem No. 6-T	
Date MM / dd	Reference	Account Number	Cust./ Vend No.	Debit	Credit
02/28	ADJ.ENT.	3150		6925.20	
		1140			6925.20
		6140		909.81	
		1145			909.81
		6150		1286.80	
		1150			1286.80
		6110		1126.51	
		1160			1126.51
	Totals			10248.32	10248.32

OPERATING PROCEDURES

To complete the accounting cycle for a partnership, you must key the adjusting entries, display the financial statements, and perform the period-end closing. The operating procedures for each of these tasks are described in this section.

▶ Keying the Adjusting Entries

The adjusting entries are keyed into the General Journal data entry window. Because the adjusting entries all occur on the same date and have the same reference ("ADJ.ENT."), you may key as many entries as will fit in one data entry window, as illustrated in Figure 6.3. It is also acceptable to record each adjusting entry in a separate data entry window. For example, the merchandise inventory adjustment could be one entry, the office supplies adjustment another entry, and so on for each of the adjustments.

FIGURE 6.3
General Journal Data Entry Window (Adjusting Entries)

```
=                        General Journal

  Year....... 19--
  Date....... 02 / 28
  Reference.. ADJ.ENT.

  Acct.  Ven./
  No.    Cus.   Account Title              Debit      Credit

  3150          Income Summary             6925.20
  1140          Merchandise Inventory                 6925.20
  6140          Supplies Expense--Office    909.81
  1145          Supplies--Office                       909.81
  6150          Supplies Expense--Store    1286.80
  1150          Supplies--Store                       1286.80
  6110          Insurance Expense          1126.51
  1160          Prepaid Insurance                     1126.51

        [ Ok ]    [ Cancel ]    [ List ]    [ Find ]
```

▶ Financial Statements

The financial statements available vary slightly depending on options set in the General Information data entry window. If the options are set to a nondepartmentalized business organized as a partnership (as are the problems in this chapter), the two financial statements available are the income statement and the balance sheet, as shown in the Report Selection dialog window illustrated in Figure 6.4.

FIGURE 6.4
Report Selection Dialog Window

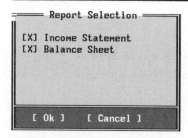

```
====== Report Selection ======

  [X] Income Statement
  [X] Balance Sheet



     [ Ok ]    [ Cancel ]
```

▶ Period-End Closing

At the end of the fiscal period in a manual accounting system, closing entries are recorded in the journal and posted to the general ledger. In an automated accounting system, the period-end closing process is performed automatically by the computer. During the period-end closing process, the computer closes all of the temporary income statement accounts to the income summary account; for sole proprietorships the computer closes the income summary account to the capital account, and closes the drawing account to the capital account. For a partnership with only two partners and equal distribution of income or loss, the computer will distribute the balance in the income summary account to the partners' capital accounts and close the partners' drawing accounts. (For a partnership with more than two partners or an unequal distribution of income or loss, refer to the Reference Guide.) In addition, the computer purges (erases) the journal entries in preparation for the beginning of a new accounting period. The computer also copies the current account balances and stores them as last fiscal period's account balances for use in financial statement analysis. When the period-end closing menu command is chosen, the dialog illustrated in Figure 6.5 appears. Respond "Ok" to proceed with the closing.

FIGURE 6.5
Perform Period-End Closing Dialog Window

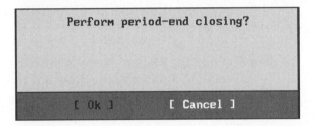

Perform period-end closing?

[Ok]   [Cancel]

TUTORIAL 6-T

In this tutorial problem, you will complete the end-of-fiscal-period processing for a merchandising business organized as a partnership. You will perform the operating procedures necessary to key the adjusting entries, generate the financial statements, and perform period-end closing. Since the partnership consists of two partners with an equal distribution of income or loss, the computer will automatically distribute the income or loss to the partners' capital accounts during closing.

Each of the steps below is a task to be completed at the computer. More detailed information on how to complete the task is provided immediately following the step. If you need additional explanation of the task, a page reference is provided from the Operating Procedures of this chapter (or a previous chapter).

Directions: The step-by-step instructions for completing the end-of-period processing for Sun City Jewelers (a partnership) for the fiscal period ended February 28 of the current year are listed below.

Step 1:   Bring up the accounting system. (page 16)

At the DOS prompt, key A1 (or follow the instructions provided by your instructor).

Step 2:   Load the opening balances template file, AA6-T. (page 19)

Pull down the File menu and choose the Open Accounting File command. When the Open File window appears, key the path and file name for the opening balances template file, AA6-T. Key into the Path field the drive and directory containing the template files. Key a file name of AA6-T and push the OK button.

Step 3:   Save the opening balances file to your drive and directory with a file name of XXX6-T (where XXX are your initials). (page 21)

Pull down the File menu and choose the Save As menu command. Key the path to the drive and directory that contains your data files (for example, if you wish to save your data to Drive B, key B: as the path name). Key a file name of XXX6-T, where XXX are your initials. Push the Ok button.

Step 4:   Enter the student name in the General Information data entry window and verify that the run date is set to February 28 of the current year. (page 21)

Pull down the Options menu and choose the General Information menu command. If necessary, set the run date to February 28 of the current year. Key your name in the Student Name field.

Step 5:   Key the adjusting entries from the general journal input form shown in Figure 6.6. (page 151)

The adjusting entries have been recorded for you and are illustrated in Figure 6.6.

Pull down the Journal menu and choose the General Journal option (unless the General Journal is already on the screen). Key the adjusting entries.

Step 6:   Display the adjusting entries. (page 152)

Pull down the Reports menu and choose the Journals command. When the Report Selection window appears, select the general journal report. When the Selection Options window shown in Figure 6.7 appears, key a date range of February 28 to February 28 (of the current year) and a Reference restriction of ADJ.ENT., so that only the adjusting entries are reported. The report appears in Figure 6.8.

FIGURE 6.6
General Journal Input Form (Adjusting Entries)

Run Date 02/28/--		GENERAL JOURNAL INPUT FORM		Problem No. 6-T	
Date MM / dd	Reference	Account Number	Cust./ Vend No.	Debit	Credit
02/28	ADJ.ENT.	3150		6925.20	
		1140			6925.20
		6140		909.81	
		1145			909.81
		6150		1286.80	
		1150			1286.80
		6110		1126.51	
		1160			1126.51
Totals				10248.32	10248.32

FIGURE 6.7
Selection Options

```
=        Selection Options
              (Journals)

Date range: 02/28/-- to 02/28/--

Reference restriction: ADJ.ENT.

         [ Ok ]     [ Cancel ]
```

FIGURE 6.8
General Journal Report (Adjusting Entries)

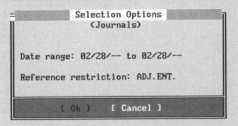

```
                         Sun City Jewelers
                          General Journal
                            02/28/--
-----------------------------------------------------------------
Date    Refer.   V/C Acct. Title                  Debit    Credit
-----------------------------------------------------------------
02/28   ADJ.ENT.     3150  Income Summary         6925.20
02/28   ADJ.ENT.     1140  Merchandise Inventory            6925.20

02/28   ADJ.ENT.     6140  Supplies Expense--Office 909.81
02/28   ADJ.ENT.     1145  Supplies--Office                  909.81

02/28   ADJ.ENT.     6150  Supplies Expense--Store 1286.80
02/28   ADJ.ENT.     1150  Supplies--Store                  1286.80

02/28   ADJ.ENT.     6110  Insurance--Expense      1126.51
02/28   ADJ.ENT.     1160  Prepaid Insurance                1126.51
                                                  --------  --------
                           Totals                 10248.32 10248.32
                                                  ======== ========
```

Step 7:   Display the financial statements. (page 152)

Pull down the Reports menu and choose the Financial Statements menu command. When the Report Selection window shown in Figure 6.9 appears, select both financial statements. The reports are shown in Figure 6.10.

FIGURE 6.9
Report Selection Dialog Window

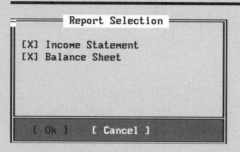

```
┌──────────── Report Selection ────────────┐
│                                           │
│  [X] Income Statement                     │
│  [X] Balance Sheet                        │
│                                           │
│                                           │
│   [ Ok ]      [ Cancel ]                  │
└───────────────────────────────────────────┘
```

FIGURE 6.10
Financial Statements (Sun City Jewelers)

```
                    Sun City Jewelers
                    Income Statement
                 For Period Ended 02/28/--

Operating  Revenue
-------------------------------------
Sales                                 30877.06
                                     ------------
Total Operating Revenue               30877.06

Cost  of  Merchandise  Sold
-------------------------------------
Beginning Inventory                  125325.20
Purchases                             14928.89
                                     ------------
Merchandise Available for Sale       140254.09
Less Ending Inventory               -118400.00
                                     ------------
Cost of Merchandise Sold              21854.09
                                     ------------
Gross Profit                           9022.97

Operating  Expenses
-------------------------------------
Insurance Expense                      1126.51
Miscellaneous Expense                   208.78
Rent Expense                           2474.00
Supplies Expense--Office                909.81
Supplies Expense--Store                1286.80
Utilities Expense                       317.87
                                     ------------
Total Operating Expenses               6323.77
                                     ------------
Net Income                             2699.20
                                     ============
```

(continued)

FIGURE 6.10 (Continued)
Financial Statements (Sun City Jewelers)

```
                        Sun City Jewelers
                          Balance Sheet
                            02/28/--

   A s s e t s
   ------------
   Cash                                  42780.93
   Petty Cash                              100.00
   Accounts Receivable                    3620.96
   Merchandise Inventory                118400.00
   Supplies--Office                        525.00
   Supplies--Store                         795.00
   Prepaid Insurance                       450.65
                                        ----------
   Total Assets                                      166672.54
                                                    ==========
   L i a b i l i t i e s
   ----------------------
   Accounts Payable                       9453.93
   Sales Tax Payable                      1746.11
                                        ----------
   Total Liabilities                                  11200.04

   O w n e r ' s E q u i t y
   --------------------------
   Joel Delano, Capital                  78095.15
   Joel Delano, Drawing                  -1550.50
   Cory Knapp, Capital                   78095.15
   Cory Knapp, Drawing                   -1866.50
   Net Income                             2699.20
                                        ----------
   Total Owner's Equity                              155472.50
                                                    ----------
   Total Liabilities & Equity                        166672.54
                                                    ==========
```

Step 8: Save your data file to disk with a file name of XXX6-TBC, where XXX are your initials. (page 21)

Pull down the File menu and choose the Save As menu command and save your file as XXX6-TBC, where XXX are your initials, 6-T is the problem number, and BC is "before closing." It is recommended that you *always* save a backup copy of your data file to disk before performing period-end closing. During the closing process, all the journal entries for the current period are erased, thus making it more difficult to make corrections after closing has been performed. If you discover an error after completing period-end closing, you can simply load the file saved in Step 8, make corrections, and proceed again with Step 9 below.

Step 9: Perform the period-end closing. (page 152)

Pull down the Options menu and select the Period-End Closing menu command. When the dialog window appears asking if you want to perform period-end closing, push the Ok button.

Step 10:   Display a post-closing trial balance. (page 63)

Pull down the Report menu and select the Ledger menu command. When the Report Selection window appears, select the Trial Balance report and push the Ok button. The trial balance report appears in Figure 6.11.

FIGURE 6.11
Trial Balance (After Closing Entries)

```
                        Sun City Jewelers
                         Trial Balance
                           02/28/--
       ----------------------------------------------------------------
       Acct.  Account
       Number Title                            Debit          Credit
       ----------------------------------------------------------------
       1110   Cash                            42780.93
       1120   Petty Cash                        100.00
       1130   Accounts Receivable             3620.96
       1140   Merchandise Inventory         118400.00
       1145   Supplies--Office                  525.00
       1150   Supplies--Store                   795.00
       1160   Prepaid Insurance                 450.65
       2110   Accounts Payable                                9453.93
       2120   Sales Tax Payable                               1746.11
       3110   Joel Delano, Capital                           77894.25
       3130   Cory Knapp, Capital                            77578.25
                                             ----------      ----------
              Totals                         166672.54       166672.54
                                             ==========      ==========
```

Step 11:   Use the Save As menu command to save your data to disk with a file name of XXX6-T, where XXX are your initials. (page 21)

Pull down the File menu and choose the Save As menu command to save your file to disk.

Step 12:   End the session. (page 22)

Choose the Quit command from the File menu.

CHAPTER 6 STUDENT EXERCISE

Directions: Write the answers to the following questions in the working papers or on a separate sheet of paper.

I. QUESTIONS

1. What is a business owned by one individual called?

2. What is a business owned by two or more individuals called?

3. List three reasons why small businesses are sometimes organized as partnerships.

4. Explain how the partners' capital accounts are affected by the period-end closing process for a partnership with a 50/50 split of income or loss.

5. List three things that happen during the period-end closing in addition to the distribution of net income or loss.

PRACTICE PROBLEM 6-P

In this problem, you will process the monthly transactions for the month of March and complete the end-of-fiscal-period processing for Sun City Jewelers, a partnership.

Directions: The step-by-step instructions for solving this practice problem are listed below.

Step 1:   Remove the input forms from the working papers. Record the following transactions for Sun City Jewelers on the proper input forms. Abbreviate the reference numbers on the input forms as follows: check no., C; memorandum, M; cash register tape, T; cash receipt no., R; sales invoice no., S; purchase invoice no., P. The chart of accounts, vendor list, and customer list are given below for reference as you complete the input forms.

```
                      Sun City Jewelers
                      Chart of Accounts
                         02/28/--
-----------------------------------------------------------------
Account     Account
Number      Title
-----------------------------------------------------------------
1110        Cash
1120        Petty Cash
1130        Accounts Receivable
1140        Merchandise Inventory
1145        Supplies--Office
1150        Supplies--Store
1160        Prepaid Insurance
2110        Accounts Payable
2120        Sales Tax Payable
3110        Joel Delano, Capital
3120        Joel Delano, Drawing
3130        Cory Knapp, Capital
3140        Cory Knapp, Drawing
3150        Income Summary
4110        Sales
5110        Purchases
6110        Insurance Expense
6120        Miscellaneous Expense
6130        Rent Expense
6140        Supplies Expense--Office
6150        Supplies Expense--Store
6160        Utilities Expense
```

```
                      Sun City Jewelers
                        Vendor List
                         02/28/--
-----------------------------------------------------------------
Vendor      Vendor
Number      Name
-----------------------------------------------------------------
210         Sterling Supply House
220         Superior Gold
230         Danielle's Designs
240         Marcel Jewelry
250         M & W Jewelers
260         Martin Supply, Inc.
270         Unique Jewels Company
280         Supply Warehouse
290         Aronoff Gems
```

```
                        Sun City Jewelers
                         Customer List
                           02/28/--
      ------------------------------------------------------------
      Customer   Customer
      Number     Name
      ------------------------------------------------------------
      110        Bayside Jewelry
      120        Kim's Jewelry Depot
      130        Ocean Shore Jewelry
      140        Barber & Wolfe Jewelry
      145        Chellis Lien
      150        McSoley's Family Jewelers
      155        Sadie's Gift Shop
      160        Brinkman's Fine Jewelry
      170        Diesel & Mercer Jewelers
      180        Ruter's Fashion Jewelry
      190        Marci's Accessories
```

Mar. 01 Sold merchandise on account to Bayside Jewelry, $4,528.86. S109.

01 03 Sold merchandise on account to Ocean Shore Jewelry, $4,827.03. S110.

04 Purchased merchandise for cash, $156.43. C80.

05 Purchased merchandise on account from Unique Jewels Company, $4,921.02. P34.

05 Paid cash for miscellaneous expense, $55.55. C81.

08 Purchased merchandise on account from Marcel Jewelry, $4,009.74. P35.

09 Paid cash on account to Sterling Supply House, $2,106.48, covering P26. C82.

10 Paid cash on account to Supply Warehouse, $629.54, covering M24. C83.

11 Paid cash for rent, $2,500.00. C84.

11 Received cash on account from Kim's Jewelry Depot, $499.61, covering S93. R157.

12 Received cash on account from Chellis Lien, $221.64, covering S98. R158.

15 Sold merchandise on account to Robert's Gemstones, $4,240.57. S111.

> Note: Add Robert's Gemstones to the customer list. Assign customer number 165 to Robert's Gemstones so that it will be positioned immediately following Brinkman's Fine Jewelry in the customer list.

16 Bought store supplies on account from Martin Supply, Inc., $331.07. M27.

17 Paid cash for insurance, $781.04. C85.

18 Sold merchandise on account to Barber & Wolfe Jewelry, $4,921.83. S112.

19 Paid cash for electric bill, $356.01. C86.

23 Bought office supplies on account from Supply Warehouse, $98.02. M28.

24 Received cash on account from McSoley's Family Jewelers, $336.94, covering S102. R159.

25 Joel Delano, partner, withdrew merchandise for personal use, $118.15. M29. Record this transaction in the general journal.

26 Purchased merchandise on account from Superior Gold, $5,006.41. P36.

29 Discovered that a transaction for store supplies bought for cash in January was journalized and posted in error as a debit to Purchases instead of Supplies--Store, $134.39. M30. Record this transaction in the General Journal.

29 Paid cash on account to Danielle's Designs, $1,699.54, covering P28. C87.

30 Paid cash on account to Aronoff Gems, $763.99, covering P31. C88.

31 Recorded cash and credit card sales, $4,927.58, plus sales tax, $246.38; total, $5,173.96. T31.

31 Cory Knapp, partner, withdrew cash for personal use, $1,000.00. C89.

31 Joel Delano, partner, withdrew cash for personal use, $825.00. C90.

31 Paid cash to replenish the petty cash fund, $84.00: office supplies, $35.40; store supplies, $48.60. C91.

Step 2: Bring up the accounting system.

Step 3: Load the opening balances template file for AA6-P.

Step 4: Use the Save As menu command to save the opening balances file to your drive and directory with a file name of XXX6-P, where XXX are your initials.

Step 5: Set the run date to March 31 of the current year and key your name into the student name field.

Step 6: Key the data from the input forms prepared in Step 1.

Step 7: Display the journal reports (general, purchases, cash payments, sales, and cash receipts) for the period March 1 through March 31 of the current year. If errors are detected, use the List button on the relevant journal data entry window to select the journal entry to correct.

Step 8: Display a trial balance, schedule of accounts payable, and schedule of accounts receivable.

Step 9: Record the adjusting entries on a general journal input form. The adjustment data are shown below. Use the trial balance generated in the previous step as the basis for making the adjusting entries. Record "ADJ.ENT." as the reference.

```
Merchandise inventory on March 31 .......$113,600.00
Office supplies inventory ....................326.00
Store supplies inventory .....................895.00
Value of insurance policies .................955.00
```

Step 10: Key the adjusting entries.

Step 11: Display the general journal report for the adjusting entries. Use a reference restriction of "ADJ.ENT.," so that only adjusting entries will be included on the report.

Step 12: Display the income statement and balance sheet.

Step 13: Use the Save As menu command to save a backup copy of your data to disk with a file name of XXX6-PBC, where XXX are your initials.

Step 14: Perform period-end closing.

Step 15: Display a post-closing trial balance.

Step 16: Use the Save As menu command to save your data with a file name of XXX6-PAC, where XXX are your initials.

AUDIT TEST PROBLEM 6-P

Directions: Write the answers to the following questions in the working papers or on a separate sheet of paper.

1. From the purchases journal report, what is the amount of the credit to Superior Gold?
2. In the cash payments journal report, what are the total debits and total credits?
3. From the sales journal report, what is the amount of sales invoice no. 112?
4. From the cash receipts journal, what is the amount of cash received from Chellis Lien for cash receipt no. 158?
5. From the schedule of accounts payable, what is the amount currently owed to Marcel Jewelry?
6. From the schedule of accounts receivable, what is the amount currently due from Robert's Gemstones?
7. What is the gross profit for the period?
8. What are the total operating expenses?
9. What is the net income?
10. What are the total assets?

M MASTERY PROBLEM 6-M

In this problem, you will process the monthly transactions for the month of April and complete the end-of-fiscal-period processing for Sun City Jewelers, a partnership. In this partnership the income or loss is divided equally among partners.

Directions:

1. Record the monthly transactions for Sun City Jewelers on the proper input forms.

2. Load the opening balances file (AA6-M).

3. Save the opening balances file to your disk or directory (XXX6-M).

4. Set the run date to April 30 of the current year.

5. Key the April transactions.

6. Display the journal reports.

7. Display a trial balance, schedule of accounts payable, and schedule of accounts receivable.

8. Record the adjusting entries on the input form.

9. Key the adjusting entries.

10. Display the adjusting entries.

11. Display the financial statements.

12. Save your data with a file name of XXX6-MBC.

13. Perform period-end closing.

14. Display a trial balance.

15. Save your data with a file name of XXX6-MAC.

16. End the session.

Transactions:

Apr. 03 Paid cash for quarterly sales tax, $1,992.49. C92.

03 Sold merchandise on account to Ruter's Fashion Jewelry, $4,323.11. S113.

04 Sold merchandise on account to Brinkman's Fine Jewelry, $3,886.52. S114.

05 Purchased merchandise on account from M & W Jewelers, $5,006.40. P37.

06 Purchased merchandise for cash, $627.54. C93.

06 Paid cash for office supplies, $79.82. C94.

07 Purchased merchandise on account from Sterling Supply House, $3,651.27. P38.

07 Paid cash for miscellaneous expense, $35.72. C95.

07 Paid cash on account to Martin Supply, Inc., $562.73, covering M23 and M27. C96.

10 Paid cash on account to M & W Jewelers, $660.11, covering P29 and P33. C97.

10 Paid cash for rent, $2,500.00. C98.

10 Received cash on account from Marci's Accessories, $782.86, covering S99 and S108. R160.

11 Received cash on account from Brinkman's Fine Jewelry, $485.66, covering S103. R161.

11 Purchased merchandise on account from Sanchez Jewelry, $2,342.17. P39.

>   Note: Add Sanchez Jewelry to the vendor list. Assign vendor number 215 for Sanchez Jewelry, so that it will be positioned immediately following Sterling Supply House in the vendor list.

12 Bought office supplies on account from Supply Warehouse, $88.82. M31.

13 Sold merchandise on account to McSoley's Family Jewelers, $3,626.83. S115.

13 Paid cash for electric bill, $388.81. C99.

14 Paid cash for insurance, $598.85. C100.

15 Sold merchandise on account to Diesel & Mercer Jewelers, $4,563.08. S116.

15 Received cash on account from Kim's Jewelry Depot, $60.49, covering S93. R162.

16 Received cash on account from Barber & Wolfe Jewelry, $306.48, covering S100. R163.

17 Cory Knapp, partner, withdrew merchandise for personal use, $328.80. M32. Record this transaction in the general journal.

24 Purchased merchandise on account from Danielle's Designs, $3,705.00. P40.

25 Discovered that a withdrawal of cash by Joel Delano, partner, was journalized and posted in error as a credit to Purchases instead of Cash, $500.00. M33. Record this transaction in the General Journal.

26 Paid cash on account to Superior Gold, $3,989.04, covering P27 and P36. C101.

27 Paid cash on account to Marcel Jewelry, $1,612.96, covering P32 and P35. C102.

28 Recorded cash and credit card sales, $5,528.40, plus sales tax, $276.42; total, $5,804.82. T28.

28 Cory Knapp, partner, withdrew cash for personal use, $1,200.00. C103.

28 Joel Delano, partner, withdrew cash for personal use, $1,500.00. 104.

28 Paid cash to replenish the petty cash fund, $93.40: office supplies, $10.06; store supplies, $18.50; Cory Knapp, partner, $25.00; miscellaneous expense, $39.84. C105.

Adjustment Data:

Merchandise Inventory on April 30. . . . . . .$111,900.00
Office supplies inventory. 400.00
Store supplies inventory 650.00
Value of insurance policies. 1,250.00

AUDIT TEST PROBLEM 6-M

Directions: Write the answers to the following questions in the working papers or on a separate sheet of paper.

1. From the purchases journal report, what is the amount of the credit to Sanchez Jewelry?
2. In the cash payments journal report, what are the total debits and total credits?
3. From the sales journal report, what is the amount of sales invoice no. 115?
4. From the cash receipts journal, what is the amount of cash received from Marci's Accessories for cash receipt no. 160?
5. From the schedule of accounts payable, what is the amount currently owed to all vendors?
6. From the schedule of accounts receivable, what is the amount currently due from Ruter's Fashion Jewelry?
7. What is the gross profit for the period?
8. What are the total operating expenses?
9. What is the net income?
10. What are the total assets?

C COMPREHENSIVE PROBLEM C-2

Zajac Tire Distributors sells automobile and truck tires to tire retailers. In Comprehensive Problem Two, you will process the monthly transactions for February and complete the end-of-fiscal-period processing, for Zajac Tire Distributors.

Directions: The step-by-step instructions for solving this practice problem are listed below.

Step 1:

Remove the input forms from the working papers. Record the following transactions for Zajac Tire Distributors on the input forms. Abbreviate the reference numbers on the input forms as follows: check no., C; memorandum, M; cash register tape, T; cash receipt no., R; sales invoice no., S; purchase invoice no., P. Refer to the chart of accounts, vendor list, and customer list below to locate account numbers as you complete the input forms.

```
                    Zajac Tire Distributors
                       Chart of Accounts
                          02/01/--
        -----------------------------------------------------
        Account    Account
        Number     Title
        -----------------------------------------------------
        1110       Cash
        1120       Petty Cash
        1130       Accounts Receivable
        1140       Merchandise Inventory
        1145       Supplies--Office
        1150       Supplies--Store
        1160       Prepaid Insurance
        2110       Accounts Payable
        2120       Sales Tax Payable
        3110       Barbara Zajac, Capital
        3120       Barbara Zajac, Drawing
        3130       Jason Zajac, Capital
        3140       Jason Zajac, Drawing
        3150       Income Summary
        4110       Sales
        5110       Purchases
        6110       Insurance Expense
        6120       Miscellaneous Expense
        6130       Rent Expense
        6140       Supplies Expense--Office
        6150       Supplies Expense--Store
        6160       Utilities Expense
```

```
                    Zajac Tire Distributors
                          Vendor List
                          02/01/--
        -----------------------------------------------------
        Vendor     Vendor
        Number     Name
        -----------------------------------------------------
        310        Spencer Tire Company
        320        Rapid City Tires, Inc.
        330        Collier Mfg. Co.
        340        Madison Corporation
        350        Sutton Car Parts Company
        360        Corsmeier Products, Inc.
        370        Siegel Car Parts Co.
        380        Daniels Tire & Rubber Co.
        390        Vaughn Supplies
```

```
                    Zajac Tire Distributors
                         Customer List
                          02/01/--
    -----------------------------------------------------------
    Customer    Customer
    Number      Name
    -----------------------------------------------------------
    110         B&B Tire
    120         Tire Discounts
    130         Monroe Repair & Service
    140         Kemper Service Garage
    150         Blaine Stewart
    160         St. Clair Garage
    170         Pete's Car Shop
    180         Mattie's Repairs
    190         Sander's Service
    200         Ann Marie Reupert
    210         Car & Tire Service
```

Feb. 01 Paid cash for sales tax, $1,333.76. C921.

01 Sold merchandise on account to Monroe Repair & Service, $1,642.21. S1004.

01 Sold merchandise on account to B&B Tire, $2,106.83. S1005.

02 Sold merchandise on account to Car & Tire Service, $1,700.05. S1006.

02 Paid cash for rent, $2,700.00. C922.

02 Paid cash for electric bill, $469.88. C923.

03 Bought store supplies on account from Vaughn Supplies, $115.68. M112.

03 Received cash on account from Ann Marie Reupert, $421.04, covering S995. R816.

03 Purchased merchandise on account from Rapid City Tires, Inc., $1,429.07. P506.

04 Purchased merchandise for cash, $791.01. C924.

04 Paid cash for miscellaneous expense, $294.76. C925.

05 Bought office supplies on account from Vaughn Supplies, $407.63. M113.

05 Sold merchandise on account to Monroe Repair & Service, $1,507.30. S1007.

06 Sold merchandise on account to Mattie's Repairs, $1,882.22. S1008.

06 Sold merchandise on account to Tire Discounts, $1,693.68. S1009.

06 Paid cash for insurance, $1,328.05. C926.

06 Recorded cash and credit card sales, $2,034.87, plus sales tax, $111.92; total, $2,146.79. T6.

06   Discovered that a purchase of merchandise for cash was journalized and posted in error as a debit to Supplies—Office instead of Purchases, $331.03. M114. Record this transaction in the general journal.

08   Delete Pete's Car Shop from the customer list.

08   Purchased merchandise on account from Collier Mfg. Co., $1,101.87. P507.

08   Purchased merchandise on account from Daniels Tire & Rubber Co., $1,475.85. P508.

09   Paid cash on account to Spencer Tire Company, $1,399.41, covering P500. C927.

09   Received cash on account from St. Clair Garage, $2,508.76, covering S996. R817.

10   Received cash on account from Sander's Service, $1,105.74, covering S997. R818.

10   Purchased merchandise on account from Sutton Car Parts Company, $1,301.96. P509.

10   Paid cash for utilities expense, $399.09. C928.

11   Received cash on account from Car & Tire Service, $2,888.35, covering S998. R819.

12   Sold merchandise on account to Sue Bishop, $185.60, plus sales tax, $10.21; total, $195.81. S1010.

> Note: Add Sue Bishop to the customer list. Assign customer number 220 for Sue Bishop, so that it will be positioned immediately following Car & Tire Service in the customer list.

12   Paid cash on account to Rapid City Tires, Inc., $3,334.45, covering S501 and S506. C929.

12   Delete Siegel Car Parts Co. from the vendor list.

13   Paid cash on account to Vaughn Supplies, $450.67, covering M111. C930.

13   Paid cash on account to Sutton Car Parts Company, $1,390.22, covering P502. C931.

13   Purchased merchandise on account from VonHagel's Parts Co., $1,006.89. P510.

> Note: Add VonHagel's Parts Co. to the vendor list. Assign vendor number 400 for VonHagel's Parts Co., so that it will be positioned immediately following Vaughn Supplies in the vendor list.

13   Recorded cash and credit card sales, $1,675.42, plus sales tax, $92.15; total, $1,767.57. T13.

15 Discovered that a payment for rent was journalized and posted in error as a debit to Purchases instead of Rent Expense, $2,700.00. M115. Record this transaction in the general journal.

15 Bought store supplies on account from Vaughn Supplies, $88.21. M116.

16 Received cash on account from B&B Tire, $3,452.72, covering S999 and S1005. R820.

16 Received cash on account from Tire Discounts, $1,678.23, covering S1002. R821.

16 Purchased merchandise for cash, $909.89. C932.

17 Barbara Zajac, partner, withdrew merchandise for personal use, $225.23. M117. Record this transaction in the general journal.

17 Sold merchandise on account to Sander's Service, $1,005.47. S1011.

18 Purchased merchandise on account from Corsmeier Products, Inc., $929.83. P511.

18 Delete Madison Corporation from the vendor list.

18 Purchased merchandise on account from Sutton Car Parts Company, $1,397.14. P512.

19 Bought office supplies on account from Vaughn Supplies, $333.03. M118.

20 Discovered that a withdrawal of merchandise by Barbara Zajac for personal use was journalized and posted in error as a debit to Jason Zajac, Drawing, instead of Barbara Zajac, Drawing, $500.00. M119. Record this transaction in the general journal.

20 Purchased merchandise for cash, $650.27. C933.

20 Paid cash for miscellaneous expense, $229.30. C934.

20 Jason Zajac, partner, withdrew merchandise for personal use, $477.80. M120. Record this transaction in the general journal.

20 Paid cash for store supplies, $50.20. C935.

20 Recorded cash and credit card sales, $2,340.88, plus sales tax, $128.75; total, $2,469.63. T20.

22 Received cash on account from Monroe Repair & Service, $1,642.21, covering S1004. R822.

22 Received cash on account from Mattie's Repairs, $1,888.03, covering S1003. R823.

23 Sold merchandise on account to Lois Gilbert, $491.26, plus sales tax, $27.02; total, $518.28. S1012.

Note: Add Lois Gilbert to the customer list. Assign customer number 230 for Lois Gilbert, so that it will be positioned immediately following Sue Bishop in the customer list.

23 Sold merchandise on account to St. Clair Garage, $2,150.45. S1013.

24 Paid cash for office supplies, $101.50. C936.

24 Discovered that a payment for a miscellaneous expense was journalized and posted in error as a debit to Rent Expense instead of Miscellaneous Expense, $91.00. M121. Record this transaction in the general journal.

25 Received cash on account from Monroe Repair & Service, $1,507.30, covering S1006. R824.

25 Received cash on account from Sue Bishop, $195.81, covering S1009. R825.

26 Sold merchandise on account to B&B Tire, $1,995.43. S1014.

26 Sold merchandise on account to Mattie's Repairs, $1,701.51. S1015.

26 Purchased merchandise on account from Daniels Tire & Rubber Co., $1,103.97. P513.

26 Received cash on account from Blaine Stewart, $654.33, covering S1000. R826.

27 Paid cash on account to Vaughn Supplies, $944.55, covering M112, M113, M116, and M118. C937.

27 Barbara Zajac, partner, withdrew cash for personal use, $2,800.00. C938.

27 Jason Zajac, partner, withdrew cash for personal use, $2,800.00. C939.

27 Paid cash to replenish the petty cash fund, $92.00: office supplies, $15.00; store supplies, $34.50; Barbara Zajac, partner, $30.00; miscellaneous expense, $12.50. C940.

27 Recorded cash and credit card sales, $1,541.37, plus sales tax, $84.78; total, $1,626.15. T27.

Step 2:   Bring up the accounting system.

Step 3:   Load the opening balances template file for AAC-2.

Step 4:   Use the Save As menu command to save the opening balances file to your drive and directory with a file name of XXXC-2, where XXX are your initials.

Step 5:   Set the run date to February 28 of the current year, and key your name into the student name field.

Step 6:   Key the data from the input forms prepared in Step 1.

Step 7:   Display the journal reports (general, purchases, cash payments, sales, and cash receipts) for the period February 1 through February 28 of the current year. If errors are detected, use the List button on the relevant journal data entry window to select the journal entry to correct.

Step 8:   Display a trial balance, schedule of accounts payable, and schedule of accounts receivable.

Step 9:   Record the adjusting entries on a general journal input form. The adjustment data are shown below. Use the trial balance generated in the previous step as the basis for making the adjusting entries. Record "ADJ.ENT." as the reference.

```
Merchandise inventory on March 31  .......$83,250.00
Office supplies inventory  ..................725.00
Store supplies inventory  ...................591.00
Value of insurance policies  .............2,200.00
```

Step 10:   Key the adjusting entries.

Step 11:   Display the general journal report for the adjusting entries. Use a reference restriction of "ADJ.ENT.," so that only adjusting entries will be included on the report.

Step 12:   Display the income statement and balance sheet.

Step 13:   Use the Save As menu command to save a backup copy of your data to disk with a file name of XXXC-2BC.

Step 14:   Perform period-end closing.

Step 15:   Display a post-closing trial balance.

Step 16:   Use the Save As menu command to save your data with a file name of XXXC-2, where XXX are your initials.

AUDIT TEST PROBLEM C-2

Directions: Write the answers to the following questions in the working papers or on a separate sheet of paper.

JOURNALS

1. From the general journal, what is the total of the credit column?
2. From the purchases journal report, what is the amount of the credit to Collier Mfg. Co.?
3. In the cash payments journal report, what are the total debits and total credits?

4. From the sales journal report, what is the amount of sales invoice no. 1006?

5. From the cash receipts journal, what is the amount of cash received from Sander's Service for cash receipt no. 818?

LEDGERS

6. From the schedule of accounts payable, what is the amount currently owed to all vendors?

7. From the schedule of accounts receivable, what is the amount currently due from Mattie's Repairs?

FINANCIAL STATEMENTS

8. What is the gross profit for the period?

9. What are the total operating expenses?

10. What is the net income?

11. What are the total liabilities?

7

Discounts, Debit Memorandums, and Credit Memorandums

LEARNING OBJECTIVES ▶ UPON COMPLETION OF THIS CHAPTER, you will be able to:

1. Process purchases discounts.
2. Process debit memorandums.
3. Process sales discounts.
4. Process credit memorandums.

INTRODUCTION

In this chapter you will learn how to process purchases discounts, debit memorandums, sales discounts, and credit memorandums. You will learn how to record these transactions on the proper input form, and how to process the transactions at the computer.

Buyers are often given a deduction on the invoice amount of credit sales in order to encourage early payment. From the seller's point of view, this deduction is refered to as a **sales discount**. From the buyer's point of view, the deduction is called a **purchases discount**. If the invoice amount is paid within the time period specified on the invoice, the discount may be deducted from the payment.

Buyers are sometimes granted credit for returned or damaged merchandise. From the seller's point of view, this type of transaction results in a credit to the customer's account and is called a **credit memorandum**. From the buyer's point of view, this type of transaction results in a debit to the vendor's account and is called a **debit memorandum**.

▶ Recording Purchases Discounts

It is not necessary to record the credit to Cash, since that part of the entry is made automatically by the computer.

A purchases discount is an incentive offered by the vendor to pay the invoice before the due date. If the invoice is paid within the specified time period (10 days or 15 days, for example), a discount amount may be deducted from the invoice amount. The specified time period is called the **discount period**. The discount amount is usually based on a percentage (1% or 2%, for example). The amount of discount allowed is typically shown on the invoice. The sample transaction shown below has been recorded on the cash payments journal in Figure 7.1.

Feb. 01 Paid cash on account to Babcock, Inc., $3,967.81, covering P520 for $4,007.89, less 1% discount, $40.08. C906.

FIGURE 7.1
Cash Payments Journal Input Form (Purchases Discount)

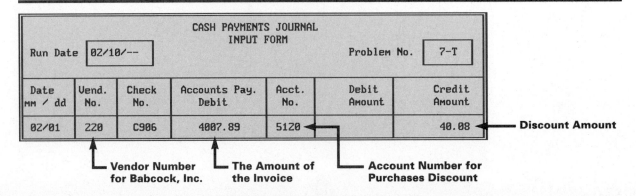

It is not necessary to record the debit to Cash, since that part of the entry is made automatically by the computer.

▶ Recording Sales Discounts

Sales discounts are recorded on the cash receipts input form at the time the cash is received on account. The sample transaction shown below has been recorded on the cash receipts input form in Figure 7.2.

Feb. 02 Received cash on account from Baxter's, $5,137.76, covering S328 for $5,189.66, less 1% discount, $51.90. R307.

FIGURE 7.2
Cash Receipts Journal Input Form (Sales Discount)

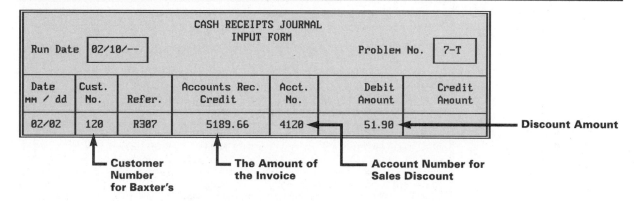

▶ Recording Debit Memorandums

A debit memorandum results when a buyer receives credit from a vendor for merchandise returned or receives an allowance for inferior or damaged merchandise. Debit memorandums are recorded on the general journal input form. A sample transactions involving a debit memorandum is listed below.

Feb. 02 Returned merchandise to S&M Shoe Corporation, $1,232.88, against P518. DM12.

The above transaction has been recorded on the general journal input form shown in Figure 7.3. To record the debit memorandum, a debit of $1,232.88 is recorded to Accounts Payable (account no. 2130) and S&M Shoe Corporation (vendor no. 230). As shown on the second line, a credit of $1,232.88 is recorded to Purchase Returns & Allowances (account no. 5130).

▶ Recording Credit Memorandums

A credit memorandum results when a seller grants credit to a customer for merchandise returned or grants an allowance for inferior or damaged merchandise. Credit memorandums are recorded on the general journal input form. A sample transaction involving a credit memorandum is listed below.

Feb. 04 Granted credit to Weinstein's for merchandise returned, $376.25, against S331. CM22.

FIGURE 7.3
General Journal Input Form (Debit Memorandum)

Run Date 02/10/--		GENERAL JOURNAL INPUT FORM		Problem No.	7-T
Date MM / dd	Reference	Account Number	Cust./ Vend No.	Debit	Credit
02/02	DM12	2130	230	1232.88	
		5130			1232.88

FIGURE 7.4
General Journal Input Form (Credit Memorandum)

Run Date 02/10/--		GENERAL JOURNAL INPUT FORM		Problem No.	7-T
Date MM / dd	Reference	Account Number	Cust./ Vend No.	Debit	Credit
02/04	CM22	4130		376.25	
		1150	110		376.25

The credit memorandum transaction has been recorded on the general journal input form shown in Figure 7.4. To record the credit memorandum, a debit of $376.25 to Sales Returns & Allowances (account no. 4130). Also, a credit of $376.25 is recorded to Accounts Receivable (account no. 1150) and Weinstein's (customer no. 110).

OPERATING PROCEDURES

Operating procedures are covered in this chapter for keying transactions involving purchases discounts and sales discounts. In addition, operating procedures for keying debit memorandum and credit memorandum transactions are covered.

▶ Keying a Purchases Discount Transaction

With the *Automated Accounting 6.0* software, purchases discounts are keyed at the time the invoice is paid. Figure 7.5 shows a completed Cash Payments Journal data entry window for the purchases discount transaction illustrated earlier on the cash payments journal input form in Figure 7.1 on page 174.

FIGURE 7.5
Cash Payments Journal Data Entry Window (Purchases Discount)

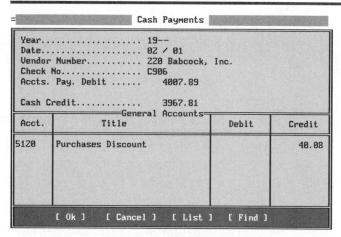

```
=▮▮▮▮▮▮▮▮▮▮▮▮▮▮ Cash Payments ▮▮▮▮▮▮▮▮▮▮▮▮
 ┌────────────────────────────────────────────────────────┐
 │ Year................... 19--                            │
 │ Date................... 02 / 01                         │
 │ Vendor Number.......... 220 Babcock, Inc.               │
 │ Check No............... C906                            │
 │ Accts. Pay. Debit ......    4007.89                     │
 │                                                         │
 │ Cash Credit............    3967.81                      │
 │              ═══════General Accounts═══════             │
 │ Acct. │      Title       │   Debit   │   Credit        │
 │───────┼──────────────────┼───────────┼─────────────────│
 │ 5120  │ Purchases Discount│          │      40.08       │
 │       │                  │           │                  │
 │       │                  │           │                  │
 │       │                  │           │                  │
 ├───────┴──────────────────┴───────────┴─────────────────┤
 │    [ Ok ]    [ Cancel ]   [ List ]   [ Find ]           │
 └────────────────────────────────────────────────────────┘
```

▶ Keying a Cash Payment with a Purchases Discount

1 Key the day of the month (01).

2 Key the Vendor No. (220 for Babcock, Inc.)

3 Key the Check No. (C906).

4 Key the Accounts Payable Debit amount, which is the invoice amount of 4007.89.

5 Key the account number for Purchases Discounts (5120).

6 Key into the Credit column the amount of the discount (40.08).

 Notice that the amount to be credited to Cash, 3967.81, was automatically calculated and displayed.

7 Push the Ok button.

When the Posting Summary shown in Figure 7.6 appears, push the Post button.

FIGURE 7.6
Posting Summary (Purchases Discount)

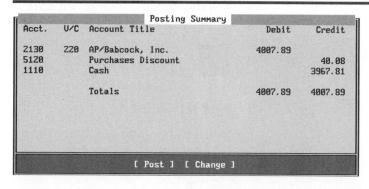

Acct.	V/C	Account Title	Debit	Credit
2130	220	AP/Babcock, Inc.	4007.89	
5120		Purchases Discount		40.08
1110		Cash		3967.81
		Totals	4007.89	4007.89

[Post] [Change]

▶Keying a Sales Discount Transaction

In this system, sales discounts are entered at the time cash is received. Figure 7.7 shows a completed Cash Receipts Journal data entry window for the sales discount transaction illustrated earlier on the cash receipts journal input form in Figure 7.2 on page 175.

FIGURE 7.7
Cash Receipts Journal Data Entry Window (Sales Discount)

```
=▭▭▭▭▭▭▭▭▭▭▭▭    Cash Receipts   ▭▭▭▭▭▭▭▭

  Year....................  19--
  Date....................  02 / 02
  Customer No.............  120 Baxter's
  Reference...............  R307
  Accts. Receivable Credit  5189.66

  Cash Debit..............     5137.76
                   ┌General Accounts┐
  ┌──────┬───────────────────┬──────────┬──────────┐
  │ Acct.│       Title       │  Debit   │  Credit  │
  ├──────┼───────────────────┼──────────┼──────────┤
  │ 4120 │ Sales Discount    │   51.90  │          │
  │      │                   │          │          │
  │      │                   │          │          │
  └──────┴───────────────────┴──────────┴──────────┘

        [ Ok ]    [ Cancel ]    [ List ]    [ Find ]
```

▶Keying a Cash Receipt with a Sales Discount

1   Key the day of the month (02).

2   Key the Vendor No. (120 for Baxter's)

3   Key the Reference. (R307).

4   **Key the Accounts Receivable Credit amount, which is the invoice amount of 5189.66.**

5   Key the account number for Sales Discounts (4120).

6   Key into the Debit column the amount of the discount (51.90).

 Notice that the amount to be debited to Cash, 5137.76, was automatically calculated and displayed.

7   Push the Ok button.

When the Posting Summary shown in Figure 7.8 appears, push the Post button.

FIGURE 7.8
Posting Summary (Cash Receipt with Sales Discount)

```
                       Posting Summary
  Acct.   V/C  Account Title              Debit      Credit

  1110         Cash                      5137.76
  4120         Sales Discount              51.90
  1150    120  AR/Baxter's                          5189.66

               Totals                    5189.66    5189.66


               [ Post ]   [ Change ]
```

▶ Keying a Debit Memorandum Transaction

Figure 7.9 illustrates a completed General Journal data entry window for the debit memorandum transaction shown earlier in Figure 7.3 on page 176.

FIGURE 7.9
General Journal Data Entry Window (Debit Memorandum)

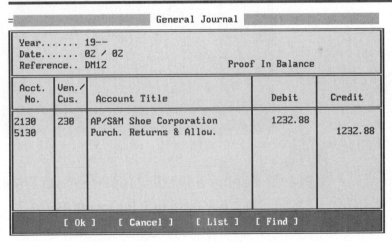

```
=                        General Journal

  Year....... 19--
  Date....... 02 / 02
  Reference.. DM12                     Proof In Balance

  Acct.  Ven./
  No.    Cus.   Account Title              Debit      Credit

  2130   230    AP/S&M Shoe Corporation    1232.88
  5130          Purch. Returns & Allow.               1232.88




            [ Ok ]     [ Cancel ]    [ List ]    [ Find ]
```

▶ Keying a Debit Memorandum Transaction

1   Key the day of the month (02).

2   Key the reference (DM12).

3   Key the Account Number for Accounts Payable (2130).

4   Key the Vendor Number for S&M Shoe Corporation (230).

5   Key the Debit amount ($1,232.88).

6   Key the Account Number for Purch. Returns & Allow. (5130).

7   Key the Credit amount ($1,232.88).

8   Push the Ok button

When the posting summary appears, push the Post button to post the transaction.

▶Keying a Credit Memorandum Transaction

Figure 7.10 illustrates a completed General Journal data entry window for the credit memorandum transaction shown earlier in Figure 7.4 on page 176.

FIGURE 7.10
General Journal Data Entry Window (Credit Memorandum)

```
=▆▆▆▆▆▆▆▆▆▆▆▆         General Journal ▆▆▆▆▆▆▆▆▆▆▆▆▆▆▆
 ┌─────────────────────────────────────────────────────────┐
 │ Year....... 19--                                          │
 │ Date....... 02 / 04                                       │
 │ Reference.. CM22                       Proof In Balance   │
 ├──────┬──────┬───────────────────────┬──────────┬─────────┤
 │ Acct.│ Uen./│                       │          │         │
 │ No.  │ Cus. │ Account Title         │  Debit   │ Credit  │
 ├──────┼──────┼───────────────────────┼──────────┼─────────┤
 │ 4130 │      │ Sales Returns & Allow.│  376.25  │         │
 │ 1150 │ 110  │ AR/Weinstein's        │          │ 376.25  │
 │      │      │                       │          │         │
 │      │      │                       │          │         │
 │      │      │                       │          │         │
 │      │      │                       │          │         │
 │      │      │                       │          │         │
 ├──────┴──────┴───────────────────────┴──────────┴─────────┤
 │    [ Ok ]    [ Cancel ]    [ List ]    [ Find ]          │
 └─────────────────────────────────────────────────────────┘
```

▶Keying a Credit Memorandum Transaction

1   Key the day of the month (04).

2   Key the reference (CM22).

3   Key the Account Number for Sales Returns & Allow. (4130).

4   Key the Debit amount ($376.25).

5   Key the Account Number for Accounts Receivable (1150).

6   Key the Customer Number for Weinstein's (110).

7   Key the Credit amount ($376.25).

8   Push the Ok button

When the posting summary appears, push the Post button to post the transaction.

TUTORIAL 7-T

In this tutorial problem, you will key the journal entries for transactions involving sales discounts, purchases discounts, sales returns and allowances, and purchases returns and allowances. In addition, you will generate journal entries reports, a trial balance, and schedules of accounts payable and accounts receivable.

The steps below list tasks to be completed at the computer. In case you need it, more detailed information on how to complete the task is provided immediately following the step. If you need additional explanation for the task, a page reference is provided from the Operating Procedures of this chapter (or a previous chapter).

Transactions:

Note: Do not key from these transaction statements, since they have already been recorded for you on the journal input forms in Figures 7.11 through 7.15. The reference numbers have been abbreviated on the input forms as follows: purchase invoice no., P; check no., C; sales invoice no., S; cash receipt no., C; cash register tape, T; memorandum, M.

Feb. 01 Paid cash on account to Babcock, Inc., $3,967.81, covering P520 for $4,007.89, less 1% discount, $40.08. C906.

01 Purchased merchandise on account from Wisconsin Shoe Company, $2,891.11. P523.

02 Received cash on account from Baxter's, $5,137.76, covering S328 for $5,189.66, less 1% discount, $51.90. R307.

02 Sold merchandise on account to Alpine Shoes, $4,661.21. S334.

02 Returned merchandise to S&M Shoe Corporation, $1,232.88, against P518. DM12.

03 Received cash on account from Ollie's Shoe Outlet, $4,129.07, covering S329. No discount. R308.

03 Sold merchandise on account to Riverside Shoes, $5,763.28. S335.

04 Granted credit to Weinstein's for merchandise returned, $376.25, against S331. CM22.

05 Sold merchandise on account to Mesa City Shoe Outlet, $4,303.28. S336.

05 Paid cash on account to Wisconsin Shoe Company, $2,595.30, covering P516. No discount. C907.

06 Purchased merchandise on account from DeSoto Shoes, Inc., $3,335.83. P524.

06 Paid cash on account to Supply Warehouse, Inc., $493.28, covering M14 for $498.26, less 1% discount, $4.98. C908.

06 Received cash on account from Mesa City Shoe Outlet, $4,950.08, covering S332 for $5,000.08, less 1% discount, $50.00. R309.

08 Returned merchandise to SVM Shoe, Inc., $1,011.91, against P522. DM13.

08 Paid cash on account to S&M Shoe Corporation, $2,002.99 (covering P518, less DM12), no discount. C909.

09 Received cash on account from Weinstein's, $4,155.84 (covering S331, less CM22), no discount. R310.

10 Granted credit to Riverside Shoes for merchandise returned, $921.04, against S335. CM23.

10 Recorded cash and credit card sales, $3,526.08, plus sales tax, $246.83; total, $3,772.91. T7.

Directions: The step-by-step instructions for processing selected transactions for Danford Shoe Corporation for February 1 through February 10 for the current year are listed below.

Step 1:   Bring up the accounting system. (page 16)

At the DOS prompt, key A1 (or follow the instructions provided by your instructor).

Step 2:   Load the opening balances template file, AA7-T. (page 19)

Pull down the File menu and choose the Open Accounting File command. When the Open File window appears, key the path and file name for the opening balances template file, AA7-T. Push the Ok button.

Step 3:   Save the data file to your drive and directory with a file name of XXX7-T (where XXX are your initials). (page 21)

Pull down the File menu and choose the Save As menu command. Key the path to the drive and directory that contains your data files (for example, if you wish to save your data to Drive B, key B: as the path name). Key a file name of XXX7-T, where XXX are your initials. Push the Ok button.

Step 4:   Enter the student name in the General Information data entry window and set the run date to February 10 of the current year. (page 24)

Pull down the Options menu and choose the General Information menu command. Set the run date to February 10 of the current year. Key your name in the Student Name field.

Step 5: Key the data from the general journal input form shown in Figure 7.11.

Pull down the Journal menu and choose the general journal (unless the general journal is already on the screen). Key the journal entries.

FIGURE 7.11
General Journal Input Form

Date MM / dd	Reference	Account Number	Cust./ Vend No.	Debit	Credit
02/02	DM12	2130	230	1232.88	
		5130			1232.88
02/04	CM22	4130		376.25	
		1150	110		376.25
02/08	DM13	2130	260	1011.91	
		5130			1011.91
02/10	CM23	4130		921.04	
		1150	160		921.04
Totals				3542.08	3542.08

Run Date 02/10/-- GENERAL JOURNAL INPUT FORM Problem No. 7-T

Step 6: Key the data from the purchases journal input form shown in Figure 7.12.

Pull down the Journal menu and choose the purchases journal. Key the journal entries.

FIGURE 7.12
Purchases Journal Input Form

Run Date 02/10/-- PURCHASES JOURNAL INPUT FORM Problem No. 7-T

Date MM / dd	Vend. No.	Invoice No.	Invoice Amount	Acct. No.	Debit Amount	Credit Amount
02/01	210	P523	2891.11	5110	2891.11	
02/06	250	P524	3335.83	5110	3335.83	

Step 7: Key the data from the cash payments journal input form shown in Figure 7.13. (page 177)

Pull down the Journal menu and choose the cash payments journal. Key the journal entries.

FIGURE 7.13
Cash Payments Journal Input Form

		CASH PAYMENTS JOURNAL INPUT FORM				
Run Date	02/10/--				Problem No.	7-T

Date MM / dd	Vend. No.	Check No.	Accounts Pay. Debit	Acct. No.	Debit Amount	Credit Amount
02/01	220	C906	4007.89	5120		40.08
02/05	210	C907	2595.30			
02/06	270	C908	498.26	5120		4.98
02/08	230	C909	2002.99			

Step 8: Key the data from the sales journal input form shown in Figure 7.14. (page 178)

Pull down the Journal menu and choose the sales journal. Key the journal entries.

FIGURE 7.14
Sales Journal Input Form

		SALES JOURNAL INPUT FORM				
Run Date	02/10/--				Problem No.	7-T

Date MM / dd	Cust. No.	Invoice No.	Invoice Amount	Acct. No.	Debit Amount	Credit Amount
02/02	140	S334	4661.21	4110		4661.21
02/03	160	S335	5763.28	4110		5763.28
02/05	130	S336	4303.28	4110		4303.28 .

Step 9: Key the data from the cash receipts journal input form shown in Figure 7.15. (page 178)

Pull down the Journal menu and choose the cash receipts journal. Key the journal entries.

FIGURE 7.15
Cash Receipts Journal Input Form

```
                    CASH RECEIPTS JOURNAL
                         INPUT FORM
  Run Date  02/10/--                        Problem No.   7-T
```

Date MM / dd	Cust. No.	Refer.	Accounts Rec. Credit	Acct. No.	Debit Amount	Credit Amount
02/02	120	R307	5189.66	4120	51.90	
02/03	150	R308	4129.07			
02/06	130	R309	5000.08	4120	50.00	
02/09	110	R310	4155.84			
02/10		T7		4110		3526.08
				2150		246.83

Step 10: Display the journal reports. (page 129).

Pull down the Reports menu and choose the Journals command. When the Report Selection window appears, select the general journal, purchases journal, sales journal, and cash receipts journal. When the Selection Options appears, key a date range of February 1 to February 10 of the current year. The reports appear in Figures 7.16 through 7.20.

FIGURE 7.16
General Journal Report

```
                    Danford Shoe Corporation
                         General Journal
                           02/10/--
    ----------------------------------------------------------------
    Date  Refer.   V/C Acct. Title                   Debit      Credit
    ----------------------------------------------------------------
    02/02 DM12     230 2130  AP/S&M Shoe Corporation 1232.88
    02/02 DM12         5130  Purch. Returns & Allow.            1232.88

    02/04 CM22         4130  Sales Returns & Allow.   376.25
    02/04 CM22     110 1150  AR/Weinstein's                      376.25

    02/08 DM13     260 2130  AP/SVM Shoes, Inc.      1011.91
    02/08 DM13         5130  Purch. Returns & Allow.            1011.91

    02/10 CM23         4130  Sales Returns & Allow.   921.04
    02/10 CM23     160 1150  AR/Riverside Shoes                  921.04
                                                    ---------- ----------
                           Totals                    3542.08    3542.08
                                                    ========== ==========
```

FIGURE 7.17
Purchases Journal Report

```
                        Danford Shoe Corporation
                           Purchases Journal
                              02/10/--
-----------------------------------------------------------------------
Date   Refer.  V/C Acct.  Title                    Debit      Credit
-----------------------------------------------------------------------
02/01  P523        5110   Purchases                2891.11
02/01  P523    210 2130   AP/Wisconsin Shoe Company            2891.11

02/06  P524        5110   Purchases                3335.83
02/06  P524    250 2130   AP/DeSoto Shoes, Inc.                3335.83
                                                 ---------- ----------
                          Totals                   6226.94    6226.94
                                                 ========== ==========
```

FIGURE 7.18
Cash Payments Journal Report

```
                        Danford Shoe Corporation
                         Cash Payments Journal
                              02/10/--
-----------------------------------------------------------------------
Date   Refer.  V/C Acct.  Title                    Debit      Credit
-----------------------------------------------------------------------
02/01  C906    220 2130   AP/Babcock, Inc.         4007.89
02/01  C906        5120   Purchases Discount                     40.08
02/01  C906        1110   Cash                                 3967.81

02/05  C907    210 2130   AP/Wisconsin Shoe Company 2595.30
02/05  C907        1110   Cash                                 2595.30

02/06  C908    270 2130   AP/Supply Warehouse, Inc.  498.26
02/06  C908        5120   Purchases Discount                      4.98
02/06  C908        1110   Cash                                  493.28

02/08  C909    230 2130   AP/S&M Shoe Corporation  2002.99
02/08  C909        1110   Cash                                 2002.99
                                                 ---------- ----------
                          Totals                   9104.44    9104.44
                                                 ========== ==========
```

FIGURE 7.19
Sales Journal Report

```
                        Danford Shoe Corporation
                             Sales Journal
                              02/10/--
-----------------------------------------------------------------------
Date   Refer.  V/C Acct.  Title                    Debit      Credit
-----------------------------------------------------------------------
02/02  S334    140 1150   AR/Alpine Shoes          4661.21
02/02  S334        4110   Sales                                4661.21

02/03  S335    160 1150   AR/Riverside Shoes       5763.28
02/03  S335        4110   Sales                                5763.28
```

(continued)

FIGURE 7.19 (Continued)
Sales Journal Report

```
 02/05 S336    130 1150  AR/Mesa City Shoe Outlet   4303.28
 02/05 S336        4110  Sales                                 4303.28
                                                   ---------- ----------
                         Totals                     14727.77   14727.77
                                                   ========== ==========
```

FIGURE 7.20
Cash Receipts Report

```
                     Danford Shoe Corporation
                       Cash Receipts Journal
                            02/10/--
-------------------------------------------------------------------
Date  Refer. V/C Acct. Title                   Debit      Credit
-------------------------------------------------------------------
02/02 R307        1110  Cash                   5137.76
02/02 R307        4120  Sales Discount           51.90
02/02 R307    120 1150  AR/Baxter's                         5189.66

02/03 R308        1110  Cash                   4129.07
02/03 R308    150 1150  AR/Ollie's Shoe Outlet              4129.07

02/06 R309        1110  Cash                   4950.08
02/06 R309        4120  Sales Discount           50.00
02/06 R309    130 1150  AR/Mesa City Shoe Outlet            5000.08

02/09 R310        1110  Cash                   4155.84
02/09 R310    110 1150  AR/Weinstein's                      4155.84

02/10 T7          1110  Cash                   3772.91
02/10 T7          4110  Sales                               3526.08
02/10 T7          2150  Sales Tax Payable                    246.83
                                             ---------- ----------
                        Totals                22247.56   22247.56
                                             ========== ==========
```

Step 11: Display a trial balance, a schedule of accounts payable, and a schedule of accounts receivable. (pages 99-102)

Pull down the Reports menu and choose the Ledgers command. When the Report Selection window appears, select the trial balance, schedule of accounts payable, and schedule of accounts receivable reports. The reports are shown in Figures 7.21 through 7.23.

Step 12: Save your data to disk with a file name of XXX7-T, where XXX are your initials. (page 21)

Pull down the File menu and choose the Save Accounting Files command to save your file to disk.

Step 13: End the session. (page 22)

Choose the Quit command from the File menu.

FIGURE 7.21
Trial Balance

```
                    Danford Shoe Corporation
                          Trial Balance
                            02/10/--
     ------------------------------------------------------------
     Acct.   Account
     Number  Title                              Debit        Credit
     ------------------------------------------------------------
     1110    Cash                             23634.09
     1120    Petty Cash                         200.00
     1130    Notes Receivable                  7500.00
     1150    Accounts Receivable              25455.60
     1160    Merchandise Inventory            76300.00
     1170    Supplies--Office                   450.00
     1180    Supplies--Store                    850.00
     1190    Prepaid Insurance                  785.00
     1510    Office Equipment                 12550.00
     1520    Accum. Depr.--Ofc. Eqpt.                        3350.00
     1530    Store Equipment                   9875.00
     1540    Accum. Depr.--Store Eqpt.                       2245.00
     2110    Notes Payable                                  10000.00
     2130    Accounts Payable                               16860.51
     2150    Sales Tax Payable                               1259.61
     3110    Capital Stock                                  95000.00
     3120    Retained Earnings                              15967.00
     4110    Sales                                          18253.85
     4120    Sales Discount                     101.90
     4130    Sales Returns & Allow.            1297.29
     5110    Purchases                         6226.94
     5120    Purchases Discount                                 45.06
     5130    Purch. Returns & Allow.                         2244.79
                                             ----------     ----------
             Totals                          165225.82      165225.82
                                             ==========     ==========
```

FIGURE 7.22
Schedule of Accounts Payable

```
                    Danford Shoe Corporation
                    Schedule of Accounts Payable
                            02/10/--
     ------------------------------------------------------------
     Account
     Number   Name                              Balance
     ------------------------------------------------------------
     210      Wisconsin Shoe Company            2891.11
     240      Felix Shoe Company                3878.21
     250      DeSoto Shoes, Inc.                7001.85
     260      SVM Shoes, Inc.                   3089.34
                                              ----------
              Total                            16860.51
                                              ==========
```

FIGURE 7.23
Schedule of Accounts Receivable

```
                    Danford Shoe Corporation
                  Schedule of Accounts Receivable
                           02/10/--
        ------------------------------------------------------
        Account
        Number      Name                              Balance
        ------------------------------------------------------
          130       Mesa City Shoe Outlet            4303.28
          140       Alpine Shoes                     9982.99
          160       Riverside Shoes                 11169.33
                                                    ---------
                    Total                           25455.60
                                                    =========
```

CHAPTER 7 STUDENT EXERCISE

I. MATCHING

Directions: For each of the following definitions, write in the working papers or on a separate sheet of paper the number of the definition followed by the letter of the appropriate term.

(a) Purchases discount

(b) Debit memorandum

(c) Sales discount

(d) Credit memorandum

(e) Discount period

1. A transaction resulting from a buyer returning merchandise which results in a deduction from the Accounts Payable account and the vendor's account.

2. A deduction given to customers from the invoice amount of sales on account to encourage early payment.

3. A deduction given to buyers from the invoice amount to encourage early payment.

4. The specified time period within which an invoice must be paid in order to receive the discount.

5. Credit granted to a customer for returned or damaged merchandise which results in a deduction from the Accounts Receivable account and the customer's account.

II. QUESTIONS

Directions: Write the answers to the following questions in the working papers.

1. Which journal is used to enter a transaction involving a purchases discount?

2. When a transaction involving a purchases discount is entered, is the Purchases Discounts account debited or credited?

3. Which journal is used to enter a transaction involving a sales discount?

4. When a transaction involving a sales discount is entered, is the Sales Discounts account debited or credited?

5. In which journal is a debit memorandum entered?

6. Does a debit memorandum affect a vendor's account or a customer's account?

7. When a credit memorandum is entered, which general ledger account is debited?

8. When a debit memorandum is entered, which general ledger account is credited?

P PRACTICE PROBLEM 7-P

In this problem you will process selected transactions involving purchases discounts, sales discounts, debit memorandums, and credit memorandums for the period February 11 through February 20 of the current year.

Directions: Step-by-step instructions for solving this practice problem are listed below.

Step 1: Remove the input forms from the working papers. Record the following transactions for Danford Shoe Corporation. Abbreviate the reference numbers on the input forms as follows: purchase invoice no., P; check no., C; sales invoice no., S; cash receipt no., C; cash register tape, T; memorandum, M. A chart of accounts, vendor list, and customer list are shown below for reference as you complete the input forms.

```
                  Danford Shoe Corporation
                      Chart of Accounts
                          02/10/--
        ------------------------------------
        Account  Account
        Number   Title
        ------------------------------------
        1110     Cash
        1120     Petty Cash
        1130     Notes Receivable
        1140     Interest Receivable
        1150     Accounts Receivable
        1160     Merchandise Inventory
        1170     Supplies--Office
        1180     Supplies--Store
        1190     Prepaid Insurance
        1510     Office Equipment
        1520     Accum. Depr.--Ofc. Eqpt.
        1530     Store Equipment
        1540     Accum. Depr.--Store Eqpt.
        2110     Notes Payable
        2120     Interest Payable
        2130     Accounts Payable
        2140     Salaries Payable
        2150     Sales Tax Payable
        3110     Capital Stock
        3120     Retained Earnings
        3130     Dividends
        3140     Income Summary
        4110     Sales
        4120     Sales Discount
        4130     Sales Returns & Allow.
        5110     Purchases
        5120     Purchases Discount
        5130     Purch. Returns & Allow.
        6110     Advertising Expense
        6120     Depr. Exp.--Office Eqpt.
        6130     Depr. Exp.--Store Eqpt.
        6140     Insurance Expense
        6150     Miscellaneous Expense
        6160     Rent Expense
        6170     Supplies Expense
        6180     Utilities Expense
        6190     Salaries Expense
        7110     Interest Income
        8110     Interest Expense
        9110     Federal Income Tax Exp.
```

```
                  Danford Shoe Corporation
                        Vendor List
                        02/10/--
        ------------------------------------------
        Vendor     Vendor
        Number     Name
        ------------------------------------------
        210        Wisconsin Shoe Company
        220        Babcock, Inc.
        230        S&M Shoe Corporation
        240        Felix Shoe Company
        250        DeSoto Shoes, Inc.
        260        SVM Shoes, Inc.
        270        Supply Warehouse, Inc.
```

```
                  Danford Shoe Corporation
                        Customer List
                        02/10/--
        ------------------------------------------
        Customer   Customer
         Number     Name
        ------------------------------------------
        110        Weinstein's
        120        Baxter's
        130        Mesa City Shoe Outlet
        140        Alpine Shoes
        150        Ollie's Shoe Outlet
        160        Riverside Shoes
```

Feb. 11 Returned merchandise to Wisconsin Shoe Company, $301.21, against P523. DM14.

11 Sold merchandise on account to Ollie's Shoe Outlet, $2,350.90. S337.

11 Purchased merchandise on account from Felix Shoe Company, $4,070.60. P525.

12 Paid cash on account to SVM Shoes, Inc., $3,089.34 (covering P522, less DM13), no discount. C910.

12 Received cash on account from Alpine Shoes, $5,321.78, covering S330. No discount. R311.

12 Received cash on account from Alpine Shoes, $4,614.60, covering S334 for $4,661.21, less 1% discount, $46.61. R312.

13 Paid cash on account to Felix Shoe Company, $3,878.21, covering P519. No discount. C911.

13 Paid cash on account to DeSoto Shoes, Inc., $3,666.02, covering P517. No discount. C912.

13 Bought office supplies on account from Supply Warehouse, $788.02. M15.

15 Sold merchandise on account to Weinstein's, $5,006.48. S338.

15 Sold merchandise on account to Baxter's, $4,034.53. S339.

15 Received cash on account from Mesa City Shoe Outlet, $4,260.25, covering S336 for $4,303.28, less 1% discount, $43.03. R313.

16 Received cash on account from Riverside Shoes, $6,327.09, covering S333. No discount. R314.

16 Paid cash on account to DeSoto Shoes, Inc., $3,302.47, covering S524 for $3,335.83, less 1% discount, $33.36. C913.

16 Granted credit to Ollie's Shoe Outlet for merchandise returned, $461.17, against S337. CM24.

17 Purchased merchandise on account from S&M Shoe Corporation, $3,306.26. P526.

18 Sold merchandise on account to Alpine Shoes, $1,675.55. S340.

19 Returned merchandise to Wisconsin Shoe Company, $56.50, against P523. DM15.

19 Paid cash on account to Felix Shoe Company, $4,029.89, covering P525 for $4,070.60, less 1% discount, $40.71. C914.

19 Purchased merchandise on account from SVM Shoes, Inc., $3,046.77. P527.

20 Purchased merchandise on account from Babcock, Inc., $3,551.25. P528.

20 Granted credit to Alpine Shoes for merchandise returned, $125.64, against S340. CM25.

20 Recorded cash and credit card sales, $3,110.15, plus sales tax, $217.71; total, $3,327.86. T20.

Step 2: Bring up the accounting system.

Step 3: Load the opening balances template file for AA7-P.

Step 4: Use the Save As menu command to save the opening balances file to your drive and directory with a file name of XXX7-P, where XXX are your initials.

Step 5: Set the run date to February 20 of the current year and key your name into the Student Name field.

Step 6: Key the data from the input forms prepared in Step 1.

Step 7: Display the journal reports (general, purchases, cash payments, sales, and cash receipts) for the period February 11 through February 20 of the current year. If errors are detected, use the List button on the relevant journal data entry window to select the journal entry to correct.

Step 8:   Display a trial balance, schedule of accounts payable, and schedule of accounts receivable.

Step 9:   Save your data to disk.

Step 10:   End the session.

AUDIT TEST PROBLEM 7-P

Directions: Write the answers to the following questions in the working papers or on a separate sheet of paper.

JOURNALS

1. What is the amount of debit memorandum no. 14 to Wisconsin Shoe Company?
2. What is the amount of credit memorandum no. 25 to Alpine Shoes?
3. What is the amount of purchase invoice no. 525 to Felix Shoe Company?
4. What are the total debits and total credits in the purchases journal report?
5. What is the amount of check no. 910 to SVM Shoes, Inc.?
6. What are the total debits and total credits in the cash payments journal?
7. What is the amount of sales invoice no. 340 to Alpine Shoes?
8. What are the total debits and total credits in the cash receipts journal?

TRIAL BALANCE

9. What is the balance in the Cash account?
10. What is the balance is the Accounts Payable account?

SCHEDULES OF ACCOUNTS PAYABLE AND ACCOUNTS RECEIVABLE

11. What is the current balance due to the vendor, Supply Warehouse, Inc.?
12. What is the total amount owed to all vendors?
13. What is the amount due from the customer, Alpine Shoes?
14. What is the total amount due from all customers?

M MASTERY PROBLEM 7-M

In this problem, you will process selected transactions involving purchases discounts, sales discounts, debit memorandums, and credit memorandums for the period February 21 through February 28 of the current year. Refer to chart of accounts, vendor list, and customer list shown in Practice Problem 7-P as you complete the input forms.

Directions:

1. Record the transactions on the input forms.

2. Load the opening balances file (AA7-M).

3. Save the opening balances file to your disk or directory (XXX7-M).

4. Set the run date to February 28 of the current year.

5. Key the transactions.

6. Display the journal reports.

7. Display the trial balance, schedule of accounts payable, and schedule of accounts receivable.

8. Save your data with a file name of XXX7-M.

9. End the session.

Transactions:

Feb. 22 Paid cash on account to Supply Warehouse, Inc., $780.14, covering M15 for $788.02, less 1% discount, $7.88. C915.

22 Received cash on account from Weinstein's, $4,956.42, covering S338 for $5,006.48, less 1% discount, $50.06. R315.

22 Received cash on account from Baxter's, $3,994.18, covering S339 for $4,034.53, less 1% discount, $40.35. R316.

22 Sold merchandise on account to Mesa City Shoe Outlet, $5,125.75. S341.

22 Sold merchandise on account to Baxter's, $3,103.47. S342.

23 Purchased merchandise on account from Felix Shoe Company, $2,875.63. P529.

23 Purchased merchandise on account from DeSoto Shoes, Inc., $1,905.78. P530.

24 Received cash on account from Ollie's Shoe Outlet, $1,889.73 (covering S337, less CM24). No discount. R317.

24 Paid cash on account to Babcock, Inc., $3,515.74, covering P528 for $3,551.25, less 1% discount, $35.51. C916.

24 Purchased merchandise on account from SVM Shoes, Inc., $2,896.14. P531.

24 Paid cash on account to Wisconsin Shoe Company, $2,533.40 (covering P523, less DM14 and DM15). No discount. C917.

25 Sold merchandise on account to Weinstein's, $4,788.99. S343.

25 Received cash on account from Alpine Shoes, $1,549.91 (covering S340, less CM25). No discount. R318.

25 Paid cash on account to S&M Shoe Corporation, $3,273.20, covering P526 for $3,306.26, less 1% discount, $33.06. C918.

26 Sold merchandise on account to Ollie's Shoe Outlet, $5,063.47. S344.

26 Received cash on account from Riverside Shoes, $4,842.24 (covering S335, less CM23). No discount. R319.

26 Returned merchandise to Felix Shoe Company, $116.17, against P529. DM16.

26 Granted credit to Mesa City Shoe Outlet for merchandise returned, $235.43, against S341. CM26.

26 Sold merchandise on account to Riverside Shoes, $2,222.08. S345.

27 Returned merchandise to DeSoto Shoes, Inc., $98.07, against P530. DM17.

27 Granted credit to Baxter's for merchandise returned, $117.95, against S342. CM27.

27 Purchased merchandise on account from Wisconsin Shoe Company, $1,513.12. P532.

27 Paid cash on account to SVM Shoes, Inc., $3,016.30, covering P527 for $3,046.77, less 1% discount, $30.47. C919.

27 Recorded cash and credit card sales, $2,816.43, plus sales tax, $197.15; total, $3,013.58. T27.

AUDIT TEST PROBLEM 7-M

Directions: Write the answers to the following questions in the working papers or on a separate sheet of paper.

JOURNALS

1. What is the amount of debit memorandum no. 17 to DeSoto Shoes, Inc.?
2. What is the amount of credit memorandum no. 27 to Baxter's?
3. What is the amount of purchase invoice no. 532 to Wisconsin Shoe Company?
4. What are the total debits and total credits in the purchases journal report?
5. What is the amount of check no. 916 to Babcock, Inc.?
6. What are the total debits and total credits in the cash payments journal?
7. What is the amount of sales invoice no. 343 to Weinstein's?
8. What are the total debits and total credits in the cash receipts journal?

TRIAL BALANCE

9. What is the balance in the Cash account?
10. What is the balance in the Accounts Payable account?

SCHEDULES OF ACCOUNTS PAYABLE AND ACCOUNTS RECEIVABLE

11. What is the current balance due to the vendor, Felix Shoe Company?
12. What is the total amount owed to all vendors?
13. What is the amount due from the customer, Mesa Shoe Outlet?
14. What is the total amount due from all customers?

8

Plant Assets

LEARNING OBJECTIVES ▶ UPON COMPLETION OF THIS CHAPTER, you will be able to:

1. Record additions, changes, and deletions on the Plant Assets input form.
2. Enter and correct plant assets.
3. Display a plant assets report.
4. Display depreciation schedules.
5. Display a depreciation report and journal entries.

INTRODUCTION

A computerized plant asset system is used to maintain records for all plant assets for a business. The information provided by the plant asset system is used by the business in several ways. Accounting uses plant assets information to show costs, to show an asset's reduction in value due to usage, and to show asset disposition. At the end of the accounting cycle, the plant assets system can be used to generate the adjusting entries.

Plant asset information is used beyond the accounting area. For example, plant assets reports are used for insurance purposes to ensure adequate coverage. In the case of an insurance claim, these reports are often used to determine the amount of the settlement. The information can also be used to estimate the worth of an asset for trade-in value.

When an asset is purchased, it must be added to the plant asset file. Changes and corrections are made to the assets as needed. Assets removed from service are deleted. Periodically, reports are generated to provide needed information regarding plant assets.

▶ Plant Assets Input Form

Additions, changes, and deletions to plant assets are recorded on the plant assets input form as illustrated in Figure 8.1. The first entry in Figure 8.1 is an example of an addition. All data fields must be completed. The second entry is an example of a change. Only the asset number and the fields that have changed need to be completed. The last entry is an example of a deletion. The asset number and (Delete) are recorded.

FIGURE 8.1
Plant Assets Input Form

	PLANT ASSETS INPUT FORM						
Run Date 12/31/--					Problem No.	Example	
Asset No.	Asset Name	Date Acquired	Depr. Meth.	Useful Life	Original Cost	Salvage Value	
180	Laser Printer Model 2	12/02/94	SL	5	3890.60	150.00	
140		07/22/94				50.00	
105	(Delete)						

TABLE 8.1
Field Names and Descriptions of the Plant Assets Input Form

Field Name	Description
Asset Number	A three-digit number used to identify and classify each asset.
Asset Name	Descriptive information that identifies the asset.
Date Acquired	The date (in the mm/dd/yy format) on which the asset was obtained.
Depreciation Method	Identifies the depreciation method the computer will use to calculate depreciation. While the software is capable of calculating depreciation for a variety of depreciation methods, in this chapter only the straight-line method will be used. Straight-line depreciation is abbreviated as SL.
Useful Life	The useful life of the asset in years. (The allowable range is from 3 to 50 years.)
Original Cost	The cost of the asset when it was acquired.
Salvage Value	An amount representing the remaining value of the asset after the asset's useful life.

OPERATING PROCEDURES

The operating procedures covered in this chapter include adding, changing, and deleting plant assets and generating the depreciation reports.

▶ Loading the Plant Asset System

The plant asset system is contained within the second software module. The name of the second module is A2. You can bring it up by typing A2 at the DOS prompt. If you already have the first module (accounting system module) loaded, you can pull down the file menu and select the second module (Payroll/Assets/Bank Rec.).

▶ Maintain Assets Data Entry Window

When the Maintain Assets menu command is chosen from the Assets menu, the data entry window shown in Figure 8.2 will appear.

FIGURE 8.2
Maintain Assets Data Entry Window

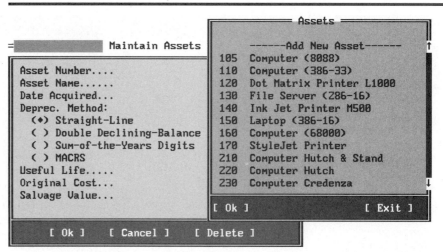

 ▶ **Adding a New Asset**

1   **Choose the ------Add New Asset------ item from the list window.**

The list window will be dismissed.

2   **Key the data fields and set the option button for the depreciation method.**

Although the Deprec. Method option button lists four depreciation methods, you should select the **straight-line** method (that is the only method used in this chapter). A completed data entry window for an asset being added is illustrated in Figure 8.3.

FIGURE 8.3
Adding a New Asset

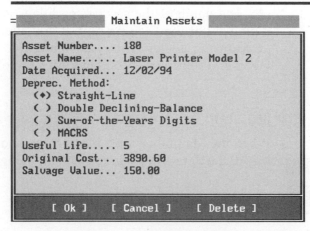

3   Push the Ok button.

▶ Changing Plant Asset Data

1   **Choose the asset you wish to change from the asset list window.**

The list window will be dismissed and the data for the chosen asset will be displayed in the data entry window.

2   **Key the correct data for the asset.**

3   **Push the Ok button.**

▶ Deleting a Plant Asset

1   **Choose the asset you wish to delete from the asset list window.**

The list window will be dismissed and the data for the chosen asset will be displayed in the data entry window.

2   **Push the Delete button.**

Press the End key to select the Delete button and press Enter to push the Delete button. If you have a mouse, click on the Delete button.

▶ Plant Asset Reports

Once the asset data has been entered, the depreciation reports can be generated. When the Reports menu is chosen, the available reports appear as shown in Figure 8.4.

FIGURE 8.4
Depreciation Reports Menu

```
 Reports
┌──────────────────────────┐
│ Plant Assets Report      │
│ Depreciation Schedule    │
│ Depreciation Report      │
└──────────────────────────┘
```

PLANT ASSETS REPORT.   The plant assets report is useful in detecting keying errors and verifying the accuracy of your input. The report also provides information concerning the cost of assets which is useful in determining asset value.

▶ Displaying the Plant Assets Reports

1 Choose the Plant Assets Report menu command from the Reports menu.

The report is illustrated in Figure 8.5.

FIGURE 8.5
Plant Assets Report

```
                        Blue Ridge Software
                        Plant Assets Report
                            12/31/94

      ----------------------------------------------------------------
      Asset      Asset               Date   Depr. Useful Original  Salvage
      Number     Name            Acquired Meth. Life    Cost     Value
      ----------------------------------------------------------------
      105  Computer (8088)         03/02/85  SL   5     2480.00    50.00
      110  Computer (386-33)       06/10/91  SL   5     2905.90   300.00
      120  Dot Matrix Printer L1000 03/01/91 SL   5      290.00    25.00
      130  File Server (286-16)    07/31/94  SL   5     1180.30   200.00
      140  Ink Jet Printer M500    07/20/94  SL   5      399.00    40.00
      150  Laptop (386-16)         03/01/93  SL   5     1500.00   120.00
      160  Computer (68000)        02/20/93  SL   5     3995.00   400.00
      170  StyleJet Printer        02/20/93  SL   5      499.00    20.00
      210  Computer Hutch & Stand  05/01/91  SL  10      220.00    30.00
      220  Computer Hutch          05/01/91  SL  10      180.00    25.00
      230  Computer Credenza       05/01/91  SL  10      110.00    20.00
      240  File Cabinet (4 Drawer) 09/02/92  SL  10      139.00    18.00
      250  Book Case (5 Shelf)     10/03/91  SL  10      123.40    30.00
      260  Copy Machine Stand      11/10/94  SL  10       95.90    10.00
      310  Typewriter              11/01/89  SL  10      220.00    20.00
      320  Copy Machine M50        04/10/91  SL  10     1280.00   110.00
                                                      ---------
      Total                                            15617.50
                                                      =========
```

DEPRECIATION SCHEDULES. Depreciation schedules can be generated for any range of asset numbers. The depreciation schedule provides annual depreciation for each year for the life of the asset. The depreciation is calculated based on the date acquired and the depreciation method. An asset purchased in any month other than January has first-year and last-year amounts that are prorated from the month the asset was purchased. In the example shown in Figure 8.7, the asset was purchased on March 2. Therefore, the first year's depreciation is for the period of March through December, which is 10 months or 10/12ths of the annual depreciation of $486.00 or $405.00. The last two months are depreciated in the last year, which is 2/12ths of the annual depreciation of $486.00, or $81.00.

When the Depreciation Schedules menu command is chosen, the Selection Options dialog window shown in Figure 8.6 appears, allowing you to select the range of assets for which depreciation schedules are to be generated. A sample depreciation schedule is shown in Figure 8.7.

FIGURE 8.6
Selection Options (Depreciation Schedules)

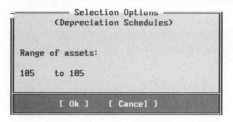

```
 ─────────────── Selection Options ───────────────
              (Depreciation Schedules)


 Range of assets:

 105     to 105


         [ Ok ]     [ Cancel ]
```

FIGURE 8.7
Depreciation Schedule

```
                      Blue Ridge Software
                      Depreciation Schedules
                           12/31/94

    Asset Number..........110
    Asset Name...........Computer (386-33)
    Date Acquired.........06/10/91
    Depreciation Method...Straight-Line
    Useful Life...........5
    Original Cost.........    2905.90
    Salvage Value.........     300.00
    -----------------------------------------------
                  Annual      Accumulated     Book
    Year      Depreciation    Depreciation    Value
    -----------------------------------------------
    1991          304.02          304.02    2601.88
    1992          521.18          825.20    2080.70
    1993          521.18         1346.38    1559.52
    1994          521.18         1867.56    1038.34
    1995          521.18         2388.74     517.16
    1996          217.16         2605.90     300.00
```

DEPRECIATION REPORT.   A depreciation report may be generated for the current month, the current year, or both, depending on the options selected in the Report Selection dialog shown in Figure 8.8. A sample yearly depreciation report is illustrated in Figure 8.9. Each report lists each asset, the depreciation method, the monthly or yearly depreciation, the accumulated depreciation, and the book value. The computer automatically generates the journal entries for the depreciation adjusting entry for the time period specified (monthly or yearly). The journal entries report is shown in Figure 8.10.

FIGURE 8.8
Report Selection

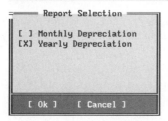

```
 ═══════ Report Selection ═══════
 [ ] Monthly Depreciation
 [X] Yearly Depreciation




   [ Ok ]     [ Cancel ]
```

FIGURE 8.9
Depreciation Report

```
                       Blue Ridge Software
                       Yearly Depreciation
                          12/31/94

 --------------------------------------------------------------
 Asset .               Depr.    Yearly    Accumulated      Book
 Name                  Meth. Depreciation Depreciation    Value
 --------------------------------------------------------------
 Computer (386-33)      SL     521.18      1867.56       1038.34
 Computer (486-66)      SL     546.78       546.78       3333.92
 Dot Matrix Printer L1000 SL    53.00       203.17         86.83
 File Server (286-16)   SL      98.03        98.03       1082.27
 Hard Disk Drive        SL      85.34        85.34        523.56
 Ink Jet Printer M500   SL      35.90        35.90        363.10
 Laptop (386-16)        SL     276.00       506.00        994.00
 Computer (68000)       SL     719.00      1378.08       2616.92
 StyleJet Printer       SL      95.80       183.62        315.38
 Hutch/Printer Stand    SL      19.00        69.67        150.33
 Computer Hutch         SL      15.50        56.83        123.17
 Computer Credenza      SL       9.00        33.00         77.00
 File Cabinet (4 Drawer) SL     12.10        28.23        110.76
 Book Case (5 Shelf)    SL       9.34        30.36         93.04
 Copy Machine Stand     SL       1.43         1.43         94.47
 File Cabinet (4 Drawer) SL      5.05         5.05        235.76
 Typewriter             SL      20.00       103.33        116.67
 Copy Machine M50       SL     117.00       438.75        841.25
 Electronic Calculator  SL       6.63         6.63        117.87
```

FIGURE 8.10
Depreciation Journal Entries

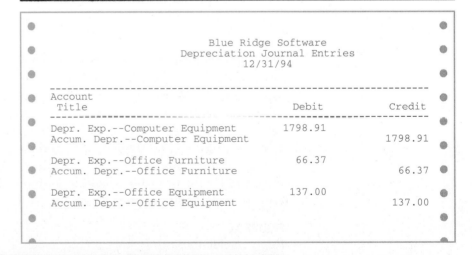

```
                      Blue Ridge Software
                   Depreciation Journal Entries
                          12/31/94

 --------------------------------------------------------------
 Account
   Title                           Debit              Credit
 --------------------------------------------------------------
 Depr. Exp.--Computer Equipment    1798.91
 Accum. Depr.--Computer Equipment                     1798.91

 Depr. Exp.--Office Furniture        66.37
 Accum. Depr.--Office Furniture                         66.37

 Depr. Exp.--Office Equipment       137.00
 Accum. Depr.--Office Equipment                        137.00
```

TUTORIAL 8-T

In this tutorial problem, you will add, change, and delete plant assets. In addition, you will generate the plant assets report, depreciation schedules, and a depreciation report.

Each of the steps below lists a task to be completed at the computer. In case you need it, more detailed information on how to complete the task is provided immediately following the step. If you need additional information on performing the task, a page reference is provided.

Directions: The step-by-step instructions for completing the plant assets processing for Blue Ridge Software are listed below.

Step 1:   Bring up the plant asset system. (page 199)

At the DOS prompt, key A2 (or follow the instructions provided by your instructor).

Step 2:   Load the opening balances template file, AA8-T. (page 19)

Pull down the File menu and choose the Open Data File option. When the Open File window appears, key the path and file name for the opening balances template file, AA8-T.

Step 3:   Save the opening balances file to your drive and directory with a file name of XXX8-T (where XXX are your initials. (page 21)

Pull down the File menu and choose the Save As menu command. Key the path to the drive and directory that contains your data files.

Step 4:   In the General Information data entry window, set the run date to December 31, 1994, and enter your name in the Student Name field.

Pull down the Options menu and choose the General Information menu command.

Step 5:   Key the data from the Plant Assets Input Form shown in Figure 8.11.

Pull down the Assets menu and choose the Maintain Assets menu command.

It is very important that you enter the correct run date (December 31, 1994) and that you enter the correct date acquired for each plant asset. Many of the calculated depreciation amounts are date sensitive and will display incorrectly if the dates are entered incorrectly.

Step 6:   Display a Plant Assets Report. (page 202)

Pull down the Reports menu and choose the Plant Assets Report. The report is shown in Figure 8.12.

FIGURE 8.11
Plant Assets Input Form

```
                        PLANT ASSETS
                        INPUT FORM

  Run Date    12/31/--                    Problem No.    8-T
```

Asset No.	Asset Name	Date Acquired	Depr. Meth.	Useful Life	Original Cost	Salvage Value
115	Computer (486-66)	03/01/94	SL	5	3880.70	600.00
135	Hard Disk Drive	04/30/94	SL	5	608.90	40.00
210	Hutch/Printer Stand					
105	(Delete)					
330	Electronic Calculator	09/30/94	SL	5	124.50	25.00
270	File Cabinet (4 Drawer)	10/31/94	SL	10	240.80	39.00

FIGURE 8.12
Plant Assets Report

```
                        Blue Ridge Software
                        Plant Assets Report
                           12/31/94

   ------------------------------------------------------------------
   Asset    Asset                   Date      Depr. Useful Original Salvage
   Number   Name                    Acquired  Meth. Life    Cost    Value
   ------------------------------------------------------------------
   110    Computer (386-33)         06/10/91  SL   5    2905.90   300.00
   115    Computer (486-66)         03/01/94  SL   5    3880.70   600.00
   120    Dot Matrix Printer L1000  03/01/91  SL   5     290.00    25.00
   130    File Server (286-16)      07/31/94  SL   5    1180.30   200.00
   135    Hard Disk Drive           04/30/94  SL   5     608.90    40.00
   140    Ink Jet Printer M500      07/20/94  SL   5     399.00    40.00
   150    Laptop (386-16)           03/01/93  SL   5    1500.00   120.00
   160    Computer (68000)          02/20/93  SL   5    3995.00   400.00
   170    StyleJet Printer          02/20/93  SL   5     499.00    20.00
   210    Hutch/Printer Stand       05/01/91  SL  10     220.00    30.00
   220    Computer Hutch            05/01/91  SL  10     180.00    25.00
   230    Computer Credenza         05/01/91  SL  10     110.00    20.00
   240    File Cabinet (4 Drawer)   09/02/92  SL  10     139.00    18.00
   250    Book Case (5 Shelf)       10/03/91  SL  10     123.40    30.00
   260    Copy Machine Stand        11/10/94  SL  10      95.90    10.00
   270    File Cabinet (4 Drawer)   10/31/94  SL  10     240.80    39.00
   310    Typewriter                11/01/89  SL  10     220.00    20.00
   320    Copy Machine M50          04/10/91  SL  10    1280.00   110.00
   330    Electronic Calculator     09/30/94  SL   5     124.50    25.00
                                                        -------
          Total                                        17992.40
                                                        =======
```

**Step 7:   Display depreciation schedules for the new
           assets: 115, 135, 270, and 330. (page 202)**

Pull down the Reports menu and select the Depreciation Schedules menu command. When the Selection Options dialog window shown in Figure 8.13 appears, key an asset range of 115 to 115 (the first asset). Repeat this process for each of the assets for which depreciation schedules are to be generated. The first depreciation schedule is illustrated in Figure 8.14.

FIGURE 8.13
Selection Options (Depreciation Schedules)

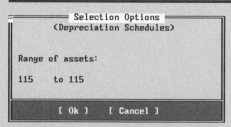

FIGURE 8.14
Depreciation Schedule

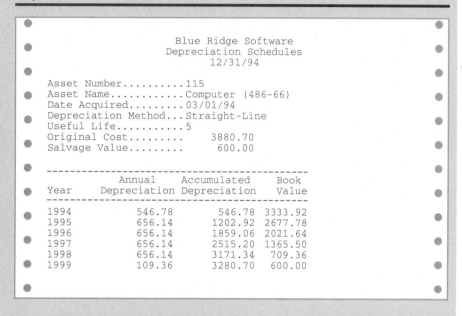

Step 8: Display a yearly depreciation report and depreciation journal entries report. (page 203)

Pull down the Reports menu and choose the Depreciation Report. When the Report Options dialog window appears, select the check box for yearly depreciation. The reports are shown in Figure 8.15.

Step 9: Save your data file to disk.

Pull down the File menu and choose the Save Data File menu command.

Step 10:   End the session.

Choose the Quit menu command from the File menu.

FIGURE 8.15
Yearly Depreciation Report and Journal Entries Report

```
                          Blue Ridge Software
                           Yearly Depreciation
                               12/31/94

-----------------------------------------------------------------
Asset                   Depr.   Yearly      Accumulated      Book
Name                    Meth.   Depreciation Depreciation    Value
-----------------------------------------------------------------
Computer (386-33)        SL      521.18      1867.56       1038.34
Computer (486-66)        SL      546.78       546.78       3333.92
Dot Matrix Printer L1000 SL       53.00       203.17         86.83
File Server (286-16)     SL       98.03        98.03       1082.27
Hard Disk Drive          SL       85.34        85.34        523.56
Ink Jet Printer M500     SL       35.90        35.90        363.10
Laptop (386-16)          SL      276.00       506.00        994.00
Computer (68000)         SL      719.00      1378.08       2616.92
StyleJet Printer         SL       95.80       183.62        315.38
Hutch/Printer Stand      SL       19.00        69.67        150.33
Computer Hutch           SL       15.50        56.83        123.17
Computer Credenza        SL        9.00        33.00         77.00
File Cabinet (4 Drawer)  SL       12.10        28.23        110.77
Book Case (5 Shelf)      SL        9.34        30.36         93.04
Copy Machine Stand       SL        1.43         1.43         94.47
File Cabinet (4 Drawer)  SL        5.05         5.05        235.75
Typewriter               SL       20.00       103.33        116.67
Copy Machine M50         SL      117.00       438.75        841.25
Electronic Calculator    SL        6.63         6.63        117.87


                          Blue Ridge Software
                        Depreciation Journal Entries
                               12/31/94

-----------------------------------------------------------------
Account
Title                                     Debit        Credit
-----------------------------------------------------------------
Depr. Exp.--Computer Equipment           2431.03
Accum. Depr.--Computer Equipment                      2431.03

Depr. Exp.--Office Furniture               71.42
Accum. Depr.--Office Furniture                          71.42

Depr. Exp.--Office Equipment              143.63
Accum. Depr.--Office Equipment                         143.63
```

CHAPTER 8 STUDENT EXERCISE

I. TRUE/FALSE

Directions: Answer the following questions in the working papers or on a separate sheet of paper. If the statement is true, write the question number followed by T. If the statement is false, write the question number followed by F.

1. The plant asset system can generate the depreciation adjusting entries automatically.
2. When recording changes on the plant assets input form, all data fields must be recorded.

3. The plant assets software is contained within the same module as the accounting system software.

4. The report that is most useful in verifying the accuracy of your input is the depreciation schedule.

5. The depreciation report can be generated for any range of assets.

6. When the depreciation report is selected, the computer generates the depreciation journal entries automatically.

II. QUESTIONS

Directions: Write the answers to the following questions in the working papers or on a separate sheet of paper.

1. List three uses of the information provided by the plant asset system.

2. Which of the reports available in the plant assets system provides annual depreciation for each year of the life of the asset?

3. Which of the reports available in the plant assets system provides monthly or yearly depreciation for each asset?

P PRACTICE PROBLEM 8-P

In this problem, you will add, change, and delete plant assets. In addition, you will generate the plant assets report, depreciation schedules, and a depreciation report.

Directions: The step-by-step instructions for completing the plant assets processing for Brownstone Company are listed below.

Step 1:   Remove the plant assets input form from the working papers and record the following additions, changes, and deletions.

Jan. 03   Purchased a desk (model A1) for $920.10; salvage value, 1994 $80.00; useful life, 10 years; depreciation method, SL; assign asset no. 125.

Note: When recording the year acquired, be sure to use a year of 1994.

03   Purchased an office chair (gray) for 362.00; salvage value, $40.00; useful life, 10 years, depreciation method, SL; assign asset no. 145.

Mar. 01   Delete the word processor from the plant assets.

June 03   Purchased a notebook computer for $2,950.00; salvage value, 250.00; useful life, 5 years; depeciation method, SL; assign asset no. 260.

Aug. 06   Change the date acquired for the laser printer to 10/01/92.

Oct. 28   Purchased a CD ROM disk for $520.00; salvage value, $50.00; useful life, 5 years, depreciation method, SL; assign asset no. 270.

Dec. 02 Purchased a telephone system, $2,890.00; salvage value, $300.00; useful life, 8 years, depreciation method, SL; assign asset no. 215.

Step 2:   Key A2 at the DOS prompt to bring up the plant asset system.

Step 3:   Load the opening balances template file, AA8-P.

Step 4:   Save the opening balances file to your drive and directory with a file name of XXX8-P (where XXX are your initials).

Step 5:   In the General Information data entry window, set the run date to December 31, 1994, and enter your name in the Student Name field.

Step 6:   Key the data from the plant assets input form completed in Step 1.

Step 7:   Display a plant assets report.

Step 8:   Display depreciation schedules for the new assets.

Step 9:   Display a yearly depreciation report.

Step 10:   Save your data file to disk with a file name of XXX8-P, where XXX are your initials.

Step 11:   End the session.

AUDIT TEST PROBLEM 8-P

Directions: Write the answers to the following questions in the working papers or on a separate sheet of paper.

1. What is the total value of all assets based on original costs?
2. On what date was the laser printer acquired?
3. For asset no. 125, the desk (model A1), what will the accumulated depreciation be as of the end of 1997?
4. For asset no. 145, the office chair (gray), what will the book value be as of the end of 1998?
5. For asset no. 260, the notebook computer, what is the annual depreciation for 1994?
6. For asset no. 270, the CD ROM disk, what will the book value be at the end of 1998?
7. For asset no. 215, the telephone system, what will the annual depreciation be for the year 2002?
8. From the yearly depreciation report, what is the accumulated depreciation for the CD ROM disk?
9. From the journal entries report, what is the amount to be debited to Depreciation Expense—Office Furniture?
10. From the journal entries report, what is the amount to be credited to Accumulated Depreciation—Office Equipment?

M MASTERY PROBLEM 8-M

In this problem, you will add, change, and delete plant assets. In addition, you will generate the plant assets report, depreciation schedules, and a depreciation report for the Brookwood Company.

Directions: To solve the mastery problem, complete the tasks listed below.

1. Record the following transactions on the plant assets input form.
2. Load the opening balances template file (AA8-M).
3. Save the opening balances data to your data disk or directory.
4. Set the run date to December 31, 1994.
5. Key the additions, changes, and deletions to plant assets.
6. Display the following reports:
   Plant assets report.
   Depreciation schedules for each of the new assets.
   Yearly depreciation report (and resulting journal entries).

Transactions:

Feb. 10 Purchased a copy machine for $3,160.00; salvage value,
1994 $200.00; useful life, 8 years; depreciation method, SL; assign asset no. 260.

Apr. 06 Purchased a Model 600 computer for $1,860.00; salvage value, $120.00; useful life, 5 years; depreciation method, SL; assign asset no. 270.

06 Purchased an MT printer for $699.00; salvage value, $50.00; useful life, 5 years; depreciation method, SL; assign asset no. 280.

May 19 Change the useful life for the fax machine to 6 years.

June 10 Delete the word processor from the plant assets.

Oct. 02 Purchased a cash register for $1,800.00; salvage value, $180.00; useful life, 8 years, depreciation method, SL; assign asset no. 350.

Nov. 01 Purchased a security display case for $2,780.00; salvage value, $120.00; useful life, 12 years, depreciation method, SL; assign asset no. 325.

AUDIT TEST PROBLEM 8-M

Directions: Write the answers to the following questions in the working papers or on a separate sheet of paper.

1. What is the total value of all assets based on original costs?
2. On what date was the C-25 delivery van acquired?

3. For asset no. 260, the copy machine, what will the accumulated depreciation be as of the end of 1997?

4. For asset no. 270, the model 600 computer, what will the book value be as of the end of 1998?

5. For asset no. 280, the MT printer, what is the annual depreciation for 1994?

6. For asset no. 350, the cash register, what will the book value be at the end of 1998?

7. For asset no. 325, the security display case, what is the annual depreciation for the year 2002?

8. From the yearly depreciation report, what is the accumulated depreciation for the company car (Apex model)?

9. From the journal entries report, what is the amount to be debited to Depreciation Expense—Vehicles?

10. From the journal entries report, what is the amount to be credited to Accumulated Depreciation—Store Equipment?

9

Corporations

LEARNING OBJECTIVES ▶ UPON COMPLETION OF THIS CHAPTER, you will be able to:

1. Process the monthly transactions for a corporation.

2. Generate accounts payable checks.

3. Generate monthly statements.

4. Complete the end-of-period processing for a corporation.

INTRODUCTION

This chapter covers the monthly processing and end-of-fiscal-period processing for a corporation. The use of a multicolumn income statement, accounts payable checks generated by the computer, and accounts receivable monthly statement are also covered.

A corporation is an organization that exists separately from its owners. A corporation has many of the legal rights of a person. It is typically owned by many people. The ownership is divided into units referred to as **shares of stock.** The owners' equity in a corporation is called **capital stock.** Owners of the corporation are called **shareholders**. A **board of directors** is elected by the shareholders to manage the corporation.

In a sole proprietorship or partnership, assets withdrawn from the business are recorded in the owner's drawing account. Shareholders may not withdraw assets from the corporation. Earnings distributed to shareholders are called **dividends.** All of the earnings may be retained by the corporation for future expansion; this is referred to as **retained earnings.**

For sole proprietorships and partnerships, the income tax liability for net income rests with the owners. Corporations must pay income tax on their earnings.

▶ General Information Data Entry Window Settings

Several features introduced in this chapter are affected by settings in the General Information data entry window. The General Information data entry window for Weil's Beauty Supply is shown in Figure 9.1. Notice that the Business Organization option button is set to a corporation, the Checks/Statements option button is set to Prepared by Computer, and the Income Stmt. (Income Statement) option button is set to Month & Year.

FIGURE 9.1
General Information Data Entry Window

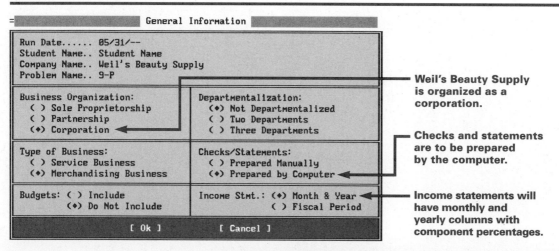

▶Journal Entries

Several journal entries related to corporations are introduced in this chapter. Also, the cash payments journal entries are slightly different when the computer is generating the accounts payable checks. A chart of accounts and a vendor list for Weil's Beauty Supply are shown in Figure 9.2 for reference.

CASH PAYMENTS.   There are several slight differences in the way that cash payment transactions are recorded when the checks are prepared by the computer. Each cash payment for which the computer is to write a check must include the vendor number to whom the check is to be written. When checks are prepared manually, a vendor number is required only for payments on account. If you leave the Vendor No. field blank for a direct payment, the computer will not prepare a check. If the Vendor No. field is blank, the computer assumes that a check has already been written manually or is not required (a bank charge, for example). Two sample transactions are recorded in the cash payments journals shown in Figure 9.3. The first transaction is an example of a cash payment on account with a discount. The second transaction is an example of a direct payment (not on account).

Mar. 06 Paid cash on account to Amity Supply Warehouse, $847.03, covering M26 for $864.32, less 2% discount, $17.29.

06 Paid cash to East Coast Utilities Co. for electric bill, $504.66.

FIGURE 9.2
Chart of Accounts and Vendor List

```
              Weil's Beauty Supply
                Chart of Accounts
                    04/01/--
       ------------------------------------
       Account   Account
       Number    Title
       ------------------------------------
       1110      Cash
       1120      Petty Cash
       1130      Accounts Receivable
       1140      Merchandise Inventory
       1150      Supplies--Office
       1160      Supplies--Store
       1170      Prepaid Insurance
       1510      Office Equipment
       1520      Accum. Depr.--Ofc. Eqpt.
       1530      Store Equipment
       1540      Accum. Depr.--Store Eqpt.
       2110      Accounts Payable
       2120      Sales Tax Payable
       2130      Employee Income Tax Pay.
       2140      Federal Income Tax Pay.
       2150      FICA Tax Payable
       2160      Medicare Tax Payable
       2170      Unemploy. Tax Pay.--Fed.
       2180      Unemploy. Tax Pay.--State
       2190      Health Ins. Premium Pay.
       2200      Disability Insurance Pay.
       2210      Dividends Payable
       3110      Capital Stock
       3120      Retained Earnings
```

(continued)

FIGURE 9.2 (Continued)
Chart of Accounts and Vendor List

```
  3130      Dividends
  3140      Income Summary
  4110      Sales
  4120      Sales Discount
  4130      Sales Returns & Allow.
  5110      Purchases
  5120      Purchases Discount
  5130      Purch. Returns & Allow.
  6110      Advertising Expense
  6120      Depr. Exp.--Office Eqpt.
  6130      Depr. Exp.--Store Eqpt.
  6140      Insurance Expense
  6150      Miscellaneous Expense
  6160      Rent Expense
  6170      Office Supplies Expense
  6180      Store Supplies Expense
  6190      Utilities Expense
  6200      Salaries Expense
  6210      Payroll Taxes Expense
  6220      Credit Card Fee Expense
  9110      Federal Income Tax Exp.


                Weil's Beauty Supply
                     Vendor List
                      04/01/--
          ---------------------------------
          Vendor    Vendor
          Number    Name
          ---------------------------------
           210      Harris Leasing Company
           220      Cape Cod Press
           230      Petals & Blooms
           240      Amity Supply Warehouse
           250      East Coast Utilities Co.
           260      Payroll Bank Account
           270      Commissioner of Revenue
           280      Aquarius Insurance Co.
           290      Internal Revenue Service
           300      Shareholders Bank Account
           310      Peterson's Equipment Co.
           320      Hunt & Reilly Mfg. Co.
           330      Sheldon & Sheldon, Inc.
           340      Terrace & Webster Corp.
           350      Macmillan & Dillon Co.
           360      Horner Chemicals, Inc.
           370      K&K Hair Products, Inc.
           380      Petty Cash Account
```

FIGURE 9.3
Cash Payments Journal Input Form

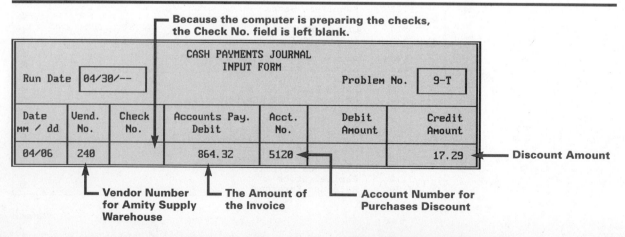

Because the computer is preparing the checks, the Check No. field is left blank.

Date MM / dd	Vend. No.	Check No.	Accounts Pay. Debit	Acct. No.	Debit Amount	Credit Amount
04/06	240		864.32	5120		17.29

Run Date 04/30/--   Problem No. 9-T

Vendor Number for Amity Supply Warehouse — The Amount of the Invoice — Account Number for Purchases Discount — Discount Amount

FIGURE 9.3 (Continued)
Cash Payments Journal Input Form

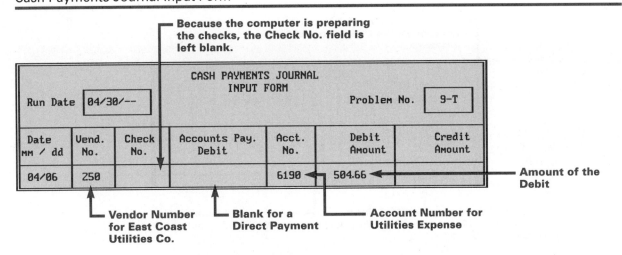

DECLARING A DIVIDEND.   The decision by the board of directors to distribute earnings to the shareholders is called **declaring a dividend**. The dividend is often not distributed at the time it is declared. However, the declaration creates a liability to the corporation and requires a journal entry.

Mar. 10 Weil's Beauty Supply's board of directors declared a dividend, $3,000.00. M22.

The above entry is recorded on the general journal input form, as illustrated in Figure 9.4.

FIGURE 9.4
General Journal Input Form (Declaring a Dividend)

Date mm / dd	Reference	Account Number	Cust./ Vend No.	Debit	Credit
03/10	M22	3130		3000.00	
		2210			3000.00

Run Date 03/10/--   GENERAL JOURNAL INPUT FORM   Problem No. Example

To record this entry, debit the Dividends account (3130) and credit the Dividends Payable account (2210).

PAYING A DIVIDEND   The dividends are paid by recording a cash payment transaction for the amount of the dividends payable to Shareholders Bank Account. This check is then deposited in a special bank account on which the individual checks to the shareholders are drawn. The cash payments journal entry to record the payment of dividends is illustrated in Figure 9.5.

Apr. 23 Paid cash to Shareholders Bank Account for first-quarter dividends declared in March, $3,000.00.

FIGURE 9.5
Cash Payments Journal Input Form

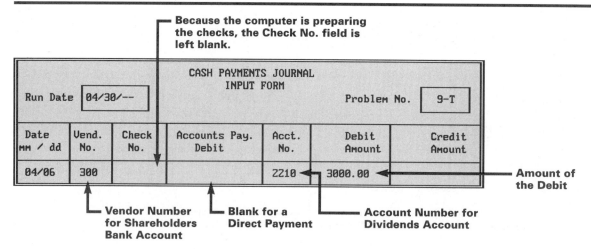

CORPORATE INCOME TAX.   Corporations are required to pay taxes on their income. The corporation pays the taxes each quarter, based on estimated tax liability. The estimated taxes are based on estimated net income. At the end of the year, the corporation must file a tax return with the Internal Revenue Service based on actual earnings. If additional tax is owed beyond the estimate, the additional tax must be paid when the return is filed. If the estimate exceeds the actual taxes, the corporation may either ask for a refund of the difference or apply the excess to the estimated tax for the following year. Because Weil's Beauty Supply completes the accounting cycle each month, an income tax adjustment is made each month. Quarterly, the corporation pays the estimated tax to the Internal Revenue Service. The payment of the quarterly estimated income tax is shown in Figure 9.6, and the monthly federal income tax adjustment is shown in Figure 9.7.

Apr. 13 Paid cash to Internal Revenue Service for quarterly estimated federal income tax, $990.00.

     30 Adjustment for estimated federal income tax, 330.00.

FIGURE 9.6
Cash Payments Journal Input Form

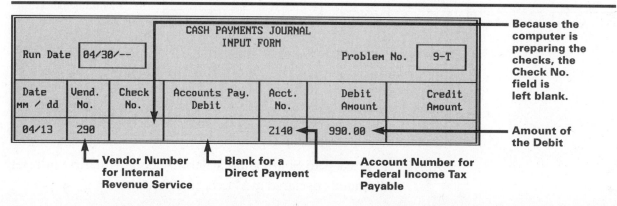

FIGURE 9.7
General Journal Input Form (Federal Income Tax Adjusting Entry)

Run Date	04/30/--		GENERAL JOURNAL INPUT FORM		Problem No.	9-T

Date MM / dd	Reference	Account Number	Cust./ Vend No.	Debit	Credit
04/30	ADJ.ENT.	9110		330.00	
		2140			330.00

To record this adjusting entry, debit Federal Income Tax Exp. (9110) and credit Federal Income Tax Pay. (2140).

OPERATING PROCEDURES

Most of the operating procedures necessary to solve the problems in this chapter have been covered in previous chapters and will not be repeated here. Operating procedures that are new to this chapter are (1) entering transactions in the Cash Payments data entry window when the computer is generating the checks; (2) printing accounts payable checks; (3) printing monthly statements of accounts; and (4) generating an income statement with monthly and yearly columns.

▶ Cash Payments Journal Data Entry Window

When checks are being prepared manually, a vendor number is not required for direct cash payments (payments that are *not* on account). When checks **are** being prepared by the computer, a vendor number **is** required for all direct payments for which a check is to be generated. If you leave the Vendor No. field blank, a check will not be generated for that cash payment. The computer assumes that either the check was prepared manually, or none is needed (as in the case of a bank charge). A vendor number is always required for a payment on account.

When checks are being prepared manually, the check number of the manually written check is recorded in the Check No. data field. When checks are being prepared by the computer, the computer skips over the Check No. field, because check numbers are assigned by the computer as they are being printed. The Check No. field is automatically updated by the computer as the checks are being printed. Therefore, if you were to make a correction to a cash payment transaction **after** checks are printed, the assigned check number will appear in the Check No. field. A completed Cash Payments data entry window for a direct payment where the computer is to write the check is illustrated in Figure 9.8.

FIGURE 9.8
Cash Payments Data Entry Window

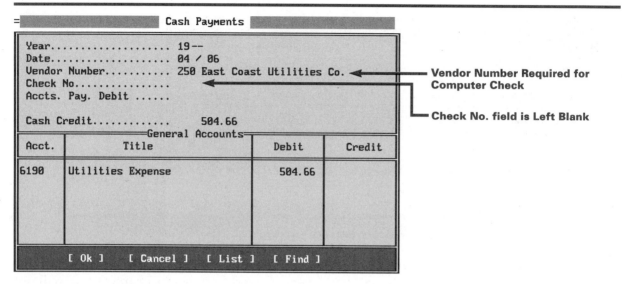

▶ Accounts Payable Checks and Accounts Receivable Statements

If the Checks/Statements option button on the General Information data entry window is set to Prepared Manually, the Checks/Statements command on the Reports menu is dimmed. Since Weil's Beauty Supply has this option button set to Prepared by Computer, the Checks/Statements command is not dimmed and can be chosen.

▶ Displaying Checks and Statements

1   **Choose the Checks/Statements command from the Reports menu.**

The Report Selection dialog window shown in Figure 9.9 will appear, allowing you to select whether you wish to display checks, statements, or both checks and statements.

2   **Select the desired reports and push the Ok button.**

If the Checks option is selected, the Selections Options dialog window shown in Figure 9.10 will appear.

3   **Key the range of dates for which you would like checks displayed.**

FIGURE 9.9
Report Selection Dialog Window

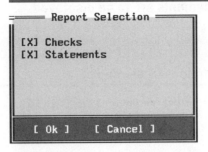

```
══════ Report Selection ══════

[X] Checks
[X] Statements



      [ Ok ]      [ Cancel ]
```

FIGURE 9.10
Selection Options (Checks)

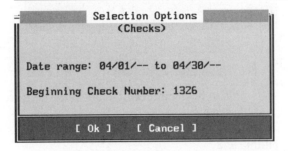

```
              Selection Options
                  (Checks)


Date range: 04/01/-- to 04/30/--

Beginning Check Number: 1326


         [ Ok ]      [ Cancel ]
```

4 Key the beginning check number.

5 Push the Ok button.

The first check is shown in Figure 9.11 as an example.

FIGURE 9.11
First Check

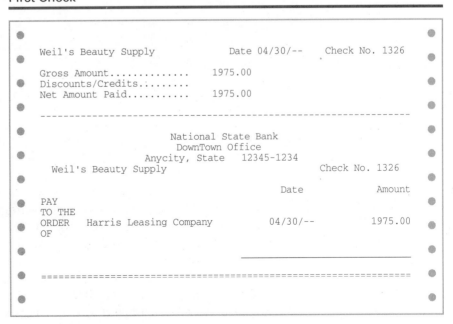

```
Weil's Beauty Supply              Date 04/30/--    Check No. 1326

Gross Amount..............    1975.00
Discounts/Credits.:........
Net Amount Paid..........     1975.00

----------------------------------------------------------------

                        National State Bank
                          DownTown Office
                    Anycity, State   12345-1234
        Weil's Beauty Supply                     Check No. 1326

                                        Date           Amount
PAY
TO THE
ORDER   Harris Leasing Company        04/30/--         1975.00
OF

                                    _____

        ================================================================
```

6   **When the Selection Options dialog window shown in Figure 9.12 appears, key the range of customers for which customer statements are to be displayed.**

FIGURE 9.12
Selection Options (Statements)

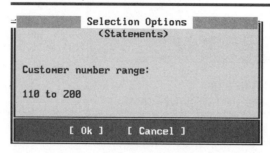

7   **Push the Ok button.**

The first statement is shown in Figure 9.13 as an example.

FIGURE 9.13
First Statement

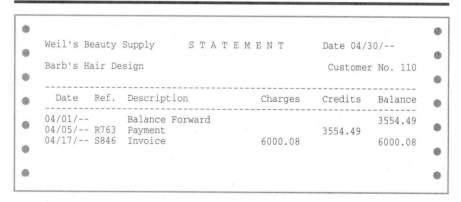

INCOME STATEMENT.   If the Income Stmt. option button on the general information data entry window is set to Month & Year, the format of the income statement will be as shown in Figure 9.14. The report includes columns for the month and for the year. Also included for each column is a percentage, indicating the percent each amount is of total operating revenue. When this format of the income statement is used, adjusting entries (for the month) are recorded and entered and financial statements are generated at the end of each month. The adjusting entries must be entered each month in order for the Monthly column to be up to date and correct. However, the period-end closing is not performed until the end of the fiscal period.

FIGURE 9.14
Income Statement

```
                           Weil's Beauty Supply
                             Income Statement
                         For Period Ended 04/30/--
------------------------------------------------------------------------
                            *****Monthly*****      *****Yearly******
                            Amount    Percent       Amount    Percent
------------------------------------------------------------------------
O p e r a t i n g   R e v e n u e
------------------------------------
Sales                      52251.75    100.45    202886.94    102.20
Sales Discount              -165.52      -.32      -1719.49      -.87
Sales Returns & Allow.       -65.95      -.13      -2653.75     -1.34
                          ---------- ----------   ---------- ----------
Total Operating Revenue    52020.28    100.00    198513.70    100.00

C o s t   o f   M e r c h a n d i s e   S o l d
------------------------------------------------
Beginning Inventory        59828.16    115.01     60715.53     30.59
Purchases                  36125.69     69.45    129807.57     65.39
Purchases Discount          -244.69      -.47      -1727.97      -.87
Purch. Returns & Allow.     -221.05      -.42      -2461.80     -1.24
                          ---------- ----------   ---------- ----------
Merchandise Available for Sale 95488.11 183.56   186333.33     93.86
Less Ending Inventory      -61700.00   -118.61    -61700.00    -31.08
                          ---------- ----------   ---------- ----------
Cost of Merchandise Sold   33788.11     64.95    124633.33     62.78
                          ---------- ----------   ---------- ----------
Gross Profit               18232.17     35.05     73880.37     37.22

O p e r a t i n g   E x p e n s e s
------------------------------------
Advertising Expense          463.55       .89      2773.65      1.40
Depr. Exp.--Office Eqpt.     191.67       .37       766.67       .39
Depr. Exp.--Store Eqpt.      150.00       .29       600.00       .30
Insurance Expense            159.38       .31       637.53       .32
Miscellaneous Expense        120.10       .23       406.24       .20
Rent Expense                1975.00      3.80      7900.00      3.98
Office Supplies Expense      565.72      1.09       786.89       .40
Store Supplies Expense       323.20       .62       519.77       .26
Utilities Expense            504.66       .97      2786.33      1.40
Salaries Expense            9372.16     18.02     37353.66     18.82
Payroll Taxes Expense        754.46      1.45      3006.96      1.51
Credit Card Fee Expense      222.20       .43       922.71       .46
                          ---------- ----------   ---------- ----------
Total Operating Expenses   14802.10     28.45     58460.41     29.45
                          ---------- ----------   ---------- ----------
Net Income from Operations  3430.07      6.59     15419.96      7.77
                          ---------- ----------   ---------- ----------
Net Income before Income Tax 3430.07     6.59     15419.96      7.77

I n c o m e   T a x
--------------------
Federal Income Tax Exp.      330.00       .63      1320.00       .66
                          ---------- ----------   ---------- ----------
Net Income after Income Tax 3100.07      5.96     14099.96      7.10
                          ========== ==========   ========== ==========
```

T TUTORIAL 9-T

In this tutorial problem, you will process the monthly transactions, generate accounts payable checks, generate monthly statements, and complete the end-of-month processing for a corporation.

The steps below list tasks to be completed at the computer. More detailed information on how to complete the task is provided immediately following the step. If you need additional explanation for the task, a page reference is provided from the Operating Procedures of this chapter (or a previous chapter).

Transactions:

> Note: Do not key from these transaction statements, since they have already been recorded for you on the journal input forms in Figures 9.15 through 9.20. The reference numbers have been abbreviated on the input forms as follows: purchase invoice no., P; sales invoice no., S; cash receipt no., C; cash register tape, T; memorandum, M.

Apr. 02 Granted credit to New Dimension Hair Salon for merchandise returned, $65.95, against S840. CM18.

02 Purchased merchandise on account from Horner Chemicals, Inc., $4,006.72. P600.

03 Sold merchandise on account to The Cutting Edge, $6,681.16. S843.

04 Bought advertising on account from Cape Cod Press, $463.55. P601.

05 Received cash on account from Barb's Hair Design, $3,518.95, covering S836 for $3,554.49, less 1% discount, $35.54. R763.

05 Received cash on account from Philippe's, $4,842.41, covering S841 for $4,891.32, less 1% discount, $48.91. R764.

06 Paid cash on account to Amity Supply Warehouse, $847.03, covering M26 for $864.32, less 2% discount, $17.29.

06 Paid cash to East Coast Utilities Co. for electric bill, $504.66.

07 Received cash on account from Nail Care & Hair, $3,968.13, covering S842 for $4,008.21, less 1% discount, $40.08. R765.

07 Purchased merchandise on account from Peterson's Equipment Co., $5,673.21. P602.

09 Paid cash on account to Hunt & Reilly Mfg. Co., $1,464.14, covering P595 for $1,478.93, less 1% discount, $14.79.

09 Returned merchandise to Peterson's Equipment Co., $221.05, against P599. DM29.

09 Paid cash to Petals & Blooms for miscellaneous expense, $103.63.

10 Bought office supplies on account from Amity Supply Warehouse, $318.66. M27.

10 Paid cash on account to Terrace & Webster Corp., $998.54, covering P594 for $1,008.63, less 1% discount, $10.09.

11 Purchased merchandise on account from Hunt & Reilly Mfg. Co., $4,761.11. P603.

11 Sold merchandise on account to Dee Dee's Hair Studio, $6,891.23. S844.

12 Paid cash to Commissioner of Revenue for quarterly sales tax, $1,205.08.

12 Paid cash to Aquarius Insurance Co. for liability for first-quarter insurance premiums: health insurance, $2,868.41; disability insurance, $838.02; total, $3,706.43.

13 Paid cash on account to Cape Cod Press, $458.92, covering P601 for $463.55, less 1% discount, $4.63.

13 Paid cash to Internal Revenue Service for payroll taxes: employee income tax, $6,155.43; FICA tax, $1,734.85; and Medicare tax, $405.73; total, $8,296.01.

13 Paid cash to Internal Revenue Service for quarterly estimated federal income tax, $990.00.

14 Paid cash on account to Macmillan & Dillon Co., $2,499.53, covering P598 for $2,550.54, less 2% discount, $51.01.

14 Received cash on account from Dominique's, $4,057.58, covering S838 for $4,098.57, less 1% discount, $40.99. R766.

16 Bought store supplies on account from Amity Supply Warehouse, $512.10. M28.

16 Sold merchandise on account to Styles with Flair, $5,881.13. S845.

16 Paid cash on account to K&K Hair Products, Inc., $4,265.82, covering P596 for $4,308.91, less 1% discount, $43.09.

17 Purchased merchandise on account from Sheldon & Sheldon, Inc., $4,950.41. P604.

17 Sold merchandise on account to Barb's Hair Design, $6,000.08. S846.

18 Paid cash to Harris Leasing Company for monthly rent, $1,975.00.

19 Sold merchandise on account to Ann Sagretti, $98.54, plus sales tax, $3.94; total, $102.48. S847.

Note: Add Ann Sagretti to the customer list. Assign customer number 200 for Ann Sagretti so that it will be positioned immediately following Second Street Salon in the customer list.

19 Purchased merchandise on account from Macmillan & Dillon Co., $3,956.21. P605.

20 Received cash on account from New Dimension Hair Salon, $5,541.88 (covering S840, less CM18), no discount. R767.

20 Paid cash on account to Amity Supply Warehouse, $814.14, covering M27 and M28 for $830.76, less 2% discount, $16.62.

21 Paid cash on account to Hunt & Reilly Mfg. Co., $4,713.50, covering P603 for $4,761.11, less 1% discount, $47.61.

23 Paid cash to Shareholders Bank Account for first-quarter dividends declared in March, $3,000.00.

23 Bought office supplies on account from Amity Supply Warehouse, $786.43. M29.

25 Sold merchandise on account to Nail Care & Hair, $4,901.29. S848.

26 Purchased merchandise on account from Hunt & Reilly Mfg. Co., $5,010.10. P606.

26 Paid cash on account to Sheldon & Sheldon, Inc., $2,107.32, covering P597, no discount.

26 Recorded credit card fee expense for March, $222.20.

27 Paid cash on account to Macmillan & Dillon Co., $3,916.65, covering P605 for $3,956.21, less 1% discount, $39.56.

28 Purchased merchandise on account from K&K Hair Products, Inc., $3,466.63. P607.

28 Purchased merchandise on account from Terrace & Webster Corp., $4,301.30. P608.

30 Paid cash to Payroll Bank Account for monthly payroll, $5,368.04. Total payroll, $9,372.16, less deductions: employee income tax, $2,051.67; FICA tax, $581.07; Medicare tax, $135.90; health insurance premium, $956.14; disability insurance premium, $279.34.

Note: The net payroll amount of $5,368.04 is derived by subtracting the deductions from the total gross payroll. The computer automatically makes the $5,368.04 credit to Cash.

30 Recorded employer payroll taxes expense, $754.46 (FICA tax, $581.07; Medicare tax, $135.90; federal unemployment tax, $28.12; state unemployment tax, $9.37). M30. Record this transaction in the general journal.

30 Paid cash to Petty Cash Account to replenish petty cash fund, $93.20: office supplies, $35.63; store supplies, $41.10; miscellaneous expense, $16.47.

30 Recorded cash and credit card sales, $21,798.32, plus sales tax, $871.93; total, $22,670.25. T30.

Directions: The step-by-step instructions for the monthly processing cycle for Weil's Beauty Supply for the month of April for the current year are listed below.

Step 1: Bring up the accounting system. (page 16)

At the DOS prompt, key A1 (or follow the instructions provided by your instructor).

Step 2: Load the opening balances template file, AA9-T. (page 19)

Pull down the File menu and choose the Open Accounting File command. When the Open File window appears, key the path and file name for the opening balances template file, AA9-T. Push the Ok button.

Step 3: Save the data file to your drive and directory with a file name of XXX9-T (where XXX are your initials). (page 21)

Pull down the File menu and choose the Save As menu command. Key the path to the drive and directory that contains your data files (for example, if you wish to save your data to Drive B, key B: as the path name). Key a file name of XXX9-T, where XXX are your initials. Push the Ok button.

Step 4: Enter the student name in the General Information data entry window and set the run date to April 30 of the current year. (page 24)

Pull down the Options menu and choose the General Information menu command. Set the run date to April 30 of the current year. Key your name in the Student Name field.

Step 5: Key the data from the customer input form shown in Figure 9.15.

Pull down the Ledgers menu and choose the Maintain Customers menu command. Key the customer data.

FIGURE 9.15
Customers Input Form

CUSTOMERS INPUT FORM		
Run Date 04/30/--	Problem No.	9-T

Cust. No.	Customer Name
200	Ann Sagretti

Step 6: Key the data from the general journal input form shown in Figure 9.16. (page 42)

Pull down the Journal menu and choose the general journal (unless the general journal is already on the screen). Key the journal entries.

FIGURE 9.16
General Journal Input Form

| Run Date | 04/30/-- | | GENERAL JOURNAL INPUT FORM | | Problem No. | 9-T |

Date MM / dd	Reference	Account Number	Cust./ Vend No.	Debit	Credit
04/02	CM18	4130		65.95	
		1130	120		65.95
04/09	DM29	2110	310	221.05	
		5130			221.05
04/30	M30	6210		754.46	
		2150			581.07
		2160			135.90
		2170			28.12
		2180			9.37
	Totals			1041.46	1041.46

Step 7:   Key the data from the purchases journal input form shown in Figure 9.17. (page 90)

Pull down the Journal menu and choose the purchases journal. Key the journal entries.

FIGURE 9.17
Purchases Journal Input Form

| Run Date | 04/30/-- | | PURCHASES JOURNAL INPUT FORM | | | Problem No. | 9-T |

Date MM / dd	Vend. No.	Invoice No.	Invoice Amount	Acct. No.	Debit Amount	Credit Amount
04/02	360	P600	4006.72	5110	4006.72	
04/04	220	P601	463.55	6110	463.55	
04/07	310	P602	5673.21	5110	5673.21	
04/10	240	M27	318.66	1150	318.66	
04/11	320	P603	4761.11	5110	4761.11	
04/16	240	M28	512.10	1160	512.10	
04/17	330	P604	4950.41	5110	4950.41	
04/19	350	P605	3956.21	5110	3956.21	
04/23	240	M29	786.43	1150	786.43	
04/26	320	P606	5010.10	5110	5010.10	
04/28	370	P607	3466.63	5110	3466.63	
04/28	340	P608	4301.30	5110	4301.30	

Step 8:   Key the data from the cash payments journal input form shown in Figure 9.18. (page 92)

Pull down the Journal menu and choose the cash payments journal. Key the journal entries.

FIGURE 9.18

Cash Payments Journal Input Form

CASH PAYMENTS JOURNAL INPUT FORM

Run Date 04/30/--   Problem No. 9-T

Date MM / dd	Vend. No.	Check No.	Accounts Pay. Debit	Acct. No.	Debit Amount	Credit Amount
04/06	240		864.32	5120		17.29
04/06	250			6190	504.66	
04/09	320		1478.93	5120		14.79
04/09	230			6150	103.63	
04/10	340		1008.63	5120		10.09
04/12	270			2120	1205.08	
04/12	280			2190	2868.41	
				2200	838.02	
04/13	220		463.55	5120		4.63
04/13	290			2130	6155.43	
				2150	1734.85	
				2160	405.73	
04/13	290			2140	990.00	
04/14	350		2550.54	5120		51.01
04/16	370		4308.91	5120		43.09
04/18	210			6160	1975.00	
04/20	240		830.76	5120		16.62
04/21	320		4761.11	5120		47.61
04/23	300			2210	3000.00	
04/26	330		2107.32			
04/26				6220	222.20	
04/27	350		3956.21	5120		39.56

CASH PAYMENTS JOURNAL INPUT FORM

Run Date 04/30/--   Problem No. 9-T

Date MM / dd	Vend. No.	Check No.	Accounts Pay. Debit	Acct. No.	Debit Amount	Credit Amount
04/30	260			6200	9372.16	
				2130		2051.67
				2150		581.07
				2160		135.90
				2190		956.14
				2200		279.34
04/30	380			1150	35.63	
				1160	41.10	
				6150	16.47	

Step 9: Key the data from the sales journal input form shown in Figure 9.19. (page 124)

Pull down the Journal menu and choose the sales journal. Key the journal entries.

FIGURE 9.19
Sales Journal Input Form

			SALES JOURNAL INPUT FORM			
Run Date	04/30/--				Problem No.	9-T
Date MM / dd	Cust. No.	Invoice No.	Invoice Amount	Acct. No.	Debit Amount	Credit Amount
04/03	170	S843	6681.16	4110		6681.16
04/11	160	S844	6891.23	4110		6891.23
04/16	130	S845	5881.13	4110		5881.13
04/17	110	S846	6000.08	4110		6000.08
04/19	200	S847	102.48	4110		98.54
				2120		3.94
04/25	140	S848	4901.29	4110		4901.29

Step 10: Key the data from the cash receipts journal input form shown in Figure 9.20. (page 127)

Pull down the Journal menu and choose the cash receipts journal. Key the journal entries.

FIGURE 9.20
Cash Receipts Journal Input Form

			CASH RECEIPTS JOURNAL INPUT FORM			
Run Date	04/30/--				Problem No.	9-T
Date MM / dd	Cust. No.	Refer.	Accounts Rec. Credit	Acct. No.	Debit Amount	Credit Amount
04/05	110	R763	3554.49	4120	35.54	
04/05	150	R764	4891.32	4120	48.91	
04/07	140	R765	4008.21	4120	40.08	
04/14	180	R766	4098.57	4120	40.99	
04/20	120	R767	5541.88			
04/30		T30		4110		21798.32
				2120		871.93

Step 11: Display the journal reports. (page 129)

Pull down the Reports menu and choose the Journals command. When the Report Selection window appears, select the general journal, purchases journal, sales journal, and cash receipts journal. When the Selection Options appears, key a date range of April 1 to April 30 of the current year. The reports appear in Figures 9.21 through 9.25.

FIGURE 9.21
General Journal Report

```
                        Weil's Beauty Supply
                          General Journal
                             04/30/--
-----------------------------------------------------------------
Date   Refer.  V/C Acct. Title                    Debit    Credit
-----------------------------------------------------------------
04/02 CM18         4130  Sales Returns & Allow.    65.95
04/02 CM18     120 1130  AR/New Dimension Hair Salon        65.95

04/09 DM29     310 2110  AP/Peterson's Equipment Co. 221.05
04/09 DM29         5130  Purch. Returns & Allow.           221.05

04/30 M30          6210  Payroll Taxes Expense     754.46
04/30 M30          2150  FICA Tax Payable                  581.07
04/30 M30          2160  Medicare Tax Payable              135.90
04/30 M30          2170  Unemploy. Tax Pay.--Fed.           28.12
04/30 M30          2180  Unemploy. Tax Pay.--State           9.37
                                                 --------  --------
                         Totals                  1041.46  1041.46
                                                 ========  ========
```

FIGURE 9.22
Purchases Journal Report

```
                        Weil's Beauty Supply
                          Purchases Journal
                             04/30/--
-----------------------------------------------------------------
Date   Refer.  V/C Acct. Title                    Debit    Credit
-----------------------------------------------------------------
04/02 P600         5110  Purchases                4006.72
04/02 P600     360 2110  AP/Horner Chemicals, Inc.         4006.72

04/04 P601         6110  Advertising Expense       463.55
04/04 P601     220 2110  AP/Cape Cod Press                  463.55

04/07 P602         5110  Purchases                5673.21
04/07 P602     310 2110  AP/Peterson's Equipment Co.       5673.21

04/10 M27          1150  Supplies--Office          318.66
04/10 M27      240 2110  AP/Amity Supply Warehouse          318.66

04/11 P603         5110  Purchases                4761.11
04/11 P603     320 2110  AP/Hunt & Reilly Mfg. Co.         4761.11

04/16 M28          1160  Supplies--Store           512.10
04/16 M28      240 2110  AP/Amity Supply Warehouse          512.10
```

(continued)

FIGURE 9.22 (Continued)
Purchases Journal Report

```
    04/17  P604           5110  Purchases                   4950.41
    04/17  P604      330  2110  AP/Sheldon & Sheldon, Inc.              4950.41

    04/19  P605           5110  Purchases                   3956.21
    04/19  P605      350  2110  AP/Macmillan & Dillon Co.               3956.21

    04/23  M29            1150  Supplies--Office             786.43
    04/23  M29       240  2110  AP/Amity Supply Warehouse                786.43

    04/26  P606           5110  Purchases                   5010.10
    04/26  P606      320  2110  AP/Hunt & Reilly Mfg. Co.               5010.10

    04/28  P607           5110  Purchases                   3466.63
    04/28  P607      370  2110  AP/K&K Hair Products, Inc.              3466.63

    04/28  P608           5110  Purchases                   4301.30
    04/28  P608      340  2110  AP/Terrace & Webster Corp.             4301.30
                                                          --------- --------
                                Totals                    38206.43 38206.43
                                                          ========= ========
```

FIGURE 9.23
Cash Payments Journal Report

```
                      Weil's Beauty Supply
                      Cash Payments Journal
                            04/30/--
    -----------------------------------------------------------------
    Date   Refer.  V/C Acct. Title                 Debit      Credit
    -----------------------------------------------------------------
    04/06          240  2110  AP/Amity Supply Warehouse  864.32
    04/06               5120  Purchases Discount   .                  17.29
    04/06               1110  Cash                                   847.03

    04/06               6190  Utilities Expense         504.66
    04/06          250  1110  Cash                                   504.66

    04/09          320  2110  AP/Hunt & Reilly Mfg. Co. 1478.93
    04/09               5120  Purchases Discount                      14.79
    04/09               1110  Cash                                  1464.14

    04/09               6150  Miscellaneous Expense     103.63
    04/09          230  1110  Cash                                   103.63

    04/10          340  2110  AP/Terrace & Webster Corp. 1008.63
    04/10               5120  Purchases Discount                      10.09
    04/10               1110  Cash                                   998.54

    04/12               2120  Sales Tax Payable        1205.08
    04/12          270  1110  Cash                                  1205.08

    04/12               2190  Health Ins. Premium Pay.  2868.41
    04/12               2200  Disability Insurance Pay.  838.02
    04/12          280  1110  Cash                                  3706.43

    04/13          220  2110  AP/Cape Cod Press         463.55
    04/13               5120  Purchases Discount                       4.63
    04/13               1110  Cash                                   458.92
```

(continued)

FIGURE 9.23 (Continued)
Cash Payments Journal Report

```
   04/13          2130  Employee Income Tax Pay.  6155.43
   04/13          2150  FICA Tax Payable          1734.85
   04/13          2160  Medicare Tax Payable       405.73
   04/13     290  1110  Cash                                 8296.01

   04/13          2140  Federal Income Tax Pay.    990.00
   04/13     290  1110  Cash                                  990.00

   04/14     350  2110  AP/Macmillan & Dillon Co.  2550.54
   04/14          5120  Purchases Discount                     51.01
   04/14          1110  Cash                                 2499.53

   04/16     370  2110  AP/K&K Hair Products, Inc.  4308.91
   04/16          5120  Purchases Discount                     43.09
   04/16          1110  Cash                                 4265.82

   04/18          6160  Rent Expense              1975.00
   04/18     210  1110  Cash                                 1975.00

   04/20     240  2110  AP/Amity Supply Warehouse  830.76
   04/20          5120  Purchases Discount                     16.62
   04/20          1110  Cash                                  814.14

   04/21     320  2110  AP/Hunt & Reilly Mfg. Co.  4761.11
   04/21          5120  Purchases Discount                     47.61
   04/21          1110  Cash                                 4713.50

   04/23          2210  Dividends Payable         3000.00
   04/23     300  1110  Cash                                 3000.00

   04/26     330  2110  AP/Sheldon & Sheldon, Inc. 2107.32
   04/26          1110  Cash                                 2107.32

   04/26          6220  Credit Card Fee Expense    222.20
   04/26          1110  Cash                                  222.20

   04/27     350  2110  AP/Macmillan & Dillon Co.  3956.21
   04/27          5120  Purchases Discount                     39.56
   04/27          1110  Cash                                 3916.65

   04/30          6200  Salaries Expense          9372.16
   04/30          2130  Employee Income Tax Pay.             2051.67
   04/30          2150  FICA Tax Payable                      581.07
   04/30          2160  Medicare Tax Payable                  135.90
   04/30          2190  Health Ins. Premium Pay.              956.14
   04/30          2200  Disability Insurance Pay.             279.34
   04/30     260  1110  Cash                                 5368.04

   04/30          1150  Supplies--Office            35.63
   04/30          1160  Supplies--Store             41.10
   04/30          6150  Miscellaneous Expense       16.47
   04/30     380  1110  Cash                                   93.20
                                                  --------  --------
                        Totals                    51798.65  51798.65
                                                  ========  ========
```

Note: Notice that the Refer. column of the cash payments journal is blank in this example. This is because the check numbers are assigned as the checks are generated. If you have previously displayed the checks, the reference column will show the check number.

FIGURE 9.24
Sales Journal Report

```
                          Weil's Beauty Supply
                             Sales Journal
                               04/30/--
     -----------------------------------------------------------------
     Date   Refer.  V/C Acct. Title                    Debit   Credit
     -----------------------------------------------------------------
     04/03  S843   170 1130  AR/The Cutting Edge      6681.16
     04/03  S843       4110  Sales                             6681.16

     04/11  S844   160 1130  AR/Dee Dee's Hair Studio 6891.23
     04/11  S844       4110  Sales                             6891.23

     04/16  S845   130 1130  AR/Styles with Flair     5881.13
     04/16  S845       4110  Sales                             5881.13

     04/17  S846   110 1130  AR/Barb's Hair Design    6000.08
     04/17  S846       4110  Sales                             6000.08

     04/19  S847   200 1130  AR/Ann Sagretti           102.48
     04/19  S847       4110  Sales                               98.54
     04/19  S847       2120  Sales Tax Payable                    3.94

     04/25  S848   140 1130  AR/Nail Care & Hair      4901.29
     04/25  S848       4110  Sales                             4901.29
                                                     --------  --------
                          Totals                     30457.37 30457.37
                                                     ========  ========
```

FIGURE 9.25
Cash Receipts Journal Report

```
                          Weil's Beauty Supply
                          Cash Receipts Journal
                               04/30/--
     -----------------------------------------------------------------
     Date   Refer.  V/C Acct. Title                    Debit   Credit
     -----------------------------------------------------------------
     04/05  R763       1110  Cash                     3518.95
     04/05  R763       4120  Sales Discount             35.54
     04/05  R763   110 1130  AR/Barb's Hair Design             3554.49

     04/05  R764       1110  Cash                     4842.41
     04/05  R764       4120  Sales Discount             48.91
     04/05  R764   150 1130  AR/Philippe's                     4891.32

     04/07  R765       1110  Cash                     3968.13
     04/07  R765       4120  Sales Discount             40.08
     04/07  R765   140 1130  AR/Nail Care & Hair               4008.21

     04/14  R766       1110  Cash                     4057.58
     04/14  R766       4120  Sales Discount             40.99
     04/14  R766   180 1130  AR/Dominique's                    4098.57

     04/20  R767       1110  Cash                     5541.88
     04/20  R767   120 1130  AR/New Dimension Hair Salon       5541.88

     04/30  T30        1110  Cash                    22670.25
     04/30  T30        4110  Sales                            21798.32
     04/30  T30        2120  Sales Tax Payable                  871.93
                                                     --------- --------
                          Totals                     44764.72 44764.72
                                                     ========= ========
```

If you have a printer attached to your computer, you may wish to print the trial balance report so that it can be used as the basis for recording the adjusting entries.

Step 12: Display a trial balance, a schedule of accounts payable, and a schedule of accounts receivable. (pages 99-102)

Pull down the Reports menu and choose the Ledgers command. When the Report Selection window appears, select the trial balance, schedule of accounts payable, and schedule of accounts receivable reports. The reports are shown in Figures 9.26 through 9.28.

FIGURE 9.26
Trial Balance

```
                    Weil's Beauty Supply
                       Trial Balance
                         04/30/--
-----------------------------------------------------------------
Acct.   Account
Number  Title                          Debit            Credit
-----------------------------------------------------------------
1110    Cash                          10693.44
1120    Petty Cash                      100.00
1130    Accounts Receivable          45855.22
1140    Merchandise Inventory        59828.16
1150    Supplies--Office              2115.72
1160    Supplies--Store               1173.20
1170    Prepaid Insurance             1100.00
1510    Office Equipment             13575.00
1520    Accum. Depr.--Ofc. Eqpt.                        2300.00
1530    Store Equipment               8775.00
1540    Accum. Depr.--Store Eqpt.                       1800.00
2110    Accounts Payable                               32855.28
2120    Sales Tax Payable                                875.87
2130    Employee Income Tax Pay.                        2051.67
2150    FICA Tax Payable                                1162.14
2160    Medicare Tax Payable                             271.80
2170    Unemploy. Tax Pay.--Fed.                         112.06
2180    Unemploy. Tax Pay.--State                         37.35
2190    Health Ins. Premium Pay.                         956.14
2200    Disability Insurance Pay.                        279.34
3110    Capital Stock                                  70500.00
3120    Retained Earnings                              19066.00
3130    Dividends                     3000.00
3140    Income Summary                 887.37
4110    Sales                                         202886.94
4120    Sales Discount                1719.49
4130    Sales Returns & Allow.        2653.75
5110    Purchases                   129807.57
5120    Purchases Discount                              1727.97
5130    Purch. Returns & Allow.                         2461.80
6110    Advertising Expense           2773.65
6120    Depr. Exp.--Office Eqpt.       575.00
6130    Depr. Exp.--Store Eqpt.        450.00
6140    Insurance Expense              478.15
6150    Miscellaneous Expense          406.24
6160    Rent Expense                  7900.00
6170    Office Supplies Expense        221.17
6180    Store Supplies Expense         196.57
6190    Utilities Expense             2786.33
6200    Salaries Expense             37353.66
6210    Payroll Taxes Expense         3006.96
6220    Credit Card Fee Expense        922.71
9110    Federal Income Tax Exp.        990.00
                                   ----------        ----------
        Totals                     339344.36         339344.36
                                   ==========        ==========
```

FIGURE 9.27
Schedule of Accounts Payable

```
                    Weil's Beauty Supply
                  Schedule of Accounts Payable
                          04/30/--
        ----------------------------------------------------
        Account
        Number    Name                         Balance
        ----------------------------------------------------
        240       Amity Supply Warehouse         786.43
        310       Peterson's Equipment Co.      8460.48
        320       Hunt & Reilly Mfg. Co.        5010.10
        330       Sheldon & Sheldon, Inc.       4950.41
        340       Terrace & Webster Corp.       4301.30
        360       Horner Chemicals, Inc.        5879.93
        370       K&K Hair Products, Inc.       3466.63
                                              ----------
                  Total                        32855.28
```

FIGURE 9.28
Schedule of Accounts Receivable

```
                    Weil's Beauty Supply
                Schedule of Accounts Receivable
                          04/30/--
        ----------------------------------------------------
        Account
        Number    Name                         Balance
        ----------------------------------------------------
        110       Barb's Hair Design            6000.08
        130       Styles with Flair             9082.48
        140       Nail Care & Hair              4901.29
        160       Dee Dee's Hair Studio         9592.97
        170       The Cutting Edge             12768.40
        190       Second Street Salon           3407.52
        200       Ann Sagretti                   102.48
                                              ----------
                  Total                        45855.22
                                              ==========
```

Step 13:   Display the checks and statements. (page 220)

Pull down the Reports menu and choose the Checks/Statements menu command. When the Report Selection window appears, select checks and statements. When the Checks Selection Options window shown in Figure 9.29 appears, verify that the date range is set to April 1 through April 30 of the current year. Key a beginning check number of 1326. When the Statements Seletion Options window illustrated in Figure 9.30 appears, verify that the customer range is set to the full range of customers and push the Ok button. The first check and the first statement are shown in Figure 9.31 as examples.

FIGURE 9.29
Selection Options (Checks)

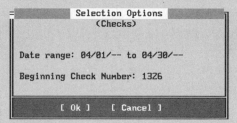

FIGURE 9.30
Selection Options (Statements)

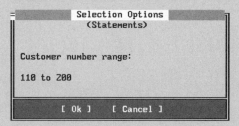

FIGURE 9.31
First Check and First Statement

```
  ●                                                                              ●
  ●     Weil's Beauty Supply            Date 04/30/--        Check No. 1326      ●
  ●     Gross Amount.............    1975.00                                     ●
  ●     Discounts/Credits........                                                ●
  ●     Net Amount Paid..........    1975.00                                     ●
  ●     ---------------------------------------------------------------------    ●
  ●                         National State Bank                                  ●
  ●                           DownTown Office                                    ●
  ●                     Anycity, State    12345-1234                             ●
  ●        Weil's Beauty Supply                         Check No. 1326           ●
  ●                                           Date               Amount          ●
  ●     PAY                                                                      ●
  ●     TO THE                                                                   ●
  ●     ORDER    Harris Leasing Company         04/30/--             1975.00     ●
  ●     OF                                                                       ●
  ●                                         _____     ●
  ●                                                                              ●
  ●     ===================================================================     ●
  ●     Weil's Beauty Supply    S T A T E M E N T    Date 04/30/--               ●
  ●     Barb's Hair Design                            Customer No. 110           ●
  ●     ---------------------------------------------------------------------    ●
  ●      Date    Ref.    Description       Charges    Credits    Balance         ●
  ●     ---------------------------------------------------------------------    ●
  ●     04/01/--         Balance Forward                         3554.49         ●
  ●     04/05/-- R763    Payment                      3554.49                    ●
  ●     04/17/-- S846    Invoice          6000.08                6000.08         ●
  ●                                                                              ●
```

Step 14: Key the adjusting entries from the general journal input form shown in Figure 9.32. (page 42)

Pull down the Journal menu and choose the general journal option (unless the general journal is already on the screen). Key the adjusting entries.

Adjustment Data: The adjustment data for the month of April for Weil's Beauty Supply is listed below.

```
Merchandise inventory...................... $61,700.00
Office supplies inventory..................    1,550.00
Store supplies inventory...................      850.00
Value of insurance policies on April 30....      940.62
Depreciation for the month:
  Office equipment...........................      191.67
  Store equipment............................      150.00
Estimated federal income tax...............      330.00
```

The adjusting entries have been recorded for you and are illustrated in Figure 9.32.

FIGURE 9.32
Adjusting Entries

Run Date 04/30/--	GENERAL JOURNAL INPUT FORM		Problem No. 9-T		
Date MM / dd	Reference	Account Number	Cust./ Vend No.	Debit	Credit
04/30	ADJ.ENT.	1140		1871.84	
		3140			1871.84
		6170		565.72	
		1150			565.72
		6180		323.20	
		1160			323.20
		6140		159.38	
		1170			159.38
		6120		191.67	
		1520			191.67
		6130		150.00	
		1540			150.00
		9110		330.00	
		2140			330.00
Totals				3591.81	3591.81

Step 15: Display the adjusting entries. (page 45)

Pull down the Reports menu and choose the Journals command. When the Report Selection window appears, select the general journal report. When the Selection Options window appears, key a date range of February 28 to February 28 (of the current year) and a reference restriction of ADJ.ENT. so that only the adjusting entries are reported. The report appears in Figure 9.33.

FIGURE 9.33
General Journal Report (Adjusting Entries)

```
                              Weil's Beauty Supply
                                 General Journal
                                   04/30/--
          ---------------------------------------------------------------
          Date   Refer.    V/C Acct. Title                   Debit    Credit
          ---------------------------------------------------------------
          04/30  ADJ.ENT.    1140  Merchandise Inventory    1871.84
          04/30  ADJ.ENT.    3140  Income Summary                     1871.84

          04/30  ADJ.ENT.    6170  Office Supplies Expense   565.72
          04/30  ADJ.ENT.    1150  Supplies--Office                    565.72

          04/30  ADJ.ENT.    6180  Store Supplies Expense    323.20
          04/30  ADJ.ENT.    1160  Supplies--Store                     323.20

          04/30  ADJ.ENT.    6140  Insurance Expense         159.38
          04/30  ADJ.ENT.    1170  Prepaid Insurance                   159.38

          04/30  ADJ.ENT.    6120  Depr. Exp.--Office Eqpt.  191.67
          04/30  ADJ.ENT.    1520  Accum. Depr.--Ofc. Eqpt.            191.67

          04/30  ADJ.ENT.    6130  Depr. Exp.--Store Eqpt.   150.00
          04/30  ADJ.ENT.    1540  Accum. Depr.--Store Eqpt.           150.00

          04/30  ADJ.ENT.    9110  Federal Income Tax Exp.   330.00
          04/30  ADJ.ENT.    2140  Federal Income Tax Pay.             330.00
                                                            --------  -------
                                   Totals                   3591.81  3591.81
                                                            ========  =======
```

Step 16: Display a general ledger report for the cash account.

Pull down the Reports menu and choose the Ledgers command. When the Report Selection window appears, select the general ledger report. When the Selection Options window appears, key an account number range of 1110 to 1110 (cash account only). The report is shown in Figure 9.34.

Step 17: Display the financial statements. (page 60)

Pull down the Reports menu and choose the Financial Statements menu command. When the Report Selection window appears, select all three financial statements. The reports are shown in Figure 9.35.

FIGURE 9.34
General Ledger Report

```
                    Weil's Beauty Supply
                      General Ledger
                        04/30/--
------------------------------------------------------------------
Account      Journal   Date  Refer.     Debit    Credit    Balance
------------------------------------------------------------------
1110-Cash
             Bal. Fwd.                                     13644.08
             Cash Rcpt 04/05 R763     3518.95             17163.03
             Cash Rcpt 04/05 R764     4842.41             22005.44
             Cash Pymt 04/06 C1329               847.03   21158.41
             Cash Pymt 04/06 C1330               504.66   20653.75
             Cash Rcpt 04/07 R765     3968.13             24621.88
             Cash Pymt 04/09 C1336              1464.14   23157.74
             Cash Pymt 04/09 C1328               103.63   23054.11
             Cash Pymt 04/10 C1338               998.54   22055.57
             Cash Pymt 04/12 C1332              1205.08   20850.49
             Cash Pymt 04/12 C1333              3706.43   17144.06
             Cash Pymt 04/13 C1327               458.92   16685.14
             Cash Pymt 04/13 C1334              8296.01    8389.13
             Cash Pymt 04/13 C1334               990.00    7399.13
             Cash Pymt 04/14 C1339              2499.53    4899.60
             Cash Rcpt 04/14 R766     4057.58              8957.18
             Cash Pymt 04/16 C1340              4265.82    4691.36
             Cash Pymt 04/18 C1326              1975.00    2716.36
             Cash Pymt 04/20 C1329               814.14    1902.22
             Cash Rcpt 04/20 R767     5541.88              7444.10
             Cash Pymt 04/21 C1336              4713.50    2730.60
             Cash Pymt 04/23 C1335              3000.00     269.40
             Cash Pymt 04/26 C1337              2107.32    2376.72
             Cash Pymt 04/26                     222.20    2598.92
             Cash Pymt 04/27 C1339              3916.65    6515.57
             Cash Rcpt 04/30 T30     22670.25             16154.68
             Cash Pymt 04/30 C1331              5368.04   10786.64
             Cash Pymt 04/30 C1341                93.20   10693.44
```

FIGURE 9.35
Financial Statements

```
                    Weil's Beauty Supply
                      Income Statement
                   For Period Ended 04/30/--
----------------------------------------------------------------------
                       *****Monthly*****      *****Yearly******
                       Amount    Percent      Amount    Percent
----------------------------------------------------------------------
O p e r a t i n g   R e v e n u e
----------------------------------------
Sales                  52251.75   100.45    202886.94    102.20
Sales Discount          -165.52    -.32      -1719.49     -.87
Sales Returns & Allow.   -65.95    -.13      -2653.75    -1.34
                       ---------- ----------  ---------- ----------
Total Operating Revenue 52020.28  100.00    198513.70    100.00

C o s t   o f   M e r c h a n d i s e   S o l d
---------------------------------------------------
Beginning Inventory     59828.16  115.01     60715.53    30.59
Purchases               36125.69   69.45    129807.57    65.39
Purchases Discount       -244.69    -.47      -1727.97     -.87
Purch. Returns & Allow.  -221.05    -.42      -2461.80    -1.24
                       ---------- ----------  ---------- ----------
Merchandise Available for Sale
                        95488.11  183.56    186333.33    93.86
Less Ending Inventory  -61700.00  -118.61   -61700.00   -31.08
                       ---------- ----------  ---------- ----------
```

(continued)

FIGURE 9.35 (Continued)
Financial Statements

```
Cost of Merchandise Sold        33788.11     64.95   124633.33     62.78
                               ----------   ------   ---------   --------
Gross Profit                    18232.17     35.05    73880.37     37.22

O p e r a t i n g   E x p e n s e s
-----------------------------------
Advertising Expense               463.55       .89     2773.65      1.40
Depr. Exp.--Office Eqpt.          191.67       .37      766.67       .39
Depr. Exp.--Store Eqpt.           150.00       .29      600.00       .30
Insurance Expense                 159.38       .31      637.53       .32
Miscellaneous Expense             120.10       .23      406.24       .20
Rent Expense                     1975.00      3.80     7900.00      3.98
Office Supplies Expense           565.72      1.09      786.89       .40
Store Supplies Expense            323.20       .62      519.77       .26
Utilities Expense                 504.66       .97     2786.33      1.40
Salaries Expense                 9372.16     18.02    37353.66     18.82
Payroll Taxes Expense             754.46      1.45     3006.96      1.51
Credit Card Fee Expense           222.20       .43      922.71       .46
                               ----------   ------   ---------   --------
Total Operating Expenses        14802.10     28.45    58460.41     29.45
                               ----------   ------   ---------   --------
Net Income from Operations       3430.07      6.59    15419.96      7.77
                               ----------   ------   ---------   --------
Net Income before Income Tax     3430.07      6.59    15419.96      7.77

I n c o m e   T a x
-------------------
Federal Income Tax Exp.           330.00       .63     1320.00       .66
                               ----------   ------   ---------   --------
Net Income after Income Tax      3100.07      5.96    14099.96      7.10
                               ==========   ======   =========   ========
```

```
                      Weil's Beauty Supply
                         Balance Sheet
                           04/30/--

A s s e t s
-----------
Cash                                10693.44
Petty Cash                            100.00
Accounts Receivable                 45855.22
Merchandise Inventory               61700.00
Supplies--Office                     1550.00
Supplies--Store                       850.00
Prepaid Insurance                     940.62
Office Equipment                    13575.00
Accum. Depr.--Ofc. Eqpt.            -2491.67
Store Equipment                      8775.00
Accum. Depr.--Store Eqpt.           -1950.00
                                   ----------
Total Assets                                   139597.61
                                               ==========
L i a b i l i t i e s
---------------------
Accounts Payable                    32855.28
Sales Tax Payable                     875.87
Employee Income Tax Pay.             2051.67
Federal Income Tax Pay.               330.00
FICA Tax Payable                     1162.14
Medicare Tax Payable                  271.80
Unemploy. Tax Pay.--Fed.              112.06
Unemploy. Tax Pay.--State              37.35
Health Ins. Premium Pay.              956.14
Disability Insurance Pay.             279.34
                                   ----------
Total Liabilities                               38931.65
```

(continued)

FIGURE 9.35 (Continued)
Financial Statements

```
   S t o c k h o l d e r s '   E q u i t y
   ----------------------------------------
   Capital Stock                    70500.00
   Retained Earnings                19066.00
   Dividends                        -3000.00
   Net Income                       14099.96
                                   ----------
   Total Stockholders' Equity                100665.96
                                             ----------
   Total Liabilities & Equity                139597.61
                                             ==========

                      Weil's Beauty Supply
                   Retained Earnings Statement
                    For Period Ended 04/30/--

   Retained Earnings (Beg. of Period)        19066.00
   Dividends                                 -3000.00
   Net Incpme                                14099.96
                                            ----------
   Retained Earnings (End of Period)         30165.96
                                            ==========
```

Step 18: Use the Save menu command to save your data. (page 20)

Pull down the File menu and choose the Save menu command to save your file to disk.

Step 19: End the session. (page 22)

Choose the Quit command from the File menu.

CHAPTER 9 STUDENT EXERCISE

I. TRUE/FALSE

Directions: Answer the following questions in the working papers or on a separate sheet of paper. If the statement is true, write the question number followed by T. If the statement is false, write the question number followed by F.

1. A partnership is an organization that exists separately from its owners.
2. A corporation has many of the legal rights of a person.
3. A corporation is typically owned by many people.
4. The ownership of a corporation is divided into units referred to as shares of stock.
5. The owners' equity in a corporation is called retained earnings.
6. Owners of the corporation are called shareholders.
7. Shareholders may withdraw assets from the corporation.
8. Earnings distributed to shareholders are called dividends.
9. Earnings that are not distributed are called capital stock.
10. Corporations must pay income tax on their earnings.

II. QUESTIONS

Directions: Write the answers to the following questions in the working papers or on a separate sheet of paper. For the following questions, assume that the accounts payable checks and customer statements are being prepared by the computer.

1. Why is the Check No. field left blank on the cash payments journal input form?
2. What happens if you leave the Vendor No. field blank for a direct cash payment?
3. What is the decision by the board of directors of a corporation to distribute earnings to shareholders called?
4. Why is the check to pay dividends written to Shareholders Bank Account?
5. Which account is debited and which account is credited to record the adjusting entry for corporate income tax?
6. The income statement illustrated in this chapter has a percent column next to the monthly amount column and another percent column next to the yearly amount column. What do these percents represent?

PRACTICE PROBLEM 9-P

In this problem, you will process the monthly transactions, generate accounts payable checks, generate accounts receivable monthly statements, and complete the end-of-month processing for Weil's Beauty Supply for the month of May of the current year.

Directions: The step-by-step instructions for solving this practice problem are listed below.

Step 1: Remove the input forms from the working papers. Record the following transactions for Weil's Beauty Supply. Abbreviate the reference numbers on the input forms as follows: purchase invoice no., P; sales invoice no., S; cash receipt no., C; cash register tape, T; memorandum, M. As you complete the problem, refer to the chart of accounts, vendor list, and customer list shown below.

```
            Weil's Beauty Supply
             Chart of Accounts
                05/01/--
        -----------------------------------
        Account   Account
        Number    Title
        -----------------------------------
        1110      Cash
        1120      Petty Cash
        1130      Accounts Receivable
        1140      Merchandise Inventory
        1150      Supplies--Office
        1160      Supplies--Store
        1170      Prepaid Insurance
        1510      Office Equipment
        1520      Accum. Depr.--Ofc. Eqpt.
        1530      Store Equipment
        1540      Accum. Depr.--Store Eqpt.
        2110      Accounts Payable
        2120      Sales Tax Payable
        2130      Employee Income Tax Pay.
        2140      Federal Income Tax Pay.
        2150      FICA Tax Payable
        2160      Medicare Tax Payable
```

(continued)

```
2170   Unemploy. Tax Pay.--Fed.
2180   Unemploy. Tax Pay.--State
2190   Health Ins. Premium Pay.
2200   Disability Insurance Pay.
2210   Dividends Payable
3110   Capital Stock
3120   Retained Earnings
3130   Dividends
3140   Income Summary
4110   Sales
4120   Sales Discount
4130   Sales Returns & Allow.
5110   Purchases
5120   Purchases Discount
5130   Purch. Returns & Allow.
6110   Advertising Expense
6120   Depr. Exp.--Office Eqpt.
6130   Depr. Exp.--Store Eqpt.
6140   Insurance Expense
6150   Miscellaneous Expense
6160   Rent Expense
6170   Office Supplies Expense
6180   Store Supplies Expense
6190   Utilities Expense
6200   Salaries Expense
6210   Payroll Taxes Expense
6220   Credit Card Fee Expense
9110   Federal Income Tax Exp.
```

```
           Weil's Beauty Supply
              Vendor List
               05/01/--
---------------------------------------
Vendor    Vendor
Number    Name
---------------------------------------
210       Harris Leasing Company
220       Cape Cod Press
230       Petals & Blooms
240       Amity Supply Warehouse
250       East Coast Utilities Co.
260       Payroll Bank Account
270       Commissioner of Revenue
280       Aquarius Insurance Co.
290       Internal Revenue Service
300       Shareholders Bank Account
310       Peterson's Equipment Co.
320       Hunt & Reilly Mfg. Co.
330       Sheldon & Sheldon, Inc.
340       Terrace & Webster Corp.
350       Macmillan & Dillon Co.
360       Horner Chemicals, Inc.
370       K&K Hair Products, Inc.
380       Petty Cash Account
```

```
           Weil's Beauty Supply
              Customer List
               05/01/--
---------------------------------------
Customer  Customer
Number    Name
---------------------------------------
110       Barb's Hair Design
120       New Dimension Hair Salon
130       Styles with Flair
140       Nail Care & Hair
150       Philippe's
160       Dee Dee's Hair Studio
170       The Cutting Edge
180       Dominique's
190       Second Street Salon
200       Ann Sagretti
```

May 01 Received cash on account from Nail Care & Hair, $4,852.28, covering S848 for $4,901.29, less 1% discount, $49.01. R768.

01 Purchased merchandise on account from Macmillan & Dillon Co., $5,099.80. P609.

02 Received cash on account from Ann Sagretti, $102.48, no discount. R769.

03 Paid cash on account to Hunt & Reilly Mfg. Co., $4,960.00, covering P606 for $5,010.10, less 1% discount, $50.10.

03 Received cash on account from Styles with Flair, $9,082.48, covering S839 and S845, no discount. R770.

04 Purchased merchandise on account from Terrace & Webster Corp., $6,825.14. P610.

05 Paid cash on account to K&K Hair Products, Inc., $3,431.96, covering P607 for $3,466.63, less 1% discount, $34.67.

07 Bought office equipment on account from Peterson's Equipment Co., $2,563.13. P611.

08 Paid cash on account to Terrace & Webster Corp., $4,258.29, covering P608 for $4,301.30, less 1% discount, $43.01.

08 Paid cash to East Coast Utilities Co. for electric bill, $482.30.

09 Returned merchandise to Horner Chemicals, Inc., $1,566.40, against P600. DM30.

10 Paid cash on account to Macmillan & Dillon Co. $4,997.80, covering P609 for $5,099.80, less 2% discount, $102.00.

11 Purchased merchandise on account from Hunt & Reilly Mfg. Co., $6,114.77. P612.

12 Paid cash to Aquarius Insurance Co. for liability insurance, $476.90.

12 Paid cash on account to Terrace & Webster Corp., $6,756.89, covering P610 for $6,825.14, less 1% discount, $68.25.

14 Sold merchandise on account to Dominique's, $3,203.33. S849.

15 Received cash on account from The Cutting Edge, $12,768.40, covering S834 and S843, no discount. R771.

16 Granted credit to Barb's Hair Design for merchandise returned, $2,560.29, against S846. CM19.

17 Paid cash on account to Peterson's Equipment Co., $2,787.27 (covering P599, less DM29).

18 Purchased merchandise on account from Macmillan & Dillon Co., $4,828.07. P613.

19 Sold merchandise on account to Philippe's, $2,116.38. S850.

19 Paid cash to Harris Leasing Company for monthly rent, $1,975.00.

21 Paid cash on account to Hunt & Reilly Mfg. Co., $6,053.62, covering P611 for $6,114.77, less 1% discount, $61.15.

22 Bought office supplies on account from Amity Supply Warehouse, $91.76. M31.

23 Received cash on account from Dominique's, $3,171.30, covering S849 for $3,203.33, less 1% discount, $32.03. R772.

24 Bought store supplies on account from Amity Supply Warehouse, $206.70. M32.

25 Sold merchandise on account to Ann Sagretti, $72.21, plus sales tax, $2.89; total, $75.10. S851.

26 Paid cash on account to Macmillan & Dillon Co., $4,731.51, covering P612 for $4,828.07, less 2% discount, $96.56.

26 Received cash on account from Philippe's, $2,095.22 covering S850 for $2,116.38, less 1% discount, $21.16. R773.

28 Sold merchandise on account to New Dimension Hair Salon, $8,629.83. S852.

28 Recorded credit card fee expense for April, $467.25.

29 Sold merchandise on account to Styles with Flair, $6,221.10. S853.

30 Paid cash on account to Horner Chemicals, Inc., $1,873.21, no discount.

30 Purchased merchandise on account from K&K Hair Products, Inc., $8,651.33. P614.

31 Sold merchandise on account to The Cutting Edge, $5,999.07. S854.

31 Paid cash to Payroll Bank Account for monthly payroll, $4,835.04. Total payroll, $8,629.03, less deductions: employee income tax, $1,898.39; FICA tax, $535.00; Medicare tax, $125.12; health insurance premium, $956.14; disability insurance premium, $279.34.

31 Recorded employee payroll taxes expense, $694.64 (FICA tax, $535.00; Medicare tax, $125.12; federal unemployment tax, $25.89; state unemployment tax, $8.63). M33. Record this transaction in the general journal.

31 Paid cash to Petty Cash Account to replenish petty cash fund, $81.33: office supplies, $5.96; store supplies, $22.98; miscellaneous expense, $52.39.

31 Recorded cash and credit card sales, $21,889.06, plus sales tax, $515.96; total, $22,405.02. T31.

Step 2: Bring up the accounting system.

Step 3: Load the opening balances template file for AA9-P.

Step 4: Use the Save As menu command to save the opening balances file to your drive and directory with a file name of XXX9-P, where XXX are your initials.

Step 5: Set the run date to May 31 of the current year and key your name into the Student Name field.

Step 6: Key the data from the input forms prepared in Step 1.

Step 7: Display the journal reports (general, purchases, cash payments, sales, and cash receipts) for the month of may of the current year. If any errors are detected, use the List button on the relevant journal data entry window to select the journal entry to correct.

Step 8: Display a trial balance, schedule of accounts payable, and schedule of accounts receivable.

Step 9: Display checks and statements. Use a beginning check number of 1342.

Adjustment Data: The adjustment data for the month of May for Weil's Beauty Supply is listed below.

```
Merchandise inventory ...................... $62,700.00
Office supplies inventory .................       750.00
Store supplies inventory ...................       700.00
Value of insurance policies on May 31 .......    1,000.00
Depreciation for the month:
  Office equipment .........................       245.00
  Store equipment ..........................       150.00
Estimated federal income tax ...............       330.00
```

Step 10: Record the adjusting entries on a general journal input form. Use a reference of "ADJ.ENT.,"

Step 11: Key the adjusting entries.

Step 12: Display the general journal report for the adjusting entries. Use a reference restriction of "ADJ.ENT.," so that only adjusting entries will be included in the report.

Step 13: Display a general ledger report for the cash account.

Step 14: Display the financial statements.

Step 15: Save your data.

Step 16: End the session.

AUDIT TEST PROBLEM 9-P

Directions: Write the answers to the following questions in the working papers or on a separate sheet of paper.

JOURNALS

1. What is the amount of the debit to payroll taxes expense?
2. What is the amount of purchase invoice no. 609 to Macmillan & Dillon Co.?
3. What is the total of the debit column in the cash payments journal?
4. What is the amount of sales invoice no. 853 to Styles with Flair?
5. What is the total of the credit column in the cash receipts journal?

SCHEDULES OF ACCOUNTS PAYABLE AND RECEIVABLE

6. What is the amount owed to Horner Chemicals, Inc.?
7. What is the amount due from all customers?

CHECKS AND STATEMENTS

8. What is the net amount paid for check no. 1347 to Hunt & Reilly Mfg. Co.?
9. What is the amount due from The Cutting Edge?

GENERAL LEDGER REPORT

10. What is the amount of check no. 1346?
11. What is the ending balance in the Cash account?

FINANCIAL STATEMENTS

12. What are the sales for the year?
13. What are the sales for the month?
14. What are the purchases for the year as a percentage of sales?
15. What are the total operating expenses for the month as a percentage of sales?
16. What are the total assets?
17. What is the total stockholders' equity?
18. What is the amount of retained earnings at the end of the month?

M MASTERY PROBLEM 9-M

In this problem, you will process the monthly transactions, generate accounts payable checks, generate accounts receivable monthly statements, and complete the end-of-month processing for Weil's Beauty Supply for the month of June of the current year. As you complete this problem, refer to the chart of accounts, vendor list, and customer list in Problem 9-P to locate the account numbers needed for the input forms.

Directions:

1. Record the transactions on the input forms.
2. Load the opening balances file (AA9-M).

3. Save the opening balances file to your disk or directory (XXX9-M).

4. Set the run date to June 30 of the current year.

5. Key the transactions.

6. Display the journal reports.

7. Display the trial balance, schedule of accounts payable, and schedule of accounts receivable.

8. Display checks and statements. Use a beginning check number of 1350.

9. Display a general ledger report for the cash account.

10. Record the adjusting entries on the general journal input form.

11. Key the adjusting entries.

12. Display the adjusting entries.

13. Display financial statements.

14. Save your data with a file name of XXX9-M.

15. End the session.

Transactions:

June 01 Received cash on account from Ann Sagretti, $75.10, no discount. R774.

02 Sold merchandise on account to Philippe's, $7,628.07. S855.

04 Granted credit to Dee Dee's Hair Studio for merchandise returned, $1,460.03, against S837. CM20.

05 Purchased merchandise on account from Hunt & Reilly Mfg. Co., $7,698.10. P615.

06 Paid cash to East Coast Utilities Co., $528.21.

07 Paid cash to Aquarius Insurance Co. for insurance premium, $925.70.

08 Received cash on account from New Dimension Hair Salon, $8,543.53, covering S852 for $8,629.83, less 1% discount, $86.30. R775.

09 Received cash on account from Styles with Flair, $6,158.89, covering S853 for $6,221.10, less 1% discount, $62.21. R776.

09 Received cash on account from The Cutting Edge, $5,939.08, covering S854 for $5,999.07, less 1% discount, $59.99. R777.

09 Paid cash on account to K&K Hair Products, Inc., $8,564.82, covering P614 for $8,651.33, less 1% discount, $86.51.

11 Purchased merchandise on account from Sheldon & Sheldon, Inc., $6,817.03. P616.

12 Paid cash to Petals & Blooms for miscellaneous expense, $141.10.

13 Bought office supplies on account from Amity Supply Warehouse, $206.33. M34.

15 Paid cash on account to Hunt & Reilly Mfg. Co., $7,621.12, covering P615 for $7,698.10, less 1% discount, $76.98.

16 Returned merchandise to Peterson's Equipment Co., $1,101.60, against P603. DM31.

18 Sold merchandise on account to Second Street Salon, $6,981.15. S856.

19 Paid cash to Harris Leasing Company for monthly rent, $1,975.00.

20 Recorded credit card fee expense for May, $496.09.

21 Paid cash on account to Sheldon & Sheldon, Inc., $6,748.86, covering P616 for $6,817.03, less 1% discount, $68.17.

21 Received cash on account from Dee Dee's Hair Studio, $1,241.71 (covering S837, less CM20), no discount. R778.

22 Sold merchandise on account to Nail Care & Hair, $7,014.16. S857.

23 Purchased merchandise on account from Terrace & Webster Corp., $7,877.16. P617.

25 Bought advertising on account from Cape Cod Press, $581.20. P618.

25 Sold merchandise on account to Ann Sagretti, $65.85, plus sales tax, $2.63; total, $68.48. S858.

26 Bought store equipment on account from Peterson's Equipment Co., $409.84. P619.

27 Paid cash on account to Horner Chemicals, Inc., $2,440.32 (covering P600, less DM30), no discount.

28 Bought store supplies on account from Amity Supply Warehouse, $199.44. M35.

30 Paid cash on account to Payroll Bank Account for monthly payroll, $4,566.42. Total payroll, $8,076.20, less deductions: employee income tax, $1,776.76; FICA tax, $500.72; Medicare tax, $117.10; health insurance premium, $881.10; disability insurance premium, $234.10.

30 Recorded employee payroll taxes expense, $650.12 (FICA tax, $500.72; Medicare tax, $117.10; federal unemployment tax, $24.22; state unemployment tax, $8.08). M36. Record this transaction in the general journal.

30 Paid cash to Petty Cash Account to replenish petty cash fund, $90.03: office supplies, $73.38; store supplies, $16.65.

30 Recorded cash and credit card sales, $18,075.39, plus sales tax, $723.02; total, $18,798.41. T30.

Adjustment Data: The adjustment data for the month of June for Weil's Beauty Supply is listed below.

Merchandise inventory	$60,750.00
Office supplies inventory	850.00
Store supplies inventory	425.00
Value of insurance policies on June 30	950.00
Depreciation for the month:	
Office equipment	245.00
Store equipment	165.00
Estimated federal income tax	330.00

AUDIT TEST PROBLEM 9-M

Directions: Write the answers to the following questions in the working papers or on a separate sheet of paper.

JOURNALS

1. What is the amount of the credit to FICA Tax Payable?
2. What is the amount of purchase invoice no. 618 to Cape Cod Press?
3. What is the total of the debit column in the cash payments journal?
4. What is the amount of sales invoice no. 856 to Second Street Salon?
5. What is the total of the credit column in the cash receipts journal?

SCHEDULES OF ACCOUNTS PAYABLE AND RECEIVABLE

6. What is the amount owed to Amity Supply Warehouse?
7. What is the amount due from all customers?

CHECKS AND STATEMENTS

8. What is the net amount paid on check no. 1355 to Hunt & Reilly Mfg. Co.?
9. What is the amount of the credit memo to Dee Dee's Hair Studio?

GENERAL LEDGER REPORT

10. What is the amount of check no. 1350?
11. What is the ending balance in the Cash account?

FINANCIAL STATEMENTS

12. What are the sales for the year?
13. What are the sales discounts for the month?
14. What are cost of merchandise sold for the year as a percentage of sales?
15. What is the advertising expense for the month as a percentage of sales?
16. What are the total assets?
17. What are the total liabilities?
18. What is the amount of retained earnings at the end of the month?

COMPREHENSIVE PROBLEM C-3

In this problem, you will process the monthly transactions for April, generate accounts payable checks, generate monthly statements, and complete the end-of-month processing for Foster & Gibbons, Inc.

Directions: The step-by-step instructions for solving this practice problem are listed below.

Step 1:

Remove the input forms from the working papers. Record the following transactions for Foster & Gibbons, Inc., on the input forms. Abbreviate the reference numbers on the input forms as follows: check no., C; memorandum, M; cash register tape, T; cash receipt no., R; sales invoice no., S; purchase invoice no., P. Refer to the chart of accounts, vendor list, and customer list shown below to locate the account numbers needed to complete the input forms.

```
                    Foster & Gibbons, Inc.
                     Chart of Accounts
                        04/01/--
-----------------------------------------------------------------
Account   Account
Number    Title
-----------------------------------------------------------------
1110      Cash
1120      Petty Cash
1130      Accounts Receivable
1140      Merchandise Inventory
1150      Supplies—Office
1160      Supplies—Store
1170      Prepaid Insurance
1510      Office Equipment
1520      Accum. Depr.—Ofc. Eqpt.
1530      Store Equipment
1540      Accum. Depr.—Store Eqpt.
2110      Accounts Payable
2120      Sales Tax Payable
2130      Employee Income Tax Pay.
2140      Federal Income Tax Pay.
2150      FICA Tax Payable
2160      Medicare Tax Payable
2170      Unemploy. Tax Pay.—Fed.
2180      Unemploy. Tax Pay.—State
2190      Health Ins. Premium Pay.
2200      Disability Insurance Pay.
2210      Dividends Payable
3110      Capital Stock
3120      Retained Earnings
3130      Dividends
3140      Income Summary
4110      Sales
4120      Sales Discount
4130      Sales Returns & Allow.
5110      Purchases
5120      Purchases Discount
5130      Purch. Returns & Allow.
6110      Advertising Expense
6120      Depr. Exp.—Office Eqpt.
6130      Depr. Exp.—Store Eqpt.
6140      Insurance Expense
6150      Miscellaneous Expense
6160      Rent Expense
6170      Office Supplies Expense
6180      Store Supplies Expense
6190      Utilities Expense
6200      Salaries Expense
```

(continued)

```
    6210      Payroll Taxes Expense
    6220      Credit Card Expense
    9110      Federal Income Tax Exp.
```

```
                    Foster & Gibbons, Inc.
                         Vendor List
                          04/01/--
    --------------------------------------------------------------
    Vendor    Vendor
    Number    Name
    --------------------------------------------------------------
    210       Payroll Bank Account
    220       Commissioner of Revenue
    230       Internal Revenue Service
    240       Shareholders Bank Account
    250       Petty Cash Account
    260       Northern Utilities
    270       Plogsted's Insurance Co.
    280       Simmons Leasing Co.
    290       Regent's Co.
    300       R & L Mfg., Inc.
    310       Broderick Supplies
    320       Cramer, Inc.
    330       Tress & Thomas Co.
    340       Price Manufacturing, Inc.
    350       McFarland Company
    360       Samuel & Samuel, Inc.
    370       Winstel Video Mfg., Inc.
    380       Electronic Toys
    390       Sampson's Gift Shop
```

```
                    Foster & Gibbons, Inc.
                        Customer List
                          04/01/--
    --------------------------------------------------------------
    Customer  Customer
    Number    Name
    --------------------------------------------------------------
    110       Vince's Video Games
    120       Games Galore
    130       Video World
    140       Fun Times
    150       Land of Video
    160       Video Connection
    170       Bill Phillips
    180       Bixbee's
    190       Elsbrock's Video Games
    200       Applegate Video
```

Apr. 01 Paid cash on account to Regent's Co., $33,082.12, covering P3354 for $33,416.28, less 1% discount, $334.16.

01 Purchased merchandise on account from R & L Mfg., Inc., $55,098.35. P3359.

02 Paid cash to Sampson's Gift Shop for miscellaneous expense, $328.91.

02 Received cash on account from Land of Video, $48,574.45, covering S4921 for $49,065.10, less 1% discount, $490.65. R1935.

03 Paid cash on account to Cramer, Inc., $50,114.82, covering P3355 for $50,621.03, less 1% discount, $506.21.

04 Received cash on account from Elsbrock's Video Games, $54,352.25, covering S4928 for $54,901.26, less 1% discount, $549.01. R1936.

04 Paid cash on account to R & L Mfg., Inc., $39,027.44, covering S3351 for $39,421.66, less 1% discount, $394.22.

06 Received cash on account from Video World, $38,032.95, covering S4930 for $38,417.12, less 1% discount, $384.17. R1937.

07 Purchased merchandise on account from Winstel Video Mfg., Inc., $51,118.15. P3360.

07 Paid cash on account to Broderick Supplies, $6,796.15, covering P3357, no discount.

08 Received cash on account from Video Connection, $29,819.90, covering S4926 for $30,121.11, less 1% discount, $301.21. R1938.

09 Sold merchandise on account to Fun Times, $116,309.66. S4931.

09 Paid cash on account to Samuel & Samuel, Inc., $64,110.97, covering P3356 for $65,419.36, less 2% discount, $1,308.39.

09 Returned merchandise to Tress & Thomas Co., $10,506.81, against P3350. DM115.

10 Paid cash on account to R & L Mfg., Inc., $54,647.37, covering P3359 for $55,098.35, less 1% discount, $550.98.

10 Granted credit to Applegate Video for merchandise returned, $6,920.65, against S4922. CM101.

10 Bought office supplies on account from Broderick Supplies, $1,507.10. M156.

11 Purchased merchandise on account from Tress & Thomas Co., $40,486.13. P3361.

11 Sold merchandise on account to Video Connection, $112,506.13. S4932.

13 Paid cash to Commissioner of Revenue for March sales tax, $4,679.00.

14 Purchased merchandise on account from Samuel & Samuel, Inc., $58,698.23. P3362.

15 Granted credit to Fun Times for merchandise returned, $8,006.50, against S4924. CM102.

15 Paid cash to Plogsted's Insurance Co. for liability for March insurance premiums: health insurance, $12,893.20; disablity insurance, $5,157.28; total, $18,050.48.

15 Paid cash to Internal Revenue Service for payroll taxes: employee income tax, $36,100.89; FICA tax, $10,658.36; and Medicare tax, $2,492.68; total, $49,251.93.

15 Paid cash to Internal Revenue Service for quarterly estimated federal income tax, $15,000.

16 Bought store supplies on account from Broderick Supplies,
$1,807.63. M157.

16 Sold merchandise on account to Elsbrock's Video Games,
$128,001.10. S4933.

17 Received cash on account from Applegate Video, $45,704.18
(covering S4922, less CM101), no discount. R1939.

17 Paid cash to Northern Utilities for electric bill, $1,453.06.

17 Paid cash on account to Winstel Video Mfg., Inc., $50,606.97,
covering P3360 for $51,118.15, less 1% discount, $511.18.

18 Received cash on account from Fun Times, $115,146.56, cover-
ing S4931 for $116,309.66, less 1% discount, $1,163.10. R1940.

18 Purchased merchandise on account from Cramer, Inc.,
$59,820.15. P3363.

18 Paid cash to Simmons Leasing Co. for monthly rent, $5,200.00.

18 Returned merchandise to Winstel Video Mfg., Inc., $5,111.63,
against P3352. DM116.

20 Sold merchandise on account to Bob Bagwell, $16,005.18,
plus sales tax, $800.26; total, $16,805.44. S4934.

> Note: Add Bob Bagwell to the customer list. Assign customer
> number 210 for Bob Bagwell so that it will be posi-
> tioned immediately following Dagwood's Sports Bar in
> the customer list.

20 Paid cash on account to Tress & Thomas Co., $14,561.54
(covering P3350, less DM115), no discount.

20 Purchased merchandise on account from Regent's Co.,
$40,111.01. P3364.

20 Bought advertising on account from Electronic Toys,
$4,421.64. P3365.

21 Received cash on account from Video Connection,
$111,381.07, covering S4932 for $112,506.13, less 1% discount, $1,125.06. R1941.

21 Paid cash on account to Tress & Thomas Co., $40,081.27,
covering P3361 for $40,486.13, less 1% discount, $404.86.

22 Paid cash to Shareholders Bank Account for first-quarter
dividends declared in March, $90,000.00.

22 Received cash on account from Bixbee's, $26,415.27, no dis-
count. R1942.

22 Granted credit to Vince's Video Games for merchandise
returned, $7,060.33, against S4923. CM103.

23 Bought store equipment on account from Broderick Supplies, $5,010.55. P3366.

23 Sold merchandise on account to Video World, $124,633.40. S4935.

24 Paid cash on account to Samuel & Samuel, Inc., $57,524.27, covering P3362 for $58,698.23, less 2% discount, $1,173.96.

24 Received cash on account from Fun Times, $38,980.81 (covering S4924, less CM102), no discount. R1943.

25 Bought office equipment on account from Broderick Supplies, $6,063.91. P3367.

25 Received cash on account from Elsbrock's Video Games, $126,721.09, covering S4933 for $128,001.10, less 1% discount, $1,280.01. R1944.

25 Sold merchandise on account to Bixbee's, $120,548.30. S4936.

25 Purchased merchandise on account from R & L Mfg., Inc., $75,829.66. P3368.

25 Recorded credit card fee expense for March, $604.83.

27 Received cash on account from Bill Phillips, $5,001.26, against S4929, no discount. R1945.

27 Paid cash on account to Cramer, Inc., $59,221.95, covering P3363 for $59,820.15, less 1% discount, $598.20.

27 Paid cash on account to Winstel Video Mfg., Inc., $33,081.36 (covering P3352, less DM116), no discount.

27 Returned merchandise to Price Manufacturing, Inc., $8,889.62, against P3358. DM117.

28 Purchased merchandise on account from Samuel & Samuel, Inc., $68,021.89. P3369.

28 Purchased merchandise on account from Cramer, Inc., $83,829.41. P3370.

29 Paid cash on account to Regent's Co., $39,709.90, covering P3364 for $40,111.01, less 1% discount, $401.11.

29 Sold merchandise on account to Applegate Video, $60,598.05. S4937.

29 Sold merchandise on account to Bill Phillips, $6,012.34, plus sales tax, $300.62; total, $6,312.96. S4938.

30 Paid cash to Payroll Bank Account for monthly payroll, $104,606.59. Total payroll, $171,909.00, less deductions: employee income tax, $36,100.89; FICA tax, $10,658.36; Medicare tax, $2,492.68; health insurance premium, $12,893.20; disability insurance premium, $5,157.28.

30 Recorded employer payroll taxes expense, $18,480.22 (FICA tax, $10,658.36; Medicare tax, $2,492.68; federal unemployment

tax, $687.64; state unemployment tax, $4,641.54). M158. Record this transaction in the general journal.

30 Paid cash to Petty Cash Account to replenish petty cash fund, $179.26: office supplies, $104.61; store supplies, $58.02; miscellaneous expense, $16.63.

30 Received cash on account from Bixbee's, $119,342.82, covering S4936 for $120,548.30, less 1% discount, $1,205.48. R1946.

30 Paid cash on account to Electronic Toys, $3,979.48, covering P3365 for $4,421.64, less 1% discount, $442.16.

30 Recorded cash and credit card sales, $92,506.58, plus sales tax, $4,625.33; total, $97,131.91. T30.

Step 2: Bring up the accounting system.

Step 3: Load the opening balances template file for AAC-3.

Step 4: Use the Save As menu command to save the opening balances file to your drive and directory with a file name of XXXC-3, where XXX are your initials.

Step 5: Set the run date to April 30 of the current year, and key your name into the Student Name field.

Step 6: Key the data from the input forms prepared in Step 1.

Step 7: Display the journal reports (general, purchases, cash payments, sales, and cash receipts) for the period April 1 through April 30 of the current year. If any errors are detected, use the List button on the relevant journal data entry window to select the journal entry to correct.

Step 8: Display a trial balance, schedule of accounts payable, and schedule of accounts receivable.

Step 9: Display the checks and statements (beginning check no. 5083).

Step 10: Display a general ledger report for the cash account.

Step 11: Record the adjusting entries on a general journal input form. The adjustment data are shown below. Use the trial balance generated in the previous step as the basis for making the adjusting entries. Record "ADJ.ENT." as the reference.

```
Merchandise Inventory on March 31 .......$574,000.00
Office supplies inventory .................3,500.00
Store supplies inventory .................2,500.00
Value of insurance policies ...............4,999.77
Depreciation for the period:
  Office equipment .........................2,006.67
  Store equipment ..........................1,500.00
Estimated Federal Income Tax ..............5,000.00
```

Step 12:   Key the adjusting entries.

Step 13:   Display the general journal report for the adjusting entries. Use a reference restriction of "ADJ.ENT.," so that only adjusting entries will be included on the report.

Step 14:   Display the income statement, balance sheet, and retained earnings statement.

Step 15:   Use the Save As menu command to save a backup copy of your data to disk with a file name of XXXC-3.

Step 16:   End the session.

AUDIT TEST PROBLEM C-3

Directions: Write the answers to the following questions in the working papers or on a separate sheet of paper.

JOURNALS

1. In the general journal, what is the amount of the debit to Payroll Tax Expense?
2. What is the amount of purchase invoice no. 3361 to Tress & Thomas Co.?
3. What is the total of the debit column in the cash payments journal?
4. What is the amount of sales invoice no. 4933 to Elsbrock's Video Games?
5. What is the total of the credit column in the cash receipts journal?

SCHEDULES OF ACCOUNTS PAYABLE AND RECEIVABLE

6. What is the amount owed to Cramer, Inc.?
7. What is the amount due from all customers?

CHECKS AND STATEMENTS

8. What is the net amount of check no. 5091 to Regent's Co.?
9. What is the amount of the credit memo to Applegate Video?

GENERAL LEDGER REPORT

10. What is the amount of check no. 5089?
11. What is the ending balance in the Cash account?

FINANCIAL STATEMENTS

12. What are the sales for the year?
13. What is the sales discount amount for the month?
14. What is the cost of merchandise sold for the year as a percentage of sales?
15. What is the amount of salaries expense for the month as a percentage of sales?
16. What are the total current assets?
17. What are the total liabilities?
18. What is the amount of retained earnings at the end of the month?

10

Payroll

1. Complete the payroll input forms.

2. Add, change, and delete employees from the payroll.

3. Enter and correct payroll transactions.

4. Display payroll reports.

INTRODUCTION

In a computerized payroll system, the computer stores data such as the employee's name, address, Social Security number, marital status, number of withholding allowances, pay rate, and voluntary deductions, for each employee. At the end of each pay period, all payroll transaction data, such as regular and overtime hours for each employee, are keyed into the computer. As the data is entered into the computer, the computer calculates all withholding taxes and other deductions and accumulates and updates the earnings and withholdings.

Before data for a new payroll period is entered, the payroll transaction data from the previous payroll must be cleared. After payroll transactions for the new payroll period have been entered, a payroll report may be displayed to verify the information. While processing this report, the computer calculates the totals for salary expense, payroll taxes expense, and withholding liabilities. These totals are presented in general journal format after the payroll report. If you wish, these payroll journal entries may be exported to a file and later imported into the accounting system as general journal entries. After the payroll report is displayed and verified, the payroll checks are printed.

At the end of the quarter, the quarterly report is displayed. At the end of the year, the W-2 statements of earnings and withholdings are displayed from the earnings and withholdings fields that have accumulated during the year.

▶ Employee Input Form

In this payroll system, additions, changes, and deletions to employee data are recorded on an employee input form, then keyed into the Maintain Employees data entry window. Figures 10.1 through 10.3 show examples of completed employee input forms for Water Sports, Inc. Figure 10.1 is an example of the addition of a new employee. The marital status and number of withholding allowances are being changed in the second example. An example of an employee deletion is illustrated in Figure 10.3.

Each field in the form corresponds to a data field in the Maintain Employees data entry window. Table 10.1 shows the field names and description of each field in the input form.

TABLE 10.1
Field Names and Descriptions for Employee Input Form

Field Name	Description
Employee No.	This field contains a unique number used to identify each employee.
Name	Record the last name first, and place a comma between the last and first names.
	(continued)

TABLE 10.1 (Continued)
Field Names and Descriptions for Employee Input Form

Field Name	Description
Address	This field contains the street address and is limited to 25 characters.
City/State/Zip	This field contains the employee's city, state abbreviation, and postal ZIP code.
Soc. Sec. No.	This field contains the employee's Social Security number, required for tax reporting.
Marital Status	Place an x in the parentheses next to married or single.
Pay Type	Place an x in the parentheses next to hourly or salaried.
Rate/Salary Amount	If you marked hourly in the previous field, record the hourly rate. If you marked salaried in the previous field, record the salary amount.
No. Pay Periods	Record in this field the number of times the employee is paid per year.
Withholding #	Record in this field the number of withholding allowances being claimed for tax purposes.
Voluntary Deductions	These three fields contain voluntary deductions which are withheld from the employee's pay each period, such as health insurance, union dues, and savings bonds.
Department No.	This field contains a one-digit department number identifying the department in which the employee works. The computer provides earnings totals for each department used when generating the payroll journal entries. This field may be left blank.

FIGURE 10.1
Employee Input Form (New Employee)

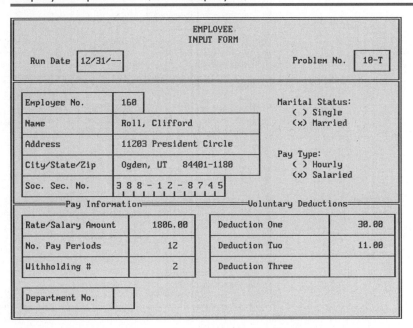

FIGURE 10.2
Employee Input Form (Changes to Employee)

```
                              EMPLOYEE
                            INPUT FORM
    Run Date  12/31/--                        Problem No.    10-T

   ┌─────────────────────────────────────────────────────────────┐
   │ Employee No.     110                    Marital Status:       │
   │                                          ( ) Single           │
   │ Name                                    (x) Married           │
   │                                                               │
   │ Address                                                       │
   │                                         Pay Type:             │
   │ City/State/Zip                           ( ) Hourly           │
   │                                          ( ) Salaried         │
   │ Soc. Sec. No.          -       -                              │
   ├═══Pay Information═══════════════════════Voluntary Deductions══│
   │ Rate/Salary Amount                 Deduction One              │
   │ No. Pay Periods                    Deduction Two              │
   │ Withholding #            2         Deduction Three            │
   │                                                               │
   │ Department No.                                                │
   └─────────────────────────────────────────────────────────────┘
```

FIGURE 10.3
Employee Input Form (Deletion)

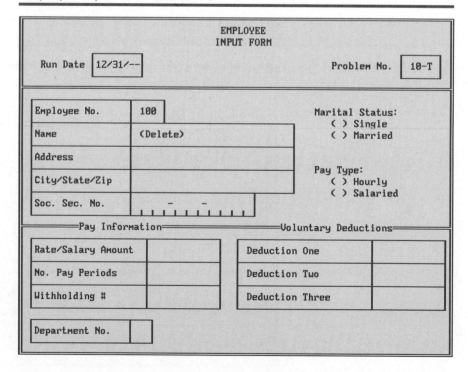

```
                              EMPLOYEE
                            INPUT FORM
    Run Date  12/31/--                        Problem No.    10-T

   ┌─────────────────────────────────────────────────────────────┐
   │ Employee No.     100                    Marital Status:       │
   │                                          ( ) Single           │
   │ Name            (Delete)                 ( ) Married          │
   │                                                               │
   │ Address                                                       │
   │                                         Pay Type:             │
   │ City/State/Zip                           ( ) Hourly           │
   │                                          ( ) Salaried         │
   │ Soc. Sec. No.          -       -                              │
   ├═══Pay Information═══════════════════════Voluntary Deductions══│
   │ Rate/Salary Amount                 Deduction One              │
   │ No. Pay Periods                    Deduction Two              │
   │ Withholding #                      Deduction Three            │
   │                                                               │
   │ Department No.                                                │
   └─────────────────────────────────────────────────────────────┘
```

▶ Payroll Input Form

With this payroll system, the data required to process the payroll is recorded on the payroll input form and then keyed into the Payroll Transactions data entry window. A completed input form for Water Sports, Inc., is shown in Figure 10.4. Table 10.2 shows the field names and a description of each column in the input form.

FIGURE 10.4
Payroll Transactions Input Form

PAYROLL TRANSACTIONS
INPUT FORM

Run Date 12/31/--   Problem No. 10-T

Employee Number	Regular Hours	OverTime Hours	Extra Pay	
120	176	5.50	28.90	◀— **Hourly employee with extra pay**
130				◀— **Salaried employee**

TABLE 10.2
Field Names and Descriptions for the Payroll Transactions Input Form

Field Name	Description
Employee Number	This field contains the employee number used to identify the employee to be paid.
Regular Hours	This field contains the total number of regular hours worked during the current pay period by an hourly employee.
OverTime Hours	This field contains the total number of overtime hours worked (if any) during the current pay period by an hourly employee.
Extra Pay	This field contains the amount of any additional pay to be received for the current pay period for either salaried or hourly employees.

OPERATING PROCEDURES

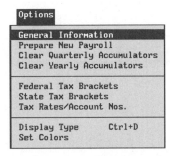

The payroll operating procedures consist of preparing a new payroll, keying employee maintenance (additions, changes, and deletions), keying payroll transactions, and generating payroll reports. At the end of the quarter, the quarterly report is printed and the quarterly accumulators are cleared. At the end of the year, the W-2 statements are printed and the yearly accumulators are cleared.

▶ General Information Data Entry Window

The General Information data entry window is illustrated in Figure 10.5. You will notice that the fields are identical to the first four fields of the General Information data entry window used in the Accounting System. The option buttons available on the Accounting System General Information data entry window are not included because they do not apply to the Payroll System.

FIGURE 10.5
General Information Data Entry Window

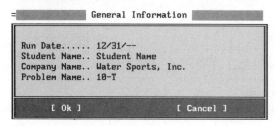

```
=▮▮▮▮▮▮▮▮▮▮  General Information  ▮▮▮▮▮▮▮▮▮▮

  ┌─────────────────────────────────────────────┐
  │                                             │
  │  Run Date...... 12/31/--                     │
  │  Student Name.. Student Name                 │
  │  Company Name.. Water Sports, Inc.           │
  │  Problem Name.. 10-T                         │
  │                                             │
  ├─────────────────────────────────────────────┤
  │      [ Ok ]              [ Cancel ]          │
  └─────────────────────────────────────────────┘
```

▶ Prepare New Payroll

```
┌─Options──────────────────────┐
│                              │
│ General Information          │
│ Prepare New Payroll          │
│ Clear Quarterly Accumulators │
│ Clear Yearly Accumulators    │
│                              │
│ Federal Tax Brackets         │
│ State Tax Brackets           │
│ Tax Rates/Account Nos.       │
│                              │
│ Display Type     Ctrl+D      │
│ Set Colors                   │
└──────────────────────────────┘
```

Choose Prepare New Payroll to erase the previous pay period transactions data before keying the current pay period data. You can correct the payroll transactions and reprint the payroll reports at any time **until** the Prepare New Payroll command is chosen to begin the next payroll period. If you do not select the Prepare New Payroll command before entering transactions for a new period, the computer assumes that you are correcting transactions for the previous pay period rather than entering transactions for a new period. You must select Prepare New Payroll option before entering the current period's transactions.

▶ Preparing a New Payroll

1 **Choose Prepare New Payroll from the Options menu.**

2 **When the dialog window shown in Figure 10.6 appears, push the Ok button.**

FIGURE 10.6
Prepare New Payroll Dialog Window

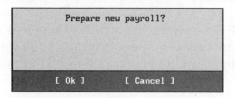

```
┌─────────────────────────────────────────┐
│          Prepare new payroll?           │
│                                         │
│                                         │
│                                         │
├─────────────────────────────────────────┤
│     [ Ok ]        [ Cancel ]            │
└─────────────────────────────────────────┘
```

▶ Clear Quarterly Accumulators

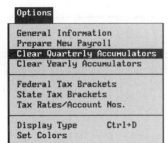

After printing and verifying the quarterly report and before processing the first payroll of the new quarter, you must instruct the computer to reset the quarterly accumulators to zero so that the next quarter's totals can be accumulated. When the Clear Quarterly Accumulators command is chosen, the current payroll data is also cleared.

▶ Clearing Quarterly Accumulators

1   Choose Clear Quarterly Accumulators from the Options menu.

2   When the dialog window shown in Figure 10.7 appears, push the Ok button.

FIGURE 10.7
Clear Quarterly Accumulators Dialog Window

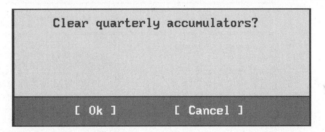

▶ Clear Yearly Accumulators

After the W-2 statements are run and before the first payroll of the new year is run, the yearly accumulators must be reset to zero so that the totals for the next year can be accumulated. The Clear Yearly Accumulators option also clears the quarterly accumulators and the current payroll data.

▶ Clearing Yearly Accumulators

1   Choose Clear Yearly Accumulators from the Options menu.

2   When the dialog window shown in Figure 10.8 appears, push the Ok button.

FIGURE 10.8
Clear Yearly Accumulators Dialog Window

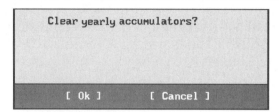

▶ Employee Maintenance

Whenever necessary, new employees must be added, data must be changed, and employees no longer employed must be deleted. The Maintain Employees data entry window is illustrated in Figure 10.9.

FIGURE 10.9
Maintain Employees Data Entry Window

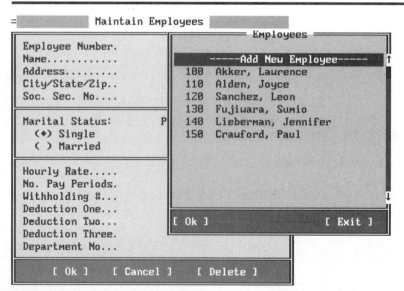

▶ Adding a New Employee

1   Choose -----Add New Employee----- from the list window.

2   Key the employee data and set the Marital Status and Pay Type option buttons. Key the pay and deductions information.

3   Push the Ok button.

▶ Changing Employee Data

1   Choose the employee you wish to change from the list window.

The list window will be dismissed, and the data for the chosen employee will be displayed.

2   Use the Tab key to position the cursor to the field you wish to change and rekey the correct data.

3   Push the Ok button.

▶ Deleting an Employee

1   Choose the employee you wish to delete.

2   Push the delete button.

When the dialog window shown in Figure 10.10 appears, push the Ok button.

FIGURE 10.10
Delete Employee Dialog Window

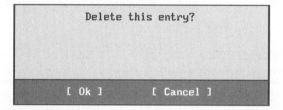

▶ Payroll Transactions Data Entry Window

Transactions

Opening Balances

Payroll Transactions   F3

You will not be allowed to delete an employee with cumulative earnings for the current year until after the Clear Yearly Accumulators command has been selected.

The purpose of the Payroll Transactions data entry window is to identify the employees to be paid for the current pay period, to key the hours worked for hourly employees, and to enter any extra pay. After a transaction is entered, the computer performs the payroll calculations and updates the employee's record. The transaction remains in memory until the computer is directed to prepare a new payroll. When the Payroll Transactions command is chosen from the Transactions menu, the data entry window with an employee list window will appear, as shown in Figure 10.11.

FIGURE 10.11
Payroll Transactions Data Entry Window

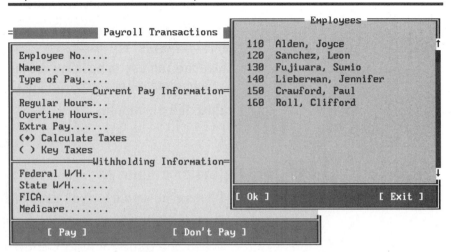

▶ Paying an Employee

1   Choose the employee to be paid from the employee list window.

The list window will be dismissed, and the Employee No., Name, and Type of Pay will be displayed as shown in Figure 10.12.

FIGURE 10.12
Payroll Transactions

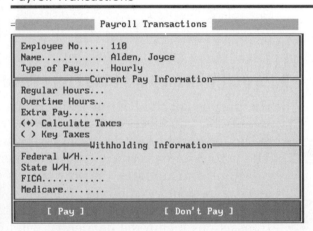

After you have chosen the employee to pay, you may add a new employee to the payroll while keying payroll transactions by pressing the F2 hot key (or by pulling down the Employees menu and choosing the Maintain Employees command).

To erase transaction data already entered and remove an employee from the pay status, select the employee, then push the Don't Pay button.

2   Key the Current Pay Information. If the employee is paid hourly, key the Regular Hours and Overtime Hours. If the employee is to be paid additional pay, key the Extra Pay.

Leave the option button set to Calculate Taxes unless you wish to key the withholding tax information rather than have the computer calculate taxes.

3   Push the Pay button.

If you must change employee data that affects payroll calculations (marital status, pay type, pay rate, pay periods per year, withholding allowances, or voluntary deductions), use this procedure: (1) correct the employee's data using the Maintain Employees option, (2) return to the Payroll Transactions data entry window, (3) choose the employee, and (4) push the Pay button so the computer can recalculate the payroll information.

▶ Payroll Reports

The procedure to display and print the payroll reports is identical to the procedure you have already used in previous chapters of this text. Once a report is displayed, it may be printed to an attached printer by choosing the Print command (in the File menu) or by pressing the F9 hot key. Each payroll report is described in the following section.

PAYROLL REPORT.   The payroll report, which must be generated each pay period, actually includes two reports. The first report lists employee data, with current, quarterly, and yearly earnings and withholdings. A payroll summary appears at the end of the report. The second report provides the journal entries resulting from the current payroll.

```
Reports

Payroll Report
Payroll Checks
Quarterly Report
W-2 Statements
```

Use the F1 hot key to obtain a list window containing the numbers and names of all employees.

▶ Display the Payroll Report

1   Choose the Payroll Report command from the Reports menu.

The Selection Options dialog window shown in Figure 10.13 will appear, allowing you to select the employees that you wish to appear on the report.

FIGURE 10.13
Selection Options (Payroll Report)

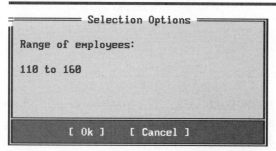

```
═════════════ Selection Options ═════════════

Range of employees:

110 to 160



          [ Ok ]        [ Cancel ]
```

2   Key the range of employees.

The payroll report for one employee is shown in Figure 10.14. The journal entries report is shown in Figure 10.15.

FIGURE 10.14
Payroll Report

```
                          Water Sports, Inc.
                            Payroll Report
                               12/31/--
         -----------------------------------------------------------
                                    Current   Quarterly     Yearly
         -----------------------------------------------------------
         110-Alden, Joyce        Gross Pay    2410.94   9301.34   27514.44
         4849 Timbers Dr.        Federal W/H   229.14   1116.46    3525.50
         Ogden, UT   84402-1270  State W/H      71.19    400.40    1349.59
         581-28-3942             FICA W/H      149.48    576.68    1705.90
         W/H Allow   2   Married Medicare       34.96    134.87     398.96
         Department  0           Deduction 1    40.00
         Pay Periods 12          Deduction 2    24.00
         Reg. Hrs.   176.00      Deduction 3
         O.T. Hrs.    11.25      Net Pay      1862.17
         Extra Pay
         Hourly Rate 12.50
```

FIGURE 10.15
Journal Entries Report

```
                          Water Sports, Inc.
                            Journal Entries
                               12/31/--
         -----------------------------------------------------------
         Account Title                        Debit       Credit
         -----------------------------------------------------------
         Salary Expense                     11988.39
         Employees' Federal Income Tax Payable            1183.70
         Employees' State Income Tax Payable               327.51
         FICA Tax Payable                                  743.28
         Medicare Payable                                  173.84
         Deduction 1 Payable                               212.00
         Deduction 2 Payable                               123.00
         Deduction 3 Payable                                23.60
         Salaries Payable                                 9201.46

         Payroll Taxes Expense               1074.42
         FICA Tax Payable                                  743.28
         Medicare Payable                                  173.84
         State Unemployment Tax Payable                    756.00
         Federal Unemployment Tax Payable                  112.00
```

PAYROLL CHECKS.   The payroll checks have two parts: (1) the check stub, which contains all current, quarterly, and year-to-date earnings and withholding information; and (2) the check itself.

▶Display Payroll Checks

1 Choose the Payroll Checks command from the Reports menu

The Selection Options dialog window shown in Figure 10.16 will appear, allowing you to select the employees for whom checks are to be prepared and the beginning check number.

FIGURE 10.16
Selection Options (Payroll Checks)

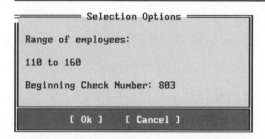

```
========= Selection Options =========
Range of employees:

110 to 160

Beginning Check Number: 803


        [ Ok ]      [ Cancel ]
```

2 Key the range of employees for which the checks are to be printed and the beginning check number.

A sample payroll check appears in Figure 10.17.

FIGURE 10.17
Payroll Check

```
Check No. 803                                        Date 12/31/--

                                  Current   Quarterly    Yearly
110-Alden, Joyce       Gross Pay  2410.94    9301.34    27514.44
4849 Timbers Dr.       Federal W/H  229.14   1116.46     3525.50
Ogden, UT  84402-1270  State W/H     71.19    400.40     1349.59
581-28-3942            FICA W/H     149.48    576.68     1705.90
W/H Allow  2  Married  Medicare      34.96    134.87      398.96
Department  0          Deduction 1   40.00
Pay Periods 12         Deduction 2   24.00
Reg. Hrs.   176.00     Deduction 3
O.T. Hrs.    11.25     Net Pay     1862.17
Extra Pay
Hourly Rate  12.50

-------------------------------------------------------------------
                        National State Bank
                          DownTown Office
                  Anycity, State  12345-1234

Water Sports, Inc.                              Check No. 803

PAY                              Date               Amount
TO THE
ORDER   Alden, Joyce
OF                             12/31/--             1862.17

                           _____

-------------------------------------------------------------------
```

Reports

Payroll Report
Payroll Checks
Quarterly Report
W-2 Statements

QUARTERLY REPORT   At the end of each quarter, the quarterly report must be run. The company uses it to report FICA and Medicare taxable wages to the Internal Revenue Service.

▶ Display the Quarterly Report

Choose the Quarterly Report command from the Reports menu.

An example of the report appears in Figure 10.18.

FIGURE 10.18
Quarterly Report

```
                        Water Sports, Inc.
                        Quarterly Report
                            12/31/--

     --------------------------------------------------------------
       Social        Employee                  Taxable      Taxable
       Security #    Name                       FICA        Medicare
     --------------------------------------------------------------
       581-28-3942   Alden, Joyce              9301.34      9301.34
       563-18-3409   Sanchez, Leon             9246.25      9246.25
       599-23-0956   Fujiwara, Sumio           6810.00      6810.00
       598-09-2381   Lieberman, Jennifer       7100.00      7100.00
       554-09-9090   Crawford, Paul             731.00       731.00
       388-12-8745   Roll, Clifford            1806.00      1806.00
                                             ----------   ---------
       Totals                                 34994.59     34994.59
                                             ==========   =========
       Total Employees 6
```

Reports

Payroll Report
Payroll Checks
Quarterly Report
W-2 Statements

W-2 STATEMENTS.   At the end of the year, the company must provide a W-2 statement to each employee paid during the past year. The W-2 statement is used for individual tax reporting purposes.

▶ Displaying W-2 Statements

1   **Choose the W-2 Statements option from the Reports menu.**

The Selection Options dialog window shown in Figure 10.19 will appear, allowing you to select the employees you wish to appear on the report.

FIGURE 10.19
Selection Options (W-2 Statements)

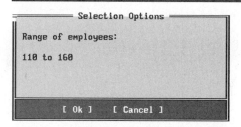

```
═══════ Selection Options ═══════
Range of employees:

110 to 160


        [ Ok ]      [ Cancel ]
```

2   Key the range of employees.

A sample W-2 statement is shown in Figure 10.20.

FIGURE 10.20
W-2 Statement

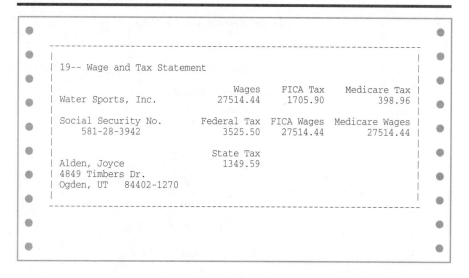

```
-------------------------------------------------------------
| 19-- Wage and Tax Statement                                |
|                                                            |
|                            Wages    FICA Tax   Medicare Tax |
| Water Sports, Inc.        27514.44   1705.90       398.96  |
|                                                            |
| Social Security No.     Federal Tax  FICA Wages  Medicare Wages |
|    581-28-3942             3525.50   27514.44      27514.44 |
|                                                            |
|                           State Tax                        |
| Alden, Joyce               1349.59                         |
| 4849 Timbers Dr.                                           |
| Ogden, UT   84402-1270                                     |
|                                                            |
-------------------------------------------------------------
```

T TUTORIAL 10-T

In this tutorial problem you will process the December payroll for Water Sports, Inc. You will perform the operating procedures necessary to add new employees, make changes to employee data, and delete employees. In addition, you will process the monthly payroll. Since this is the last payroll of the year, it will include the end-of-quarter and end-of-year reports. The information required to complete the December 31 payroll is listed below. The data has been recorded for you on the payroll forms.

Addition of New Employee

Roll, Clifford
1203 President Circle
Ogden, UT 84401-1180

Assign employee number 160; Social Security number, 388-12-8745; married; salaried; $1,806.00; pay periods per year, 12; withholding allowances, two; deduction one, $30.00; deduction two, $11.00; department number not used.

Changes to Current Employees

Alden, Joyce: Change marital status to married and number of withholding allowances to 2.

Lieberman, Jennifer: Change street address to 9060 Apple Tree Lane.

Deletion of Employee

Delete Employee No. 100

Employees to Be Paid This Pay Period

Employee Number	Employee Name	Regular Hours	Overtime Hours	Extra Pay
110	Alden, Joyce	176	11.25	
120	Sanchez, Leon	176	5.50	28.90
130	Fujiwara, Sumio			
140	Lieberman, Jennifer			80.00
150	Crawford, Paul	86		
160	Roll, Clifford			

Directions: Each of the step-by-step instructions below lists a task to be completed at the computer. If you need additional explanation for the task, a page reference is provided from the Operating Procedures section of this chapter (or a previous chapter).

Step 1: Bring up the second module of the accounting system (A2). (page 199)

At the DOS prompt, key A2 (or follow the instructions provided by your instructor).

Step 2: Load the opening balances template file, AA10-T. (page 19)

Pull down the File menu and choose the Open Data File menu command. Key into the Path field the drive and directory containing the template files. Key a file name of AA10-T and push the Ok button.

If the AA10-T template file does not appear in the template directory, you may have loaded the incorrect accounting system module. In this case, pull down the file menu and choose the "Payroll/Assets/Bank Rec." menu command.

Step 3: Use the Save As command to save data to disk with a file name of XXX10-T (where XXX are your initials). (page 21)

Pull down the File menu and choose the Save As menu command. Key the path to the drive and directory that contains your data files. Key a file name of XXX10-T, where XXX are your initials. Push the Ok button.

Step 4: Enter your name in the General Information data entry window and set the run date to December 31 of the current year. (page 24)

Pull down the Options menu and choose the General Information menu command. Set the run date to December 31 of the current year. Key your name in the Student Name field.

Step 5: Key the employee data from the employee input forms shown in Figure 10.21. (page 266)

Pull down the Employees menu and choose the Maintain Employees command. Key the employee data.

Step 6: Prepare a new payroll. (page 264)

Pull down the Options menu and choose the Prepare New Payroll menu command. When the decision dialog window shown in Figure 10.22 on page 277 appears, push the Ok button to erase the transaction data for the previous pay period.

FIGURE 10.21
Employee Input Forms

```
                              EMPLOYEE
                             INPUT FORM

   Run Date  12/31/--                         Problem No.   10-T


   ┌─────────────────────────────────┐        Marital Status:
   │ Employee No.      160           │          ( ) Single
   ├─────────────────────────────────┤          (x) Married
   │ Name          Roll, Clifford    │
   ├─────────────────────────────────┤
   │ Address       11203 President Circle │     Pay Type:
   ├─────────────────────────────────┤          ( ) Hourly
   │ City/State/Zip  Ogden, UT  84401-1180 │     (x) Salaried
   ├─────────────────────────────────┤
   │ Soc. Sec. No.  388 - 12 - 8745  │

   ══Pay Information══              ══Voluntary Deductions══
   ┌──────────────────────┐        ┌──────────────────────────┐
   │ Rate/Salary Amount  1806.00 │  │ Deduction One      30.00 │
   ├──────────────────────┤        ├──────────────────────────┤
   │ No. Pay Periods     12  │      │ Deduction Two      11.00 │
   ├──────────────────────┤        ├──────────────────────────┤
   │ Withholding #       2   │      │ Deduction Three          │
   └──────────────────────┘        └──────────────────────────┘

   ┌──────────────────────┐
   │ Department No.       │
   └──────────────────────┘
```

EMPLOYEE INPUT FORM

Run Date 12/31/--   Problem No. 10-T

Employee No. 110

Name

Address

City/State/Zip

Soc. Sec. No. ___ - __ - ____

Marital Status:
( ) Single
(x) Married

Pay Type:
( ) Hourly
( ) Salaried

Pay Information

Rate/Salary Amount

No. Pay Periods

Withholding #   2

Voluntary Deductions

Deduction One

Deduction Two

Deduction Three

Department No.

EMPLOYEE INPUT FORM

Run Date 12/31/--   Problem No. 10-T

Employee No. 140

Name

Address 9060 Apple Tree Lane

City/State/Zip

Soc. Sec. No. ___ - __ - ____

Marital Status:
( ) Single
( ) Married

Pay Type:
( ) Hourly
( ) Salaried

Pay Information

Rate/Salary Amount

No. Pay Periods

Withholding #

Voluntary Deductions

Deduction One

Deduction Two

Deduction Three

Department No.

EMPLOYEE INPUT FORM

Run Date 12/31/--   Problem No. 10-T

Employee No. 100

Name (Delete)

Address

City/State/Zip

Soc. Sec. No. ___ - __ - ____

Marital Status:
( ) Single
( ) Married

Pay Type:
( ) Hourly
( ) Salaried

Pay Information

Rate/Salary Amount

No. Pay Periods

Withholding #

Voluntary Deductions

Deduction One

Deduction Two

Deduction Three

Department No.

FIGURE 10.22
Prepare New Payroll Dialog Window

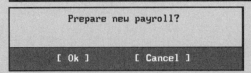

```
Prepare new payroll?


        [ Ok ]            [ Cancel ]
```

Step 7: Key the payroll transactions. (page 267)

Pull down the Transactions menu and choose the Payroll Transactions menu command. Key the data from the payroll transactions input form shown in Figure 10.23. Use the Calculate Taxes option.

FIGURE 10.23
Payroll Transactions Input Form

```
             PAYROLL TRANSACTIONS
                 INPUT FORM

 Run Date  12/31/--      Problem No.  10-T
```

Employee Number	Regular Hours	OverTime Hours	Extra Pay
110	176	11.25	
120	176	5.50	28.90
130			
140			80.00
150	86		
160			

Step 8: Display the Payroll Report and Journal Entries Report.

Pull down the Reports menu and choose the Payroll Report menu command. When the Selection Options dialog window shown in Figure 10.24 appears, key a range of employees from 110 to 160. The reports are shown in Figures 10.25 and 10.26.

FIGURE 10.24
Selection Options (Payroll Report)

```
=========== Selection Options ===========
Range of employees:

110 to 160




        [ Ok ]     [ Cancel ]
```

FIGURE 10.25
Payroll Report

```
                        Water Sports, Inc.
                          Payroll Report
                            12/31/--
        ------------------------------------------------------------
                                   Current   Quarterly    Yearly
        ------------------------------------------------------------
        110-Alden, Joyce        Gross Pay    2410.94    9301.34   27514.44
        4849 Timbers Dr.        Federal W/H   229.14    1116.46    3525.50
        Ogden, UT   84402-1270  State W/H      71.19     400.40    1349.59
        581-28-3942             FICA W/H      149.48     576.68    1705.90
        W/H Allow   2   Married  Medicare      34.96     134.87     398.96
        Department  0           Deduction 1    40.00
        Pay Periods 12          Deduction 2    24.00
        Reg. Hrs.   176.00      Deduction 3
        O.T. Hrs.    11.25      Net Pay      1862.17
        Extra Pay
        Hourly Rate  12.50

        120-Sanchez, Leon       Gross Pay    2350.45    9246.25   28218.05
        9870 Quade Lane         Federal W/H   327.38    1257.67    3665.74
        Ogden, UT   84401-1420  State W/H      70.88     410.06    1394.01
        563-18-3409             FICA W/H      145.73     573.26    1749.52
        W/H Allow   1   Single   Medicare      34.08     134.07     409.16
        Department  0           Deduction 1    40.00
        Pay Periods 12          Deduction 2    24.00
        Reg. Hrs.   176.00      Deduction 3
        O.T. Hrs.    5.50       Net Pay      1708.38
        Extra Pay    28.90
        Hourly Rate  12.60

        130-Fujiwara, Sumio     Gross Pay    2270.00    6810.00   27240.00
        8244 Bird Trace         Federal W/H   179.25     537.75    2151.00
        Ogden, Ut   84404-1280  State W/H      61.74     185.22     740.88
        599-23-0956             FICA W/H      140.74     422.22    1688.88
        W/H Allow   3   Married  Medicare      32.92      98.76     395.04
        Department  0           Deduction 1    45.00
        Pay Periods 12          Deduction 2    18.00
        Reg. Hrs.               Deduction 3    12.60
        O.T. Hrs.               Net Pay      1779.75
        Extra Pay
        Salary      2270.00

        140-Lieberman, Jennifer Gross Pay    2420.00    7100.00   28160.00
        9060 Apple Tree Lane    Federal W/H   259.25     753.75    2979.00
        Ogden, UT   84404-1495  State W/H      74.25     215.01     848.43
        598-09-2381             FICA W/H      150.04     440.20    1745.92
        W/H Allow   1   Married  Medicare      35.09     102.95     408.32
        Department  0           Deduction 1    45.00
        Pay Periods 12          Deduction 2    28.00
        Reg. Hrs.               Deduction 3    11.00
        O.T. Hrs.               Net Pay      1817.37
        Extra Pay    80.00
        Salary      2340.00

        150-Crawford, Paul      Gross Pay     731.00     731.00     731.00
        8828 Lincoln Lane       Federal W/H    50.28      50.28      50.28
        Ogden, UT   84405-1120  State W/H       7.57       7.57       7.57
        554-09-9090             FICA W/H       45.32      45.32      45.32
        W/H Allow   1   Single   Medicare      10.60      10.60      10.60
        Department  0           Deduction 1    12.00
        Pay Periods 12          Deduction 2    18.00
        Reg. Hrs.    86.00      Deduction 3
        O.T. Hrs.               Net Pay       587.23
        Extra Pay
        Hourly Rate   8.50
```

(continued)

FIGURE 10.25 (Continued)
Payroll Report

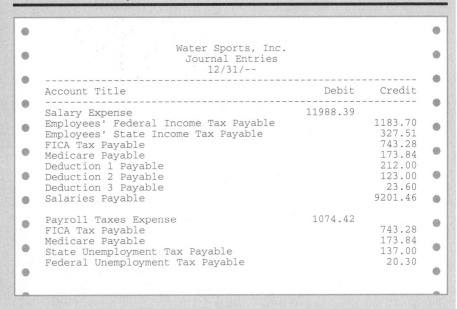

```
  160-Roll, Clifford        Gross Pay    1806.00   1806.00   1806.00
  11203 President Circle     Federal W/H   138.40    138.40    138.40
  Ogden, Ut  84401-1180      State W/H      41.88     41.88     41.88
  388-12-8745                FICA W/H      111.97    111.97    111.97
  W/H Allow   2    Married   Medicare       26.19     26.19     26.19
  Department  0              Deduction 1    30.00
  Pay Periods 12             Deduction 2    11.00
  Reg. Hrs.                  Deduction 3
  O.T. Hrs.                  Net Pay      1446.56
  Extra Pay
  Salary      1806.00


  Payroll summary:           Gross Pay   11988.39  34994.59 113669.49
                             Federal W/H  1183.70   3854.31  12509.92
                             State W/H     327.51   1260.14   4382.36
                             FICA W/H      743.28   2169.65   7047.51
                             Medicare W/H  173.84    507.44   1648.27
                             Deduction 1   212.00
                             Deduction 2   123.00
                             Deduction 3    23.60
                             Net Pay      9201.46
```

FIGURE 10.26
Journal Entries Report

When the payroll report is displayed, the resulting journal entries report is displayed automatically.

```
                        Water Sports, Inc.
                          Journal Entries
                            12/31/--
          -----------------------------------------------------------
          Account Title                       Debit        Credit
          -----------------------------------------------------------
          Salary Expense                     11988.39
          Employees' Federal Income Tax Payable            1183.70
          Employees' State Income Tax Payable               327.51
          FICA Tax Payable                                  743.28
          Medicare Payable                                  173.84
          Deduction 1 Payable                               212.00
          Deduction 2 Payable                               123.00
          Deduction 3 Payable                                23.60
          Salaries Payable                                 9201.46

          Payroll Taxes Expense               1074.42
          FICA Tax Payable                                  743.28
          Medicare Payable                                  173.84
          State Unemployment Tax Payable                    137.00
          Federal Unemployment Tax Payable                   20.30
```

Step 9: Display payroll checks. (page 271)

Pull down the Reports menu and choose the Payroll Checks menu command. When the Selection Options window appears, key an employee range of 110 to 160 and a beginning check number of 803, as shown in Figure 10.27. Then push the Ok button to display the checks for all employees. The first check is illustrated in Figure 10.28 (your display will include checks for all employees).

FIGURE 10.27
Selections Options (Checks)

```
╔══════════ Selection Options ═══════════╗
║                                         ║
║ Range of employees:                     ║
║                                         ║
║ 110 to 160                              ║
║                                         ║
║ Beginning Check Number: 803             ║
║                                         ║
╠═════════════════════════════════════════╣
║        [ Ok ]       [ Cancel ]          ║
╚═════════════════════════════════════════╝
```

FIGURE 10.28
Payroll Checks

```
  ●                                                              ●

  ●   Check No. 803                              Date 12/31/--   ●

  ●                                Current  Quarterly    Yearly  ●
      110-Alden, Joyce     Gross Pay 2410.94  9301.34  27514.44
  ●   4849 Timbers Dr.     Federal W/H 229.14  1116.46   3525.50  ●
      Ogden, UT   84402-1270 State W/H   71.19   400.40   1349.59
  ●   581-28-3942          FICA W/H   149.48   576.68   1705.90  ●
      W/H Allow   2    Married Medicare  34.96   134.87    398.96
  ●   Department  0       Deduction 1   40.00                   ●
      Pay Periods 12      Deduction 2   24.00
  ●   Reg. Hrs.  176.00    Deduction 3                          ●
      O.T. Hrs.   11.25    Net Pay    1862.17
  ●   Extra Pay                                                 ●
      Hourly Rate  12.50
  ●                                                             ●

  ●   ------------------------------------------------------    ●
                     National State Bank
  ●                   DownTown Office                           ●
                 Anycity, State  12345-1234
  ●                                                             ●
      Water Sports, Inc.                      Check No. 803
  ●                                                             ●
      PAY                          Date            Amount
  ●   TO THE                                                    ●
      ORDER   Alden, Joyce
  ●   OF                      12/31/--           1862.17        ●

  ●                         _____            ●

  ●   ------------------------------------------------------    ●
```

Step 10: Display the quarterly report. (page 272)

Pull down the Reports menu, choose the Quarterly Report menu command, and display the quarterly report as of the end of the fourth quarter (December 31, 19—).The report is shown in Figure 10.29.

Step 11: Display the W-2 statements. (page 272)

Pull down the Reports menu, choose the W-2 Statements menu command, and display the W-2 statements as of the end of the year.When the Selections Optons dialog window appears, select an employee range of 110 to 160 (all employees). The first statement is shown in Figure 10.30 (your display will show statements for all employees).

FIGURE 10.29
Quarterly Report

```
                            Water Sports, Inc.
                            Quarterly Report
                                12/31/--

    ----------------------------------------------------------------
      Social          Employee                    Taxable     Taxable
      Security #      Name                         FICA        Medicare
    ----------------------------------------------------------------
      581-28-3942     Alden, Joyce                 9301.34     9301.34
      563-18-3409     Sanchez, Leon                9246.25     9246.25
      599-23-0956     Fujiwara, Sumio              6810.00     6810.00
      598-09-2381     Lieberman, Jennifer          7100.00     7100.00
      554-09-9090     Crawford, Paul                731.00      731.00
      388-12-8745     Roll, Clifford               1806.00     1806.00
                                                  ---------   ---------
                      Totals                      34994.59    34994.59
                                                  =========   =========
                      Total Employees 6
```

FIGURE 10.30
W-2 Statement

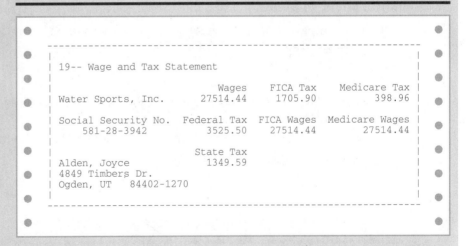

```
    ----------------------------------------------------------------
    |                                                                |
    | 19-- Wage and Tax Statement                                    |
    |                                                                |
    |                          Wages     FICA Tax    Medicare Tax    |
    | Water Sports, Inc.     27514.44     1705.90         398.96     |
    |                                                                |
    | Social Security No.  Federal Tax  FICA Wages  Medicare Wages   |
    |     581-28-3942          3525.50    27514.44       27514.44    |
    |                                                                |
    |                         State Tax                              |
    | Alden, Joyce             1349.59                               |
    | 4849 Timbers Dr.                                               |
    | Ogden, UT   84402-1270                                         |
    |                                                                |
    ----------------------------------------------------------------
```

Step 12: **Save your data to disk with a file name of XXX10-T (where XXX are your initials). (page 21)**

Step 13: **End the session. (page 22)**

From the File menu, choose the Quit command.

CHAPTER 10 STUDENT EXERCISE

I. TRUE/FALSE

Directions: Answer the following questions in the working papers or on a separate sheet of paper. If the statement is true, write the question number followed by T. If the statement is false, write the question number followed by F.

1. Before data for a new payroll period is entered, the payroll transaction data for the previous payroll period must be cleared.

2. When recording changes to employee data on the employee input form, all data fields must be recorded (whether they have changed or not).

3. You can correct the payroll transactions and reprint the payroll reports at any time until the Prepare New Payroll command is chosen to begin the next payroll period.

4. The Clear Quarterly Accumulators command directs the computer to prepare a quarterly report.

5. The Clear Yearly Accumulators command must be performed prior to running the first payroll of the new year.

6. An employee can be deleted from the payroll at any time.

7. After a payroll transaction is entered, the computer performs the payroll calculations and updates the employee's record.

8. A report that provides the journal entries resulting from the payroll is automatically generated after the checks have finished printing.

II. QUESTIONS

Directions: Write the answers to the following questions in the working papers or on a separate sheet of paper.

1. If an employee is paid biweekly (every two weeks), what would you record in the employee data field, No. Pay Periods?

2. Explain the differences between the Prepare New Payroll, Clear Quarterly Accumulators, and Clear Yearly Accumulators commands.

3. Explain the process for erasing transaction data already entered and removing an employee from pay status.

4. How does the computer know what check numbers to assign to current payroll checks?

5. What is the purpose of the quarterly report?

P PRACTICE PROBLEM 10-P

In this problem, you will process the September and October monthly payrolls for A & B Products. You will perform the operating procedures necessary to add new employees, make changes to employee data, and delete employees. In addition, you will process the payroll for the months of September and October. Since September is the end of a quarter, the September payroll will include the end-of-quarter report.

September Payroll: The step-by-step instructions for completing the September payroll for A & B Products are listed below.

Step 1:	Remove one of the payroll transactions input forms from the working papers and record the following information.

Employees to Be Paid This Pay Period

Employee Number	Employee Name	Regular Hours	Overtime Hours	Extra Pay
210	Foster, Barbara			80.00
220	Spencer, Donald			
230	Moya, Virginia	176	2.5	
240	Mendez, Diana	176		
250	Winston, Carmen	176	1.5	
260	Freman, James	176		

Step 2:	Bring up the second module of the accounting system (A2).
	At the DOS prompt, key A2 (or follow the instructions provided by your instructor).
Step 3:	Load the opening balances template file, AA10-P.
Step 4:	Use the Save As command to save data to disk with a file name of XXX10-P1 (where XXX are your initials).
Step 5:	Enter your name in the General Information data entry window and set the run date to September 30 of the current year.
Step 6:	Prepare a new payroll.
Step 7:	Key the data from the payroll transactions input form prepared in Step 1.
Step 8:	Display a payroll report for all employees.
Step 9:	Display payroll checks for all employees.Begin check numbering with check no. 765.
Step 10:	Display a quarterly report.
Step 11:	Save your data file to disk with a file name of XXX10-P1 (where XXX are your initials).
Step 12:	End the session.
	October Payroll: The step-by-step instructions for completing the October payroll for A & B Products are listed below.
Step 1:	Use the input forms from the working papers to record the following payroll transactions.

Addition of New Employee

Terganza, Oliver
1290 Clark Road
Jackson, MS 39203-1110

Assign employee number 280; Social Security number, 418-90-6713; married; salaried; salary amount, $2,304.50; pay periods per year, 12; withholding allowances, two; deduction one, $50.00; deduction two, 85.00; department number not used.

Changes to Current Employees

Foster, Barbara: Change address to 3487 Sandpiper Drive.

Moya, Virginia: Change Social Security number to 654-28-8744.

Kramer, Leonard: Delete from the payroll file.

Employees to Be Paid This Pay Period

Employee Number	Employee Name	Regular Hours	Overtime Hours	Extra Pay
210	Foster, Barbara			
220	Spencer, Donald			30.00
230	Moya, Virginia	168	3.25	
240	Mendez, Diana	168		
250	Winston, Carmen	168	4.5	
260	Freman, James	168		
280	Terganza, Oliver			

Step 2:   Bring up the second module of the accounting system (A2).

At the DOS prompt, key A2 (or follow the instructions provided by your instructor).

Step 3:   Load the payroll data file saved in Step 12 above (XXX10-P1).

Step 4:   Use the Save As command to save data to disk with a file name of XXX10-P2 (where XXX are your initials).

Step 5:   In the General Information data entry window, set the run date to October 31 of the current year.

Step 6:   Clear the quarterly accumulators.

Note: Since October begins a new quarter, the quarterly accumulators must be cleared before processing the October payroll.

Step 7:   Key the employee data from the employees input forms recorded in Step 1.

Step 8:   Key the data from the payroll transactions input form.

Step 9:   Display a payroll report for all employees.

Step 10:   Display payroll checks for all employees.Begin check numbering with check no. 771.

Step 11:   Save your data file to disk with a file name of XXX10-P2 (where XXX are your initials).

Step 12:   End the session.

AUDIT TEST PROBLEM 10-P

Directions: Write the answers to the following questions in the working papers or on a separate sheet of paper.

September Payroll: Use the payroll file you saved under file name XXX10-P1 to answer the following questions about the September payroll.

PAYROLL REPORT

1. What is the number of withholding allowances for Barbara Foster?
2. What is the current gross pay for Donald Spencer?
3. What is the amount withheld for the quarter for Medicare for Carmen Winston?
4. What is the total current net pay for all employees?
5. What is the total yearly gross pay for all employees?

JOURNAL ENTRIES REPORT

6. What is the amount of the debit to Salaries Expense?
7. What is the amount of the debit to Payroll Taxes Expense?
8. What is the amount of the credit to Salaries Payable?

PAYROLL CHECKS

9. What is the number of the check written to Donald Spencer?
10. What is the amount of the check written to Diana Mendez?

QUARTERLY REPORT

11. What is the taxable FICA amount for James Freman?
12. What is the total taxable Medicare amount for all employees for the quarter?

October Payroll: Use the payroll file you saved under file name XXX10-P2 to answer the following questions about the October payroll.

PAYROLL REPORT

1. What is the salary amount for Oliver Terganza?
2. What is the current federal withholding amount for Virginia Moya?
3. What is the FICA amount withheld for the year for Barbara Foster?
4. What is the total amount withheld for Deduction 3 for all employees?
5. What is the total yearly gross pay for all employees?

JOURNAL ENTRIES REPORT

6. What is the amount of the debit to Salaries Expense?

7. What is the amount of the debit to Payroll Taxes Expense?

8. What is the amount of the credit to Salaries Payable?

PAYROLL CHECKS

9. What is the number of the check written to Donald Spencer?

10. What is the amount of the check written to Oliver Terganza?

M MASTERY PROBLEM 10-M

In this problem, you will process the November and December payrolls for A & B Products. Since December 31 is the end of the year, you will also display the quarterly report and W-2 statements.

November Payroll: The payroll data for the November payroll are listed below.

Addition of New Employee

Wainsworth, Laura
9838 Grand View Way
Jackson, MS 39203-1210

Assign employee number 290; Social Security number, 518-90-8721; married; salaried; salary, $2,602.50; pay periods per year, 12; withholding allowances, four; deduction one, $80.00; deduction two, $35.00; department number not used.

Changes to Current Employees

Foster, Barbara: Change deduction number three to $75.00.

Spencer, Donald: Change number of withholding allowances to three.

Employees to Be Paid This Pay Period

Employee Number	Employee Name	Regular Hours	Overtime Hours	Extra Pay
210	Foster, Barbara			80.00
220	Spencer, Donald			
230	Moya, Virginia	168		
240	Mendez, Diana	168	6.0	
250	Winston, Carmen	168		
260	Freman, James	168		
280	Terganza, Oliver			
290	Wainsworth, Laura			

December Payroll: The payroll data for the December payroll are listed on page 287.

Employee Number	Employee Name	Regular Hours	Overtime Hours	Extra Pay
210	Foster, Barbara			50.00
220	Spencer, Donald			50.00
230	Moya, Virginia	176		50.00
240	Mendez, Diana	176		50.00
250	Winston, Carmen	176		50.00
260	Freman, James	176		50.00
280	Terganza, Oliver			50.00
290	Wainsworth, Laura			50.00

Directions: To solve this problem, complete the tasks listed below.

1. Record the November payroll transactions on the input forms.

2. Load the opening balances file, AA10-M.

3. Save the data to your data disk or directory with a name of XXX10-M1.

4. Set the run date to November 30 of the current year.

5. Process the November payroll.

6. Display the November payroll report and payroll checks (starting check number, 778).

7. Save your data with a file name of XXX10-M1.

8. End the session.

9. Record the December payroll transactions on the input forms.

10. Load your payroll data file (XXX10-M1).

11. Save the data to your data disk or directory with a name of XXX10-M2.

12. Set the run date to December 31 of the current year.

13. Process the December payroll.

14. Display a payroll report, payroll checks (starting check number, 786), quarterly report, and W-2 statements.

15. Save your data with a file name of XXX10-M2.

16. End the session.

AUDIT TEST PROBLEM 10-M

Directions: Write the answers to the following questions in the working papers or on a separate sheet of paper.

November Payroll: Use the payroll file you saved under file name XXX10-M1 to answer the following questions about the November payroll.

PAYROLL REPORT

1. What is the number of regular hours worked by James Freman?
2. What is the current gross pay for Laura Wainsworth?
3. What is the amount withheld for the quarter for Medicare for Virginia Moya?
4. What is the total current net pay for all employees?
5. What is the total yearly gross pay for all employees?

JOURNAL ENTRIES REPORT

6. What is the amount of the credit to Federal Income Tax Payable?
7. What is the amount of the credit to Medicare Payable?
8. What is the amount of the credit to Salaries Payable?

PAYROLL CHECKS

9. What is the gross pay shown on the check stub for the check written to Oliver Terganza?
10. What is the amount of the check written to Donald Spencer?

December Payroll: Use the payroll file you saved under file name XXX10-M2 to answer the following questions about the December payroll.

PAYROLL REPORT

1. What is the salary amount for Laura Wainsworth?
2. What is the current federal withholding amount for Barbara Foster?
3. What is the Medicare amount withheld for the year for Donald Spencer?
4. What is the total amount withheld for Deduction 2 for all employees?
5. What is the total yearly FICA withheld for all employees?

JOURNAL ENTRIES REPORT

6. What is the amount of the credit to Medicare Payable?
7. What is the amount of the debit to Payroll Taxes Expense?
8. What is the amount of the credit to Salaries Payable?

PAYROLL CHECKS

9. What is the number of the check written to Oliver Terganza?
10. What is the amount of current FICA withheld as shown on the check stub for Virginia Moya?

QUARTERLY REPORT

11. What is the taxable FICA amount for Virginia Moya?
12. What is the total taxable Medicare amount for all employees for the quarter?

W-2 STATEMENTS

13. What is the amount of state tax withheld for Carmen Winston?
14. What is the Medicare tax for James Freman?

11

Inventory

LEARNING OBJECTIVES ▶ UPON COMPLETION OF THIS CHAPTER, you will be able to:

1. Complete inventory input forms.

2. Maintain inventory by adding, changing, and deleting inventory items.

3. Enter and correct inventory transactions.

4. Display inventory transactions.

5. Display inventory reports.

INTRODUCTION

With the *Automated Accounting 6.0* inventory system, data for each stock item included in merchandise inventory is stored in the computer. This information must be maintained by adding new items, making changes and corrections to existing items, and deleting obsolete items. Periodically (usually daily), the transactions that affect inventory must be processed. These transactions consist of sales, sales returns, purchase orders, items received into inventory, and purchase returns.

Additions, changes, and deletions to inventory items are recorded on an inventory stock items input form. The inventory transactions are recorded on the inventory transactions input form. Once this inventory data has been keyed into the computer, useful management information reports are available. These management reports provide valuable information on stock levels, inventory exceptions (out-of-stock items, for example), sales history, profitability, and inventory valuation.

The examples used in this chapter are for R & W Business Machines, a retail business. R & W Business Machines sells copiers, facsimile machines, and laser printers to other businesses.

> A business must know which items are selling well and which are not. Otherwise, the inventory might include items that are not selling well, yet are very expensive to maintain.

▶ Inventory Stock Items Input Form

Whenever necessary, new items must be added, existing stock item data changed, or obsolete items deleted. When a new stock item is added, each of the columns on the input form must be completed. Table 11.1 contains a description of each of the data fields. Table 11.2 contains a description of additional data fields that are stored with each new inventory item. These fields start out with zero values. As transactions are processed, these data fields are used to accumulate useful information.

TABLE 11.1
Descriptions of Inventory Stock Items Input Form Fields

Field Name	Description
Stock Number	A unique, four-character code (numbers or letters) is assigned to each inventory item for identification. The first digit of the stock item should be used to classify the asset. R & W Business Machines uses the following classifications: 1=copiers 2=facsimile machines 3=copier supplies 4=laser printers 5=cartridges 6=toner *(continued)*

TABLE 11.1 (Continued)
Descriptions of Inventory Stock Items Input Form Fields

Field Name	Description
Description	This field contains a description (maximum of 25 characters) of the inventory item.
Unit of Measure	The unit of measure is a two-character abbreviation that indicates how the item is sold (each, by the dozen, by the box, by the foot, etc.)
Reorder Point	When the quantity on hand reaches this point, additional items are to be reordered.
Retail Price	This field contains the current retail selling price per unit for this item.

When recording changes to data fields for an inventory item, you must include the stock number field as well as the data field(s) to be changed. Any data fields that have not changed may be left blank. To delete a stock item, record the stock number and the notation (Delete) in the description field. An addition, a change, and a deletion are illustrated on the inventory stock items input form shown in Figure 11.1.

FIGURE 11.1
Inventory Stock Items Input Form

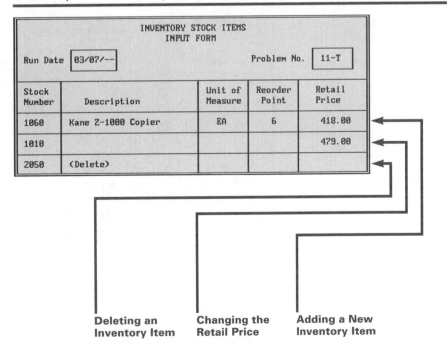

TABLE 11.2
Descriptions of Additional Inventory Data Fields

Field Name	Description
Quantity on Hand	Stored in this field is a count of the quantity of this particular item included in the merchandise inventory at the present time.
Quantity on Order	This field contains the quantity of this item that is currently on order.
Yearly Quantity Sold	This field stores an accumulation of the number of this inventory item sold so far this year.
Yearly Dollars Sold	Contained in this field is an accumulation of the dollar value sold for this item this year.
Last Cost Price	This field contains the price paid per unit for the most recent purchase of this item.
Average Cost	This field contains a per-unit average cost for this inventory item.

▶ Inventory Transactions Input Form

In this inventory system, each of the five different types of transactions are recorded on the inventory transactions input form. The inventory transactions input form in Figure 11.2 shows an example of each type of transaction.

FIGURE 11.2
Inventory Transactions Input Form (Examples)

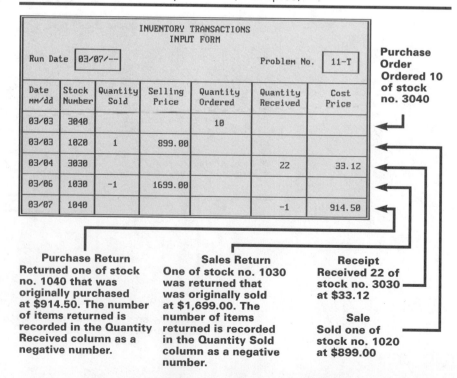

Purchase Order Ordered 10 of stock no. 3040

Purchase Return Returned one of stock no. 1040 that was originally purchased at $914.50. The number of items returned is recorded in the Quantity Received column as a negative number.

Sales Return One of stock no. 1030 was returned that was originally sold at $1,699.00. The number of items returned is recorded in the Quantity Sold column as a negative number.

Receipt Received 22 of stock no. 3030 at $33.12

Sale Sold one of stock no. 1020 at $899.00

OPERATING PROCEDURES

The operating procedures covered in this chapter include maintaining inventory items, keying inventory transactions, correcting inventory transactions, finding previously entered transactions, and displaying the inventory reports.

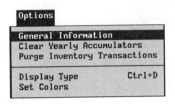

▶ General Information Data Entry Window

The General Information data entry window is illustrated in Figure 11.3. You will notice that the fields are identical to the first four fields of the General Information data entry window used in the Accounting System. The option buttons available on the Accounting System General Information data entry window are not included because they do not apply to the Inventory System.

FIGURE 11.3
General Information Data Entry Window

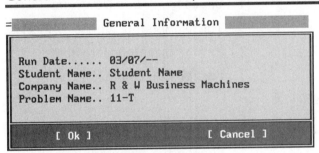

CLEAR YEARLY ACCUMULATORS. The Clear Yearly Accumulators command clears (zeros out) the yearly sales figures. At the end of the year, the yearly sales figures must be reset to zero to accumulate the figures for the next year.

PURGE INVENTORY TRANSACTIONS. The inventory system has a capacity of 500 transactions. If this capacity is exceeded, a dialog window will inform you. Before you can enter additional transactions, the previously entered transactions must be erased by choosing the Purge Inventory Transactions command from the Options menu. Since stock items are updated when transactions are entered into the computer, purging inventory transactions will not cause any information to be lost.

▶ Maintain Inventory Data Entry Window

The Maintain Inventory data entry window is used to add, change, or delete inventory items. The Maintain Inventory data entry window is illustrated in Figure 11.4.

FIGURE 11.4
Maintain Inventory Data Entry Window

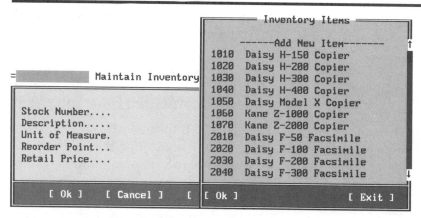

▶ Adding a New Inventory Item

1   Choose ------Add New Item------ from the list window.

The list window will be dismissed.

2   Key the inventory data fields.

3   Push the Ok button.

▶ Changing Inventory Data

1   Choose the inventory item you wish to change from the list window.

The list window will be dismissed, and the data for the chosen item will be displayed in the data entry window.

2   Use the Tab key to position the cursor to the field you wish to change and rekey the correct data.

3   Push the Ok button.

▶ Deleting an Inventory Item

1   Choose the item you wish to delete from the list window.

The list window will be dismissed, and the data for the chosen item will be displayed in the data entry window.

2   Push the delete button.

The confirmation dialog shown in Figure 11.5 will appear. Push the Ok button to delete the item.

If the item being deleted has a quantity on hand or has sales history, a dialog window will appear issuing a warning and asking if you want to delete the item anyway.

FIGURE 11.5
Delete Confirmation Dialog Window

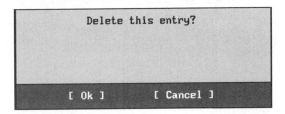

> Delete this entry?
>
> [Ok]   [Cancel]

▶ Inventory Transactions Data Entry Window

The Inventory Transactions data entry window is used to enter, correct, and delete all five types of inventory transactions. A completed Inventory Transactions data entry window for a purchase order is illustrated in Figure 11.6.

When the Inventory Transactions data entry window first appears, the Year and Date data fields will contain the year and date of the last transaction that was entered (even if it was entered in an earlier session).

FIGURE 11.6
Inventory Transactions Data Entry Window

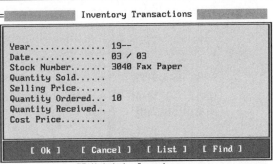

```
=                Inventory Transactions

   Year.............. 19--
   Date.............. 03 / 03
   Stock Number....... 3040 Fax Paper
   Quantity Sold......
   Selling Price......
   Quantity Ordered... 10
   Quantity Received..
   Cost Price........

      [ Ok ]    [ Cancel ]  [ List ]   [ Find ]
F1=Items List  F2=Maintain Inventory
```

You may add a stock item to the inventory while keying inventory transactions. Simply press the F2 hot key (or pull down the Item menu and choose the Maintain Inventory command).

Transactions

Opening Balances

Inventory Transactions

▶ Keying an Inventory Transaction

1   Key the two-digit day of the month (or press Tab if it is correct as is).

2   Key the data fields.

While the cursor is positioned at the Stock Number field, you can press the F1 key to choose an inventory item from a list window.

3   When the inventory transaction is complete, push the Ok button.

▶ Changing or Deleting an Inventory Transaction

1   **Push the List command button near the bottom of the data entry window.**

A list of inventory transactions will appear as shown in Figure 11.7.

FIGURE 11.7
Inventory Transactions List

```
╔══════════════════════ Transactions ══════════════════════╗
║ Date  Stk.# Description         Qty. Sold    Price Ord. Rec.   Cost ║
║ 03/03 3040  Fax Paper                              10          ▲
║ 03/03 3020  Copy Paper 20 lb.                      10
║ 03/03 1020  Daisy H-200 Copier      1     899.00
║ 03/03 5020  Daisy H-200 Cartridge   3      64.50
║ 03/04 1060  Kane Z-1000 Copier                  3
║ 03/04 1070  Kane Z-2000 Copier                  2
║ 03/04 3030  Copy Paper 24 lb.                      24   33.12
║ 03/04 3010  Copy Paper 16 lb.                       6   13.18
║ 03/05 1040  Daisy H-400 Copier                      4  914.50
║ 03/05 2030  Daisy F-200 Facsimile   1     969.00
║ 03/05 1040  Daisy H-400 Copier      1    1800.00
║ 03/05 6030  Toner 32 oz. Container  5      26.00            ▼
║                                                             ║
║ [ Ok ]                                        [ Cancel ]    ║
╚═══════════════════════════════════════════════════════════╝
```

2   **Choose the transaction you wish to change or delete.**

The chosen transaction will be displayed in the data entry window so that it may be changed or deleted.

3   **Key the corrections to the transaction and push the Ok button (or if you wish to delete the transaction, push the Delete command button).**

▶ Finding an Inventory Transaction

1   **Push the Find command button.**

The Find What dialog window shown in Figure 11.8 will appear.

2   **Key the complete date, stock number, quantity sold, selling price, quantity ordered, quantity received, or cost price for the transaction you want to find.**

3   **Push the Ok button.**

4   **If a matching transaction is found, it will be displayed in the data entry window so that it may be changed or deleted.**

FIGURE 11.8
Find What? Dialog Window

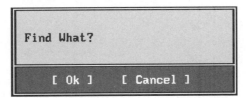

Find What?

[Ok]   [Cancel]

▶Inventory Reports

Reports

Inventory Items
Opening Balances
Inventory Transactions
Inventory Exceptions
Inventory Valuation
Yearly Sales

The procedure to display and print the inventory reports is identical to the procedure you used while working with other systems in previous chapters of this text. Only those reports that are used to solve the problems in this chapter will be covered here.

INVENTORY ITEMS.   The inventory items report provides the current status of each inventory item for reference. The report is also useful in verifying the accuracy of inventory maintenance.

▶Display the Inventory Items Report

1   **Choose the Inventory Items command from the Reports menu.**

The Report Selection dialog window shown in Figure 11.9 will appear, allowing you to select the sequence in which you would like the report to appear.

FIGURE 11.9
Report Selection Dialog Window (Inventory Items)

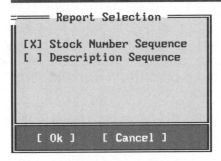

Report Selection

[X] Stock Number Sequence
[ ] Description Sequence

[Ok]   [Cancel]

2   **Select the sequence you want and push the Ok button.**

If both sequences are selected, two reports will be generated—one in each sequence. An inventory items report in stock number sequence is illustrated in Figure 11.10.

FIGURE 11.10
Inventory Items Report

```
                        R & W Business Machines
                             Inventory Items
                                03/07/--
    -------------------------------------------------------------------
    Stock                      Unit  On   On  Reorder Average Last  Retail
    No.   Description          Meas. Hand Order Point  Cost   Cost  Price
    -------------------------------------------------------------------
    1010 Daisy H-150 Copier     EA    12    0    10   396.70 396.70  479.00
    1020 Daisy H-200 Copier     EA    10    3     7   768.00 768.00  899.00
    1030 Daisy H-300 Copier     EA     7    0     6   940.83 970.00 1699.00
    1040 Daisy H-400 Copier     EA     2    0     3   914.50 914.50 1899.00
    1050 Daisy Model X Copier   EA     0    0    10   886.00 886.00 1750.00
    1060 Kane Z-1000 Copier     EA     0    3     6                  418.00
    1070 Kane Z-2000 Copier     EA     0    2     4                  944.50
    2010 Daisy F-50 Facsimile   EA    12    3    10   270.00 270.00  349.95
    2020 Daisy F-100 Facsimile  EA    10    4     9   324.00 324.00  499.00
    2030 Daisy F-200 Facsimile  EA    11    0     5   650.00 650.00  969.00
    2040 Daisy F-300 Facsimile  EA     1    2     3'  989.00 989.00 1899.00
    3010 Copy Paper 16 lb.      CS    31    0    20    15.14  13.18   29.50
    3020 Copy Paper 20 lb.      CS     9   10    25    29.00  29.00   39.95
    3030 Copy Paper 24 lb.      CS    35    0    15    32.77  33.12   45.95
    3040 Fax Paper              RL     7   22    10    26.00  26.00   45.90
    4010 Laser Printer MM2      EA     0    0     3   589.00 589.00  989.40
    5010 Daisy H-150 Cartridge  EA    16    0     4    38.00  38.00   59.00
    5020 Daisy H-200 Cartridge  EA    15    0     6    44.30  44.30   69.00
    6010 Toner 12 oz. Container EA    20    0    12     8.45   8.45   10.80
    6020 Toner 24 oz. Container EA    20    0     6    10.40  10.40   16.50
    6030 Toner 32 oz. Container EA     2    0     4    16.90  16.90   26.00
```

Reports

Inventory Items
Opening Balances
Inventory Transactions
Inventory Exceptions
Inventory Valuation
Yearly Sales

INVENTORY TRANSACTIONS. The inventory transactions report lists selected groups of inventory transactions. You should display this report whenever you enter or correct inventory transactions, to verify that all data have been recorded and entered correctly.

▶ **Displaying Inventory Transactions**

1 **Choose the Inventory Transactions command from the Reports menu.**

The Selection Options dialog window shown in Figure 11.11 will appear.

2 **Key the range of dates to be included in the inventory transactions report. Key a stock number restriction if you wish to restrict the report to only one stock number.**

An inventory transactions report is shown in Figure 11.12.

FIGURE 11.11
Selection Options for Inventory Transactions

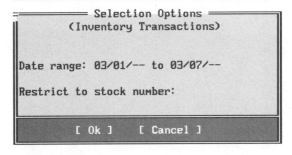

```
================ Selection Options ================
             (Inventory Transactions)


Date range: 03/01/-- to 03/07/--

Restrict to stock number:


        [ Ok ]      [ Cancel ]
```

FIGURE 11.12
Inventory Transactions Report

```
                        R & W Business Machines
                         Inventory Transactions
                                03/07/--
         -----------------------------------------------------------
         Stock                      Quantity Selling Quan.  Quan.  Cost
  Date   No.   Description             Sold    Price  Ord.  Recd.  Price
         -----------------------------------------------------------
  03/03  3040  Fax Paper                              10
  03/03  3020  Copy Paper 20 lb.                      10
  03/03  1020  Daisy H-200 Copier        1    899.00
  03/03  5020  Daisy H-200 Cartridge     3     64.50
  03/04  1060  Kane Z-1000 Copier                      3
  03/04  1070  Kane Z-2000 Copier                      2
  03/04  3030  Copy Paper 24 lb.                             24    33.12
  03/04  3010  Copy Paper 16 lb.                              6    13.18
  03/05  1040  Daisy H-400 Copier                             4   914.50
  03/05  2030  Daisy F-200 Facsimile     1    969.00
  03/05  1040  Daisy H-400 Copier        1   1800.00
  03/05  6030  Toner 32 oz. Container    5     26.00
  03/05  3020  Copy Paper 20 lb.         3     39.95
  03/05  3040  Fax Paper                 2     45.90
  03/06  1030  Daisy H-300 Copier       -1   1699.00
  03/07  1040  Daisy H-400 Copier                            -1   914.50
                                       ----          ----  ----
               Totals                    15           25    33
                                       ====          ====  ====
```

```
Reports
┌──────────────────────────┐
│ Inventory Items          │
│ Opening Balances         │
│ Inventory Transactions   │
│ Inventory Exceptions     │
│ Inventory Valuation      │
│ Yearly Sales             │
└──────────────────────────┘
```

INVENTORY EXCEPTIONS. The inventory exceptions report lists items in the inventory that are out of stock (quantity on hand of zero or less) and items that are at or below the reorder point (quantity on hand less than or equal to the reorder point). This report alerts management to items in inventory that need attention.

▶ Displaying an Inventory Exceptions Report

1 **Choose the Inventory Exceptions command from the Reports menu.**

The exceptions report for R & W Business Machines is shown in Figure 11.13.

FIGURE 11.13
Inventory Exceptions Report

```
                  R & W Business Machines
                  Inventory Exceptions
                       03/07/--
-----------------------------------------------------------------
Stock                     Unit  On  On  Reorder Exceptional
  No. Description         Meas. Hand Order Point  Condition
-----------------------------------------------------------------
1040 Daisy H-400 Copier    EA    2          3   At/below reorder point
1050 Daisy Model X Copier  EA    0         10   Out of stock
1060 Kane Z-1000 Copier    EA    0   3      6   Out of stock
1070 Kane Z-2000 Copier    EA    0   2      4   Out of stock
2040 Daisy F-300 Facsimile EA    1   2      3   At/below reorder point
3020 Copy Paper 20 lb.     CS    9  10     25   At/below reorder point
3040 Fax Paper             RL    7  22     10   At/below reorder point
4010 Laser Printer MM2     EA    0          3   Out of stock
6030 Toner 32 oz. Container EA   2          4   At/below reorder point
```

YEARLY SALES.   The yearly sales report provides management with unit and dollar sales for each item in inventory. The report may be sequenced by stock number or by yearly sales. When sequenced by yearly sales, the report is arranged from the item with the least sales to the item with the most sales.

▶ Displaying a Yearly Sales Report

1   Choose the Yearly Sales command from the Reports menu.

The Report Selection dialog window shown in Figure 11.14 will appear, allowing you to select the sequence in which you would like the report to appear.

2   Select the sequence of the report and push the Ok button.

If both sequences are selected, two reports will be generated—one in each sequence. A yearly sales report in yearly sales sequence is illustrated in Figure 11.15.

FIGURE 11.14
Report Selection Dialog Window (Yearly Sales Report)

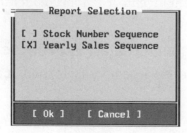

FIGURE 11.15
Sales Report in Yearly Sales Sequence

```
                        R & W Business Machines
                             Yearly Sales
                              03/07/--
        --------------------------------------------------------------
        Stock                              Unit   Yearly      Yearly
        No.   Description                  Meas.  Quantity    Amount
        --------------------------------------------------------------
        1050  Daisy Model X Copier         EA
        1060  Kane Z-1000 Copier           EA
        1070  Kane Z-2000 Copier           EA
        4010  Laser Printer MM2            EA
        6020  Toner 24 oz. Container       EA        76        810.00
        6010  Toner 12 oz. Container       EA       230       1756.00
        5010  Daisy H-150 Cartridge        EA       118       4457.30
        6030  Toner 32 oz. Container       EA       325       5531.00
        5020  Daisy H-200 Cartridge        EA       131       5933.50
        3030  Copy Paper 24 lb.            CS       340      15043.00
        1010  Daisy H-150 Copier           EA        35      16789.00
        3010  Copy Paper 16 lb.            CS       589      17002.00
        3040  Fax Paper                    RL       504      19934.80
        2010  Daisy F-50 Facsimile         EA        59      20340.00
        1030  Daisy H-300 Copier           EA        14      26955.47
        3020  Copy Paper 20 lb.            CS       793      30908.45
        2030  Daisy F-200 Facsimile        EA        33      31776.00
        2040  Daisy F-300 Facsimile        EA        18      33456.00
        2020  Daisy F-100 Facsimile        EA        82      39457.23
        1040  Daisy H-400 Copier           EA        26      47676.00
        1020  Daisy H-200 Copier           EA        63      55669.00
                                                   -----   ----------
                                                   3436    373494.75
                                                   =====   ==========
```

TUTORIAL 11-T

In this problem, you will process the inventory transactions for the week of March 1 through March 7 of the current year for R & W Business Machines. You will perform the operating procedures necessary to add new inventory items, make changes to existing inventory items, and delete inventory items. In addition, you will process the inventory transactions (orders, sales, receipts, sales returns, and purchases returns). The data required to complete the weekly inventory processing is listed below. The data has been recorded for you on the inventory input forms.

New Inventory Items

Stock no. 1060; Kane Z-1000 Copier; unit of measure, EA (each); reorder point, 6; retail price, 418.00.

Stock no. 1070; Kane Z-2000 Copier; unit of measure, EA (each); reorder point, 4; retail price, 944.50.

Changes to Inventory Items

Retail price of Daisy H-150 Copier (stock no. 1010), $479.00.

Retail price of Daisy F-200 Facsimile (stock no. 2030), $969.00.

Reorder point of Daisy F-50 Facsimile (stock no. 2010), 10.

Delete

Daisy Combo Fax (stock no. 2050)

It is important that you enter the transactions in the same order in which they are recorded on the input form; otherwise, your reports will be incorrect because the computer calculates perpetual inventory according to the transactions' dates. The following transactions occurred during the first week of March of the current year. The transactions have been recorded for you on the input forms that appear within the step-by-step instructions. Proceed to Step 1 of the step-by-step instructions.

Weekly Transactions:

Mar 03   Ordered the following merchandise:

Description	Quantity Ordered
Fax Paper	10
Copy Paper 20 lb.	10

03   Sold the following merchandise:

Description	Quantity Sold	Selling Price
Daisy H-200 Copier	1	899.00
Daisy H-200 Cartridge	3	64.50

04   Ordered the following merchandise:

Description	Quantity Ordered
Kane Z-1000 Copier	3
Kane Z-2000 Coper	2

04   Received the following merchandise:

Description	Quantity Received	Cost
Copy Paper 24 lb.	24	33.12
Copy Paper 16 lb.	6	13.18

05   Received the following item:

Description	Quantity Received	Cost
Daisy H-400 Copier	4	914.50

05   Sold the following merchandise:

Description	Quantity Sold	Selling Price
Daisy F-200 Facsimile	1	969.00
Daisy H-400 Copier	1	1800.00
Toner 32 oz. Container	5	26.00
Copy Paper 20 lb.	3	39.95
Fax Paper	2	45.90

06 The following item was returned to R & W Business Machines by a customer:

Description	Quantity Returned	Price
Daisy H-300 Copier	1	1,699.00

07 R & W Business Machines returned the following merchandise to a vendor:

Description	Quantity Returned	Cost
Daisy H-400 Copier	1	914.50

Directions: Each of the step-by-step instructions listed below contains a task to be completed at the computer. Detailed information on how to complete the task is provided immediately following the step. If you need additional explanation for the task, a page number is shown that references that topic in the Operating Procedures section of this or a previous chapter.

If the AA11-T template file does not appear in your directory, you may have loaded an incorrect accounting system module. In this case, pull down the File menu and choose the "Inventory" menu command.

Step 1: Bring up the inventory module of the accounting system (A3).

At the DOS prompt, key A3 (or follow the instructions provided by your instructor). If you already have one of the other two modules loaded, pull down the File menu and choose the Inventory command.

Step 2: Load the opening balances template file, AA11-T. (page 19)

Pull down the File menu and choose the Open Data File menu command. Key into the Path field the drive and directory containing the template files. Key a file name of AA11-T and push the Ok button.

Step 3: Use the Save As command to save the data file loaded in the previous step to disk with a file name of XXX11-T (where XXX are your initials). (page 21)

Pull down the File menu and choose the Save As menu command. Key the path to the drive and directory that contains your data files. Key a file name of XXX11-T. Push the Ok button.

Step 4:   Key your name in the General Information data entry window and set the run date to March 7 of the current year. (page 293)

Pull down the Options menu and choose the General Information menu command. Set the run date to March 7 of the current year. Key your name in the Student Name field.

Step 5:   Key the data from the inventory stock items input form shown in Figure 11.16. (page 293)

Pull down the Items menu and choose the Maintain Inventory menu command. Key the inventory data.

FIGURE 11.16
Inventory Stock Items

```
                       INVENTORY STOCK ITEMS
                            INPUT FORM

  Run Date   03/07/--                        Problem No.    11-T
```

Stock Number	Description	Unit of Measure	Reorder Point	Retail Price
1060	Kane Z-1000 Copier	EA	6	418.00
1070	Kane Z-2000 Copier	EA	4	944.50
1010				479.00
2030				969.00
2010			10	
2050	(Delete)			

Step 6:   Key the data from the inventory transactions input form shown in Figure 11.17. (page 295)

Pull down the Transactions menu and choose the Inventory Transactions menu command. Key the inventory transactions data.

Step 7:   Make the following corrections to the inventory transactions keyed in the previous step. (page 296)

The quantity received for stock number 3030, Copy Paper 24 lb., on March 4, should have been 24 instead of 22.

The quantity sold for stock number 6030, Toner 32 oz. Container, on March 5, should have been 5 instead of 7.

In the Inventory Transactions data entry window, push the List button. A list of transactions as shown in Figure 11.18 will appear. Select the receipt transaction for stock number 3030 on March 4 and push the Ok button. The transaction will appear in the inventory transaction window so that it can be corrected. Make the necessary correction and push the Ok button. Repeat the process for the sales transaction for stock number 6030 on March 5.

FIGURE 11.17
Inventory Transactions Input Form

```
                        INVENTORY TRANSACTIONS
                              INPUT FORM

Run Date  03/07/--                              Problem No.   11-T
```

Date mm/dd	Stock Number	Quantity Sold	Selling Price	Quantity Ordered	Quantity Received	Cost Price
03/03	3040			10		
03/03	3020			10		
03/03	1020	1	899.00			
03/03	5020	3	64.50			
03/04	1060			3		
03/04	1070			2		
03/04	3030				22	33.12
03/04	3010				6	13.18
03/05	1040				4	914.50
03/05	2030	1	969.00			
03/05	1040	1	1800.00			
03/05	6030	7	26.00			
03/05	3020	3	39.95			
03/05	3040	2	45.90			
03/06	1030	-1	1699.00			
03/07	1040				-1	914.50

FIGURE 11.18
Inventory Transactions List

```
══════════════════════ Transactions ══════════════════════
Date   Stk.# Description           Qty. Sold      Price Ord. Rec.    Cost
03/03  3040  Fax Paper                                   10
03/03  3020  Copy Paper 20 lb.                           10
03/03  1020  Daisy H-200 Copier         1     899.00
03/03  5020  Daisy H-200 Cartridge      3      64.50
03/04  1060  Kane Z-1000 Copier                          3
03/04  1070  Kane Z-2000 Copier                          2
03/04  3030  Copy Paper 24 lb.                               22  33.12
03/04  3010  Copy Paper 16 lb.                                6  13.18
03/05  1040  Daisy H-400 Copier                               4  914.50
03/05  2030  Daisy F-200 Facsimile      1     969.00
03/05  1040  Daisy H-400 Copier         1    1800.00
03/05  6030  Toner 32 oz. Container     7      26.00

[ Ok ]                                                      [ Cancel ]
```

Step 8: Display an inventory items report in stock number sequence. (page 297)

Pull down the Reports menu and choose the Inventory Items menu command. When the Report Selection dialog window shown in

Figure 11.19 appears, select the Stock Number Sequence check box. The report is shown in Figure 11.20.

FIGURE 11.19
Report Selection (Inventory Items)

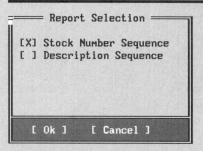

```
┌══════ Report Selection ══════┐
│                              │
│  [X] Stock Number Sequence   │
│  [ ] Description Sequence     │
│                              │
│                              │
│                              │
│                              │
│    [ Ok ]      [ Cancel ]    │
└──────────────────────────────┘
```

FIGURE 11.20
Inventory Items Report

```
                    R & W Business Machines
                        Inventory Items
                          03/07/--

    ------------------------------------------------------------------
    Stock                 Unit  On   On   Reorder Average Last  Retail
    No.    Description     Meas. Hand Order Point   Cost    Cost  Price
    ------------------------------------------------------------------
    1010 Daisy H-150 Copier    EA   12    0     10    396.70 396.70  479.00
    1020 Daisy H-200 Copier    EA   10    3      7    768.00 768.00  899.00
    1030 Daisy H-300 Copier    EA    7    0      6    940.83 970.00 1699.00
    1040 Daisy H-400 Copier    EA    2    0      3    914.50 914.50 1899.00
    1050 Daisy Model X Copier  EA    0    0     10    886.00 886.00 1750.00
    1060 Kane Z-1000 Copier    EA    0    3      6                   418.00
    1070 Kane Z-2000 Copier    EA    0    2      4                   944.50
    2010 Daisy F-50 Facsimile  EA   12    3     10    270.00 270.00  349.95
    2020 Daisy F-100 Facsimile EA   10    4      9    324.00 324.00  499.00
    2030 Daisy F-200 Facsimile EA   11    0      5    650.00 650.00  969.00
    2040 Daisy F-300 Facsimile EA    1    2      3    989.00 989.00 1899.00
    3010 Copy Paper 16 lb.     CS   31    0     20     15.14  13.18   29.50
    3020 Copy Paper 20 lb.     CS    9   10     25     29.00  29.00   39.95
    3030 Copy Paper 24 lb.     CS   35    0     15     32.77  33.12   45.95
    3040 Fax Paper             RL    7   22     10     26.00  26.00   45.90
    4010 Laser Printer MM2     EA    0    0      3    589.00 589.00  989.40
    5010 Daisy H-150 Cartridge EA   16    0      4     38.00  38.00   59.00
    5020 Daisy H-200 Cartridge EA   15    0      6     44.30  44.30   69.00
    6010 Toner 12 oz. Container EA  20    0     12      8.45   8.45   10.80
    6020 Toner 24 oz. Container EA  20    0      6     10.40  10.40   16.50
    6030 Toner 32 oz. Container EA   2    0      4     16.90  16.90   26.00
```

Step 9:   Display the inventory transactions for the period March 1 through March 7. (page 298)

Pull down the Reports menu and select the Inventory Transactions menu command. When the Selection Options dialog window shown in Figure 11.21 appears, select the dates for the period March 1 through March 7 of the current year. The report is shown in Figure 11.22.

FIGURE 11.21
Selection Options (Inventory Transactions)

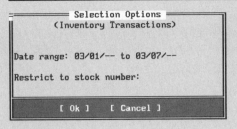

```
┌══════ Selection Options ══════┐
│         (Inventory Transactions)        │
│                                         │
│                                         │
│ Date range: 03/01/-- to 03/07/--        │
│                                         │
│ Restrict to stock number:               │
│                                         │
├─────────────────────────────────────────┤
│      [ Ok ]        [ Cancel ]           │
└─────────────────────────────────────────┘
```

FIGURE 11.22
Inventory Transactions Report

```
                    R & W Business Machines
                      Inventory Transactions
                            03/07/--
-----------------------------------------------------------------
        Stock                    Quantity Selling Quan. Quan.  Cost
  Date   No.  Description          Sold    Price  Ord. Recd.  Price
-----------------------------------------------------------------
  03/03 3040  Fax Paper                                 10
  03/03 3020  Copy Paper 20 lb.                         10
  03/03 1020  Daisy H-200 Copier      1    899.00
  03/03 5020  Daisy H-200 Cartridge   3     64.50
  03/04 1060  Kane Z-1000 Copier                    3
  03/04 1070  Kane Z-2000 Copier                    2
  03/04 3030  Copy Paper 24 lb.                          24  33.12
  03/04 3010  Copy Paper 16 lb.                           6  13.18
  03/05 1040  Daisy H-400 Copier                          4 914.50
  03/05 2030  Daisy F-200 Facsimile   1    969.00
  03/05 1040  Daisy H-400 Copier      1   1800.00
  03/05 6030  Toner 32 oz. Container  5     26.00
  03/05 3020  Copy Paper 20 lb.       3     39.95
  03/05 3040  Fax Paper               2     45.90
  03/06 1030  Daisy H-300 Copier     -1   1699.00
  03/07 1040  Daisy H-400 Copier                         -1 914.50
                                    ----        ---- ----
         Totals                      15          25   33
                                    ====        ==== ====
```

Step 10: Display the inventory exceptions report. (page 299)

Pull down the Reports menu and choose the Inventory Exceptions menu command. The report appears in Figure 11.23.

Step 11: Display the yearly sales report sequenced by yearly sales. (page 300)

Pull down the Reports menu and choose the Yearly Sales menu command. When the Report Selection dialog shown in Figure 11.24 appears, select the Yearly Sales check box. The report is shown in Figure 11.25.

Step 12: Save your data file to disk with a file name of XXX11-T where XXX are your initials.

FIGURE 11.23
Inventory Exceptions Report

```
                    R & W Business Machines
                      Inventory Exceptions
                           03/07/--
    -----------------------------------------------------------
    Stock                          Unit  On  On  Reorder Exceptional
    No.  Description               Meas. Hand Order Point  Condition
    -----------------------------------------------------------
    1040 Daisy H-400 Copier        EA    2        3   At/below reorder point
    1050 Daisy Model X Copier      EA    0       10   Out of stock
    1060 Kane Z-1000 Copier        EA    0    3   6   Out of stock
    1070 Kane Z-2000 Copier        EA    0    2   4   Out of stock
    2040 Daisy F-300 Facsimile     EA    1    2   3   At/below reorder point
    3020 Copy Paper 20 lb.         CS    9   10  25   At/below reorder point
    3040 Fax Paper                 RL    7   22  10   At/below reorder point
    4010 Laser Printer MM2         EA    0        3   Out of stock
    6030 Toner 32 oz. Container    EA    2        4   At/below reorder point
```

FIGURE 11.24
Report Selection (Yearly Sales Report)

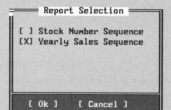

```
 ┌─ Report Selection ──────────┐
 │                             │
 │ [ ] Stock Number Sequence   │
 │ [X] Yearly Sales Sequence   │
 │                             │
 │                             │
 ├─────────────────────────────┤
 │   [ Ok ]      [ Cancel ]    │
 └─────────────────────────────┘
```

FIGURE 11.25
Yearly Sales Report

```
                    R & W Business Machines
                         Yearly Sales
                           03/07/--
    -----------------------------------------------------------
    Stock                          Unit    Yearly      Yearly
    No.   Description              Meas.   Quantity     Amount
    -----------------------------------------------------------
    1050  Daisy Model X Copier     EA
    1060  Kane Z-1000 Copier       EA
    1070  Kane Z-2000 Copier       EA
    4010  Laser Printer MM2        EA
    6020  Toner 24 oz. Container   EA         76        810.00
    6010  Toner 12 oz. Container   EA        230       1756.00
    5010  Daisy H-150 Cartridge    EA        118       4457.30
    6030  Toner 32 oz. Container   EA        325       5531.00
    5020  Daisy H-200 Cartridge    EA        131       5933.50
    3030  Copy Paper 24 lb.        CS        340      15043.00
    1010  Daisy H-150 Copier       EA         35      16789.00
    3010  Copy Paper 16 lb.        CS        589      17002.00
    3040  Fax Paper                RL        504      19934.80
    2010  Daisy F-50 Facsimile     EA         59      20340.00
    1030  Daisy H-300 Copier       EA         14      26955.47
    3020  Copy Paper 20 lb.        CS        793      30908.45
    2030  Daisy F-200 Facsimile    EA         33      31776.00
    2040  Daisy F-300 Facsimile    EA         18      33456.00
    2020  Daisy F-100 Facsimile    EA         82      39457.23
    1040  Daisy H-400 Copier       EA         26      47676.00
    1020  Daisy H-200 Copier       EA         63      55669.00
                                            -----   ----------
                                            3436    373494.75
                                            =====   ==========
```

CHAPTER 11 STUDENT EXERCISE

I. MATCHING

Directions: For each of the following definitions, write in the working papers or on a separate sheet of paper the number of the definition followed by the letter of the appropriate term.

(a) purge inventory transactions

(b) inventory stock items input form

(c) inventory transactions input form

(d) unit of measure

(e) reorder point

(f) quantity on hand

(g) quantity on order

(h) yearly dollars sold

(i) retail price

(j) average cost

1. A two-character abbreviation that indicates how the item is sold (each, by the dozen, by the box, etc.)

2. A count of the quantity of this particular item currently included in merchandise inventory.

3. A per-unit average cost for this inventory item.

4. The current selling price per unit for this item.

5. The input form used to record additions, changes, and deletions to inventory items.

6. The input form that is used to record sales.

7. When the quantity on hand reaches this point, additional items are to be ordered.

8. The process in which previously entered transactions are erased when capacity is exceeded.

9. An accumulation of the dollar value sold for this item this year.

10. The quantity of this item for which stock is ordered but not yet received.

II. QUESTIONS

Directions: Write the answers to the following questions in the working papers or on a separate sheet of paper.

1. List five types of inventory transactions.

2. What is the purpose of the inventory exceptions report?

3. What will happen if you attempt to delete an item that currently has a quantity on hand or a sales history?

4. List the two sequences in which the inventory items report may be displayed.

5. List the two sequences in which the sales report may be displayed.

PRACTICE PROBLEM 11-P

In this problem, you will process the inventory transactions for the week of March 8 through March 14 for R & W Business Machines. You will perform the operating procedures necessary to add new inventory items, make changes to inventory data, and delete inventory items. In addition, you will process the weekly inventory transactions.

Directions: The step-by-step instructions for completing the inventory processing are listed below:

Step 1:   Remove the input forms from the working papers and record the following transactions.

New Inventory Items

Stock no. 1080; Kane Z-2500 Copier; unit of measure, EA (each); reorder point, 4; retail price, $1,499.00.

Stock no. 2060; Benz J-21 Facsimile; unit of measure, EA (each); reorder point, 3; retail price, $1,160.00.

Changes to Inventory Items

Retail price of Daisy H-150 Cartridge (stock no. 5010), $45.99.

Retail price of Daisy H-200 Cartridge (stock no. 5020), $ 65.99.

Reorder point of Toner 12 oz. Container (stock no. 6010), 10.

Delete

Daisy Model X Copier (stock no. 1050).

Weekly Transactions:

Mar 10   Received the following merchandise:

Description	Quantity Received	Cost Price
Kane Z-1000 Copier	3	268.40
Kane Z-2000 Copier	2	618.00
Fax Paper	22	24.20
Copy Paper 20 lb.	10	28.10
Daisy F-300 Facsimile	2	959.80
Daisy H-200 Copier	3	721.30

10   Sold the following merchandise:

Description	Quantity Sold	Selling Price
Daisy I I-150 Copier	1	479.00
Daisy H-150 Cartridge	3	45.99
Copy Paper 20 lb.	2	39.95

11   Ordered the following merchandise:

Description	Quantity Ordered
Daisy H-400 Copier	2
Daisy F-300 Facsimile	2

12   The following item was returned to R & W Business Machines by a customer:

Description	Quantity Returned	Selling Price
Toner 32 oz. Container	2	26.00

12 Sold the following merchandise:

Description	Quantity Sold	Selling Price
Daisy F-300 Facsimile	1	1825.00
Copy Paper 20 lb.	2	39.95
Toner 24 oz. Containe	3	16.50

13 Ordered the following merchandise:

Description	Quantity Ordered
Kane Z-2500 Copier	3
Benz J-21 Facsimile	2

13 R & W Business Machines returned the following item to a vendor:

Description	Quantity Returned	Cost Price
Kane Z-1000 Copier	1	268.40

14 Sold the following merchandise:

Description	Quantity Sold	Selling Price
Daisy H-200 Copier	6	825.00
Daisy H-200 Cartridge	12	50.00

Step 2:   Bring up the inventory module of the accounting system by keying A3 at the DOS prompt (or choose the Inventory menu command from the File menu).

Step 3:   Load the opening balances template file, AA11-P.

Step 4:   Use the Save As menu command to save the data file with a file name of XXX11-P.

Step 5:   Key your name in the General Information data entry window and set the run date to March 14 of the current year.

Step 6:   Key the data from the inventory stock items input form prepared in Step 1.

Step 7:   Key the data from the inventory transactions form prepared in Step 1.

Step 8:   Display an inventory items report in stock number sequence.

Step 9:   Display the inventory transactions for the period March 8 through March 14 of the current year.

Step 10:   Display the inventory exceptions report.

Step 11:   Display the yearly sales report sequenced by yearly sales.

Step 12:   Save your data to disk.

Step 13:   End the session.

AUDIT TEST PROBLEM 11-P

Directions: Write the answers to the following questions in the working papers or on a separate sheet of paper.

INVENTORY ITEMS REPORT

1. How many items are currently on hand for Daisy F-100 Facsimile?
2. What is the last cost price for the Daisy H-200 Copier?
3. What is the retail price of the Kane Z-2500 copier?
4. What is the average cost of the Daisy F-300 Facsimile?
5. What is the reorder point for Fax Paper?

INVENTORY TRANSACTIONS REPORT

6. What is the total quantity sold for all items?
7. What is the total quantity ordered?

INVENTORY EXCEPTIONS REPORT

8. List the items that are out of stock.
9. List the items that are at or below the reorder point for which there are no items currently on order.

YEARLY SALES REPORT

10. Which item has the greatest sales volume based on dollar amount?
11. Which item has the greatest sales volume based on quantity sold?

M MASTERY PROBLEM 11-M

In this problem, you will process the inventory transactions for the week of March 15 through March 21 for R & W Business Machines. You will perform the operating procedures necessary to add new inventory items, make changes to inventory data, and delete inventory items. In addition, you will process the weekly inventory transactions.

Inventory Data for Week of March 15 to March 21: The inventory data for March 15 through March 21 are listed below.

New Inventory Items

Stock no. 4020; Kane Z-50 Laser Printer; unit of measure, EA (each); reorder point, 3; retail price, $749.00.

Stock no. 4030; Kane Z-60 Laser Printer; unit of measure, EA (each); reorder point, 4; retail price, $1,199.00.

Stock no. 5030; Kane Z-50 Cartridge; unit of measure, EA (each); reorder point, 10; retail price, $48.80.

Stock no. 5040; Kane Z-60 Cartridge; unit of measure, EA (each); reorder point, 12; retail price, $51.60.

Stock no. 5050; Kane Z-1000 Cartridge; unit of measure, EA (each); reorder point, 12; retail price, $34.60.

Changes to Inventory Items

Retail price of Daisy F-50 Facsimile to $369.00.

Retail price of Daisy F-100 Facsimile to $510.00.

Retail price of Fax Paper to $38.70.

Reorder point of Copy Paper 20 lb. to 12.

Reorder point of Kane Z-1000 Copier to 2.

Delete

Laser Printer MM2 (stock no. 4010)

Weekly Transactions:

Mar. 17 Ordered the following merchandise:

Description	Quantity Ordered
Daisy H-200 Cartridge	6
Kane Z-2000 Copier	4

18 Received the following merchandise:

Description	Quantity Received	Cost Price
Benz J-21 Facsimile	2	588.00
Daisy F-300 Facsimile	2	968.00
Kane Z-2500 Copier	3	860.00
Daisy H-400 Copier	2	970.00

19 Sold the following merchandise:

Description	Quantity Sold	Selling Price
Daisy F-100 Facsimile	1	499.00
Fax Paper	3	38.70

19 Ordered the following merchandise:

Description	Quantity Ordered
Kane Z-50 Laser Printer	5
Kane Z-60 Laser Printer	5
Kane Z-50 Cartridge	24
Kane Z-60 Cartridge	24
Kane Z-1000 Cartridge	24

20   Sold the following merchandise:

Description	Quantity Sold	Selling Price
Kane Z-2000 Copier	1	944.50
Copy Paper 20 lb.	6	39.95
Toner 24 oz. Container	4	16.50
Benz J-21 Facsimile	1	1,160.00
Fax Paper	3	38.70

21   The following item was returned to R & W Business Machines by a customer:

Description	Quantity Returned	Selling Price
Daisy H-150 Cartridge	1	45.99

21   Sold the following merchandise:

Description	Quantity Sold	Selling Price
Daisy H-400 Copier	1	1,899.00
Copy Paper 20 lb.	6	39.95
Toner 24 oz. Container	4	16.50

21   Sold the following merchandise:

Quantity Description	Selling Sold	Price
Daisy F-100 Facsimile	1	480.00
Fax Paper	3	38.70
Daisy H-150 Copier	1	479.00
Daisy H-150 Cartridge	3	45.99
Copy Paper 24 lb.	6	45.95

21   R & W Business Machines returned the following merchandise to a vendor:

Description	Quantity Returned	Cost Price
Kane Z-1000 Copier	1	268.40

Directions: To solve problem 11-M, complete the tasks listed below.

1. Record the inventory transactions on the input forms.

2. Load the opening balances template file, AA11-M.

3. Save the data to your data disk or directory with a name of XXX11-M (where XXX are your initials).

4. Set the run date to March 21 of the current year.

5. Process the inventory data for the period March 15 to March 21.

6. Display an inventory items report in stock number sequence.

7. Display the inventory transactions for the period March 15 through March 21 of the current year.

8. Display the inventory exceptions report.

9. Display the yearly sales report sequenced by yearly sales.

10. Save your data.

11. End the session.

AUDIT TEST PROBLEM 11-M

Directions: Write the answers to the following questions in the working papers or on a separate sheet of paper.

INVENTORY ITEMS REPORT

1. How many items are currently on hand of the Kane Z-2000 Copier?

2. What is the last cost price for the Copy Paper 16 lb?

3. What is the retail price of the Kane Z-1000 Cartridge?

4. What is the average cost of the Fax Paper?

5. What is the reorder point for the Daisy H-200 Copier?

INVENTORY TRANSACTIONS REPORT

6. What is the total quantity sold for all items?

7. What is the total quantity ordered?

INVENTORY EXCEPTIONS REPORT

8. List the items that are out of stock.

9. Of the items in Question 8 that are out of stock, how many are currently on order?

YEARLY SALES REPORT

10. What is the yearly amount of sales for the Daisy H-150 Copier?

11. What is the yearly quantity of sales for Toner 32 oz. Container?

12

Accounting System Setup

LEARNING OBJECTIVES ▶ UPON COMPLETION OF THIS CHAPTER, you will be able to:

1. Establish company information, required accounts, account classifications, extended classifications, and account subtotals.

2. Establish the chart of accounts and opening balances.

3. Perform plant assets, payroll, and inventory setup.

4. Display and print setup information.

INTRODUCTION

Because many software packages are written to handle a wide variety of business processing tasks, it is unlikely that a business user will use all of the capabilities and capacities of a given system.

To solve the problems in this text, you have loaded template files for accounting systems that were already established. Because the accounting systems were already established, you were not required to use several of the data entry windows designed to tailor the accounting system and enter opening balance data. For example, either a service or a merchandising business can be set up as a sole proprietorship, a partnership, or a corporation. The accounting system can be set up so that accounts payable checks are prepared manually or so that they are automatically generated by the computer. Many other options are available that allow the software to be tailored to a specific business.

In this chapter, you will learn how to set up opening balance data for The Stereo Warehouse. The Stereo Warehouse is a merchandising wholesale business organized as a corporation. The Stereo Warehouse wholesales automobile stereos to automobile dealerships.

OPERATING PROCEDURES

Automated Accounting 6.0 is made up of three modules: (1) the accounting system (module A1); (2) bank reconciliation, fixed assets, and payroll (module A2); and (3) inventory (module A3). The operating procedures for setting up each of the components of the accounting system will be covered in this section.

▶ Accounting System Setup

```
File
New
Open Accounting File    Ctrl+O
Save Accounting File    Ctrl+S
Save As
Erase Accounting File

Import                  F8
Print                   F9

Payroll/Assets/Bank Rec.
Inventory
Quit                    Ctrl+Q
```

The tasks necessary to set up the accounting system are covered in the sequence in which they must be performed. Those menu commands and data entry windows that were used in earlier chapters for accounting system processing will not be covered extensively in this chapter. All of the menu commands and data entry windows required to complete the accounting system setup that were not covered in earlier chapters will be illustrated and explained.

NEW. The New menu command clears any existing data from memory in preparation for setting up a new accounting system. If you have data in memory, you should save it before you choose the New command.

GENERAL INFORMATION. The General Information data entry window shown in Figure 12.1 is used to provide information to the accounting system, such as the run date and the company name that is to appear on the various reports. In addition, several option buttons must be set to tailor the accounting system to the needs of the business being established. These option buttons are described in Table 12.1.

FIGURE 12.1
General Information Data Entry Window

```
=▓▓▓▓▓▓▓▓▓▓▓▓▓▓▓▓▓   General Information   ▓▓▓▓▓▓▓▓▓▓▓▓▓▓▓▓▓

  Run Date...... 03/01/--
  Student Name.. Student Name
  Company Name.. The Stereo Warehouse
  Problem Name.. 12-T

  Business Organization:          Departmentalization:
    ( ) Sole Proprietorship         (•) Not Departmentalized
    ( ) Partnership                 ( ) Two Departments
    (•) Corporation                 ( ) Three Departments

  Type of Business:               Checks/Statements:
    ( ) Service Business            (•) Prepared Manually
    (•) Merchandising Business      ( ) Prepared by Computer

  Budgets: (•) Include            Income Stmt.: ( ) Month & Year
           ( ) Do Not Include                   (•) Fiscal Period

                [ Ok ]              [ Cancel ]
```

TABLE 12.1
Option Button Settings

Option Button	Description
Business Organization	The business organization button setting is used by the software during financial statement preparation and period-end closing.
Type of Business	The type of business option is used by the software to determine the format of the income statement. If the type of business is set to a merchandising business, the software will include a cost of goods sold section in the income statement.
Budgets	If this option is set to include budgets, the software will make available (in the Options menu) a data entry window for entering yearly budget amounts. Also, a performance report will be made available (in the Financial Statements menu) that compares actual amounts to budgeted amounts for the income statement accounts.
Departmentalization	If this option is set to two departments or to three departments, the software will change the format of the Maintain Accounts data entry window to include a department number, so that separate accounts can be set up for each of the departmentalized accounts. In addition, a departmentalized statement of gross profit will be available.
Checks/Statements	If this option is set to have the computer prepare accounts payable checks and accounts receivable statements, the checks/statements option of the Reports menu is activated. Also, the Check No. field of the cash payments journal is not accessible (since the check numbers are now assigned by the computer). When the checks are displayed, the cash payments transactions are updated to include the assigned check number.
Income Stmt.	If this option button is set to month and year, the income statement will include a column for the current month and a column for the year. If the option button is set for fiscal period, the income statement will list only amounts for the fiscal period.

▶ General Information Data Entry

1   From the Options menu, choose the General Information menu command.

2   Key any changes to the data fields.

3   Set the option buttons (use the Up and Down Arrow keys to select the button option, then press the Space Bar to choose the option or click on the option button).

If the Partnership option button is selected, the decision window shown in Figure 12.2 will appear. If you respond Yes, the software will split any income or loss equally between two partners during the period-end closing. In addition, the software will close the two partners' drawing accounts to their respective capital accounts. If you respond No, the software will close the net income or loss to the Income Summary account, and you must make the journal entries necessary to distribute the net income or loss to the respective capital accounts. In addition, you must make the journal entries to close each of the partners' drawing accounts to their respective capital accounts.

4   Push the Ok button to accept and store your changes.

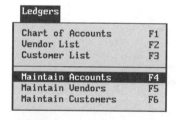

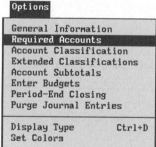

ACCOUNT MAINTENANCE.   Once the general information has been entered, the chart of accounts, vendor, and customer data must be entered. This process was described in Chapter 2. If you need additional information on maintaining accounts, refer to Chapter 2.

REQUIRED ACCOUNTS.   Because you have a great deal of flexibility in assigning account numbers and titles, you must provide the computer with the account numbers assigned to key accounts. The computer needs this information to prepare financial statements and to perform period-end closing. The Required Accounts data entry window for The Stereo Warehouse is shown in Figure 12.3.

FIGURE 12.2
Partnership Decision Window

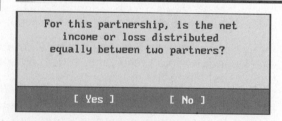

Several of the accounts in the Required Accounts column may appear dimmed, based on the type of business and departmentalization option button settings in the General Information data entry window. For a service business, all the Merchandise Inventory required accounts are dimmed. For a merchandising business, a Merchandise Inventory and an Income Summary account are required for each department. For a sole proprietorship and a partnership, the Stock Dividends account is dimmed. The Stock Dividends account is required for a corporation. If your corporation does not have stock dividends, key the Cash Dividends account number.

FIGURE 12.3
Required Accounts Data Entry Window

Acct.	Title	Required Accounts
1110	Cash	Cash
1120	Accounts Receivable	Accounts Receivable
1130	Merchandise Inventory	Merchandise Inventory
		Merchandise Inventory
		Merchandise Inventory
2110	Accounts Payable	Accounts Payable
3120	Retained Earnings	Capital/Retained Earnings
3130	Dividends	Drawing/Cash Dividends
3130	Dividends	Stock Dividends
3140	Income Summary	Income Summary
		Income Summary
		Income Summary

[Ok]   [Cancel]

F1=Chart

▶ **Required Accounts Data Entry**

1   **From the Options menu, choose the Required Accounts menu command.**

2   **Key the account number for each of the nondimmed accounts.**

Press the F1 function key to display a chart of accounts, from which an account may be selected.

3   **When all of the account numbers have been entered, push the Ok button.**

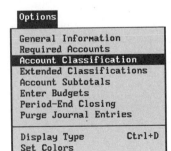

ACCOUNT CLASSIFICATION.   The Account Classification data entry window allows you to classify the accounts based on account number ranges. The data entry window illustrated in Figure 12.4 contains the account number ranges for The Stereo Warehouse.

When classifying accounts, do *not* key the actual range of account numbers: Enter the *potential* range. For example, if your chart of accounts currently has five assets ranging from account number 1110 to account number 1150, you should not specify the actual range, 1110 to 1150. Specify a potential range, such as 1000 to 1999, so that asset accounts added later will automatically be included in the assets classification. If your chart of accounts does not include a certain classification, key the anticipated account number range, for that classification. For example, if your chart of accounts does not include Other Expenses, include a range of account numbers that are to be reserved for Other Expenses in case they are added to the chart of accounts at a later date.

FIGURE 12.4
Account Classification Data Entry Window

Account Classification	From	To
Assets	1000	1999
Liabilities	2000	2999
Capital/Equity	3000	3999
Revenue	4000	4999
Cost	5000	5999
Expenses	6000	6999
Other Revenue	7000	7999
Other Expenses	8000	8999
Corporate Income Tax	9000	9999

[Ok]   [Cancel]

▶ **Account Classification Data Entry**

1   **From the Options menu, choose the Account Classification menu command.**

2   **Key the account number range for each of the classes of accounts.**

    Press the F1 function key to display a chart of accounts.

3   **When all of the account number ranges have been entered, push the Ok button.**

EXTENDED CLASSIFICATION.   In order to perform financial statement analysis, the computer needs to know the range of account numbers for long-term assets and long-term liabilities. This data is provided in the Extended Classification data entry window, as illustrated for The Stereo Warehouse in Figure 12.5.

Options	
General Information	
Required Accounts	
Account Classification	
Extended Classifications	
Account Subtotals	
Enter Budgets	
Period-End Closing	
Purge Journal Entries	
Display Type	Ctrl+D
Set Colors	

FIGURE 12.5
Extended Classifications Data Entry Window

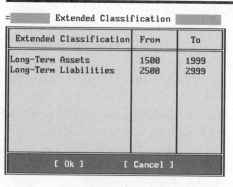

Extended Classification	From	To
Long-Term Assets	1500	1999
Long-Term Liabilities	2500	2999

[Ok]   [Cancel]

▶ Extended Classification Data Entry

1 **From the Options menu, choose the Extended Classification menu command.**

2 **Key the account number range for each of the extended classifications.**

Press the F1 function key to display a chart of accounts.

3 **When all of the account number ranges have been entered, push the Ok button.**

```
┌─Options────────────────┐
│ Options │              │
├─────────┴──────────────┤
│ General Information     │
│ Required Accounts      │
│ Account Classification │
│ Extended Classifications│
│ Account Subtotals      │
│ Enter Budgets          │
│ Period-End Closing     │
│ Purge Journal Entries  │
│                        │
│ Display Type    Ctrl+D │
│ Set Colors             │
└────────────────────────┘
```

ACCOUNT SUBTOTALS.   The purpose of the Accounts Subtotals data entry window is to allow you to select where subtotals are to be printed on the financial statements. For example, you may wish to tailor the income statement so that a subtotal prints after selling expenses and another after administrative expenses. To set up subtotals, key the account number range of the accounts to be included in the subtotal and the title to be printed on the subtotal line. The account number ranges need not reference actual accounts. Instead, the potential range should be entered so that it will not be necessary to modify the account number range as accounts are added to the chart of accounts. The Account Subtotals data entry window for The Stereo Warehouse is shown in Figure 12.6.

FIGURE 12.6
Account Subtotals Data Entry Window

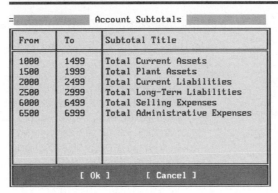

▶ Account Subtotals Data Entry Window

1 **From the Options menu, choose the Account Subtotals menu command.**

2 **Key the account number range and title for each of the subtotals.**

Press the F1 function key to display a chart of accounts.

3 **When all of the account number ranges and titles have been entered, push the Ok button.**

Options

```
General Information
Required Accounts
Account Classification
Extended Classifications
Account Subtotals
Enter Budgets
Period-End Closing
Purge Journal Entries

Display Type        Ctrl+D
Set Colors
```

ENTER BUDGETS.   The purpose of the Enter Budgets data entry window is to allow you to key the budgeted amounts for the income statement accounts. A budgeted amount is the estimated balance for that particular account at the end of the fiscal period. The account titles and currently stored budget amounts are displayed in the data entry window, as illustrated in Figure 12.7, so that you may either key new budget amounts (or correct existing budgeted amounts).

FIGURE 12.7
Enter Budgets Data Entry Window

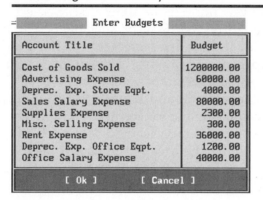

```
=                 Enter Budgets

 Account Title                      Budget

 Cost of Goods Sold              1200000.00
 Advertising Expense               60000.00
 Deprec. Exp. Store Eqpt.           4000.00
 Sales Salary Expense              80000.00
 Supplies Expense                   2300.00
 Misc. Selling Expense               300.00
 Rent Expense                      36000.00
 Deprec. Exp. Office Eqpt.          1200.00
 Office Salary Expense             40000.00

              [ Ok ]          [ Cancel ]
```

▶Enter Budgets Data Entry

1 **Key the budgeted amount for the first account.**

2 **Press the Tab key to move to the next account.**

The accounts are scrollable. When you have keyed the amount for the last account shown on the screen, the accounts will scroll up so that you can key the next budget amount (assuming that the last account on the screen is not the last account in the chart of accounts). Similarly, if the cursor is positioned at the first account and you press the Up Arrow key, the accounts will scroll down (assuming that the first account on the screen is not the first income statement account in the chart of accounts).

3 **When all budget amounts have been entered, push the Ok button.**

Journals

Opening Balances

```
General Journal        S+F1
Purchases Journal      S+F2
Cash Payments Journal  S+F3
Sales Journal          S+F4
Cash Receipts Journal  S+F5
```

OPENING BALANCES.   The Opening Balances data entry window is identical to the General Journal data entry window you used when entering general journal entries in earlier chapters. Figure 12.8 illustrates the data entry window used to enter the opening balances for The Stereo Warehouse.

FIGURE 12.8
Opening Balances Data Entry Window

```
=▭▭▭▭▭▭▭▭▭▭▭▭▭▭   Opening Balances  ▭▭▭▭▭▭▭▭▭▭▭▭
┌────────────────────────────────────────────────────────────┐
│ Year....... 19--                                           │
│ Date....... 03 / 01                                        │
│ Reference.. Balance                 Proof   37965.46 Debit │
│                                                            │
│ ┌──────┬──────┬──────────────────────────┬─────────┬────────┐
│ │ Acct.│ Ven./│                          │         │        │
│ │ No.  │ Cus. │ Account Title            │  Debit  │ Credit │
│ ├──────┼──────┼──────────────────────────┼─────────┼────────┤
│ │ 1110 │      │ Cash                     │19807.70 │        │
│ │ 1120 │ 210  │ AR/Midtown Automart      │ 2309.40 │        │
│ │ 1120 │ 230  │ AR/Wheels Auto Market    │ 1208.00 │        │
│ │ 1120 │ 250  │ AR/Cox Sports Cars       │ 1876.40 │        │
│ │ 1120 │ 270  │ AR/Bonnie Parker Automobiles │ 756.00 │      │
│ │ 1130 │      │ Merchandise Inventory    │ 8848.88 │        │
│ │ 1140 │      │ Prepaid Insurance        │ 1280.00 │        │
│ │ 1150 │      │ Supplies                 │ 1879.00 │        │
│ └──────┴──────┴──────────────────────────┴─────────┴────────┘
│       [ Ok ]      [ Cancel ]      [ List ]     [ Find ]     │
└────────────────────────────────────────────────────────────┘
```

Use the same procedure to key the accounting system opening balances that you used to enter the general journal entries in Chapter 2. Figure 12.8 shows the opening balances for the first several general accounts, including the opening balances for the customers. When the accounts receivable account number is entered, the customer number and balance due from that customer should also be entered. The total of the balances for all the customers will be the balance of the Accounts Receivable general ledger account. Likewise, when the Accounts Payable general ledger account number is entered, the vendor numbers and the balance owed to each vendor should also be entered. Again, the total of the balances owed to all vendors will be the balance of the Accounts Payable account.

▶ Plant Assets System Setup

The Plant Assets System is contained within the second software module (A2). The second module can be accessed by keying A2 at the DOS prompt or by selecting the Payroll/Assets/Bank Rec. command from the Accounting System File menu. To prepare for plant assets system setup, pull down the File menu and choose the New command. The New menu command clears any existing data from memory in preparation for setting up a new plant assets system. The New command causes the computer to clear (or erase) data from memory for all three systems (plant assets, payroll, and bank reconciliation).

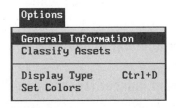

GENERAL INFORMATION.   Since the Plant Assets system is included in the second software module (a separate program), the general information for The Stereo Warehouse as illustrated in Figure 12.9 must be entered again. Once this information is entered, it will be available to the payroll and bank reconciliation systems, which are also contained within module 2.

FIGURE 12.9
General Information Data Entry Window

▶ General Information Data Entry

1 From the Options menu, choose the General Information command.

2 Key the run date, your name, the company name, and the problem name.

3 Push the Ok button.

CLASSIFY ASSETS.   The purpose of the Classify Assets data entry window is to group the assets based on the general ledger accounts affected. The Stereo Warehouse has two classes of assets: (1) store equipment and (2) office equipment. Store equipment assets will be assigned asset numbers in the range 100 to 199. Office equipment assets will be assigned asset numbers in the range 200 to 299. The account number for the Accumulated Depreciation general ledger account for store equipment is 1520. The account number for the Depreciation Expense account for store equipment is 6120. The account number for the Accumulated Depreciation account for office equipment is 1540, and the account number for Depreciation Expense for office equipment is 6520. The account numbers are used in conjunction with the export feature. While the plant assets journal entries report is displayed, plant asset journal entries can be exported to a data file (via the Export option of the File menu). This data file containing journal entries can then be imported by choosing the Import command from the accounting system File menu. The completed Classify Assets data entry window for The Stereo Warehouse is shown in Figure 12.10.

▶ Classify Assets Data Entry

1 From the Options menu, choose the Classify Assets command.

2 Key the range of asset numbers in the From and To columns.

3 Key the asset classification.

4 Key the accumulated depreciation account number for the specified class of assets.

5 Key the depreciation expense account number for the specified class of assets.

FIGURE 12.10
Classify Assets Data Entry Window

From	To	Asset Classification	Accum. Depr.	Depr. Exp.
100	199	Store Equipment	1520	6120
200	299	Office Equipment	1540	6520

[Ok]   [Cancel]

6   Repeat the process for each of the asset classifications.

7   Push the Ok button.

MAINTAIN ASSETS.   Once the general information has been established and the assets classified, each of the plant assets must be keyed into the computer. This process was described in Chapter 8. If you need more information on adding plant assets, refer to Chapter 8.

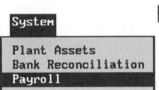

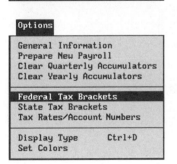

▶Payroll Setup

The Payroll system is also contained within the second software module (A2). If module 2 is already loaded, you can access the Payroll system by pulling down the System menu and choosing the Payroll command.

FEDERAL TAX BRACKETS.   Federal tax rates are supplied with the software. You may update the federal withholding rates by referring to IRS Circular E (Employer's Tax Guide), Table 7 (Annual Payroll). It is recommended that you not change these rates when working the payroll problems in this text. If the rates or percentages are changed, the calculated withholding amounts will no longer match the solutions provided to your instructor. The Federal Tax Brackets data entry window is illustrated in Figure 12.11.

FIGURE 12.11
Federal Tax Brackets Data Entry Window

Federal Tax Brackets

******Single******		******Married******	
Amount	Percent	Amount	Percent
2450	15	6000	15
22750	28	39500	28
47450	31	78700	31

[Ok]   [Cancel]   [Defaults]

▶ Changing Federal Tax Brackets

1 **From the Options menu, choose the Federal Tax Brackets command.**

2 **Position the cursor on the appropriate field and key the change(s) to the amounts and percentages.**

3 **When the changes are complete, push the Ok Button.**

The new rates will be saved to disk along with your data and will be used to compute withholding rates for future payrolls.

To restore previously changed rates to the 1992 withholding rates provided with the software, push the Default button.

STATE TAX BRACKETS.   You may update the state withholding rates supplied with this software by referring to your state's Employer's Tax Guide. Like the federal tax bracket data, these rates should not be changed when working the problems in this text. If the amounts or percentages are changed, the calculated withholding amounts will not match your instructor's solutions. The State Tax Brackets data entry window showing the default amounts and rates is shown in Figure 12.12.

FIGURE 12.12
State Tax Brackets Data Entry Window

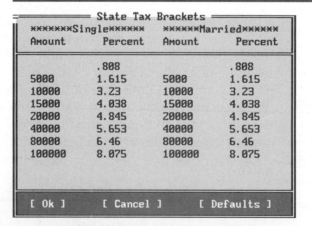

▶ Changing State Tax Brackets

1 **From the Options menu, choose the State Tax Brackets command.**

2 **Position the cursor on the appropriate field and key the change(s) to the amounts and percentages.**

3 When the changes are complete, push the Ok Button.

The new rates will be saved to disk along with your data and will be used to compute withholding rates for future payrolls.

To restore previously changed rates to the withholding rates provided with the software, push the Default button.

TAX RATES/ACCOUNT NUMBERS. There are two sections in the Tax Rates/Account Numbers data entry window. The Tax Rates section contains the various tax rates, upper limits, and allowance amounts required by the software to calculate employee and employer payroll taxes. The Account Numbers section is used to collect the general ledger account numbers required to export the payroll journal entries to the accounting system. If you do not wish to export journal entries, you may leave the account numbers blank. The Tax Rates/Account Numbers data entry window for The Stereo Warehouse is shown in Figure 12.13.

FIGURE 12.13
Tax Rates/Account Numbers Data Entry Window

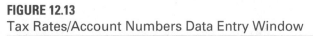

Tax Rates		Account Numbers	
FICA Rate	6.20	Salary Expense 1	6130
FICA Limit	55500	Salary Expense 2	6530
Medicare Rate	1.45	Salary Expense 3	
Medicare Limit	130200	Emp. Fed. Inc. Tax Pay.	2130
State W/H Allowance	650	Emp. State Inc Tax Pay.	2140
Federal W/H Allowance	2300	FICA Tax Payable	2150
State Unemploy. Rate	5.40	Medicare Payable	2160
State Unemploy. Limit	7000	Deduction 1 Payable	2170
Federal Unemploy. Rate	0.80	Deduction 2 Payable	2180
Federal Unemploy. Limit	7000	Deduction 3 Payable	
		Salaries Payable	2190
		Payroll Taxes Expense	6560
		State Unemp. Tax Pay	2200
		Federal UnEmp. Tax Pay.	2210

[Ok]   [Cancel]   [Defaults]

▶ Tax Rates/Account Numbers Data Entry

1 From the Options menu, choose the Tax Rates/Account Numbers command.

2 Position the cursor on the appropriate field and key the change(s) to the amounts and percentages.

3   Position the cursor to the Account Numbers section and key the appropriate account numbers.

If you do not wish to export the payroll journal entries to the accounting system, you may leave the account numbers blank.

4   When the changes are complete, push the Ok Button.

The new rates will be saved to disk along with your data and will be used to compute withholding rates for future payrolls.

To restore previously changed rates and limits to the rates and limits provided with the software, push the Default button.

MAINTAIN EMPLOYEES.   Once the general information has been established and the tax tables updated (if necessary), each of the employees must be keyed into the computer. This process was described in Chapter 10. If you need more information on adding employees, refer to Chapter 10.

PAYROLL OPENING BALANCES.   The Payroll Opening Balances data entry window illustrated in Figure 12.14 allows you to enter historical data for an employee. Because *Automated Accounting 6.0* prepares the quarterly report and the annual W-2 statements, complete payroll data must be available for all of the current year. The Payroll Opening Balances data entry window allows you to enter that historical data.

FIGURE 12.14
Payroll Opening Balances Data Entry Window

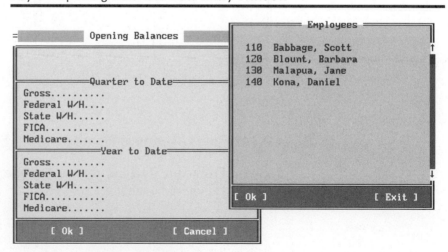

▶ Entering or Correcting Payroll Opening Balance Data

1   From the Transactions menu, choose the Opening Balances command.

2   Choose the employee for whom you wish to enter or change historical data.

> The employee number, employee name, quarterly historical data (if any), and yearly historical data (if any) will be displayed in the data entry window as illustrated in Figure 12.15.

FIGURE 12.15
Opening Balances Data Entry Window

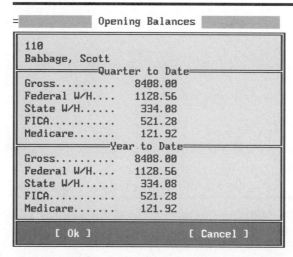

3   Key the quarterly and yearly historical data.

4   Push the Ok button.

5   Repeat the process for each employee for whom historical data is to be entered.

▶ Inventory System Setup

The inventory system is contained with the third module (A3). The inventory system can be accessed by keying A3 at the DOS prompt or by selecting Inventory from the file menu from modules 1 or 2.

Three tasks are required to set up an inventory system: (1) enter the data into the General Information data entry window; (2) key the data for each stock item; and (3) enter opening balance historical data.

GENERAL INFORMATION.   The General Information data entry window in the inventory system is identical to the General Information data entry window described earlier under the Plant Assets system and illustrated in Figure 12.9.

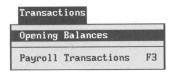

MAINTAIN INVENTORY. Each of the inventory stock items must be keyed into the computer. This process was described in Chapter 11. If you need more information on adding inventory items, refer to Chapter 11.

INVENTORY OPENING BALANCES. After the company's stock items have been entered, the historical data may be entered. The Inventory Opening Balances data entry window is illustrated in Figure 12.16. Refer to Table 12.2 for a description of each of the data fields.

FIGURE 12.16
Inventory Opening Balances Data Entry Window

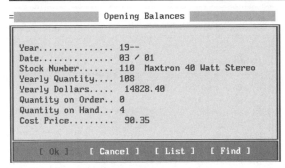

TABLE 12.2
Field Names and Descriptions of the Inventory Opening Balances Data Fields.

Field Name	Description
Date	The date the opening balance transaction is entered.
Stock Number	The number used to identify the stock item.
Yearly Quantity	The total number of units sold for the current year for this stock item.
Yearly Dollars	The total dollar amount sold for this stock item for the current year.
Quantity on Order	The number of units currently ordered but not yet received for this stock item.
Quantity on Hand	The current quantity of this item on hand that were purchased at the cost price shown in the next field.
Cost Price	This data field is related directly to the previous (Quantity on Hand) data field. If items currently on hand were purchased at different prices, a separate entry is required for each different cost price, listing the quantity on hand at that cost price. A separate entry for each cost price is required because the computer uses this data for inventory valuation.

▶ **Keying Inventory Opening Balances**

   1   **From the Transactions menu, choose the Opening Balances command.**

2   Key the opening balance data fields.

3   Push the Ok button.

▶Making Corrections to Opening Balances

1   Push the List button on the Opening Balances data entry window.

A list of opening balances will be displayed as shown in Figure 12.17.

FIGURE 12.17
Opening Balances List

```
╔═══════════════════════ Opening Balances ═══════════════════════╗
║ Date  Stk.# Description          Qty. Sold   Yrly. $ Ord. Hand  Cost ║
║ 03/01 110   Maxtron 40 Watt Stereo      108  14828.40       4   90.35 ↑║
║ 03/01 110   Maxtron 40 Watt Stereo                          2   87.50 ║
║ 03/01 120   Maxtron 50 Watt CD Player    82  39764.00  10   2  325.60 ║
║ 03/01 120   Maxtron 50 Watt CD Player                       3  344.00 ║
║ 03/01 120   Maxtron 50 Watt CD Player                       1  302.00 ║
║ 03/01 130   Maxtron 40 Watt Auto Rev.   202  37174.78       2  130.00 ║
║ 03/01 130   Maxtron 40 Watt Auto Rev.                       3  136.00 ║
║ 03/01 130   Maxtron 40 Watt Auto Rev.                       1  145.00 ║
║ 03/01 130   Maxtron 40 Watt Auto Rev.                       2  123.00 ║
║ 03/01 140   Maxtron 50 Watt Amplifier   245  22809.00  10   3   66.00 ║
║ 03/01 140   Maxtron 50 Watt Amplifier                       2   56.00 ║
║ 03/01 140   Maxtron 50 Watt Amplifier                       4   71.00 ↓║
╠══════════════════════════════════════════════════════════════════╣
║ [ Ok ]                                                   [ Cancel ] ║
╚══════════════════════════════════════════════════════════════════╝
```

2   Select the opening balance transaction to be corrected and push the Ok button.

The selected transaction will be displayed in the Opening Balances data entry window for correction.

TUTORIAL 12-T

In this problem, you will set up a complete accounting system. You will complete the processing necessary to set up the Accounting System, the Plant Assets System, the Payroll System, and the Inventory System for The Stereo Warehouse as of March 1 of the current year. To complete the tutorial problem, follow the step-by-step instructions provided. More detailed information on how to complete the task is provided immediately following the step.

Directions for Setting up the Accounting System:

Step 1:   Bring up the accounting system. (page 16)

Key A1 at the DOS prompt (or follow the instructions provided by your instructor).

Step 2:   Use the New command to erase the data in memory (if any) and prepare the computer for setup. (page 318)

Pull down the File menu and choose the New command.

Step 3:   Set the data fields or option buttons in the General Information data entry window as follows: (page 319)

```
Run Date................ 03/01/--(--represents the
                                     current year)
Student Name........... Your Name
Company Name........... The Stereo Warehouse
Problem Name........... 12-T
Business Organization... Corporation
Departmentalization..... Not Departmentalized
Type of Business....... Merchandising Business
Checks/Statements...... Prepared Manually
Budgets................ Include
Income Statement....... By Fiscal Period
```

Step 4:   Key the data from the chart of accounts input forms shown in Figure 12.18. (page 320)

Pull down the Ledgers menu and choose the Maintain Accounts command.

Step 5:   Key the data from the vendors input form shown in Figure 12.19. (page 89)

Pull down the Ledgers menu and choose the Maintain Customers command.

Step 6:   Key the data from the customers input form shown in Figure 12.20. (page 123)

Pull down the Ledgers menu and choose the Maintain Customers command.

FIGURE 12.18
Chart of Accounts Input Forms

CHART OF ACCOUNTS INPUT FORM	
Run Date 03/01/--	Problem No. 12-T

Acct. No.	Account Title
1110	Cash
1120	Accounts Receivable
1130	Merchandise Inventory
1140	Prepaid Insurance
1150	Supplies
1510	Store Equipment
1520	Accum. Depr. Store Eqpt.
1530	Office Equipment
1540	Accum. Depr. Office Eqpt.
2110	Accounts Payable
2120	Sales Tax Payable
2130	Emp. Fed. Inc. Tax Pay.
2140	Emp. State Inc. Tax Pay.
2150	FICA Tax Payable
2160	Medicare Payable
2170	Health Insurance Payable
2180	Dental Insurance Payable
2190	Salaries Payable
2200	State Unemp. Tax Payable
2210	Federal Unemp. Tax Pay.

FIGURE 12.18 (Continued)
Chart of Accounts Input Forms

```
┌─────────────────────────────────────────────────────────────┐
│                      CHART OF ACCOUNTS                        │
│                        INPUT FORM                             │
│                                                               │
│   Run Date  [03/01/--]          Problem No.    [ 12-T ]       │
└─────────────────────────────────────────────────────────────┘
```

Acct. No.	Account Title
2510	Note Payable
3110	Capital Stock
3120	Retained Earnings
3130	Dividends
3140	Income Summary
4110	Sales
4120	Sales Discounts
4130	Sales Returns & Allow.
5110	Purchases
5120	Purchases Discounts
5130	Purch. Returns & Allow.
6110	Advertising Expense
6120	Depr. Expense Store Eqpt.
6130	Sales Salary Expense
6140	Supplies Expense
6150	Misc. Selling Expense
6510	Rent Expense
6520	Depr. Exp. Office Eqpt.
6530	Office Salary Expense
6540	Insurance Expense

FIGURE 12.18 (Continued)
Chart of Accounts Input Forms

CHART OF ACCOUNTS
INPUT FORM

Run Date 03/01/--   Problem No. 12-T

Acct. No.	Account Title
6550	Misc. General Expense
7110	Interest Income
8110	Interest Expense
9110	Corporate Income Tax

FIGURE 12.19
Vendors Input Form

VENDORS
INPUT FORM

Run Date 03/01/--   Problem No. 12-T

Vend. No.	Vendor Name
110	Long Electronics
120	Western Digital
130	Far East Manufacturing
140	K C Development Co.
150	Statewide Power & Light
160	Winston Office Supply
170	Payroll Bank Account
180	Elite Electronics
190	Brookville Insurance
195	Tri-State Advertising

FIGURE 12.20
Customers Input Form

```
                           CUSTOMERS
                          INPUT FORM

    Run Date  03/01/--              Problem No.    12-T
```

Cust. No.	Customer Name
210	Midtown Automart
220	Spencer Auto Sales
230	Wheels Auto Mart
240	Discount Auto Store
250	Cox Sports Cars
260	Waters Edge Imports
270	Bonnie Parker Automobiles

Step 7: Enter the required account data shown below. (page 321)

Pull down the Options menu and choose the Required Accounts command.

Acct No.	Required Account
1110	Cash
1120	Accounts Receivable
1130	Merchandise Inventory
2110	Accounts Payable
3120	Capital/Retained Earnings
3130	Cash Dividends
3130	Stock Dividends
3140	Income Summary

If the company does not have a Stock Dividends account in the general ledger, enter the Cash Dividends account number for Stock Dividends in the Required Accounts data entry.

Step 8: Enter the account classification data. (page 322)

Pull down the Options menu and choose the Account Classification command.

Assets	1000-1999
Liabilities	2000-2999
Capital/Equity	3000-3999
Revenue	4000-4999

```
Cost              5000-5999
Expenses          6000-6999
Other Revenue     7000-7999
Other Expense     8000-8999
Income Tax        9000-9999
```

Step 9: Enter the extended account classifications. (page 323)

Pull down the Options menu and choose the Extended Classifications command.

```
Long-Term Assets        1500-1999
Long-Term Liabilities   2500-2999
```

Step 10: Enter the account subtotals. (page 323)

Pull down the Options menu and choose the Account Subtotals command.

```
1000-1499      Total Current Assets
1500-1999      Total Plant Assets
2000-2499      Total Current Liabilities
2500-2999      Total Long-Term Liabilities
6000-6499      Total Selling Expenses
6500-6999      Total Administrative Expenses
```

Step 11: Key the general ledger opening balances shown in Figure 12.21. (page 324)

Pull down the Journals menu and choose the Opening Balances option. All of the opening balances cannot be entered on one screen; you can enter and post only eight opening balances at a time. It is also acceptable to enter and post the opening balances one at a time.

Step 12: Display a chart of accounts, vendor, and customer list. (page 13)

Pull down the Reports menu and choose the Accounts option. Select the chart of accounts, vendor list, and customer list. The reports appear in Figure 12.22.

Step 13: Display an opening balances report. (page 45)

Pull down the Reports menu and choose the Journals command. Select opening balances. The report appears in Figure 12.23.

FIGURE 12.21
General Ledger Opening Balances Input Forms

Run Date 03/01/--		OPENING BALANCES INPUT FORM		Problem No.	12-T
Date MM / dd	Reference	Account Number	Cust./ Vend No.	Debit	Credit
03 / 01	Balance	1110		19807.70	
		1120	210	2309.40	
		1120	230	1208.00	
		1120	250	1876.40	
		1120	270	756.00	
		1130		8848.88	
		1140		1280.00	
		1150		1879.00	
		1510		29800.00	
		1520			5870.00
		1530		13900.00	
		1540			2860.00
		2110	110		7860.00
		2110	120		12900.00
		2110	130		1818.00
		2110	180		6450.00
		2120			1670.00
		2130			1925.80
		2140			462.89
		2150			784.51
	Totals				

Run Date 03/01/--		OPENING BALANCES INPUT FORM		Problem No.	12-T
Date MM / dd	Reference	Account Number	Cust./ Vend No.	Debit	Credit
03 / 01	Balance	2160			183.48
		2170			413.00
		2180			72.50
		2200			319.95
		2210			47.40
		2510			6008.00
		3110			24000.00
		3120			8019.85
	Totals			81665.38	81665.38

FIGURE 12.22
Chart of Accounts, Vendor List, and Customer List

```
              The Stereo Warehouse
               Chart of Accounts
                   03/01/--
------------------------------------
Account   Account
Number    Title
------------------------------------
1110      Cash
1120      Accounts Receivable
1130      Merchandise Inventory
1140      Prepaid Insurance
1150      Supplies
1510      Store Equipment
1520      Accum. Depr. Store Eqpt.
1530      Office Equipment
1540      Accum. Depr. Office Eqpt.
2110      Accounts Payable
2120      Sales Tax Payable
2130      Emp. Fed. Inc. Tax Pay.
2140      Emp. State Inc. Tax Pay.
2150      FICA Tax Payable
2160      Medicare Payable
2170      Health Insurance Payable
2180      Dental Insurance Payable
2190      Salaries Payable
2200      State Unemp. Tax Payable
2210      Federal UnEmp. Tax Pay.
2510      Note Payable
3110      Capital Stock
3120      Retained Earnings
3130      Dividends
3140      Income Summary
4110      Sales
4120      Sales Discounts
4130      Sales Returns & Allow.
5110      Purchases
5120      Purchases Discounts
5130      Purch. Returns & Allow.
6110      Advertising Expense
6120      Depr. Expense Store Eqpt.
6130      Sales Salary Expense
6140      Supplies Expense
6150      Misc. Selling Expense
6510      Rent Expense
6520      Depr. Exp. Office Eqpt.
6530      Office Salary Expense
6540      Insurance Expense
6550      Misc. General Expense
7110      Interest Income
8110      Interest Expense
9110      Corporate Income Tax
```

```
              The Stereo Warehouse
                  Vendor List
                   03/01/--
------------------------------------
Vendor    Vendor
Number    Name
------------------------------------
110       Long Electronics
120       Western Digital
130       Far East Manufacturing
140       K C Development Co.
150       Statewide Power & Light
160       Winston Office Supply
170       Payroll Bank Account
180       Elite Electronics
```

(continued)

FIGURE 12.22 (Continued)
Chart of Accounts, Vendor List, and Customer List

```
  190        Brookville Insurance
  195        Tri-State Advertising

           The Stereo Warehouse
              Customer List
                03/01/--

  ------------------------------------
  Customer   Customer
   Number     Name
  ------------------------------------
  210        Midtown Automart
  220        Spencer Auto Sales
  230        Wheels Auto Market
  240        Discount Auto Store
  250        Cox Sports Cars
  260        Waters Edge Imports
  270        Bonnie Parker Automobiles
```

FIGURE 12.23
Opening Balances Report

```
                    The Stereo Warehouse
                      Opening Balances
                         03/01/--
  --------------------------------------------------------------------
  Date   Refer.   V/C Acct. Title                    Debit     Credit
  --------------------------------------------------------------------
  03/01 Balance       1110  Cash                  19807.70
  03/01 Balance   210 1120  AR/Midtown Automart     2309.40
  03/01 Balance   230 1120  AR/Wheels Auto Market   1208.00
  03/01 Balance   250 1120  AR/Cox Sports Cars      1876.40
  03/01 Balance   270 1120  AR/Bonnie Parker Automobiles  756.00
  03/01 Balance       1130  Merchandise Inventory   8848.88
  03/01 Balance       1140  Prepaid Insurance       1280.00
  03/01 Balance       1150  Supplies                1879.00

  03/01 Balance       1510  Store Equipment        29800.00
  03/01 Balance       1520  Accum. Depr. Store Eqpt.           5870.00
  03/01 Balance       1530  Office Equipment       13900.00
  03/01 Balance       1540  Accum. Depr. Office Eqpt.          2860.00
  03/01 Balance   110 2110  AP/Long Electronics                7860.00
  03/01 Balance   120 2110  AP/Western Digital                12900.00
  03/01 Balance   130 2110  AP/Far East Manufacturing          1818.00
  03/01 Balance   180 2110  AP/Elite Electronics               6450.00

  03/01 Balance       2120  Sales Tax Payable                  1670.00
  03/01 Balance       2130  Emp. Fed. Inc. Tax Pay.            1925.80
  03/01 Balance       2140  Emp. State Inc. Tax Pay.            462.89
  03/01 Balance       2150  FICA Tax Payable                    784.51
  03/01 Balance       2160  Medicare Payable                    183.48
  03/01 Balance       2170  Health Insurance Payable            413.00
  03/01 Balance       2180  Dental Insurance Payable             72.50
  03/01 Balance       2200  State Unemp. Tax Payable            319.95

  03/01 Balance       2210  Federal UnEmp. Tax Pay.             47.40
  03/01 Balance       2510  Note Payable                       6008.00
  03/01 Balance       3110  Capital Stock                     24000.00
  03/01 Balance       3120  Retained Earnings                  8019.85

                                                  ---------- ---------
                            Totals               81665.38   81665.38
                                                  ========== =========
```

Step 14: Display a trial balance, schedule of accounts payable, and schedule of accounts receivable. (page 131)

Pull down the Reports menu and choose the Ledgers command. Select the trial balance, schedule of accounts payable, and schedule of accounts receivable reports. The reports appear in Figure 12.24.

Step 15: Use the Save As menu command to save your data file with a name of XXX12-T. (page 21)

Pull down the File menu and choose the Save As command and save your file to disk with a name of XXX12-T (where XXX are your initials).

FIGURE 12.24
Trial Balance, Schedule of Accounts Payable, and Schedule of Accounts Receivable

```
                    The Stereo Warehouse
                       Trial Balance
                        03/01/--
-----------------------------------------------------------
Acct.  Account
Number Title                          Debit          Credit
-----------------------------------------------------------
1110   Cash                          19807.70
1120   Accounts Receivable           6149.80
1130   Merchandise Inventory         8848.88
1140   Prepaid Insurance             1280.00
1150   Supplies                      1879.00
1510   Store Equipment               29800.00
1520   Accum. Depr. Store Eqpt.                      5870.00
1530   Office Equipment              13900.00
1540   Accum. Depr. Office Eqpt.                     2860.00
2110   Accounts Payable                             29028.00
2120   Sales Tax Payable                             1670.00
2130   Emp. Fed. Inc. Tax Pay.                       1925.80
2140   Emp. State Inc. Tax Pay.                       462.89
2150   FICA Tax Payable                               784.51
2160   Medicare Payable                               183.48
2170   Health Insurance Payable                       413.00
2180   Dental Insurance Payable                        72.50
2200   State Unemp. Tax Payable                       319.95
2210   Federal UnEmp. Tax Pay.                         47.40
2510   Note Payable                                  6008.00
3110   Capital Stock                                24000.00
3120   Retained Earnings                             8019.85
                                     ----------     ----------
       Totals                        81665.38       81665.38
                                     ==========     ==========

                    The Stereo Warehouse
                 Schedule of Accounts Payable
                        03/01/--
-----------------------------------------------------------
Account
Number   Name                             Balance
-----------------------------------------------------------
110      Long Electronics                 7860.00
120      Western Digital                 12900.00
130      Far East Manufacturing           1818.00
180      Elite Electronics                6450.00
                                         ----------
         Total                           29028.00
                                         ==========
```

(continued)

FIGURE 12.24 (Continued)
Trial Balance, Schedule of Accounts Payable, and Schedule of
Accounts Receivable

```
                    The Stereo Warehouse
                 Schedule of Accounts Receivable
                          03/01/--
        ----------------------------------------------------
        Account
        Number    Name                            Balance
        ----------------------------------------------------
        210       Midtown Automart                2309.40
        230       Wheels Auto Market              1208.00
        250       Cox Sports Cars                 1876.40
        270       Bonnie Parker Automobiles        756.00
                                                 ----------
                  Total                           6149.80
                                                 ==========
```

Directions for Setting up the Plant Assets System:

Step 1:   Load module 2 (Payroll/Assets/Bank Rec.). (page 325)

Pull down the File menu and choose the Payroll/Assets/Bank Rec.
option.

Step 2:   Choose the Plant Assets system. (page 325)

Pull down the System menu and choose the Plant Assets system. If
the Plant Assets command is dimmed, you are already in the Plant
Assets system, so this step is unnecessary.

Step 3:   Prepare the computer for setup by choosing the New command. (page 318)

Pull down the File menu and choose the New command.

Step 4:   Set the general information. (pages 325-326)

Pull down the Options menu and choose the General Information
command. Key the data as shown.

```
Run Date .......03/01/-- (--represents the current year)
Student Name ...Your Name
Company Name ...The Stereo Warehouse
Problem Name ...12-T
```

Step 5:   Classify the assets. (page 326)

Pull down the Options menu and choose the Classify Assets command. Key the asset classifications and account numbers shown below.

Range	Classification	Accum. Depr.	Deprec. Expense
100-199	Store Equipment	1520	6120
200-299	Office Equipment	1540	6520

Step 6: Key the data to set up the plant assets. (page 199)

Pull down the Assets menu and choose the Maintain Assets command. Key the data shown in Figure 12.25.

FIGURE 12.25
Plant Assets Input Form

PLANT ASSETS
INPUT FORM

Run Date   03/01/--   Problem No.   12-T

Asset No.	Asset Name	Date Acquired	Depr. Meth.	Useful Life	Original Cost	Salvage Value
110	Display Case	10/01/90	SL	10	8000.00	250.00
120	Cash Register	07/02/91	SL	10	4500.00	300.00
130	Shelving	09/01/92	SL	10	17300.00	1200.00
210	Typewriter	06/30/90	SL	5	250.00	35.00
220	File Cabinet	11/30/91	SL	10	590.00	50.00
230	Copy Machine	08/31/91	SL	5	2550.00	250.00
240	Computer System	05/31/90	SL	5	10510.00	400.00

Step 7: Display a plant assets report. (pages 201-202)

Pull down the Reports menu and choose the Plant Assets report. The report is shown in Figure 12.26.

Directions for Setting up the Payroll System:

Step 1: Choose the Payroll system. (page 327)

Pull down the System menu and choose the Payroll system. Do *not* choose the New command prior to setting up payroll. Plant assets and payroll are both contained within module 2 and are both stored in the same data file. If you choose New at this point, you will erase the plant asset data already entered.

Step 2: Key the employee data. (page 266)

Pull down the Employees menu and choose the Maintain Employees command. Key the data from the employees input forms shown in Figure 12.27.

FIGURE 12.26
Plant Assets Report

```
                        The Stereo Warehouse
                         Plant Assets Report
                              03/01/--
         ------------------------------------------------------------
         Asset          Asset         Date   Depr. Useful Original   Salvage
         Number         Name          Acquired Meth. Life  Cost       Value
         ------------------------------------------------------------
          110    Display Case         10/01/90  SL    10    8000.00    250.00
          120    Cash Register        07/02/91  SL    10    4500.00    300.00
          130    Shelving             09/01/92  SL    10   17300.00   1200.00
          210    Typewriter           06/30/90  SL     5     250.00     35.00
          220    File Cabinet         11/30/91  SL    10     590.00     50.00
          230    Copy Machine         08/31/91  SL     5    2550.00    250.00
          240    Computer System      05/31/90  SL     5   10510.00    400.00
                                                           ----------
                 Total                                      43700.00
                                                           ==========
```

Step 3:   Key the opening balances historical data. (pages 330-331)

Pull down the Transactions menu and select the Opening Balances command. Key the data from the Opening Balances input form shown in Figure 12.28 on page 348.

FIGURE 12.27
Employee Input Forms

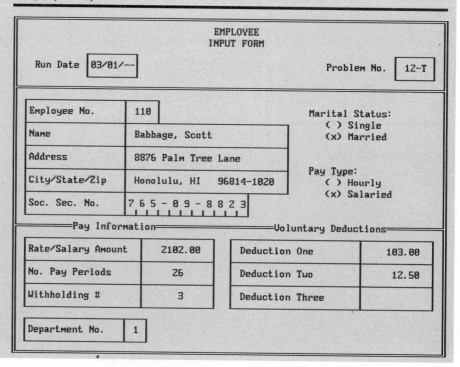

FIGURE 12.27 (Continued)
Employee Input Forms

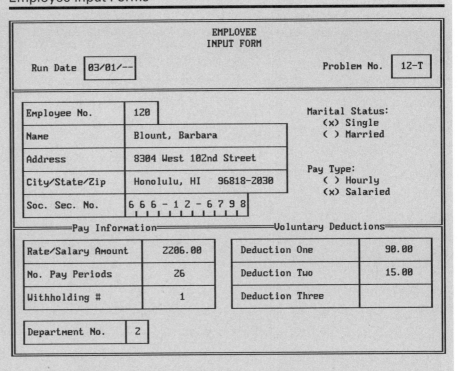

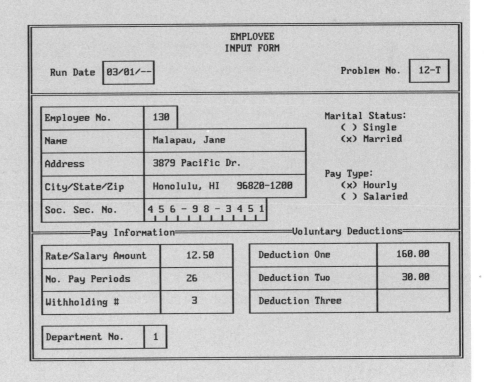

FIGURE 12.27 (Continued)
Employee Input Forms

```
                        EMPLOYEE
                       INPUT FORM
    Run Date  03/01/--                        Problem No.  12-T


    Employee No.      140               Marital Status:
                                          (x) Single
    Name         Kona, Daniel             ( ) Married

    Address      4599 58th Street
                                        Pay Type:
    City/State/Zip  Honolulu, HI   96801-8012   (x) Hourly
                                          ( ) Salaried
    Soc. Sec. No.  4 2 3 - 8 0 - 0 5 4 1

    ===Pay Information===              ===Voluntary Deductions===

    Rate/Salary Amount   12.50         Deduction One      90.00

    No. Pay Periods      26            Deduction Two      15.00

    Withholding #        1             Deduction Three

    Department No.    2
```

FIGURE 12.28
Payroll Opening Balances Input Form

```
                PAYROLL OPENING BALANCES
                     INPUT FORM
    Run Date  03/01/--                    Problem Number  12-T
```

Emp. No.	Quarter-to-Date					Year-to-Date				
	Gross	Fed.W/H	St.W/H	FICA	Medcr.	Gross	Fed.W/H	St.W/H	FICA	Medcr.
110	8408.00	1128.56	334.08	521.28	121.92	8408.00	1128.56	334.08	521.28	121.92
120	0024.00	1895.20	368.92	547.08	127.96	8824.00	1895.20	368.92	547.08	127.96
130	4037.50	307.94	106.54	250.33	58.54	4037.50	307.94	106.54	250.33	58.54
140	4037.50	519.90	116.25	250.33	58.54	4037.50	519.90	116.25	250.33	58.54

**Step 4:   Enter the payroll integration account numbers.
Refer to the chart of accounts report printed on
page 341 as a reference. (pages 329-330)**

Pull down the options menu and choose the Tax Rates/Accounts
Numbers command. Key the integration account numbers.

Step 5: Display the payroll report. (page 269)

Pull down the Reports menu and choose the Payroll Report command. The report is shown in Figure 12.29.

FIGURE 12.29
Payroll Report

```
                          The Stereo Warehouse
                              Payroll Report
                                03/01/--
    --------------------------------------------------------------------
                                         Current    Quarterly    Yearly
    --------------------------------------------------------------------
    110-Babbage, Scott        Gross Pay                8408.00    8408.00
    8876 Palm Tree Lane       Federal W/H             1128.56    1128.56
    Honolulu, HI  96814-1020  State W/H                 334.08     334.08
    765-09-8823               FICA W/H                  521.28     521.28
    W/H Allow   3    Married  Medicare                  121.92     121.92
    Department  1             Deduction 1    103.00
    Pay Periods 26            Deduction 2     12.50
    Reg. Hrs.                 Deduction 3
    O.T. Hrs.                 Net Pay
    Extra Pay
    Salary     2102.00

    120-Blount, Barbara       Gross Pay                8824.00    8824.00
    8304 West 102nd Street    Federal W/H             1895.20    1895.20
    Honolulu, HI  96818-2030  State W/H                 368.92     368.92
    666-12-6798               FICA W/H                  547.08     547.08
    W/H Allow   1    Single   Medicare                  127.96     127.96
    Department  2             Deduction 1     90.00
    Pay Periods 26            Deduction 2     15.00
    Reg. Hrs.                 Deduction 3
    O.T. Hrs.                 Net Pay
    Extra Pay
    Salary     2206.00

    130-Malapua, Jane         Gross Pay                4037.50    4037.50
    3879 Pacific Dr.          Federal W/H              307.94     307.94
    Honolulu, HI  96820-1200  State W/H                 106.54     106.54
    456-98-3451               FICA W/H                  250.33     250.33
    W/H Allow   3    Married  Medicare                   58.54      58.54
    Department  1             Deduction 1    160.00
    Pay Periods 26            Deduction 2     30.00
    Reg. Hrs.                 Deduction 3
    O.T. Hrs.                 Net Pay
    Extra Pay
    Hourly Rate 12.50

    140-Kona, Daniel          Gross Pay                4037.50    4037.50
    4599 58th Street          Federal W/H              519.90     519.90
    Honolulu, HI  96801-8012  State W/H                 116.25     116.25
    423-80-0541               FICA W/H                  250.33     250.33
    W/H Allow   1    Single   Medicare                   58.54      58.54
    Department  2             Deduction 1     90.00
    Pay Periods 26            Deduction 2     15.00
    Reg. Hrs.                 Deduction 3
    O.T. Hrs.                 Net Pay
    Extra Pay
    Hourly Rate 12.50

    Payroll summary:          Gross Pay               25307.00   25307.00
                              Federal W/H             3851.60    3851.60
                              State W/H                925.79     925.79
                              FICA W/H                1569.02    1569.02
                              Medicare W/H             366.96     366.96
                              Deduction 1
                              Deduction 2
                              Deduction 3
                              Net Pay
```

Step 6: Save your data to disk with a file name of XXX12-T (where XXX are your initials). (page 21)

Pull down the File menu and choose the Save As command. Save your file with a name of XXX12-T, where XXX are your initials.

Directions for Setting up the Inventory System:

Step 1: Load module 3 (Inventory). (page 331)

Pull down the File menu and choose the Inventory option.

Step 2: Prepare the inventory system for setup with the New command.

Pull down the File menu and choose the New command.

Step 3: Set the general information. (page 331)

Pull down the Options menu and choose the General Information command. Key the data as shown.

```
Run Date .......03/01/-- (--represents the current year)
Student Name ...Your Name
Company Name ...The Stereo Warehouse
Problem Name ...12-T
```

Step 4: Key the data from the inventory stock item input form. (pages 293-294)

Pull down the Items menu and choose the Maintain Inventory command. Key the data from the inventory stock items input form shown in Figure 12.30.

FIGURE 12.30
Inventory Stock Items Input Form

```
                    INVENTORY STOCK ITEMS
                          INPUT FORM

 Run Date  03/01/--                       Problem No.   12-T
```

Stock Number	Description	Unit of Measure	Reorder Point	Retail Price
110	Maxtron 40 Watt Stereo	EA	5	139.90
120	Maxtron 50 Watt CD Player	EA	3	499.00
130	Maxtron 40 Watt Auto Rev.	EA	3	199.00
140	Maxtron 50 Watt Amplifier	EA	5	99.00
210	Tawa 40 Watt Stereo	EA	4	170.00
220	Tawa 50 Watt Stereo	EA	3	290.00
230	Tawa 50 Watt CD Player	EA	5	389.00
240	Tawa 40 Watt Stereo DNR	EA	3	190.00

Step 5:   Key the inventory opening balances. (pages 332-333)

Pull down the Transactions menu and choose the Opening Balances command. Key the data from the Inventory Opening Balances input form in Figure 12.31.

FIGURE 12.31
Inventory Opening Balances Input Form

```
                    INVENTORY OPENING BALANCES
                            Input Form

  Run Date  03/01/--                         Problem No.    12-T
```

Date MM/dd	Stock Number	Yearly Quantity	Yearly Dollars	Quantity On Order	Quantity On Hand	Cost Price
03/01	110	108	14828.40		4	90.35
	110				2	87.50
	120	82	39764.00	10	2	325.60
	120				3	344.00
	120				1	302.00
	130	202	37174.78		2	130.00
	130				3	136.00
	130				1	145.00
	130				2	123.00
	140	245	22809.00	10	3	66.00
	140				2	56.00
	140				4	71.00
	210	402	58209.40		8	122.99
	220	286	82100.30		12	202.80
	230	120	46680.00		2	255.60
	240	98	18620.00		3	140.90
	240				2	161.40

Step 6:   Display the inventory items report in stock number sequence. (page 297)

Pull down the Reports menu and choose the Inventory Items command. When the Report Selection menu appears, select Stock Number Sequence. The report appears in Figure 12.32.

Step 7:   Display an inventory opening balances report. (page 297)

Pull down the Reports menu and choose the Opening Balances command. When the Selection Options dialog appears, key a date range of March 1 to March 1 of the current year. The report is shown in Figure 12.33.

FIGURE 12.32
Inventory Items Report

```
                          The Stereo WareHouse
                            Inventory Items
                               03/01/--
        -----------------------------------------------------------------
        Stock                      Unit  On  On   Reorder Average Last  Retail
        No.  Description           Meas. Hand Order Point  Cost   Cost  Price
        -----------------------------------------------------------------
        110  Maxtron 40 Watt Stereo    EA    6   0      5    89.40  87.50 139.90
        120  Maxtron 50 Watt CD Player EA    6  10      3   330.87 302.00 499.00
        130  Maxtron 40 Watt Auto Rev. EA    8   0      3   132.38 123.00 199.00
        140  Maxtron 50 Watt Amplifier EA    9  10      5    66.00  71.00  99.00
        210  Tawa 40 Watt Stereo       EA    8   0      4   122.99 122.99 170.00
        220  Tawa 50 Watt Stereo       EA   12   0      3   202.80 202.80 290.00
        230  Tawa 50 Watt CD Player    EA    2   0      5   255.60 255.60 389.00
        240  Tawa 40 Watt Stereo DNR   EA    5   0      3   149.10 161.40 190.00
```

FIGURE 12.33
Inventory Opening Balances Report

```
                          The Stereo WareHouse
                      Opening Balances Transactions
                               03/01/--
     -----------------------------------------------------------------------
           Stock                    Yearly    Yearly   On    On    Cost
     Date  No.  Description          Qty.     Dollars  Order Hand  Price
     -----------------------------------------------------------------------
     03/01 110  Maxtron 40 Watt Stereo.  108  14828.40              4   90.35
     03/01 110  Maxtron 40 Watt Stereo                              2   87.50
     03/01 120  Maxtron 50 Watt CD Player 82  39764.00       10     2  325.60
     03/01 120  Maxtron 50 Watt CD Player                          3  344.00
     03/01 120  Maxtron 50 Watt CD Player                          1  302.00
     03/01 130  Maxtron 40 Watt Auto Rev. 202 37174.78             2  130.00
     03/01 130  Maxtron 40 Watt Auto Rev.                          3  136.00
     03/01 130  Maxtron 40 Watt Auto Rev.                          1  145.00
     03/01 130  Maxtron 40 Watt Auto Rev.                          2  123.00
     03/01 140  Maxtron 50 Watt Amplifier 245 22809.00      10     3   66.00
     03/01 140  Maxtron 50 Watt Amplifier                          2   56.00
     03/01 140  Maxtron 50 Watt Amplifier                          4   71.00
     03/01 210  Tawa 40 Watt Stereo      402  58209.40             8  122.99
     03/01 220  Tawa 50 Watt Stereo      286  82100.30            12  202.80
     03/01 230  Tawa 50 Watt CD Player   120  46680.00             2  255.60
     03/01 240  Tawa 40 Watt Stereo DNR   98  18620.00             3  140.90
     03/01 240  Tawa 40 Watt Stereo DNR                            2  161.40
                                        ----  ---------  ----  ----
            Totals                      1543  320185.88   20    56
                                        ====  =========  ====  ====
```

Step 8: Save your data to disk with the file name of
**   XXX12-T (where XXX are your initials). (page 21)**

CHAPTER 12 STUDENT EXERCISE

I. TRUE/FALSE

Directions: Answer the following questions in the working papers or on a separate sheet of paper. If the statement is true, write the question number followed by T. If the statement is false, write the question number followed by F.

1. The New menu command clears any existing data from memory in preparation for setting up a new system.
2. *Automated Accounting 6.0* supports 12 departments.
3. *Automated Accounting 6.0* allows for checks to be prepared manually or by computer.
4. The Account Classifications data entry window can be used to specify that a subtotal is to be printed after selling expenses on the income statement.
5. The Plant Assets system is in module 2, along with the Payroll system.
6. The journal entries generated by the Plant Assets system may be exported to a data file, which in turn may be imported by the Accounting System.
7. The integration account numbers on the payroll Tax Rates/Account Numbers data entry window are required.
8. In *Automated Accounting 6.0*, inventory is in the same software module as payroll.
9. When entering the inventory opening balances data, items in inventory purchased at different prices require a separate entry for each purchase price.

II. QUESTIONS

Directions: Write the answers to the following questions in the working papers or on a separate sheet of paper.

1. *Automated Accounting 6.0* is made up of three modules. List them.
2. The Income Statement option button in the Accounting System General Information data entry window allows two settings. List the two settings and explain the difference between them.
3. How is the data collected in the Required Accounts data entry window used?
4. What is the purpose of the Account Subtotals data entry window?
5. What is the purpose of the Classify Assets data entry window?
6. Why may it be necessary to enter opening balances historical data into the Payroll system?

P PRACTICE PROBLEM 12-P

In this problem, you will perform the accounting system setup for Swan Detective Agency, a private investigation service owned and operated by Jennifer Swan. Swan Detective Agency is a service business which is organized as a sole proprietorship, is not departmentalized, does not use budgets, prepares checks manually, and generates the income statement by fiscal period. The trial balance, schedule of accounts payable, and schedule of accounts receivable for Swan Detective Agency as of February 1 of the current year are provided as follows.

General Ledger Account Titles and Balances

Account Number	Account Title	Debit	Credit
Current Assets:			
110	Cash	1905.70	
120	Accounts Receivable	6478.60	
130	Notes Receivable	1000.00	
140	Supplies	180.60	
150	Prepaid Insurance	240.00	
Plant Assets:			
190	Office Equipment	7270.00	
191	Accum. Depr. Office Eq.		2405.00
Current Liabilities:			
210	Accounts Payable		981.50
Long-Term Liabilities:			
250	Notes Payable		5000.00
Capital:			
310	Jennifer Swan, Capital		8688.40
320	Jennifer Swan, Drawing		
330	Income Summary		
Revenue:			
410	Fees Earned		
Expenses:			
510	Advertising Expense		
520	Depr. Expense Office Eq.		
530	Insurance Expense		
540	Rent Expense		
550	Utilities Expense		
560	Telephone Expense		
570	Vehicle Expense		
580	Miscellaneous Expense		
Other Revenue:			
710	Interest Income		
Other Expenses:			
810	Interest Expense		

Schedule of Accounts Payable

Account Number	Name	Balance
110	Watson Office Supply	130.00
120	The Computer Center	240.60
130	West Ad Agency	480.00
140	Baker Auto Service	130.90
	Total	981.50

Schedule of Accounts Receivable

Account Number	Name	Balance
210	Gerome Matson	1380.40
220	Airtight Security Co.	2480.80
230	Linda Gemar	809.40
240	Michael Latemer	708.00
250	Pace Manufacturing	1100.00
	Total	6478.60

Directions:

Step 1: Remove the input forms for Problem 12-P from the working papers. Record the above data on the input forms. This step is optional in that you may wish to key the above data directly into the computer rather than record it on the input forms first.

Step 2: Bring up the accounting system software (module A1).

Step 3: Use the New command from the File menu to prepare the computer for accounting system setup.

Step 4: Set the general information data.

Step 5: Key the chart of accounts data.

Step 6: Key the vendor data.

Step 7: Key the customer data.

Step 8: Key the data into the Required Accounts data entry window.

Step 9: Key the account number ranges into the Account Classification data entry window.

Step 10: Key the account number ranges into the Extended Classification data entry window.

Step 11:	Key the account subtotals data to provide the following subtotals:

> Total Current Assets
> Total Plant Assets
> Total Current Liabilities
> Total Long-Term Liabilities

Step 12:	Key the opening balances from the trial balance, schedule of accounts payable, and schedule of accounts receivable shown at the beginning of this problem.
Step 13:	Display a chart of accounts, vendor list, and customer list.
Step 14:	Display the opening balances journal report.
Step 15:	Display a trial balance, schedule of accounts payable, and schedule of accounts receivable.
Step 16:	Display a balance sheet.
Step 17:	Use the Save As command from the File menu. Save your data to disk with a file name of XXX12-P, where XXX are your initials.
Step 18:	End the session.

AUDIT TEST PROBLEM 12-P

Directions: Write the answers to the following questions in the working papers or on a separate sheet of paper.

1. What is the total of the Debit column of the opening balances journal report?
2. What is the total of the Credit column in the trial balance?
3. What is the balance in the Accounts Receivable account in the trial balance?
4. What is the balance in the Accounts Payable account in the trial balance?
5. What is the amount owed to The Computer Center?
6. What is the total owed to all vendors?
7. What is the amount due from Pace Manufacturing?
8. What is the amount due from all customers?
9. From the balance sheet, what are the total current assets?
10. From the balance sheet, what are the total plant assets?

M MASTERY PROBLEM 12-M

In this problem, you will set up a plant asset system and a payroll system for Hampton Water Purifiers. A list of Hampton Water Purifiers assets, employees, and employee opening balances as of April 1 of the current year are provided as follows:

Plant Assets

Asset No.	Asset Name	Date Acquired	Depr. Method	Useful Method	Original Cost	Salvage Value
Warehouse Equipment						
110	Fork Lift	10/31/92	SL	8	4200.00	500.00
120	Shelving	09/30/91	SL	10	12000.00	900.00
130	Hydraulic Hoist	02/20/91	SL	10	1990.00	250.00
Office Equipment						
210	Copy Machine	03/21/90	SL	6	2450.00	200.00
220	Fax Machine	01/28/91	SL	5	980.00	120.00
230	File Cabinet	04/20/91	SL	10	409.00	30.00
240	Computer System	02/24/92	SL	5	3509.00	350.00

Plant Asset Account Numbers

	Accumulated Depreciation	Depreciation Expense
Warehouse Equipment	1520	6140
Office Equipment	1540	6150

Employees

No. Name Address, City/State	SS No.	Mar. Stat.	Type Pay	Rate/ Salary	W/H Allow.	Ded. 1	Ded. 2	Ded. 3
210 Arnst, Janet 6070 Bird Tree Court Norman, Ok 73069-1100	345-22-4569	Mar.	Sal.	2280.00	3	80.12	25.00	15.00
220 Brandt, John 4586 Red River Drive Norman, OK 73071-2020	677-88-2309	Single	Sal.	2170.00	1	60.00	25.00	12.00
230 Lomax, Lance 5908 Snake Road Norman, OK 73071-2050	678-54-4402	Single	Hrly.	9.50	1	50.00	25.00	
240 Mason, Louise 9034 Coffee Lane Norman, OK 73070-1220	459-03-0033	Mar.	Hrly.	9.00	2	45.00	25.00	

Note: All employees are paid 26 times per year. Record a department number of 0 for all employees.

Employee Opening Balance Data

Emp. No.	Gross	Fed. W/H	State W/H	FICA	Medicare
	*****************Year-to-Date********************				
210	15960.00	2323.86	655.13	989.52	231.42
220	15190.00	3238.48	631.33	941.78	220.29

| 230 | 5339.00 | 609.05 | 121.52 | 331.02 | 77.42 |
| 240 | 5058.00 | 330.65 | 103.14 | 313.60 | 73.34 |

Note: Because the payroll system is being established on the first day of a new quarter, the quarter-to-date opening balance data are all zero.

Directions:

Step 1: Remove the input forms for Problem 12-M from the working papers. Record the above data on the input forms. This step is optional in that you may wish to key the above data directly into the computer.

Step 2: Bring up the accounting system software (module A2) or select Payroll/Assets/Bank Rec. from the File menu of either of the other two modules.

Step 3: Use the New command from the File menu to prepare the computer for the plant asset setup.

Step 4: Set the general information data.

Step 5: Key the asset classification data.

Step 6: Key the plant assets.

Step 7: Display the plant assets report.

Step 8: From the System menu, select the Payroll system.

Step 9: Key the integration account numbers (Options, Tax Rates/Account Numbers) as follows:

Account Title	Account No.
Salary Expense 1	6150
Salary Expense 2	
Salary Expense 3	
Emp. Fed. Inc. Tax Pay.	2130
Emp. State Inc. Tax Pay.	2140
FICA Tax Payable	2150
Medicare Payable	2160
Deduction 1 Payable	2170
Deduction 2 Payable	2180
Deduction 3 Payable	2190
Salaries Payable	2200

Payroll Taxes Expense   6160

State Unemp. Tax Pay.   2210

Federal UnEmp. Tax Pay.   2220

Step 10:   Key the employee data.

Step 11:   Key the opening balances historical data.

Step 12:   Display a payroll report for all employees.

Step 13:   Use the Save As command to save your data with a file name of XXX12-M, where XXX are your initials.

Step 14:   End the session.

AUDIT TEST PROBLEM 12-M

Directions: Write the answers to the following questions in the working papers or on a separate sheet of paper.

PLANT ASSETS SYSTEM

1. What is the salvage value of asset no. 210 (copy machine)?
2. What is the total original cost of all assets?
3. What date was asset no. 220 (fax machine) acquired?

PAYROLL

4. What is the yearly federal income tax withheld for Janet Arnst?
5. What is the salary amount for John Brandt?
6. What is the total gross pay for the year for all employees?
7. What is the total FICA withheld for the year for all employees?
8. What is the amount of Deduction 1 for Louise Mason?

Index

A

Account
Adjusting entries, recording, 58-60, 150-152, 219
   adding, 41
   deleting, 42
Account Classification data entry window, 321
Account number, changing, 41
Account Subtotals data entry window, 323-324
Account title, changing, 41-42
Accounting system setup, 317-333
Accounts payable checks, printing, 220-222
Accounts payable ledger report, 101, 102. *See also* Schedule of accounts payable report.
Accounts receivable ledger reports, 131-132
Accounts receivable statements, printing, 220-222
Add New Account, 41
Assets. *See* Plant Assets System.
Audit tests, def., 3
Automated Accounting 6.0
   data entry windows, using, 8-10
   dialog windows, using, 12-13
   features overview, 3
   graphical user interface, using with, 17-18
   icons, 3
   list windows, using, 10-12
   menu system, 4-7
   modules in, 318
   mouse, using with, 4
   network, using with, 17-18
   operating procedures, 4-27
   report windows, using, 13-15
   software overview, 2
   start-procedures, 16-18
   template disk, 3
   working papers, 3
Automated Accounting 6.0
   Reference Guide, 2

B

Balance sheet, 60, 61, 62
Bank reconciliation, 63-66
Board of directors, 214

C

Calculator, 27
Capital stock, 214
Cash account balance, 63
Cash disbursements, 88
Cash payment on account, keying, 94-95
Cash Payments Journal
   changing or deleting transactions in, 95-96
   data entry window, 92, 177, 219-220
   finding entries in, 96-97
   input form for, 88-89, 174, 216-217
   journal reports in, 97
   keying a cash payment on account into, 94-95
   keying direct payment into, 92-92
   ledger reports in, 99-102
Cash receipt on account
   def., 126
   keying, 128-129
Cash receipts journal
   data entry window, 126-129
   input form for, 122-123
Caution icon, 3
Chart of accounts, 215
   data entry window for, 40-42
   input form for, 38
   maintenance of, 40-42
Checkbook balance, 63
Classify Assets data entry window, 326-327

Commands
   Assets menu
      Asset List, 200
      Maintain Assets, 199, 327
   File menu
      Erase Accounting File, 21
      Import, 21
      New, 19, 318, 325
      Open Accounting File, 19-20
      Payroll/Assets/Bank Rec., 22
      Print, 22
      Quit, 22
      Save Accounting File, 20-21
      Save As, 21
   Help menu, 27
   Journals menu
      Cash Payments Journal, 92
      Cash Receipts Journal, 126
      General Journal, 42
      Opening Balances, 324
      Purchases Journal, 90
      Sales Journal, 124
   Ledgers menu
      Chart of Accounts
      Customer List, 123
      Maintain Accounts, 40, 320
      Maintain Customers, 123
      Maintain Vendors, 89
      Vendor List, 897
   Options menu
      Account Classification, 322
      Account Subtotals, 323
      Classify Assets, 326
      Clear Quarterly Accumulators, 265
      Clear Yearly Accumulators, 265, 293
      Display Type, 24-25
      Enter Budgets, 324
      Extended Classification, 322
      Federal Tax Brackets, 327, 328
      General Information, 22-24, 263, 293, 320, 325
      Period-End Closing, 63
      Prepare New Payroll, 264
      Purge inventory transactions, 293